YOUR
COLLEGE
EXPERIENCE
Strategies for Success

twelfthedition

YOUR COLLEGE EXPERIENCE

Strategies for Success

John N. Gardner

President, John N. Gardner Institute for Excellence in Undergraduate Education
Brevard, North Carolina

Distinguished Professor Emeritus, Library and Information Science Senior Fellow,
National Resource Center for The First-Year Experience and Students in Transition
University of South Carolina, Columbia

Betsy O. Barefoot

Senior Scholar
John N. Gardner Institute for Excellence in Undergraduate Education
Brevard, North Carolina

Bedford/St. Martin's
A Macmillan Education Imprint

Boston • New York

For Bedford/St. Martin's

Vice President, Editorial, Macmillan Higher Education Humanities: Edwin Hill
Publisher for College Success: Erika Gutierrez
Senior Executive Editor for College Success: Simon Glick
Senior Developmental Editor: Jennifer Jacobson of Ohlinger Publishing Services
Senior Production Editor: Gregory Erb
Senior Production Supervisor: Dennis J. Conroy
Senior Marketing Manager: Christina Shea
Associate Editor: Bethany Gordon
Editorial Assistant: Jonathan Douglas
Copy Editor: Christina Nolan
Indexer: Steve Csipke
Photo Researcher: Julie Tesser
Director of Rights and Permissions: Hilary Newman
Senior Art Director: Anna Palchik
Text Design: Jerilyn Bockorick, Cenveo Publisher Services
Cover Design: William Boardman
Cover Photo: © Susan Chiang/Getty Images
Composition: Cenveo Publisher Services
Printing and Binding: RR Donnelley and Sons

Manufactured in the United States of America.

0   9   8   7   6   5
f   e   d   c   b   a

For information, write: Bedford/St. Martin's, 75 Arlington Street, Boston, MA 02116
   (617-399-4000)

ISBN 978-1-4576-9966-5   (Student Edition)
ISBN 978-1-319-01251-9   (Loose-leaf Edition)
ISBN 978-1-319-01256-4   (Instructor's Annotated Edition)

Dear Student,

More than ever before, a college education is an essential step in preparing you for almost any career. A few years ago, many well-paying jobs required only a high school diploma, but most employers today require that job applicants have a college degree.

Higher education is becoming more expensive, and some people are questioning whether a college degree is worth the cost. Yes, college is expensive, but the benefits of a college education are well worth the price tag. According to current statistics, a college-educated person receives a better salary and enjoys a healthier life, more confidence, and a more promising future for his or her children than a person who does not attend college. Of course we can all name a few exceptions: Mark Zuckerberg of Facebook and Bill Gates of Microsoft were college dropouts who still managed to be highly successful. Such success stories are very rare, however.

While you might have many reasons for being in college, we hope your primary goal is graduation, and you will be more likely to graduate if you have a successful first year. When we were in our first year of college, college success courses, with few exceptions, did not exist, and there was no "textbook" like *Your College Experience* that provided strategies for making the most of college. Most colleges and universities allowed new students to sink or swim. As a result, some students did well, some hardly survived, and some dropped out or flunked out.

Beyond graduation, some of you will want to continue your education in professional or graduate school, but others will want to begin a career. While it may be tough to land your ideal job immediately, your college education is an investment that will make you competitive in the marketplace.

You are likely reading *Your College Experience* because you are enrolled in a college success course—a special course designed to help you be successful. Although this book might seem different from your other textbooks, we believe that it could be the most important book you read this term because it's all about improving your chances for success in college and in your career. This book will help you identify your own strengths, as well as areas where you need to improve. We know that if you apply the ideas in this book to your everyday life, you are more likely to enjoy your time in college, graduate, and achieve your life goals.

As college professors, researchers, and administrators with many years of experience working with first-year students, we know that starting college can be challenging. But through your college success course, the faculty, staff, and academic resources on your campus will help you meet that challenge. Welcome to college!

John N. Gardner

Betsy O. Barefoot

John N. Gardner brings unparalleled experience to this authoritative text for first-year seminar courses. He is the recipient of the University of South Carolina's highest award for teaching excellence. He has twenty-five years of experience directing and teaching in the most respected and most widely emulated first-year seminar in the country: the University 101 course at the University of South Carolina. He is recognized as one of the country's leading educators for his role in initiating and orchestrating an international reform movement to improve students' transition to college. He is also the founding leader of two influential higher education centers that support campuses in their efforts to improve the learning and retention of first-year college students: the National Resource Center for The First-Year Experience and Students in Transition at the University of South Carolina (**sc.edu/fye**), and the John N. Gardner Institute for Excellence in Undergraduate Education (**jngi.org**), based in Brevard, North Carolina. The experiential basis for all of John Gardner's work is his own miserable first year of college, which he spent on academic probation—an experience that he hopes to prevent for this book's readers.

Betsy O. Barefoot is a writer, researcher, and teacher whose special area of scholarship is the first year of college. During her tenure at the University of South Carolina from 1988 to 1999, she served as codirector for research and publications at the National Resource Center for The First-Year Experience and Students in Transition. She taught University 101, in addition to special-topics graduate courses on the first-year experience and the principles of college teaching. She conducts first-year seminar faculty training workshops around the United States and in other countries, and she is frequently called on to evaluate first-year seminar outcomes. She currently serves as Senior Scholar in the Gardner Institute for Excellence in Undergraduate Education. In her Institute role, she led a major national research project to identify institutions of excellence in the first college year. She currently works with both two- and four-year campuses to evaluate all components of the first year.

brief contents

contents

PART ONE FOUNDATIONS

David Shaffer/Getty Images

Michael Krinke/Getty Images

Indicates sections that refer to high-impact practices. See page 9 for more information.

wavebreakmedia/Shutterstock

wavebreakmedia/Shutterstock

PART TWO PREPARING TO LEARN

Phase4Studios/Shutterstock

Chris Schmidt/Getty Images

⊙ Indicates sections that refer to high-impact practices. See page 9 for more information.

wavebreakmedia/Shutterstock

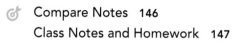
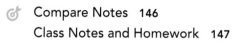

Ammentorp Photography/
Shutterstock

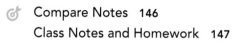

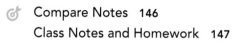
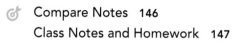

Chris Ryan/Getty Images

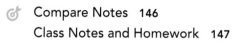
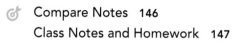 Indicates sections that refer to high-impact practices. See page 9 for more information.

Blend Images-Hill Street
Studios/Getty Images

PART THREE PREPARING FOR LIFE

William Perugini/Shutterstock

Indicates sections that refer to high-impact practices. See page 9 for more information.

⊙ Indicates sections that refer to high-impact practices. See page 9 for more information.

yourturn features

Indicates Your Turn activities that involve high-impact practices. All Work Together and Write and Reflect activities involve high-impact practices.

preface

Anyone who teaches beginning college students knows how much they have changed in recent years. Today's students are increasingly job focused, technologically adept, and concerned about the future. More than ever, students worry about how they will pay for college. Recently, popular media sources such as the *Washington Post* have raised questions about whether the benefits of college are worth the cost.[1] While it is tempting to focus on the few individuals who succeed without finishing college, we know that for the overwhelming majority of individuals, a college degree is more essential than ever before.

Today, we see diverse students of all ages and backgrounds enrolling in two- and four-year public and private institutions, bringing with them the hopes and dreams that a college education can help fulfill—as well as expectations that may or may not be realistic. *Your College Experience* is designed specifically to give all students the practical help they need to gain self-knowledge, set goals, succeed, and stay in college so that those hopes and dreams have a better chance of becoming realities.

While maintaining its approach on goal setting, the twelfth edition of this text offers a new emphasis on the ten high-impact practices identified by the American Association of Colleges & Universities, and it now incorporates information on the value of peer leaders in supporting students. *Your College Experience* teaches skills and strategies in areas where students often need the most help and that are critical for success in college and the workplace. These include time management, academic reading, test taking, research, and career preparation. At a time when institutions are increasing class sizes and mainstreaming developmental students, students will need more individual attention and the skills to ask for the help they need. Of course, concerns about student retention remain, as do pressures on college success administrators to do more with less. These realities of college and university life mean that giving students strategies they can use immediately is more important than ever.

To help you meet the challenges of engaging and retaining today's students, we have created a complete package of support materials, including an Instructor's Annotated Edition and an Instructor's Manual. In the Instructor's Annotated Edition, you will find clearly marked retention strategies and activities to help you engage and retain students. These activities, and all of the instructor support materials, are valuable for both new and experienced instructors as they prepare to teach the course.

What has not changed in the forty years since the inception of the first-year seminar is our level of commitment to and deep understanding of our students. Although this edition of *Your College Experience* has been significantly revised, it is still based on our collective knowledge and experience in teaching new students. It is grounded in the growing body of research

---

[1] www.washingtonpost.com/blogs/she-the-people/wp/2014/08/22/do-the-benefits-of-a-college-education-outweigh-the-cost

on student success and retention and includes valuable contributions from leading experts in the field. Most of all, it is a text born from our devotion to students and to their success. Simply put, we do not like to see students fail. We are confident that if students both read and heed the information herein, they will become engaged in the college experience, learn, and persist to graduation.

We have written this text for students of any age in both residential and commuter institutions. Our writing style is intended to convey respect and admiration for students while recognizing their continued need for challenge and support. We have addressed topics that our experience, our research, and our reviewers tell us are concerns for students at any type of college or university and with any kind of educational background. We have also embedded various reading and writing strategies to support students' efforts to comprehend the material and apply the skills presented in each chapter, and we have included technology tools and tips that can enhance students' studying experience.

Your College Experience uses a simple and logical organization. Part One, Foundations, sets the stage by challenging students to explore their purpose for attending college and by helping them learn how to apply that purpose to both short- and long-term goal setting. Students are armed with solid time-management strategies in Chapter Two, and then they explore the topics of emotional intelligence and learning styles. Part Two, Preparing to Learn, enumerates essential learning skills like critical thinking, reading, note taking, studying, and test taking, and guides students in communicating and finding information. Part Three, Preparing for Life, emphasizes practical and realistic considerations such as relationships, diversity, wellness, and money management. Part Four, Next Steps, features a comprehensive chapter on majors and careers with a wealth of tools and strategies that students can use during their first-year experience and beyond.

Whether you are considering this textbook for use in your first-year seminar or have already made a decision to adopt it, we thank you for your interest, and we trust that you will find it to be a valuable teaching aid. We also hope that this book will guide you and your campus in understanding the broad range of issues that can affect student success.

A Revision Focused on Research-Based Strategies to Help Students Succeed

While retaining many of the hallmark features that characterize the Gardner/Barefoot text, we have added new areas of emphasis grounded in the latest research on student success.

1. **A focus on high-impact practices.** An exciting new aspect of the twelfth edition is the inclusion of strategies for using "high-impact practices"—ten educational activities that have been shown to increase student learning, retention, and engagement throughout the undergraduate years.[2] The first chapter of the book introduces the concept of high-impact practices (HIP) for students, lists and describes

---

[2]G. D. Kuh, *High-Impact Educational Practices: What They Are, Who Has Access to Them, and Why They Matter* (Washington, DC: Association of American Colleges and Universities, 2008). www.aacu.org/leap/hips

them, and discusses their benefits. New annotations in each chapter of the Instructor's Annotated Edition feature suggestions for utilizing one or more HIPs in the context of chapter content. This new category of instructor's annotations is denoted with the heading "HIGH-IMPACT PRACTICE." Also, a special icon ⊙ identifies content in the features and narrative of the student edition that relates to HIPs. For instance, readers will see the HIP icon adjacent to the Your Turn: Work Together and Your Turn: Write and Reflect activities, and with content coverage related to writing, collaboration, diversity, global learning, or service learning. Furthermore, icons placed within the table of contents and the list of Your Turn features show you where to find HIP material.

2. **An emphasis on motivation and the importance of the choices students make.** Through the narrative and special features, the new edition helps students see how good choices bring them closer to their goals, guides them in understanding how being resilient involves bouncing back from poor choices and making increasingly smarter ones, and motivates them to make these smarter decisions. Each chapter includes a Your Turn: Stay Motivated feature, a Your Turn: Make Good Choices feature, and an ending exercise that invites students to Reflect on Choices through writing. Collegiate success is often determined by both large and small choices that students make in the first term of college, and we want students to be aware of how their choices can dramatically change the outcomes of their college experience.

3. **Updates across all chapters, with extensive revisions to fundamental coverage in one chapter in each major part.** In Chapter 3, Emotional Intelligence, we present strong links between emotional intelligence concepts and the daily events of college life. In Chapter 5, Thinking in College, students explore what college-level thinking involves. Chapter 13, Wellness, presents the mental, physical, and spiritual aspects of wellness. Chapter 15, Majors and Careers, offers effective guidance on and tools for exploring different careers and industries in today's job market and economy. See more information about changes in each chapter on pages xxiv–xxvi.

4. **Assistance for using peer leaders in college success courses.** As many colleges and universities now recognize the importance of upper-level students as coteachers or peer leaders for the first-year seminar, the Instructor's Annotated Edition now includes special annotations for and about them. Each chapter includes suggestions that peer leaders (or the instructor of record) can use in designing special activities that can be led by peer leaders. The Use Your Resources section includes peer leaders as valuable sources for student support.

5. **An increased focus on four-year higher education.** With the publication of a new edition of *Your College Experience* specifically developed for students attending two-year and community colleges, the twelfth edition now focuses more intentionally on the particular issues of students in baccalaureate colleges and universities. Given that students attending open-enrollment institutions are becoming increasingly broad and diverse, the twelfth edition provides support, information, and guidance appropriate for students at all higher education institutions.

The twelfth edition continues the Gardner and Barefoot tradition of helping students self-assess their strengths, practice goal setting, focus on purpose and motivation, and maintain their engagement in this course. A section on goal setting in Chapter 1 gets students thinking immediately about this important skill. Assess Your Strengths and Set Goals boxes early in each chapter ask students to set goals, and Reflect on Choices and Apply What You Have Learned exercises at the end of each chapter ask students to think back on how the chapter relates to choices they make and to apply what they have learned in the chapter to current and future academic work.

The following features return in the twelfth edition, with many exciting enhancements:

Chapter-opening profiles help students see themselves in the text. Each chapter of the text opens with the story of a recent first-year student who has used the strategies presented in the chapter to succeed in college. The profiled students come from diverse backgrounds and attend diverse colleges and universities around the country.

Thought-provoking photographs and cartoons in every chapter—many of them new to this edition—with carefully written titles and captions reinforce concepts in the narrative and encourage critical thinking. For instance, in the Time Management chapter, a captioned photo of NFL coach Pete Carroll and his players encourages students to "Set Priorities like the Pros." In the communication chapter, a new photo of Ellen DeGeneres hosting the Academy Awards provides a great example of audience interaction, and its caption discusses how the comedy icon used to be scared to speak before an audience. In the careers chapter, a new photo of a career fair for military veterans emphasizes the importance of making professional connections.

Your Turn **collaborative learning activities foster peer-to-peer communication, collaboration, and critical thinking.** These activities can be used in class, as homework, or as group activities to strengthen the bond between students and their college communities. They are organized into four types based on what students are asked to do or to consider: Work Together, Write and Reflect, Make Good Choices, and Stay Motivated. A complete list of all Your Turn activities, organized by type and with page numbers included to make it easy for instructors to assign them, can be found on p. xviii.

Is This You? **boxes speak directly to students in circumstances that are commonly found among students taking first-year experience courses.** Look for these special messages to first-generation college students, returning students, veterans, students with children, and student athletes. They also cover common first-year issues that many students encounter, such as being disappointed in a class, weight gain, financial problems, and the clash of new ideas with old beliefs. The feature directs students to specific content within the chapter. Here is a list of these features:

> *Is This You?* I Don't Know What I'm Doing Here (Chapter 1)
> *Is This You?* Time Flies (Chapter 2)
> *Is This You?* Older than Average (Chapter 3)
> *Is This You?* Disappointed in My Classes (Chapter 4)

Is This You? When New Knowledge and Old Beliefs Collide (Chapter 5)
Is This You? The Challenge of Being "First" (Chapter 6)
Is This You? Balancing Sports and Study (Chapter 7)
Is This You? Making *A*'s without Studying (Chapter 8)
Is This You? Bouncing Back from a Bad Grade (Chapter 9)
Is This You? Dreading Writing Assignments (Chapter 10)
Is This You? In a Long-Distance Relationship (Chapter 11)
Is This You? From Another Country (Chapter 12)
Is This You? My Favorite Pants Don't Fit (Chapter 13)
Is This You? Too Much Month, Too Little Money (Chapter 14)
Is This You? No Plan for Life after College (Chapter 15)

Coverage of technology and learning. The link between technology and learning is highlighted in every chapter of the twelfth edition with a Tech Tip feature. These features introduce critical technology skills that span the classroom and real life. All Tech Tip features have been extensively revised for the new edition, with titles such as Get Digitally Organized (Chapter 2); Use Blogs and Twitter (Chapter 3); Correlate Online Learning with Your Learning Style (Chapter 4); Take Better Notes in Better Ways (Chapter 7); Use the Cloud (Chapter 8); Conduct Effective Searches (Chapter 10); Build a Digital Persona (Chapter 11); Go Beyond the Filter (new, Chapter 12); and Join the Professional Community (Chapter 15). **Models** (including **digital models**) let students see principles in action. Because many students learn best by example, full-size models—more than in any competing book—show realistic examples of strategies for academic success such as using time-management tools, annotating a textbook, using mind maps, and taking notes in various formats. Digital models are included to reflect the tools today's students use in their everyday lives.

Expanded examples from across the curriculum. The text now includes more concrete scenarios, pages, exercises, and problems from STEM, humanities, and social science courses.

***Use Your Resources* boxes connect students to their campus, faculty, and other students.** To help students take more control of their own success, every chapter includes a quick overview of additional resources for support, including learning-assistance centers, books, Web sites, and fellow students—with a prompt for students to add their own ideas.

Skills-based practice exercises provide hands-on, point-of-use reinforcement of major concepts. Students use these exercises to practice skills that they can then apply to other academic courses. For instance, the Time Management chapter includes a tool for students to conduct a Procrastination Self-Assessment, and the test-taking chapter includes a new Test Anxiety Quiz.

Retention Strategies in every chapter of the Instructor's Annotated Edition offer best practices from John Gardner and Betsy Barefoot to help students persist in the first year. In addition, a 16-page insert at the beginning of the Instructor's Annotated Edition includes chapter-specific exercises and activities designed as retention strategies to support writing, critical thinking, working in groups, planning, reflecting, and taking action.

Key Chapter-by-Chapter Revisions

In addition to new features that appear across all chapters of the book, each chapter also features key new and updated content:

Chapter 1, Welcome to Your College Experience, introduces students to the concepts of purpose and goal setting and explores the value of higher education. New to this reorganized chapter is a summary of high-impact practices that are featured throughout the book, an introduction to the role of peer leaders in the college success course, and new material on academic planning and working with an academic adviser. In addition, the authors introduce students to the concept of resilience, a topic that is addressed throughout the new edition.

Chapter 2, Time Management, addresses the tools today's students use to stay organized. This chapter includes information about the relationship between locus of control and one's ability to manage time. Students are guided in using time-management tools and understanding how to avoid procrastination. The chapter includes a new procrastination self-assessment and a valuable tool for measuring the impact of distractions.

Chapter 3, Emotional Intelligence, has been improved by linking emotional intelligence concepts to the daily events of college life, with additional explanation on the concepts of resilience and making good choices. The chapter also includes self-assessments that help students evaluate and improve their own level of emotional intelligence.

Chapter 4, How You Learn, introduces students to learning styles and learning preferences. The chapter includes the VARK Inventory, which can be used in class. Also, three other learning-styles theories are described in the chapter: David Kolb's Experiential Learning Theory, the Myers-Briggs Type Indicator, and Howard Gardner's Theory of Multiple Intelligences. A brief version of the Multiple Intelligences Inventory is included. The chapter ends with coverage of learning disabilities to help students know how and when to seek help for themselves or other students.

Chapter 5, Thinking in College, has been heavily revised and reorganized to give students a better understanding of what is involved in college-level thinking and practical strategies on how to achieve that high level of thinking. Students are clearly shown how concepts like fast and slow thinking, problem solving, creativity, and collaboration all relate to critical thinking. The chapter includes a critical-thinking assessment that is new to this edition, as well as a new application of Bloom's Taxonomy.

Chapter 6, Reading to Learn, helps students meet the particular challenges of reading college textbooks across the various disciplines. It introduces them to the steps involved in active reading and explains how to use strategies such as outlining and mapping to understand and retain important content for tests and exams. Strategies for reading with concentration, reading improvement, and monitoring are provided. New visuals include a sample organizer, several new photos, and sample textbook pages from an economics and chemistry textbook, which reflect the text's increased attention to the STEM fields.

Chapter 7, Getting the Most from Class, covers topics such as preparing for class, listening, taking notes, and participating. The chapter introduces students to various note-taking methods, particularly the Cornell method. The chapter's Tech Tip presents helpful note-taking apps. Students are encouraged to overcome any reluctance they might have about asking a question in class or participating out loud in a group discussion.

Chapter 8, Studying, includes an essential focus on the basics—how to study and how to remember. Students are warned about the pitfalls of multitasking and the downsides of trying to study in an environment that is full of distractions. The chapter opens with a new assessment that asks students to determine their willingness to make tough choices to improve their study habits and includes a new figure showing a sample mind map.

Chapter 9, Test Taking, helps students learn how to prepare for tests and exams, understand and deal with test anxiety, and appreciate the value of maintaining academic integrity. The chapter covers different types of tests and different test environments, including online testing. A major theme in the chapter is the importance of being resilient—not allowing a poor grade on a test to negatively affect a student's motivation. A new visual showing a sample page from a math textbook reinforces the value of working practice problems as a great way to study for tests.

Chapter 10, Information Literacy and Communication, connects writing and speaking to the important topic of information literacy. The chapter now more clearly walks students through the steps of the writing process. The chapter emphasizes doing good research and getting comfortable using the resources at the campus library. Students are also introduced to ways to evaluate and cite sources and recognize bias.

Chapter 11, Relationships, includes a major focus on the value of students building positive relationships with their instructors. The chapter also addresses the changing nature of interactions with family members, roommate issues, and romantic relationships. The chapter contains a new section on communicating in a digital age, with a new table outlining best practices for online communication. The chapter's Tech Tip has been reoriented around building a digital persona in an attempt to educate students about being responsible with their online presence, especially as it relates to employment. This chapter also covers the value of involvement in campus life.

Chapter 12, Diversity, takes a broad view of diversity and considers the many advantages of a diverse campus environment that includes differences in gender, race, ethnic group, sexuality, age, economic status, religion, and learning and physical abilities. The chapter advises students to refrain from stereotyping and instead get to know others as individuals before drawing conclusions about an entire group.

Chapter 13, Wellness, takes a new, holistic view of wellness, including mental, physical, and spiritual health. A major focus of this chapter is stress and how to prevent and manage it through proper nutrition, sleep, and exercise. The chapter includes a stress self-assessment exercise and a Tech Tip that introduces students to ways that technology can help monitor health. This chapter includes new coverage of cyberbullying and the latest information about the federal government's actions against sexual assault, including strategies that students can use to protect themselves and others from becoming victims.

Chapter 14, Money, emphasizes the importance of budgeting and gives students a template for designing their own budget. The chapter also explores responsible use of credit and debit cards, and ways for students to obtain and maintain financial aid.

Chapter 15, Majors and Careers, helps students understand how to consider different majors and to make a decision that sets them up for success and fulfillment. The chapter also provides a wealth of guidance on and tools for exploring different careers and industries. This chapter offers a cutting-edge evaluation of the new economy and guidance in developing the right mind-set for creating a strong future, before moving on to discuss clear strategies for career planning, enhancing marketability, conducting industry and company research, gaining experience while in college, and searching for jobs.

Extensive Resources for Instructors

- **LaunchPad for *Your College Experience*, Twelfth Edition.** LaunchPad combines an interactive e-book with high-quality multimedia content and ready-made assessment options, including LearningCurve adaptive quizzing. Prebuilt units are easy to assign or adapt to your material, such as readings, videos, quizzes, discussion groups, and more. LaunchPad also provides access to a grade book that provides a clear window on performance for your whole class, for individual students, and for individual assignments. The result is superior, book-specific content in a breakthrough user interface in which power and simplicity go hand in hand. To package LaunchPad for *Your College Experience* with the text, use ISBN 978-1-319-03845-8. To order LaunchPad standalone, use ISBN 978-1-319-01263-2.

- ***LearningCurve for College Success 2.0.*** *LearningCurve for College Success 2.0* is an online, adaptive, self-quizzing program that quickly learns what students already know and helps them practice what they don't yet understand. LearningCurve motivates students to engage with key concepts before they come to class so that they are ready to participate; it also offers reporting tools to help you discern your students' needs. This updated version of LearningCurve features a larger question pool with new multiple-choice questions. To package *LearningCurve for College Success 2.0* for **free** with the text, use ISBN 978-1-319-03846-5. To order LearningCurve standalone, use ISBN 978-1-4576-7999-5.

- **The Academic and Career Excellence System (ACES).** This instrument measures student strengths in twelve critical areas and prompts students to reflect on their habits, behaviors, attitudes, and skills. Norm-referenced reports indicate whether students are at a high, moderate, or low skill level in particular areas. For more information, go to **macmillanhighered.com/ACES/catalog**.

- **Instructor's Annotated Edition.** A valuable tool for new and experienced instructors alike, the Instructor's Annotated Edition includes the full text of the student edition with abundant marginal annotations, chapter-specific exercises, and helpful suggestions for teaching, fully updated and revised by the authors. In this edition are numerous retention strategies and high-impact practice tips and exercises to help you help your students succeed and stay in school.

- **Instructor's Manual.** The Instructor's Manual includes chapter objectives, teaching suggestions, an introduction to the first-year experience course, a sample lesson plan for each chapter, sample syllabi, final projects for the end of the course, and various case studies that are relevant to the topics covered in the text. The Instructor's Manual is available online.

- **Computerized Test Bank.** The Computerized Test Bank contains more than 800 multiple-choice, true/false, short-answer, and essay questions designed to assess students' understanding of key concepts. This edition features 150 new multiple-choice questions and more challenging scenario-based questions that ask students to apply their understanding to concepts in the text. An answer key is included. A digital text file is also available.

- *French Fries Are Not Vegetables.* This comprehensive instructional DVD features multiple resources for class and professional use. Also available online on Video Central: College Success. ISBN 978-0-312-65073-5.

- **Custom Solutions program.** Bedford/St. Martin's Custom Publishing offers the highest-quality books and media, created in consultation with publishing professionals who are committed to the discipline. Make *Your College Experience* more closely fit your course and goals by integrating your own materials, including only the parts of the text you intend to use in your course, or both. Contact your local Bedford/St. Martin's sales representative for more information.

- **CS Select custom database.** The CS Select database allows you to create a textbook for your College Success course that reflects your course objectives and uses just the content you need. Start with one of our core texts, and then rearrange chapters, delete chapters, and add additional content—including your own original content—to create just the book you're looking for. Get started by visiting **macmillanhighered.com/csSelect**.

- **TradeUp.** Bring more value and choice to your students' first-year experience by packaging *Your College Experience*, Twelfth Edition, with one of a thousand titles from Macmillan publishers at a 50 percent discount from the regular price. Contact your local Bedford/St. Martin's sales representative for more information.

Student Resources

- **LaunchPad for *Your College Experience*, Twelfth Edition.** LaunchPad is an online course solution that offers our acclaimed content, including e-books, videos, LearningCurve adaptive quizzes, and more. For more information, see the Extensive Resources for Instructors section. To package LaunchPad for *Your College Experience* with the text, use ISBN 978-1-319-03845-8. To order LaunchPad standalone, use ISBN 978-1-319-01263-2.

- *LearningCurve for College Success 2.0.* LearningCurve *for College Success 2.0* is an online, adaptive, self-quizzing program that quickly learns what students already know and helps them practice what they don't yet understand. For more information, see the Extensive Resources for Instructors section. To package *LearningCurve for College Success 2.0* for **free** with the text, use ISBN 978-1-319-03846-5. To order LearningCurve standalone, use ISBN 978-1-4576-7999-5.

- **College Success companion site: macmillanhighered.com/collegesuccess/resources.** The College Success companion site offers a number of tools to use in class, including videos with quizzing, downloadable podcasts, flashcards of key terms, and links to apps that students can use on their phones or computers to reinforce success strategies. From the companion Web site, you can also access instructor materials whenever you need them.

- *VideoCentral: College Success* is a premiere collection of videos for the college success classroom. The site features the 30-minute documentary, *French Fries Are Not Vegetables and Other College Lessons: A Documentary of the First Year of College,* which follows five students through the life-changing transition to the first year of college. Learn more at **macmillanhighered.com/videosuccess/catalog.** *VideoCentral* also includes access to sixteen brief Conversation Starters that combine student and instructor interviews on the most important topics taught in first-year seminar courses, and sixteen accompanying video glossary definitions with questions that bring these topics to life.

- **Bedford e-Book to Go for *Your College Experience*, Twelfth Edition.** For roughly half the cost of a print book, **Bedford e-Book to Go** offers an affordable alternative for students. To learn more, visit **macmillanhighered.com/aboutebooks.**

- **Additional e-book formats.** You can also find PDF versions of our books when you shop online at our publishing partners' sites: CourseSmart, Barnes & Noble NookStudy, Kno, CafeScribe, or Chegg.

- *The Bedford/St. Martin's Planner* includes everything that students need to plan and use their time effectively, with advice on preparing schedules and to-do lists, along with blank schedules and monthly and weekly calendars for planning. Integrated into the planner are tips and advice on fixing common grammar errors, taking notes, and succeeding on tests; an address book; and an annotated list of useful Web sites. The planner fits easily into a backpack or purse, so students can take it anywhere. To order the planner standalone, use ISBN 978-0-312-57447-5.

- *Bedford/St. Martin's Insider's Guides.* These concise and student-friendly booklets on topics that are critical to college success are a perfect complement to your textbook and course. One Insider's Guide can be packaged with *any* Bedford/St. Martin's textbook at no additional cost. Additional Insider's Guides can also be packaged for additional cost. Topics include:
  - New! *Insider's Guide for Adult Learners*
  - New! *Insider's Guide to College Etiquette,* 2e
  - New! *Insider's Guide for Returning Veterans*
  - New! *Insider's Guide to Transferring*
  - *Insider's Guide to Academic Planning*
  - *Insider's Guide to Beating Test Anxiety*
  - *Insider's Guide to Building Confidence*
  - *Insider's Guide to Career Services*
  - *Insider's Guide to College Ethics and Personal Responsibility*
  - *Insider's Guide to Community College*

- *Insider's Guide to Credit Cards,* 2e
- *Insider's Guide to Getting Involved on Campus*
- *Insider's Guide to Global Citizenship*
- *Insider's Guide to Time Management,* 2e

For more information on ordering one of these guides with the text, go to **macmillanhighered.com/collegesuccess**.

- *Journal Writing: A Beginning.* Designed to give students an opportunity to use writing as a way to explore their thoughts and feelings, this writing journal includes a generous supply of inspirational quotes placed throughout the pages, tips for journaling, and suggested journal topics. To order the journal standalone, use ISBN 978-0-312-59027-7.

Acknowledgments

Special thanks to the reviewers of this edition, whose wisdom and suggestions guided the creation of the twelfth edition of the text:

Donna Dabney, Norfolk State University
Maria Flynn, West Kentucky Community and Technical College
DeLandra Hunter, Clayton State University
Hector Menchaca, Tarrant County College—Trinity River Campus
Darrah Mugrauer, Delaware Valley College

Amy Nemmetz, University of Wisconsin—Platteville
Heather Ortiz, Ranger College
Jennifer Palcich, University of North Texas
Carolyn Sanders, University of Alabama in Huntsville
Deborah Stephens, East Tennessee State University

We also thank those who reviewed the Instructor's Manual and Test Bank so thoroughly: Margaret Garroway, Howard Community College; Greta Henglein, Martin Methodist College; Patti Richter, Northwestern State University of Louisiana; Mary Kay Skrabalak, University of Alabama; Brenda Tuberville, Rogers State University. We would also like to continue to thank our reviewers from the eleventh, tenth, and ninth editions, as they helped to shape the text you see today.

Eleventh Edition: Erin Barnett, Eastern Kentucky University; Andrea Berta, University of Texas at El Paso; Christie Cruse-Cohen, Rockland Community College; Linda Frank, Harper College; Lauren Kelley, Owens Community College; Mark Lanting, Kankakee Community College; Molly Burke Leon, Indiana University at Bloomington; General McArthur, Moraine Valley Community College; Roarke O'Leary, Long Beach City College; Rachael Orr, University of Missouri; Jennifer Palcich, University of North Texas; Kelda Quintana, Humboldt State University; Carolyn Sanders, University of Alabama in Huntsville; Deb Vetter, Asbury University; Sara Weertz, Angelo State University.

Tenth Edition: Laurie Adamson, Olympic College; Jim Archer, South Plains College; Jennifer L. Guerriero, Valencia Community College; Kevin Johnson, Middle Georgia College; Joseph Kaye, Edison State College; Elizabeth Kennedy, Florida Atlantic University; Kimberly Koledoye, Houston Community College; Joseph Kornoski, Montgomery County Community College; Audra Leverton, Hinds Community College; Rhonda Lee Meadows, West Virginia University; Pamela Moss, Midwestern State University; Marissa Santos, Navarro College; Ysabel M. Sarte, Texas A&M University;

Melanie Steeves, Dean College; Susannah Waldrop, University of South Carolina Upstate; and Shoshana Zeisman, Portland State University.

Ninth Edition: Josie Adamo, Buffalo State College; Leigh A. Adams, Missouri State University—West Plains; Andrés Armijo, University of New Mexico; Camille J. Belolan, Bloomsburg University of Pennsylvania; Richard Conway, Nassau Community College; Matthew Gainous, Ogeechee Technical College; Wendy Grace, Holmes Community College; Janis M. Hausmann, Mount Marty College; Darby Johnsen, Oklahoma City Community College; Tamara Kuzmenkov, Tacoma Community College; Wendy McNeeley, Howard Payne University; Gail Malone Platt, South Plains College; Amy Reese, Baton Rouge Community College; Cristina C. Rodriguez, Los Angeles Pierce College; Rebecca Rogge, Louisiana State University; Janice Waltz, Harrisburg Area Community College; Jodi E. Webb, Bowling Green State University.

As we look to the future, we are excited about the numerous improvements to this text that our creative Bedford/St. Martin's team has made and will continue to make. Special thanks to Edwin Hill, Vice President, Editorial, Macmillan Higher Education Humanities; Simon Glick, Senior Executive Editor for College Success; Jennifer Jacobson, Development Editor of Ohlinger Publishing Services; Bethany Gordon, Associate Editor; Jonathan Douglas, Editorial Assistant; Christina Shea, Senior Marketing Manager; and Greg Erb, Senior Production Editor.

Most of all, we thank you, the users of our book, for you are the true inspirations for our work.

Contributors

Although this text speaks with the voices of its two authors, it represents contributions from many other people. We gratefully acknowledge those contributions and thank these individuals, whose special expertise has made it possible to introduce new students to their college experience through the holistic approach we deeply believe in.

 **Amber Manning-Ouellette** of Southern Illinois University provided guidance on revising the Emotional Intelligence, Thinking in College, and Wellness chapters. Amber is the Director of Enrollment Management for the SIU College of Business, focusing on recruitment and retention strategies for undergraduate students. She holds a B.S. in Psychology and an M.S. in Counselor Education and received her Doctorate in Educational Administration and Higher Education from SIU in May 2015.

Amber enjoys working with first-year students. In her previous position, she coordinated more than one hundred sections of student success courses, designed curricula, implemented faculty training, and assisted in assessment through a University College model. She was also instrumental in the implementation of the First-Year Experience program for incoming SIU students. One of her passions is coordinating a first-year women's leadership course and living learning community to empower her students. Her academic research interests surround first-year student early interventions, at-risk student development programs, sex education, sexual assault, women's leadership, women's cognitive development, and retention initiatives. She is active in the First-Year Experience movement and continues to present and publish her research at national, regional, and institutional conferences.

Given the nature of technology as a moving target, we relied on the work of **Mark Hendrix** of Palm Beach State College to update the Tech Tips for the twelfth edition. Mark heavily revised or rewrote the Tech Tips, providing new themes in several cases, with the goal of providing students with information to increase their productivity when using the apps, software, or hardware described.

Mark has been an educator for over twenty-five years. He taught in adult and community education before earning a master's degree in education from the University of St. Thomas in St. Paul, Minnesota. He has worked as a teacher or program director in a variety of adult and vocational programs and alternative high school programming, in addition to teaching at community colleges and universities in Minnesota, Kansas, and Florida. He has served on numerous boards of community organizations and has helped them creatively and enthusiastically embrace challenges and thrive in a changing environment. Currently, he is an Associate Professor at Palm Beach State College in Palm Beach County, Florida. He has been recognized for his dynamic teaching strategies, use of technology in the classroom, and his ability to work effectively across departments and outside organizations.

Lea Susan Engle rewrote and updated the chapter on information literacy for the previous edition, helping to incorporate the topics of writing and speaking. Lea is a former instructor and first-year experience librarian at Texas A&M University and currently serves as Training Coordinator for the Canvas learning management system at The University of Texas at Austin. Lea earned a B.A. in Women's Studies from the University of Maryland, College Park and holds an M.S. in Information Studies and an M.A. in Women's and Gender Studies from the University of Texas at Austin.

Her professional interests include educational technology, the first-year experience, creative outreach methods, feminist pedagogy, library service to GLBTQ users, formative assessment, taking risks, and fostering cross-campus collaborations. She is a library evangelist, fulfilling her dream of strategically positioning librarians in all areas of academia.

Casey Reid vastly updated the chapter on Time Management to reflect the needs of today's students. Casey graduated in 2002 from Missouri State University with a B.A. in Anthropology and Professional Writing, and in 2004 she received an M.A. in Writing from the same institution. From 2004 through 2011, she worked on the English faculty at Metropolitan Community College (MCC) in Kansas City. From 2011–2014, she was MCC's College Orientation Coordinator, initiating and directing a mandatory first-year seminar class for 6,000–7,000 new students each year. In 2014, she became the Director of Developmental Education Programs at East Central College, where she implements first-year seminars and programs for students in developmental education classes. When she isn't working, she adds balance to her life by running, biking, hiking, reading, spending time with her three rescued dogs, and hanging out with friends and family.

 The wealth of resources offered in the Majors and Careers chapter is due in large part to **Heather N. Maietta**. Heather is Associate Vice President of Career and Corporate Engagement at Merrimack College. While at Merrimack, she created Generation Merr1mack, a career and professional development program to support first-generation college students. Generation Merr1mack was a finalist for the 2014 Diversity and Inclusion award from the National Association of Colleges and Employers.

Heather has presented or copresented more than thirty times nationally on topics related to career and professional preparation, and she is a Certified Career Development Facilitator Instructor through the National Career Development Association. Heather has authored articles and research reports in several publications, including About Campus; Career Convergence; and ESource. Heather has also coauthored three textbooks for Kendall/Hunt Publishers. Most recently, she coauthored and edited *The Senior Year: Culminating Experiences and Transitions*, published by The National Resource Center on the First-Year Experience and Students in Transition.

Heather also serves on the Notre Dame Education Center Board of Directors, an organization that provides education and support services for adult learners in the greater Lawrence, Massachusetts, community.

 **Chris Gurrie** is an Assistant Professor and Director of the Speech Communication Program at the University of Tampa. He also teaches first-year experience seminars and advises undergraduate students. He holds a doctorate from Nova Southeastern University, and when he is not teaching he speaks about the concept of immediacy and student-instructor connections. He has published other articles about communication among the Millennial Generation. He contributed the first generation of Tech Tips, which were introduced in the tenth edition, and wrote the *Guide to Teaching with YouTube,* which is available online and as part of the Instructor's Manual.

We would also like to acknowledge and thank the numerous colleagues who have contributed to this book in its previous editions:

Chapters 2, 6, 7, 8, 9: Jeanne L. Higbee, University of Minnesota
Chapter 3: Catherine Andersen, University of Baltimore
Chapters 4, 11: Tom Carskadon, Mississippi State University
Chapter 7: Mary Ellen O'Leary, University of South Carolina
Chapter 10: Charles Curran, Distinguished Professor Emeritus, University of South Carolina at Columbia
Chapter 14: Natala Kleather (Tally) Hart, founding head of the Economic Access Initiative at The Ohio State University; and Kate Trombitas, Director of Development at The Ohio State University College of Nursing
Chapter 15: Philip D. Gardner, Michigan State University

PART ONE
FOUNDATIONS

David Shaffer/Getty Images

1 WELCOME TO YOUR COLLEGE EXPERIENCE

Student Goals

• Understand the importance of this course and this textbook
• Explore the outcomes of the college experience
• Set goals for attending college
• Adjust to college life
• Understand the basics of academic planning

Michael Krinke/Getty Images

2 TIME MANAGEMENT

Student Goals

• Gain strategies and tools to manage your time
• Understand how setting priorities leads to having more balance in your life
• Learn how to combat procrastination and avoid distractions
• Appreciate the value of time and how to use it wisely and budget it properly

wavebreakmedia/
Shutterstock

3 EMOTIONAL INTELLIGENCE

Student Goals

• Learn what emotional intelligence is
• Explore emotional intelligence in everyday life: motivation, resilience, establishing balance, prioritizing, and anger management
• Develop emotional intelligence in college
• Examine how emotions influence success
• Understand ways to improve your emotional intelligence

wavebreakmedia/
Shutterstock

4 HOW YOU LEARN

Student Goals

• Discover your learning style
• Learn how to handle a mismatch between how you learn best and how you are being taught
• Understand and recognize a learning disability

1
WELCOME TO YOUR COLLEGE EXPERIENCE

YOU WILL EXPLORE

The value of a college education, the college success course, and this textbook

What the college experience is about

The importance of exploring your purpose and setting goals for attending college

The value of academic planning and working with an academic adviser to choose a major and build a program of study

⚲ What high-impact practices are and the positive impact they can have on your learning and overall success

Rontavius Jamal Snipes, 23

Biology major
Clayton State University, Georgia

> ❝ **Working twenty-two hours while taking sixteen credits means that I rarely get enough sleep because I have to stay up late studying. So my biggest goal for now is to find a way to better manage my time.** ❞

Setting both long- and short-term goals has always been important to Rontavius Snipes. After high school, when he found himself living in Atlanta and working at a dead-end job, he set his sights on going to college and enrolled at Clayton State University. Now that he's in college, he's majoring in biology with the goal of attending dental school after graduation, and he knows that getting good grades and staying involved on campus will help him achieve that ultimate goal.

Like many students, Rontavius also needs to balance working (he works at a pharmacy 30 miles from campus) with attending and participating in school, so many of his goals have involved small steps. "I am currently the president of the pre-dental student association," he explains. "The group is small, but this semester I plan to attend a leadership seminar to get some extra motivation to be able to lead a successful student organization." He also gets involved on campus in smaller ways by promoting concerts and plays, which helps him stay connected with other students. He acknowledges, however, that working while

attending school does have its challenges, which he is still trying to solve. "Working twenty-two hours while taking sixteen credits means that I rarely get enough sleep because I have to stay up late studying. Finding a social life away from my roommates and my girlfriend can be difficult too, so my biggest goal for now is to find a way to better manage my time." Still, Rontavius knows that the hard work will pay off. "Prior to attending college, I never thought about things deeply and took everything at face value. I have greater intuition now and definitely feel that the price I pay for education is well worth it," he says.

In the future, Rontavius hopes to travel the world tackling issues such as poverty, cultural barriers, and the economic glass ceiling that many people face, and his favorite class so far, Sociology 1101, plays nicely into those goals. "That class pushes my life message," he says, "that we should try to understand other cultures and not be so close-minded. I have been the subject of negative stereotypes, and I just love how this class shows how these ways of thinking came about."

To access the LearningCurve study tool, video activities, and more, go to LaunchPad for *Your College Experience*. macmillanhighered.com /gardner12e

Rontavius knows how important a college education is to his future economic status, but he also knows that going to college presents him with many learning opportunities that he couldn't access any other way. He has already discovered how important it is to think deeply and has recognized that he has leadership skills. Rontavius is also encountering challenges, primarily in time management. He has to work and also wants a satisfying personal life. Therefore, he wants strategies to help him better manage his limited time and maintain good grades.

This book is designed to help you both overcome the struggles that face you and explore all that college has to offer. As you read this book, you will discover your own strengths, learn to be a good thinker, and become skilled at making good choices. You will develop an appreciation of the power you have to direct the aspects of your life, such as managing relationships with your friends, instructors, and family, selecting out-of-class opportunities to pursue, and allocating your time to school, work, and leisure activities. But the most important skill you will need to learn in college is how to keep learning throughout your life. As you're settling into your new college routine, we want to welcome you to the demanding and rewarding world of higher education and equip you with a set of strategies you can use to do your best.

THE VALUE OF A COLLEGE EDUCATION

American society values higher education, which explains why the United States currently has more than 4,400 colleges and universities. College is the primary way that people achieve upward social mobility or the ability to attain a higher standard of living. That might accurately describe your purpose for being in college: to attain a higher standard of living. In earlier centuries, a high standard of living was almost always a function of family background. Either you were born into power and money or you spent your life working for others who had power and money. In most countries today, however, receiving a college degree helps level the playing field for everyone. A college degree can minimize or eliminate the restrictions to achievement that stem from differences in background, race, ethnicity, family income level, national origin, immigration status, family lineage, and personal connections. Simply put, college participation is about ensuring that more people have the opportunity to be evaluated on the basis of merit rather than family status, money, or other forms of privilege. It makes achieving the American dream possible.

In 1900, fewer than 2 percent of Americans of traditional college age attended college. Today, new technologies and the information explosion are changing the workplace so drastically that to support themselves and their families adequately, most people will need some education beyond high school. In spite of the fact that today more than 67 percent of high school graduates (approximately 18 million students) are attending

IN CLASS ❯ We highly recommend some activities for getting acquainted on the first day of class to lay the foundation for active learning. If a peer leader is working in your class, you might want to assign him or her responsibility for this get-acquainted activity. Ask the students to pair up and interview a classmate they do not know. The interview should take roughly 5 to 8 minutes, and the topics for the interview might include name, hometown, college major, career thoughts, and something the individual is proud of. Have the members of each pair introduce each other to the rest of the class. Ask for anonymous feedback at the end of the first class, including thoughts on what each student hopes to learn.

IN CLASS ❯ Ask your students what college means to them. What thoughts come to mind? The discussion might explore the expectations they had before they came to college.

IN CLASS ❯ This is an opportune time to ask students what they might have heard about the differences between their high school and this particular college or university. Remind them that being successful in college is likely to take much more time than being successful in high school.

college, we are seeing a wave of questions in the media about whether or not college is really worth it.

Rontavius, the student profiled at the beginning of this chapter, likely would answer that yes, college is really worth it, but what do the data say? A *New York Times* analysis of data from the Economic Institute (**epi.com**) finds that the answer is "yes." Dramatic differences exist between the earning power of students with a high school diploma and those with a four-year college degree. In 2013, four-year college graduates earned about twice as much per hour as high school graduates. While there are concerns about the cost of college today, the cost of not attending college is even more dramatic. David Autor, an economist from the Massachusetts Institute of Technology, reported that not going to college will, over your lifetime, cost you about half a million dollars.[1]

You can also take a look at Figure 1.1 to see how earning a college degree will improve your earning potential. This figure breaks down unemployment rates and weekly earnings according to education level. The more education you have, the more likely you are to be employed, and the higher your earnings will be.

Beyond the financial benefits that earning a college degree gives to an individual, society benefits as a whole when people earn college degrees. College is an established process designed to further formal education so that students who attend and graduate will be prepared for certain roles in society. Today, for many, those roles are found predominantly in what has become known as the "information economy," which means that most college graduates will earn their living by creating,

---

[1]David Leonhardt, "Is College Worth It? Clearly, New Data Say," *The New York Times*, May 27, 2014, www.nytimes.com/2014/05/27/upshot/is-college-worth-it-clearly-new-data-say. html?_r=0, accessed August 7, 2014.

FIGURE 1.1 › Education Pays

Earning a college degree will improve your earning potential. This figure breaks down unemployment rates and weekly earnings according to education level. Use this information as motivation to make the most of college. The more education you have, the more likely you are to be employed, and the higher your earnings will be.

Source: U.S. Department of Labor, Bureau of Labor Statistics, *Current Population Survey*, 2013.

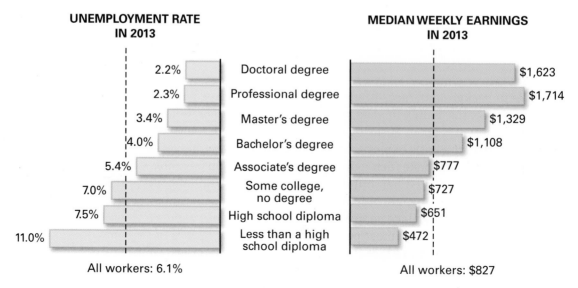

managing, and using information. For others, college is a crucial way for students to prepare for leadership roles in their communities, companies, professions, or military units.

Another reason students get a four-year college degree is to prepare them to continue their education in a graduate or professional school. If you want to become a medical doctor, dentist, lawyer, or college professor, a four-year college degree is just the beginning, but it is a required step on the path to such professions. Let's say you aspire to be a pharmacist and are planning to get a bachelor's degree in chemistry. Your primary purpose for your degree in chemistry is to gain admittance to pharmacy school. Perhaps you have also considered that if your plans should change, having a degree in chemistry will get your foot in the door in several different industries, so another purpose for your degree is having an edge in the job market upon graduation.

The Value of Your College Success Course

Since you are reading this textbook, it is likely that you are enrolled in a first-year seminar, first-year experience, or "college success" course. In this book we use all three names. The course—possibly the most important course you will take—and this textbook—possibly the most important textbook you will read—are all about improving your chances for success in college and beyond. Before you start reading, though, you probably have some questions.

Research conducted by colleges and universities has found that first-year students are far more likely to be successful if they participate in courses and programs designed to teach them how to succeed in college. This course is designed to help you avoid some of the pitfalls—both academic and personal—that trip up many beginning students.

Although your classmates might not say it out loud, many of them share your concerns, doubts, and fears about being in college. This course will provide a supportive environment in which you can share your successes and your frustrations, get to know others who are beginning college, develop lasting relationships with your instructor and some other students, and begin to think about your plans for life after college.

The Value of Your College Success Textbook

As college professors, researchers, and administrators with many years of experience working with first-year students, we're well aware that starting college can be challenging. We also know that if you apply the ideas in this book to your everyday life, you are likely to enjoy your time in college, graduate, and achieve your life goals.

Your instructor may ask you to read every chapter in this book, but even if you're not required to do so, consider this book a resource to answer questions you might have later this year and throughout your college experience. After this opening chapter, which discusses the value of college, purpose and goal setting, and academic planning, subsequent chapters cover topics such as managing your time, discovering your personal learning style, and understanding how your emotions affect your learning and interactions with others. The next chapters focus on what happens in class and cover topics such as thinking, listening, taking notes, reading, taking tests, writing and speaking, and developing information

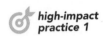

high-impact practice 1

RETENTION STRATEGY › Try to get students to understand the significance of the information about the value of a college education, which will aid motivation, commitment, and retention.

HIGH-IMPACT PRACTICE › You will note later in this chapter that research finds that the college success course, or first-year seminar, is a high-impact practice that can result in student learning, retention, and engagement.

RETENTION STRATEGY › Make a positive prediction of your students' success as a result of taking this course by briefly explaining to them the pervasive research indicating that students who participate in college success courses are more likely to persist in and graduate from college than those who do not participate.

PEER LEADERS › As a peer leader, you should take some time to relay your own experiences when you were a new college student—your hopes, doubts, and fears. If you took a college success course, be prepared to tell the students how you feel about it now. Looking back, was it fun? Was it helpful to you?

HIGH-IMPACT PRACTICE › If the college success course on your campus is required of all or almost all first-year students, it also qualifies as a "campus-wide common intellectual experience," another high-impact practice.

literacy skills. The concluding chapters address issues that are relevant both to college and to life beyond college: selecting an academic major and career, managing your money, developing healthy relationships, understanding diversity, and maintaining healthy behaviors.

Though some of the textbook's content may seem like common sense, much of it is based on research and the experiences of thousands of college students and educators. And although some topics in this book might have been presented in high school, we find that many college success strategies cannot be properly understood until students are actually in college and have an immediate "need to know."

FYI › Four types of active "Your Turn" features in each chapter are available for you and your students to use in a variety of ways. With clear directives for what we want students to do, the questions we ask can be used as triggers for student reflection (Write and Reflect), for decision making (Make Good Choices), in small- or large-group discussions (Work Together), and for motivation (Stay Motivated), or they can be used in any active learning mode you choose.

THE COLLEGE EXPERIENCE

What is the college experience? Depending on who you are, your life circumstances, and why you decided to enroll, college can mean different things. College is often portrayed in books and movies as a place where young people live away from home in ivy-covered residence halls. We frequently see college depicted with a major focus on big-time sports, heavy drinking, and partying. Yes, you'll find some of that at some colleges, but most students today don't move away from home, don't live on campus, and don't see much ivy. College is far more than any single image you might carry around in your head. And college students today come from more walks of life than ever before.

Why College Is Important for You

College is about thinking, and it will help you understand how to become a careful and critical thinker, someone who doesn't believe everything that he or she hears or reads but instead looks for evidence before forming an opinion. Developing solid thinking skills will empower you to make sound decisions throughout your life.

Although college is often thought of as a time when traditional-age students become young adults, we realize that on today's college campuses, many students are already adults. Whatever your age, college can be a time when you take risks, learn new things, and meet new and different people, all in a relatively safe environment. It's OK to experiment in college, within limits, because that's what college is designed for.

College will provide you with numerous opportunities to develop a variety of formal and informal social networks. These networks will help you make friends and develop alliances with faculty members and fellow students who share your interests and goals. Social networking sites such as Facebook and Twitter provide a way to enrich your real-life social networks in college.

College definitely can and should be fun, and we hope it will be for you. You will meet new people, go to athletic events and parties, build camaraderie with new friends, and feel a sense of school spirit. Many college graduates relive memories of college days throughout their lives, fanatically root for their institution's athletic teams, return for homecoming and class reunions, and encourage their own children to attend their alma mater. In fact, you might be a legacy student, someone whose parents or grandparents attended the same institution that you do.

In addition to being fun, college is a lot of work. Being a college student means spending many hours studying each week, staying up late at night, taking high-stakes exams, and possibly working harder than you ever have before. For many students, college becomes much like a job, with defined duties, expectations, and obligations. Most important is that college will be a set of experiences that will help you to further define your goals and achieve your own purpose.

Getting the Most Out of College: High-Impact Practices

high-impact practices 1–10

Throughout your college experience, you will have the opportunity to participate in activities known as "high-impact practices." High-impact practices are particular activities that research shows have significant positive impact on both your learning and your overall success. One high-impact practice is taking the first-year seminar, which shouldn't surprise you given what you have read in this chapter about the value of this course. Here is a comprehensive list of the ten high-impact practices in which you can participate, listed in the order you are most likely to encounter them. (In this textbook, this icon ♂ is used to alert you to these opportunities to enrich your learning.):

1. **first-year seminars** The course in which you find yourself now, designed to prepare you for your college experience.
2. **writing-intensive courses** Courses across the curriculum that engage you in multiple forms of writing for different audiences. This textbook offers various writing activities that make your first-year seminar a writing-intensive course.
3. **collaborative assignments** Learning activities in which you work and solve problems with your classmates in this and other courses.
4. **global learning or diversity experiences** Courses and programs in which you explore cultures, life experiences, and worldviews different from your own.
5. **service-learning** Programs or courses in which you engage in required field-based "experiential learning" and reflection while giving back to your community through service.
6. **learning communities** Programs in which you would take two or more "linked" courses with a group of other students and work closely with one another and with your instructors.
7. **campus-wide common intellectual experiences** Programs in which you would take required "common-core" courses, participate in a required learning community, or engage in other shared experiences such as a "common reading."
8. **undergraduate research** A program that gives you the opportunity to participate in systematic investigation and research working one-to-one with a faculty member.
9. **internships** Direct experience with service-learning or in a work setting often related to your career interests.
10. **capstone courses and projects** Courses or experiences that would require you in the senior year to reflect on what you have learned in all your courses and create a project of some sort that integrates and applies your knowledge.

Does College Seem Like a Strange Land?

Are you a student who has recently come to the United States from another country? Perhaps you have immigrated with family members or on your own. Whatever the situation, learning the unique language, culture, and expectations that exist at a U.S. college can be a challenge. Do instructors' expectations and students' behaviors seem different than what you experienced in your home country? Seek out English as a second language (ESL) courses or programs if you need help you with your English skills. Also, visit the international student counselors to find out how you can continue to increase your understanding of life in the United States, both on and off campus.

Blend Images/Arial Skelley/Getty Images

Some high-impact practices may be activities or courses that are mandatory to fulfill general education or major requirements, but others will be optional. It's a good idea to seek out as many of these practices as you can manage, because doing so will result in heightened learning and greater success for you.

---

your turn   Make Good Choices

The Decision to Become a College Student

Write five reasons that you chose to go to college at this time in your life. Share what you wrote with a classmate and see how many of your reasons are the same or different.

Traditional Students: Making the Transition

If you are a traditional student, meaning that you just graduated from high school, the transition you are making means that you have to adjust to some distinct differences between high school and college. For instance, you will probably be part of a more diverse student body, not just in terms of race but also in terms of age, religion, political opinions, and life experiences. If you attend a large college or university, you might feel like a "number" and not as special as you felt in high school. You will have more potential friends to choose from, but familiar assumptions about people based on where they live, where they go to church, or what high school they attended might not apply to the new people you're meeting.

Because of the many competing opportunities you'll be faced with both in and out of class, managing your time is sure to be more complex than it was in high school. Your classes will meet on various days and times, and you will likely have additional commitments, including work, family, activities, and sports. Your college classes might meet for longer class periods than your high school classes. Tests are given less frequently in college—sometimes only twice a term—and you will most likely spend more time writing in college than you did in high school. You will be encouraged to do original research and to investigate differing points of view on a topic. You will be expected to study outside of class, prepare assignments, do assigned reading, and be ready for in-class discussions.

If any upper-level students work as peer leaders in your college success course, get to know them. Peer leaders are selected because of their knowledge, experience, and willingness to help new students. A peer leader can serve as an informal academic adviser, mentor, and friend.

As discussed throughout this chapter, college is also the time when you will begin making serious plans for your work life after college. Although you may have thought about potential careers in high school, determining a particular career direction takes on special urgency in college. The college success course and this textbook give you tools to help you identify and choose the right career path among the endless choices offered at many colleges and universities. We'll discuss college majors toward the end of this chapter, and we'll delve into career options in the last chapter of the book.

HIGH-IMPACT PRACTICE ▶
Collaborative student work, a high-impact practice, can be easily implemented in a college success course. This Your Turn exercise gives students an opportunity to begin the process of collaboration by sharing their expectations of, and experiences in, college.

high-impact practice 3

---

yourturn Work Together

Are You Surprised?

Talk with a classmate to discover whether college life is what each of you thought it would be. Share what you have experienced and times when you have been pleasantly or unpleasantly surprised.

IN CLASS ▶ If you have both nontraditional students and traditional students in class, consider a discussion in which representatives from each group share their concerns. For example, some returning students who have been away from college for several years might believe that they will not be able to keep up with "those kids," whereas the younger students might think that the class will be more difficult because of the presence of older students.

Challenges and Opportunities for Nontraditional Students

If you are a nontraditional or adult student, you might have experience in the job market, and you might have a spouse or partner and children.

techtip

E-MAIL WITH STYLE

As you planned for college, you probably heard about all the ways you'll use technology as a student. First, you need to activate your college e-mail as soon as possible to receive information regarding class cancellations, weather-related closings, student events, and other types of communication that your college or your instructors may send you. Many colleges require you to use your student e-mail account to send and receive official communications. It is a good idea to get in the habit of checking that account daily, or at least every other day.

Whether your class meets online or face-to-face, at some point you will need to communicate with your instructor via e-mail. Although you may prefer to use Facebook or Twitter, be sure to use e-mail to communicate with your instructors unless they tell you otherwise. Writing e-mails to your instructors is different from writing e-mails or sending texts to your friends.

The Problem

You need help with an assignment or you have a question about the syllabus and have to send your professor an e-mail, but you've never sent an e-mail to any kind of teacher before.

The Fix

Take a few minutes to figure out what exactly you need to ask, jot down your main points, and then construct a clear and concise e-mail.

How to Do It

Look at the example shown here and follow its format in your e-mail.

It's best to use your college e-mail address because it has your name and your college's e-mail address, which will help your professor immediately recognize that your message has been sent by a student. If you have to use another e-mail address, use a professional, simple address that includes your name.

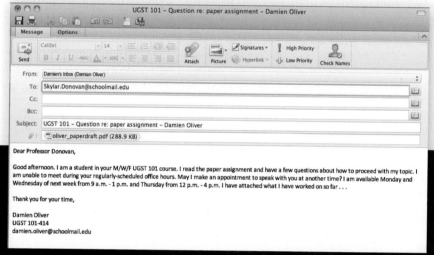

- Make the subject line informative. Your instructor might receive hundreds of e-mails every day, and a relevant subject like the name of the course or the assignment will help him or her respond to your e-mail promptly. A subject line like "Class" or "Question" isn't helpful; a blank subject line usually goes to the instructor's spam folder.

- Address your instructor with respect. Think about how you address your instructor in class, or look at your syllabus to see his or her proper title. If an instructor uses Doctor, then you should use Doctor. If you don't know your instructor's title, you can never go wrong with Dear Professor, plus your instructor's last name.

- Sign every e-mail with your full name, course number, and e-mail address.

- When attaching files to your e-mail (a skill you should have), use widely accepted file formats like .doc, .docx, or .pdf. Also, be sure your last name is included in the file name. See the example shown.

EXTRA STYLE POINTS: Set your college e-mail to feed into your phone, tablet, or regular online account. Tie it into your regular e-mail, like Google or Outlook. Most of these services can be configured so that you can receive e-mail from multiple accounts. This way, you will have all of your e-mail in one place that you're sure to check.

*Note: If you want to cut back on e-mails from Web sites that you visit, use a free service like UnRollMe (https://unroll.me) that condenses the blanket e-mails you get, but allows you to read them when you have time. You can list your instructors as "favorites" so you don't miss their e-mails.

You might be returning to college or beginning college for the first time. You will face a special set of challenges, such as trying to relate to younger students and juggling the responsibilities of work, caring for a family, and being in college. You will likely experience a challenging lack of freedom in dealing with so many important, competing responsibilities. Remember, though, that nontraditional students tend to have intrinsic motivation that comes with maturity and experience, and they appreciate the value of an education. You will have the advantage of approaching college work with a very clear purpose for why you are there.

No matter where you are on the age continuum—seventeen or eighteen or much older—you will bring certain strengths to your college experiences that will help both you and others. Older students have a lot of determination and a set of real-life experiences that they can relate to what they're learning. Eighteen- and nineteen-year-olds are comfortable with technology and social media, and they are pop-culture experts. These kinds of strengths are all important to the learning process.

Communicating with Your Instructors

In college, whether you're a nontraditional student adjusting to less freedom than you've been used to or a traditional student adjusting to more freedom, you will find that your instructors are not going to tell you what, how, or when to study. In addition, they will rarely monitor your progress. However you will have more freedom to express views that are different from theirs. They will usually have private offices and keep regular office hours when they can meet with you. Check with your instructors to find out if you need to make an appointment before coming to their office. (Read the Tech Tip: E-Mail with Style, which shows you how to communicate with your instructors appropriately via e-mail.) You might be able to ask your instructors a quick question before or after class, but you will be able to get far more help by actually visiting their offices. By taking advantage of office hours, you will also let the instructor know that you are serious about learning. You can ask the instructor for direct help with any question or misunderstanding that you have. You might also want to ask some questions about the instructor's educational career and particular research interests. Many students develop close relationships with their instructors, relationships that can be important both now and in the future.

IN CLASS > Point out that most people base their success in life on their strengths, not their weaknesses. Therefore, it is important for students to think about how college can help them build on their strengths and address their weaknesses.

OUTSIDE CLASS > Consider staying in touch with your students electronically, either by setting up a class e-mail list or by having some kind of Web presence through which students can network with their peers outside of class. Most first-year students can comfortably communicate online. At some institutions, college success classes are linked electronically with similar classes in other parts of the country. This kind of communication gives students the opportunity to develop new perspectives on beginning college successfully.

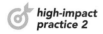 **high-impact practice 2**

HIGH-IMPACT PRACTICE ▶ Your college success course should be "writing intensive." Although most writing assignments in your course will not be lengthy, students can practice their writing skills continuously through a series of short assignments such as this one.

---

your turn — Write and Reflect

What Does "The American Dream" Mean to You?

Using Google or another search engine, look up "American Dream" images. What images appear? Choose a few that resonate with you. Write a short essay describing these images and why you find them meaningful.

IN CLASS ▶ Ask your students whether they have thought about where they would like to be in the next five years. Ten years? What skills and values drive these goals? Challenge your students to write down a five- or ten-year plan, and encourage them to refer to the plan throughout their college years as a motivational reminder.

IN CLASS ▶ Ask your students which is more important: education for its own sake or education for the sake of earning more money? This question might lead to a lively debate.

EXPLORING PURPOSE AND SETTING GOALS

You might think that you know exactly what you want to do with your life and where you want to go once you finish college. Or, like many students, you might be struggling to balance being in college, working, and having a satisfying personal life. You might be highly motivated to do your best in college, or you may be unsure about why you're in college at this time in your life. It is possible that as you discover more about yourself and your abilities, your purpose for coming to college will change.

Let's stop and think about what "purpose" means. A firefighter who enters a burning building with people trapped inside has a clear purpose: He has been trained to get those people out of the building safely. He is determined to fulfill the commitment of his job. The reason to go into the burning building is clear: to accomplish the objective of rescuing the people.

These words—determination, resolve, goal, reason, and objective—all relate to purpose. What will the training and education that you get in college teach you to do? How will succeeding in college help you succeed in the job and life that you envision for yourself? What do you feel determined to be, to have, and to accomplish? As you consider your answers to these questions, you'll get closer to understanding your purpose for being in college and setting the right goals to achieve this purpose. The more you keep the answers to these questions in the front of your mind, the more purposeful you will feel in what you do, and the more motivated you will be to do it. In this course and in this book, we'll help you answer questions about purpose, and we will equip you with strategies to help you achieve your goals.

Another concept that we stress in this book is "resilience," which is an ability to recover from or adjust easily to misfortune or change. Virtually every college student faces an occasional disappointment, whether it's a poor grade, an unsatisfactory performance on a stage or in an athletic arena, or the end of a relationship. Students who are resilient—who bounce back quickly from difficult situations—will be more successful in college and later in life. We encourage you to develop your own resilience as a tool you will use now and in the future.

Getting Started with Goal Setting

Think about how you define success. Is success about money, friendship, or power? Is it about achieving excellence in college and beyond, or is it about finding a sense of purpose in your life? For most people, success is a combination of all these factors and more. Although luck or "who you know" may play a role, first and foremost your success will be the result of intentional steps you take. So, in your quest for success, where do you start?

Identify Your Personal Strengths. Do you like to talk, deal with conflict, and stand up for yourself? Are you a good reader? If your answers to these questions are "yes," you may want to consider a career in the legal profession. Are you a good science student, and do you enjoy working with your hands? If so, you might want to think about dentistry. Your campus career center can help you discover your unique strengths—and weaknesses—which can influence your direction as you explore career choices.

Ask Yourself Tough Questions. Am I here to find out who I am and to study a subject that I am truly passionate about, regardless of whether it leads to a career? Am I here to engage in an academic program that provides an array of possibilities when I graduate? Am I here to prepare myself for a graduate program or for immediate employment? Am I here to obtain specific training in a field that I am committed to? Am I here to gain specific skills for a job I already have?

RETENTION STRATEGY > These questions are very important for solidifying the connection between a student's sense of purpose for being in college and his or her career choice. Purposeful students are more likely to persist in college than students who lack a sense of purpose.

Establish Goals for Today, This Week, This Year, and Beyond. Although some students prefer to "go with the flow" and let life happen to them, those students are more likely to flounder and less likely to achieve success in college or in a career. So, instead of "going with the flow" and simply reacting to what college and life present, think instead about how you can take more control over the decisions and choices you make now, because these decisions and choices will lay the foundation for the achievement of future life goals. It is easy to make vague plans for the future, but you must determine which short-term steps are necessary if those plans are to become a reality.

College is an ideal time to begin setting and fulfilling short- and long-term goals. A short-term goal might be to read twenty pages from your history text twice a week to prepare for an exam that will cover the first hundred pages of the book. A long-term goal might be to begin predicting which elective college courses you could choose that would help you attain your career goals.

Thinking about a career might seem unrelated to some of the general education courses you are required to take in your first year. Sometimes it's hard to see the connection between a history or literature course and what you want to do with the rest of your life. If you're open to learning, however, you may discover potential areas of interest that you have never considered before, and these areas of interest may lead you to discover a new career path.

Setting SMART Goals

Follow these guidelines to set some short-term goals and consider how they fall within the framework of setting goals that are *specific, measurable, attainable, relevant,* and achievable within a given *time* (SMART).[2] (Figure 1.2 gives you a chance to practice.)

1. Be specific about what you want to achieve and when.
2. State your goal in measurable terms.
3. Be sure that the goal is attainable. If you don't have the necessary skills, strengths, and resources to achieve your goal, change it to one that is more appropriate for you. Be sure that you really want to reach the goal. Don't set out to work toward something only because you want to please others.
4. Know how the goal is relevant to your life and why the goal matters. Be sure that your goal helps your larger life plan and gives you a sense of moving forward.
5. Consider the time frame and whether the goal is achievable within the period you desire. Allow yourself enough time to pursue it considering any difficulties you might have. Plan for ways you might deal with problems. Decide which goal comes next. How will you begin? Create steps and a time line for reaching your next goal.

For instance, let's assume that after you graduate, you think that you might want to work in an underdeveloped country, perhaps spending some time in the Peace Corps. What are some short-term goals that would help you reach this long-term objective? One goal might be to take courses focused on different countries or cultures, but that goal isn't very specific and doesn't state a particular time period. A much more specific goal would be to take one course each year that helps you build a body of knowledge about other countries and cultures. An even more specific goal would be to review the course catalog, identify the courses you want to take, and list them on a personal time line.

Before working toward any long-term goal, it's important to be realistic and honest with yourself. Is it truly *your* goal—one that you yourself value and desire to pursue—or is it a goal that a parent or friend argued was right for you? Given your abilities and interests, is the goal realistic? Remember that dreaming up long-term goals is the easy part. To reach your goals, you need to be specific and systematic about the steps you will take today, this week, and throughout your college experience.

ACADEMIC PLANNING

If you have a goal to drive across the United States, you could, in theory, hop in a car that may need an oil change and travel without GPS or an itinerary and without a carefully packed bag or a planned

---

[2]T. Doran, "There's a S.M.A.R.T. Way to Write Management's Goals and Objectives," *Management Review* 70, no. 11 (1981): 35–36.

FIGURE 1.2 > Practice Setting SMART Goals

Using this chart, try to set one goal in each of the areas listed: academic, career, personal, and financial. Follow the goal through time, from immediate to long term. An example is provided for you.

IN CLASS > Figure 1.2 gives students a chance to practice goal setting by walking through the SMART model.

Types of Goals	Immediate (this week)	Short Term (this term)	Long Term (this year)
Example: Academic	I will list all of my tests and project due dates on my academic calendar.	I will keep a file with my own test and exam grades in case of a discrepancy with my final grades.	I will research graduate programs in my field to determine if I have the grades and scores to be admitted.
Academic			
Career			
Personal			
Financial			

budget. You could simply follow the stars and road signs and hope for the best with weather, lodging, money, and the condition of the car. You might make it to your destination—which you didn't even narrow down beyond getting to the opposite coast—but what is likely to go wrong? How would some planning have improved the journey? Planning your college education is no different. Some preparation, a navigation system, and a clear destination will help you reach your goals, and smoothly.

Academic planning is a vital step in your college career, and it should be an ongoing process that starts on day one. Once you lay a foundation for your studies, you'll save time and money, avoid missing credits, and take ownership of your curriculum. You'll also stay motivated with a clear sense of how each step in your academic plan contributes to your overall purpose for being in college. It's no coincidence that students who engage in academic planning are more likely to stay in school. They are the people who know where they're going and how to get there. They have set their goals, and they know what it takes to achieve them.

Choosing a Major

Even before you have figured out your purpose for going to college, you might be required to select a program of study also referred to as a major,

RETENTION STRATEGY > Although being undecided can have a negative correlation with retention, that is not always the case. Make sure that you do not reinforce any stigma for students who are "undecided." Instead, urge them to think of themselves more positively as "exploratory." It is very important to get such students to use your career center early in the first year to influence their direction and commitment. Tell them that this course will deal with major, career, and course selection.

IN CLASS > Take a poll to determine how many students are undecided and how many have already selected a major. Assure the students that both are perfectly acceptable places to be when they first come to college. Explain that it is important for students to keep an open mind in their studies and use this time to explore their options.

an area of study like psychology, engineering, education, or nursing. Selecting a major is one step in academic planning. In every major, students take a variety of courses; some are directly related to the area of study, whereas others are general education and elective courses. For example, all students should take college-level math and English courses as part of general education, but they can choose electives depending on their interests.

Many students change majors as they better understand their strengths and weaknesses, learn more about career options, and become interested in different areas of study. Some colleges and universities allow you to be undecided for a while or to select liberal arts as your major until you make a decision about what to study.

Although it's OK to be undecided, planning your major and your college curriculum as soon as possible saves valuable time and resources. Even if you're on financial aid, you're not going to have an unlimited amount of cash. If you randomly take courses without a specific goal in mind, your tuition funds could dry up before your plan takes shape. Therefore, it's essential to have a strategy for your program of study. Start by building a solid base of general courses that could qualify you for a few different majors, but leave time in your schedule to explore other subjects that grab your interest. Do you like math? Try an accounting or economics class. Love *CSI*? Sign up for Criminology 101 or the equivalent. An academic adviser or counselor can provide you with proper information and guidance to make a decision about your major.

Working with an Academic Adviser

IN CLASS > Make sure that your students know who their academic adviser is, and that they have an appointment to see their adviser before the end of the term.

Before you register for classes next term, sit down for a strategy session with your academic adviser. On most campuses, you'll be assigned an adviser, who is usually an instructor or a staff person in your chosen field of study. Some colleges offer special advisory centers run by professional advisers. A good adviser can help you choose courses, decide on a major, weigh career possibilities, and map out your degree and certificate requirements. Your adviser can also recommend instructors and help you simplify all aspects of your academic life, so it's important to meet with your adviser right away. Here are a few ways to make sure that your first meeting is a valuable experience.

- **Prepare for the meeting by looking at the course catalog, thinking about available majors, and familiarizing yourself with campus resources.** If you haven't decided on a major, investigate opportunities for taking an aptitude test or self-assessment to help you narrow down your options; ask your adviser about these tests during your meeting. (You will read more about self-assessments and self-exploration in Chapter 15.) The early days of college are critical; once classes start, you might not have time for in-depth research.
- **Prepare materials to bring to the meeting.** Even if you submitted one with your application, take along a copy of your academic transcript.

The transcript, which contains your complete high school record, is an important tool. It shows your academic adviser where you've been, what your academic strengths are, and where your interests lie.

- **Make a list of majors that appeal to you.** Academic advisers love it when students come prepared. It shows that you're passionate and serious about your future.

- **Map out your time frame and goals.** Do you plan to enroll full-time or part-time? If you're at a four-year college or university, when do you plan to graduate and with what degree? Are you planning to go to graduate school to finish your studies? If you are at a two-year college, do you want an associate's degree or a certificate? Do you plan to transfer to a four-year institution?

- **Know the right questions to ask.** Once you've chosen a major, you'll need to understand how to move forward in your academic program to meet the necessary requirements. Fortunately, the process is straightforward. You will have prerequisites, which are the core courses that you need to take before you can enroll in upper-level classes in your major. Your major may also have corequisites, courses that you have to take in conjunction with other courses during the same term, such as a chemistry lab alongside your chemistry class. With this knowledge under your belt, here is what you need to find out:

  1. How many credits must I take each term to graduate on time? (Note: If you are on financial aid, doing a work-study program, or are a college athlete, you may have to take a minimum number of credits per term to maintain your benefits.)
  2. What are the prerequisites for my major? Corequisites?
  3. If I've taken any advanced placement credits or exams, can I use them to fulfill some of my major's requirements?
  4. What career opportunities will I have once I graduate? What will the salary potential look like?

- **Know what to take away from your meeting.** By the end of the meeting, you should have a printout of your current course schedule and plans for classes that you might take in the next term and beyond. At many institutions, you and your adviser will set up a five- to seven-term plan online.

- **Know these rules of thumb about selecting your classes:**

  1. Most full-time students take four to six courses a term. Most classes don't meet every day. With that in mind, decide which classes you want to take, find out which days and times they meet, and make sure they don't overlap.
  2. To get the classes you want, make sure to register as early as possible, either in person or online.
  3. Resist the temptation to cram all your classes into one or two days. It's better to aim for a manageable workload, so spread your classes over the week.
  4. Go for a mix of hard and easy classes. Especially at the beginning, you might not realize how challenging college classes can be or how much outside work they entail. If you load up on organic chemistry, Russian 101, and advanced thermodynamics, your grades and general well-being could suffer.

IN CLASS ❯ After the fall advising period, ask your students to reflect in class on their advising interactions by responding to questions such as these: Did they get the help they needed? Did they feel comfortable with their advisers? Are they still confused about courses and schedules? Be alert for continuing advising issues that you may need to address either in class or one-on-one with some students.

- **Know what to do if your academic adviser isn't very helpful.** If you think that you and your adviser are not a good match, talk to your college success course instructor about what you need to do to be assigned to a different adviser. Alternately, drop by the campus counseling center for assistance. But whatever you do, be resilient. Don't throw in the towel. Academic planning is so critical to your success in college that it's worth persevering until you find an adviser with whom you feel comfortable.
- **Set up subsequent meetings with your academic adviser.** Touch base with your adviser at least once a term, if not more. It's important to stay connected and make sure that you're on a positive track. Programs change requirements occasionally, so it's smart to touch base to make any necessary adjustments. Here are some questions to ask your adviser as you check in:

  1. Have there been any changes to my program of study?
  2. If I want to officially withdraw from a class, will I be penalized at a later time?
  3. Am I still taking classes in the right order?
  4. What courses do I need to take to satisfy the major requirements at the institution where I plan to transfer?
  5. For those students who are considering graduate school: Am I meeting the criteria for graduate school, and will my grades qualify me for the program I'm interested in?

high-impact practice 2

HIGH-IMPACT PRACTICE ❯ This "Your Turn" exercise suggests that students write briefly about their academic advising experience. This short writing assignment can be part of an ongoing student journal or a separate short paper. Although this is not an English composition class, use these early writing assignments to become aware of any writing problems your students have so that you can refer them for assistance either now or later in the term.

your turn Stay Motivated

Academic Planning

You have probably already met with an academic adviser, but if not, schedule a meeting right away. Think about this meeting and what you accomplished. Then write a short paper or journal entry about something you learned that increased your motivation to take academic planning seriously. Also, describe in writing at least three problems you might encounter when it comes to choosing your major or planning your program of study if you do not take academic planning seriously. How can these possible negative consequences increase your motivation to plan well for your next meeting with your adviser?

checklist for success

Welcome to Your College Experience

☐ **Know and appreciate the value of a college education, your college success course, and this textbook.** College is a major investment of both time and money, an investment that will pay rich dividends both now and in the future. This course and this textbook can help you make the right choices and increase your chances for success. Read the table of contents, skim the entire book, and access the information that you need now.

☐ **Meet with your instructors outside of class.** You can talk to your instructors before or after class, but the better option is to visit them during their office hours. You'll probably also have the opportunity to get to know your instructors in informal settings; some of them may even invite you and your classmates to their homes or to a local restaurant to share a meal and conversation.

☐ 🎯 *high-impact practice* **Pursue high-impact practices.** Throughout this textbook, we have highlighted high-impact practices. These practices will begin in the first year and continue throughout your college experience. By taking every opportunity to participate in high-impact practices, you will increase your learning and overall success in college.

☐ **Meet the challenges of making the transition from high school to college or of being a nontraditional student returning to college.** Whatever your age or stage of life, beginning college is one of life's most significant transitions. This book will help you become more aware of the particular kinds of transition experiences you will encounter either as a student fresh out of high school or one who has been working or raising a family before beginning college.

☐ **Set both short-term and long-term goals.** You are far more likely to succeed in college if your goals for today, tomorrow, and four years from now are clear. For instance, if you plan to graduate from college in four years, what goals could you set for this week or this term that would help you reach this important long-term goal?

☐ **Find a competent and caring academic adviser or counselor.** Prepare thoroughly for your first meeting with your adviser, know what questions to ask, and keep in touch throughout each term. Doing so will lead to successful academic planning. Remember that if you are not comfortable with the person who has been assigned as your academic adviser, you can request a different one.

☐ **Have realistic expectations.** If you are disappointed in your grades, remember that college is a new experience and that your grades will probably improve if you continue to work hard and apply yourself. Be sure to take advantage of the services available through your campus's learning center.

REFLECT ON CHOICES

🎯 **high-impact practice 2** | Reflect and write about what you have learned about college success in this chapter and how you are going to apply this information to the choices that you need to make this term. Select a few choices you need to make such as when to meet with an academic adviser and whether or when to visit instructors during their office hours. Write about these choices in a journal entry or readily accessible file. Revisit these questions throughout your first-year experience.

APPLY WHAT YOU'VE LEARNED

Now that you have read and discussed this chapter, consider how you can apply what you have learned to your academic and personal life. The following prompts will help you reflect on chapter material and its relevance to you, both now and in the future.

1. Why are you in college? Reflect on your decision to enter this college at this time in your life. Be honest about who or what influenced you to make this decision. What challenges do you face, and what strategies for success in this chapter can you use to overcome those challenges?

2. College students often feel the stress of trying to balance their personal and academic lives. The ups and downs of life are inevitable, but we can control our choices and attitudes. You will want to develop a personal strategy for being resilient—for bouncing back after a particularly difficult time.

USE YOUR RESOURCES

> **Academic Advising Center** Does your institution have an academic advising center, or is advising done by faculty? If you don't already know, find out this week where you can get help with selecting courses, learning how to get information on degree requirements, and deciding on a major.

> **Academic Skills Center** Whether you need help or not, explore this facility. Its services can include tutoring, help with study and memory skills, and help with studying for exams.

> **Adult Reentry Center** If you are an adult or returning student, visit this center to learn about special programs, make contacts with other adult students, and gather information about services such as child care.

> **Career Center** You may visit the career center as part of your college success course. If not, put it on your list of important campus services. Career centers usually feature a career library, interest assessments, counseling, and help in finding a major.

> **Commuter Services** Commuter students are the new majority. If you are a commuter student, find the campus office that provides lists of special services for you.

> **Counseling Center** Find out about your institution's counseling center and the services it offers, which will probably include stress-management programs and confidential counseling.

> **Financial Aid and Scholarship Office** Be sure to meet with someone in this office to learn about financial aid programs, scholarships, and grants.

> **Veterans Affairs Office** If you are a veteran, be sure to learn about the services of this office, including special financial aid.

> **Health Center** Don't wait until you need a doctor or a nurse. Locate your campus health center and learn about their services.

> **Math Center** If your math instructor hasn't already told you about help from the math center, ask whether your college or university has such a center.

> **Writing Center** As you write your first research paper, ask an expert in the writing center to read a first draft for help with proper grammar, syntax, and punctuation, as well as the appropriate method for citing and listing references.

🌀 **LaunchPad**

LaunchPad for *Your College Experience* is a great resource! Go online to master concepts using the LearningCurve study tool and much more. macmillanhighered.com/gardner12e

Michael Krinke/Getty Images

2
TIME MANAGEMENT

YOU WILL EXPLORE

Ways to manage your time

Time-management tools

Procrastination and how to overcome it

Setting priorities and achieving balance

The value of time and the importance of allocating your time wisely

⚙ High-impact practices 2 (writing) and 3 (collaboration)

Abby York, 19

Economics major
California State University, Los Angeles

> **It is difficult balancing school, volunteer work, and a job, but as long as you have everything scheduled and planned, it is easily achievable and very rewarding.**

When Abby York started college, she had already begun to build a solid foundation in time-management skills. She was born in New York City and moved to Los Angeles, California, when she was three years old. During her senior year of high school, she participated in a college preparation program, which meant taking all her classes at a local college to gain transferable credits. The curriculum included a course that focused on learning how to manage time and set priorities. She credits that course with helping her learn how to manage time in her first year of college and beyond. But even with a solid foundation, Abby didn't make it through her first year of college without a few time-management roadblocks. "Sometimes I just got overwhelmed with school and just wanted to work or hang out with my friends and would put my schoolwork on the back burner. This had some bad side effects. Once I saw the drop in my grades, I knew that I had to reprioritize and get back on track."

One key to Abby's success with time management is organization. "I use both paper and electronic organizational tools. If my computer ever goes down, I still have all my information, plans, and due dates in my planner, and vice versa, if I lose my planner, I still have everything on my computer."

Abby recognizes that prioritizing is the key to maintaining her busy schedule and her sanity. "My first priority is school, second comes work, and then everything else—volunteering, exercising, friends, and family," she says. "I find places in my schedule to fit them in every week. All these things are important and essential for me to be successful and happy. It's like each piece of my life is a puzzle piece. If I don't keep making sure that each piece fits, or if there is any piece missing, the puzzle doesn't work and breaks apart."

Abby recently changed her major from psychology to economics. She just returned from a semester abroad in England and is looking into transferring to a school more geared toward her new major. After college, she hopes to move to the East Coast, find a job in market research or finance, and possibly continue her education in graduate school. Her advice to other first-year students: "Take a class on time management and balancing all your priorities. It definitely helped me ease into college life and balance my life."

To access the LearningCurve study tool, video activities, and more, go to LaunchPad for *Your College Experience.*
macmillanhighered.com
/gardner12e

Time management is a challenge for almost all first-year college students, many of whom misallocate their time at first. Soon they realize they will have to change their behavior to ensure that they have sufficient time to give to their coursework. How did Abby deal with the time-management roadblocks that she encountered? How do you deal with those you face? This chapter covers many challenges to time management, such as procrastination and distractions, and it offers techniques you can use to meet your obligations and use your time effectively.

MANAGING YOUR TIME

People approach the concept of time differently based on their personalities and backgrounds. Some people are always punctual, while others are almost always late. Some students enter all due dates for assignments on a calendar as soon as they receive the syllabus for each class. Other students take a more laid-back approach and prefer to go with the flow rather than follow a daily or weekly schedule. These students might deal well with the unexpected, but they might also leave everything to the last minute and be less successful than if they managed their time more effectively. Even if you prefer to go with the flow, improving your organizational skills can help you do better in college, work, and life. Think of it this way: If *you* were hiring someone for a job, wouldn't you choose an organized person who gets things done on time?

Taking Control of Your Time

The first step to effective time management is recognizing that you can be in control. Psychologists use the term *locus of control*—*locus* means "place"—to refer to a person's beliefs about how much control they have over the events that affect them. Being in control means that you make your own decisions and accept responsibility for the outcomes of those decisions.

Some people believe that their locus of control is internal, or within themselves; others believe that it is external, or beyond their power. If you frequently find yourself saying "I don't have time," you likely have an external locus of control. The next time you find yourself saying this, stop and ask yourself whether it is actually true. Do you *really* not have time, or have you made a choice not to make time for a particular task or activity? When we say we don't have time, we imply that we don't have a choice. We do have a choice because we have control over how we use our time and how many commitments and small decisions we choose to make every day. For example, we have control over when we get up in the morning; how much sleep we get; and how much time we spend studying, working, and exercising. All of these small decisions have a big impact on our success in college and in life.

Your Memory Cannot Be Your Only Planner

How you manage your time reflects what you value—what is most important to you and what consequences you are willing to accept when you make

PEER LEADER > As a peer leader, you can help your students make the right choices about time management by sharing both your strategies and your challenges in managing your own time. Contribute to the class discussion on this issue or talk one-on-one with the students in your classroom.

RETENTION STRATEGY > Relate the concept of *locus of control* to wise choices in time management. Students who learn to take responsibility for their own choices increase their chances of persisting and graduating.

IN CLASS ❯ Students might question the value of spending so much time to save time. Ask them to be patient; there may be a learning curve, and time spent on the front end will save more time later. Research indicates that college students who know how to plan their time can produce good work and have fun as well.

certain choices. For instance, if you value time with friends above everything else, your academic work likely takes a backseat to social activities. How you manage your time also corresponds to how successful you will be in college and throughout life. Almost all successful people use some sort of calendar or planner to help them keep up with their appointments, assignments, tasks, and other important activities. Using your memory as your only planner—trying to remember everything you have to do without recording it anywhere—means that you will probably forget important events and deadlines.

---

your turn | Make Good Choices

Does Your Planner Work for You?

What kind of planner do you currently use, if any? Do you use a paper planner or mark the calendar on your phone? Do you think you have chosen the best kind of planner for you? Why or why not? Can you think of a different planner that might work even better?

USING TIME-MANAGEMENT TOOLS

Getting a bird's-eye view—or big picture—of each college term will allow you to plan ahead effectively. An **academic calendar** is a calendar that shows all the important dates that are specific to your campus: financial aid, registration, and add/drop deadlines; midterm and final exam dates; holidays; graduation deadlines; and so forth. You may have received an academic calendar when you registered for classes, or your campus bookstore may have one for sale.

Knowing your big-picture academic deadlines will be helpful as you add deadlines for specific assignments, papers, and exams into your calendar. It is important to refer to your college's academic calendar to add important dates and deadlines, such as when the registration period starts and ends and when you need to pay your tuition or file your application for financial aid or scholarships. Remember, also, that you have to keep track of important dates, not only in your own life, but also in the lives of those close to you—birthdays, doctor's appointments, work schedules, travel, visits from out-of-town guests, and so on. Different aspects of your life have different sorts of time requirements, and the goal is to stay on top of all of them.

You might prefer to use an electronic calendar on your phone, tablet, laptop, or desktop. (See the Tech Tip in this chapter for different options.) Regardless of whether you prefer a paper or electronic calendar, it's a good idea to begin the academic term by reviewing the syllabus for each of your courses and then completing a preview (Figure 2.1), recording all of your commitments for each day, and using different colors for each category:

- Classes
- Study time for each class you're taking
- Tests and assignment due dates
- Personal obligations such as work, family, friends
- Scheduled social events (including phone numbers in case you need to cancel)

FIGURE 2.1 > Monthly Calendar

Using the course syllabi provided by your instructors, create your own monthly calendars for your entire term. Provide details such as the number of hours you anticipate spending on each assignment or task.

MONTH: SEPTEMBER

MONDAY	TUESDAY	WEDNESDAY	THURSDAY	FRIDAY	SATURDAY	SUNDAY
					1	**2**
3 9–12 Work	**4** First Day of Classes 9–12 Psychology 2–5 Work 8–9 Psychology: Read Ch. 1	**5** 9–12 Work 1–4 Math 8–10 Math HW 1	**6** 10–1 English 2–5 Work 8–10 English: Read Ch. 1	**7** 10–12 Work 9–10 Psychology: Review Notes	**8** 10–4 Work 8–9 Math HW 1 9–10 English: Read Ch. 1	**9** 2–4 Review Math Notes 6–10 Party at Susan's
10 9–12 Work 1–5 Biology	**11** 9–12 Psychology 2–5 Work 8–10 Biology: Read Ch. 1	**12** 9–12 Work 1–4 Math 8–10 Psychology: Read Ch. 2	**13** 10–1 English 2–5 Work 7–8 Math HW 2 9–11 Biology: Read Ch. 1	**14** 10–12 Work 1–3 Lunch with Mary 6–7 Start English Summary Paper	**15** 10–4 Work 4–6 Shopping 9–10 Finish English Summary Paper	**16** 10–1 Study for Psychology Test 6–8 Review Math notes for Quiz 1
17 9–12 Work 1–5 Biology 7–10 Study for Psychology Test	**18** 9–12 Psychology Psychology Test 1 2–5 Work 8–9 Review Math notes for Quiz 1	**19** Work 9–12 Math 1–4 Math Quiz 1 8–9 Revise English Summary Paper	**20** 10–1 English English Summary Paper due 2–5 Work 8–10 Biology: Read Ch. 2	**21** 10–12 Work 1–2 Attend Student Club Meeting 6–9 Math HW 3	**22** 10–4 Work 5–7 Psychology: Read Ch. 3 9–10 English: Read Ch. 2	**23** 10–12 Biology: Read Ch. 2 9–10 Biology: Lab Report 1
24 9–12 Work 1–5 Biology 6–8 Math Tutoring 10–11 Math HW 3	**25** 9–12 Psychology 2–5 Work 8–10 Biology: Read Ch. 3 10–11 Math HW 3	**26** 9–12 Work 1–4 Math 8–9 Psychology: Read Ch. 4 9–10 Prepare English Paper Outline	**27** 10–1 English 2–5 Work 7–9 Math HW 9–10 Review Biology Notes	**28** 10–12 Work 1–3 Meet with Biology Study Group 8–9 Biology: Lab report 2 9–11 English: Read Ch. 3	**29** 10–4 Work 8–9 English: Read Ch. 3	**30** 4–8 Nina's Birthday

Recording your daily commitments allows you to examine your toughest weeks during each month and each term. If research paper deadlines and test dates fall during the same week, find time to finish some assignments early to free up study time. If you use an electronic calendar, set reminders for these important deadlines and dates.

Overall, you should create monthly (Figure 2.1), weekly (Figure 2.2), and daily (Figure 2.3) views of your calendar. All three views are available

FIGURE 2.2 ❯ Weekly Timetable

Using your term calendar, create your own weekly timetable using a conventional template or one that uses an app such as LifeTopix. At the beginning of each term, track all of your activities for a full week by entering everything you do and how much time each task requires into your schedule. Use this record to help you estimate the time you will need for similar activities in the future.

SEPTEMBER

Time	MONDAY	TUESDAY	WEDNESDAY	THURSDAY	FRIDAY	SATURDAY	SUNDAY
	3	4 _First Day of Classes_	5	6	7	8	9
5 am							
6 am							
7 am							
8 am							
9 am	_Work_	_Psychology_	_Work_				
10 am				_English_	_Work_	_Work_	
11 am							
12 pm							
1 pm			_Math_				
2 pm		_Work_		_Work_	_Mom's Doctor's Appointment_		_Review Math Notes_
3 pm							
4 pm							
5 pm							
6 pm							_Party at Susan's_
7 pm							
8 pm		_Psychology: Read Ch. 1_	_Math HW1_	_English: Read Ch. 1_		_Math HW 1_	
9 pm					_Psychology: Review Notes_	_English: Read Ch. 1_	
10 pm							
11 pm							
12 am							

FIGURE 2.3 > Daily Planner

Notice how college, work, and personal activities are noted on this daily planner.

IN CLASS > A student's schedule controls how each day and each week is structured. Discuss how a class schedule and commuting to class are factors in time management.

	FRIDAY, SEPTEMBER 14
5 am	
6 am	
7 am	
8 am	
9 am	
10 am	*Work*
11 am	
12 pm	
1 pm	*Lunch with Mary*
2 pm	
3 pm	
4 pm	
5 pm	
6 pm	*Start English Summary Paper*
7 pm	
8 pm	

in an electronic planner, but you can also create monthly, weekly, and daily calendars with paper planners.

Once you complete your monthly templates, you can put them together to preview your entire academic term. Remember to provide details such as the number of hours you anticipate spending on each assignment or task.

As you create your schedule, try to reserve study time for each class and for each assignment. Not all assignments will take an equal amount of time to complete. Estimate how much time you will need for each one, and begin your work well before the assignment is due. A good time manager frequently allows for emergencies by finishing assignments before actual due dates. If you are also working on or off campus, reconsider how many hours per week it will be reasonable for you to work on top of your academic commitments, and whether you need to reduce your credit load to ensure that you have enough time for both work and school.

Remember that managing your time effectively requires practice. You may have to rearrange your schedule a few times, rethink some priorities, and try to use your time differently. The more you apply time-management skills, the more time you can save.

Being a good student does not necessarily mean studying day and night and doing little else. Scheduling time for work and pleasure is important, too. After all, most students have to juggle a *lot* of responsibilities. You might have to work to help pay for college, and you probably want to spend time with family or friends to recharge your battery. And most people also need time to relax and unwind; that time can include getting some exercise, reading a book for pleasure, or seeing a movie. Note that the daily planner (Figure 2.3 on the previous page) includes time for other activities as well as time for classes and studying.

When using an electronic calendar, it's a good idea to print a backup copy in case you lose your phone, cannot access the Internet, experience a computer crash, or leave your charger at home or in your residence hall. Carry your calendar with you in a place where you're not likely to lose it. Checking your calendar regularly helps you keep track of commitments and maintain control of your schedule. This practice will become invaluable to you in your career. Check your calendar daily for both the current week and the coming week. It takes just a moment to be certain that you aren't forgetting something important, and it helps relieve stress. Consider setting regular times to check your calendar every day, perhaps right after eating breakfast and then again in the evening, to see what's coming in the days and weeks ahead.

Keep the following points in mind as you organize your day:

- **Set realistic goals for your study time.** Assess how long it takes to read a chapter in your different textbooks and how long it takes you to review your notes from different instructors.
- **Use waiting, commuting, and travel time to review.** Allow time to review your notes as soon as you can after class. You can review your notes if you have a break between classes or while you're waiting for or riding the bus or train. Consider formally budgeting this commuting time in your planner. If you have a long drive, consider listening to recorded notes or asking those riding with you to quiz you. Make a habit of using waiting time wisely, and it will become bonus study time to help compensate for unexpected events that might pop up in your day and throw off your schedule.
- **Limit distracting and time-consuming communications.** Check your phone, tablet, or computer for messages or updates at a set time, not whenever you're tempted to do so. Constant texting, browsing, or posting can keep you from achieving your academic goals. Remember that when time has passed, you cannot get it back.
- **Avoid multitasking.** Doing more than one thing at a time, referred to as multitasking, requires that you divide your attention among tasks. You might think that you are good at multitasking. However, the reality is (and research shows) that you can get tasks done faster and more accurately if you concentrate on one at a time.[1] Don't take our word for it: Try setting up your schedule to focus on one important task at a time. You'll probably find you do a better job on your assignment, test, or project.

- **Be flexible.** You cannot anticipate every disruption to your plans. Build extra time into your schedule so that unexpected events do not prevent you from meeting your goals.
- **Schedule breaks.** Relax, catch up with friends and family, or spend time in the cafeteria or student center.

---

[1] E. Ophir, C. Nass, and A. Wagner, "Cognitive Control in Media Multitaskers," *Proceedings of The National Academy of Sciences* 106, no. 37 (2009).

Select Your Best Study Times

What times of day or night do you usually study? Have you selected times when you can concentrate and be productive, or do you just study whenever you can fit it in, even if you're really tired and distracted? For instance, have you already figured out that early morning is your best time to read and remember what you're reading, or that studying after 10:00 p.m. is a waste? Everyone is different, so based on your college experience so far, make a list of the best and worst times for you to study. Most instructors will expect you to study two hours out of class for every hour you spend in class. Using your list as a guide, be intentional about the times you set aside for studying.

PROCRASTINATION

Procrastination is the habit of delaying something that needs your immediate attention. Putting things off can become a serious problem for college students. Dr. Piers Steel, a leading researcher and speaker on the science of motivation and procrastination, writes that procrastination is on the rise, with 80–95 percent of students in college spending time procrastinating.[2] According to Steel, half of college students report that they procrastinate on a regular basis, spending as much as one-third of their time every day in activities solely related to procrastination. All this procrastination takes place even though most people, including researchers who study the negative consequences of procrastination, view procrastination as a significant problem. These numbers, plus the widespread acknowledgment of the negative effects of procrastination, provide evidence that it is a serious issue that trips up many otherwise capable people. Researchers at Carleton University in Canada have found that college students who procrastinate in their studies also avoid confronting other tasks and problems and are more likely to develop unhealthy habits, such as higher levels of alcohol consumption, smoking, insomnia, a poor diet, or lack of exercise.[3]

The good news is that, of those people who procrastinate on a regular basis, 95 percent want to change their behavior.[4] As a first step toward initiating change, it is important to understand why people procrastinate. According to Steel, some people who are highly motivated fear failure, and

---

[2]Piers Steel, "The Nature of Procrastination: A Meta-Analytic and Theoretical Review of Quintessential Self-Regulatory Failure," *Psychological Bulletin* 133, no. 1 (2007): 65–94.

[3]Timothy A. Pychyl and Fuschia M. Sirois, "*Procrastination:* Costs to Health and Well-Being," presentation at the American Psychological Association convention, Aug. 22, 2002, Chicago.

[4]Piers Steel, "The Nature of Procrastination: A Meta-Analytic and Theoretical Review of Quintessential Self-Regulatory Failure," *Psychological Bulletin* 133, no. 1 (2007): 65–94.

GET DIGITALLY ORGANIZED

Mapping out your schedule doesn't have to be a chore. Think of a well-appointed calendar as a compass for a college student. Besides being a guide for navigating your current term, it will also keep you pointed toward your long-term goals.

The Problem

You keep forgetting assignments and can't find the paper planner that your college provided.

The Fix

Replace the lost paper planner with your phone or computer by using a free electronic calendar or phone app.

How to Do It

Select the device and platform you would be most likely to use. Don't make this complicated. You are trying to be more efficient.

- Would you check your phone, tablet, or computer?
- Do you have a Gmail or a Hotmail account already? (These will also allow you to share files with classmates for group projects using GoogleDrive or SkyDrive and will allow you to create and store files in the "cloud" using the Internet like a hard drive).
- Look at platforms like **iStudiez** (istudentpro.com) or **Studious** (studiousapp.com), which allow you to coordinate and sync your schedule across devices.

Collect schedule information. Depending on what system you are using, look at the syllabi you have gotten from your classes, especially if your instructors provided schedules for assignments, tests, quizzes, and projects. Also, go to your college's Web site and get a copy of the academic calendar, which will include dates that the college is closed, registration dates, and other important information.

Use the information you have collected. Set up your electronic calendar with important dates and your class schedule for the term. Your electronic calendar will allow you to repeat a weekly schedule so you won't have to type in each class meeting time individually. Set up alerts for major events (tests, registration deadlines, holiday closings, etc.) on your schedule so that your electronic calendar will send you text or e-mail reminders in advance. If you are confused about how to do this, go to YouTube and search "set up Google calendar to repeat and remind."

Courtesy of iStudiez Team

iStudiez Pro App for Android Devices

Pick a time every week to review your schedule. Add things you need to accomplish to the list. Make a to-do list, and cross off tasks as you complete them.

Optional: Add your work schedule or other regular commitments and social events, so that you see them in real time next to your class schedule. Doing so will help you make time for the things you really want to do.

Remember: Setting up your schedule at the beginning of the term does take time, but fortunately, this is usually the time when fewer assignments are due. Having a schedule will pay you big dividends in fewer missed assignments and deadlines or worse, showing up for class on a day when there are no classes.

EXTRA STYLE POINTS: Sync your phone or tablet with your calendar so that if you make changes on your phone, they appear on your online system (Google Calendar, etc.), and if you make changes on your online system, they appear on your phone. Go to YouTube again, and search "Sync (your phone's name) with (the name of your online system)," and view some videos that show you exactly how to sync them. If you tied your Gmail or Outlook account to your campus e-mail as suggested in the Tech Tip in Chapter 1, you should already be synced.

some people even fear success, although that might seem counterintuitive. Consequently, some students procrastinate because they are perfectionists; not doing a task might be easier than having to live up to your own very high expectations or those of your parents, teachers, or peers. Many procrastinate because they are easily distracted—a topic we'll explore below. Often they have difficulty organizing and regulating their lives, have difficulty following through on goals, view the assigned task as too far into the future, or find an assigned task boring or irrelevant[5] or consider it "busy work," believing they can learn the material just as effectively without doing the homework.

Overcoming Procrastination

Many of the traits most associated with people who chronically procrastinate can make change more difficult. Fortunately, though, there is hope. With certain changes in behaviors and mind-set, you can reduce procrastination and become more effective at managing your time. In college, changing how you think about and approach less enjoyable assignments is key to decreasing procrastination and increasing your success.

For instance, simply disliking an assignment is not a good reason to put it off; it's an *excuse*, not a valid *reason*. Throughout life you'll be faced with tasks you don't find interesting, and in many cases you won't have the option not to do them. Whether it is cleaning your house, filing your taxes, completing paperwork, or responding to hundreds of e-mails, tedious tasks will find you, and you will have to figure out strategies to complete them. College is a good time to practice and hone your skills at finishing uninteresting tasks in a timely manner. Perhaps counterintuitively, research indicates that making easier or less-interesting tasks more challenging can decrease boredom and increase your likelihood of completing the tasks on time.[6]

> ### your turn Work Together
>
> **Staying on Task and on Time**
>
> With two or three other students, discuss ways to avoid procrastination. What works for you? Share examples from your experiences.

When you're in college, procrastinating can signal that it's time to reassess your goals and objectives; maybe you're not ready to make a commitment to academic priorities at this point in your life. Only you can decide, but an academic adviser can help you sort it out. If you cannot get procrastination under control, it is in your best interest to seek help at your campus counseling service before you begin to feel as though you are also losing control of other aspects of your life. Taking the Procrastination Self-Assessment in this chapter will help give you a sense of whether or not procrastination is a problem for you.

---

[5]Ibid.

[6]Ibid.

Procrastination Self-Assessment

Place a number from 1 to 5 before each statement. (For example, if you "agree" with a statement, place a 4 before the statement.)

1 = Strongly Disagree
2 = Disagree
3 = Mildly Disagree
4 = Agree
5 = Strongly Agree

_____ I have a habit of putting off important tasks that I don't enjoy doing.

_____ My standards are so high that I'm not usually satisfied enough with my work to turn it in on time.

_____ I spend more time planning what I'm going to do than actually doing it.

_____ The chaos in my study space makes it hard for me to get started.

_____ The people I live with distract me from doing my class work.

_____ I have more energy for a task if I wait until the last minute to do it.

_____ I enjoy the excitement of living on the edge.

_____ I have trouble prioritizing all my responsibilities.

_____ Having to meet a deadline makes me really nervous.

_____ My biggest problem is that I just don't know how to get started.

If you responded that you "agree" or "strongly agree" with two questions or fewer, then you may procrastinate from time to time, but it may not be a major problem for you. Reading this chapter will help you continue to stay focused and avoid procrastination in the future.

If you responded that you "agree" or "strongly agree" with three to five questions, then you may be having difficulties with procrastination. Revisit the questions to which you answered "agree" or "strongly agree" and look in the chapter for strategies that specifically address these issues to help you overcome obstacles. You _can_ get a handle on your procrastination!

If you responded that you "agree" or "strongly agree" with six or more questions, then you may be having a significant problem with procrastination, and it could interfere with your success in college if you do not make a change. Revisit the questions to which you answered "agree" or "strongly agree" and look in the chapter for strategies that specifically address these issues. Also, if you are concerned about your pattern of procrastination and you aren't having success in dealing with it yourself, consider talking to a professional counselor in your campus counseling center. It's free and confidential, and counselors have extensive experience working with students who have problems with procrastination.

Here are some strategies for beating procrastination and staying motivated:

- Remind yourself of the possible consequences if you do not get down to work, and then get started. Also, remind yourself that simply not enjoying an assignment is not a good reason to put it off; it's an _excuse_, not a valid _reason_.
- Create a to-do list. Check off items as you get them done. Use the list to focus on the things that aren't getting done. Move them to the top of the next day's list, and make up your mind to do them. Working from a list will give you a feeling of accomplishment.

- Break big jobs into smaller steps. Tackle short, easy-to-accomplish tasks first.
- Avoid doing other things that might seem more fun, and promise yourself a reward for finishing the task, such as watching your favorite TV show or going out with friends. For completing larger tasks and assignments, give yourself bigger and better rewards.
- Find a place to study that's comfortable and doesn't allow for distractions and interruptions.
- Say *no* to friends and family members who want your attention; agree to spend time with them later, and schedule that time.
- Shut off and put away all electronic devices during planned study sessions. If you *need* to use an electronic device for studying, turn off all social media and any other applications that are not part of your studying—and *keep* them off.
- Consider asking those living with you to help keep you on track. If they see that you are not studying when you should be, ask them to remind you to get back to the books. If you study in your room, close your door.

Dealing with Distractions

Overcoming procrastination and planning your time effectively are closely associated with achieving your goals. What you do on a daily basis affects your outcomes for that week, that month, that year, and so on. Distractions may push you off course and away from your intended goals. A good first step is becoming aware of what distractions trip you up and considering how much control you have over them.

Table 2.1 lists possible distractions that may or may not be a problem for you. Choose Yes (a problem) or No (not a problem) for each one. Then note whether the distraction is controllable or uncontrollable and write down possible solutions.

IN CLASS › Ask students to think about distractions and report the kinds of distractions they have in their environments. How are distractions a problem?

IN CLASS › Time management often requires the use of the word *no*. Ask students to discuss how saying no relates to the way they manage their time.

IN CLASS › Ask students to discuss how much time they spend on the Internet each day. How much on social networking sites? Is this a time-management problem? For some students, time spent on social networks is a problem that can rise to the level of addiction. Consider inviting someone from your counseling center to speak about this issue.

TABLE 2.1

Distraction	Yes (Y) No (N)	Controllable (C) Uncontrollable (U)	Solutions
Texting/Messaging			
Social media			
Gaming/Videos/Music			
Sports/Hobbies			
Television/Streaming			
Lack of sleep			
Relationships			
Meals/Snacking			
Daydreaming			
Perfectionism			
Errands/Shopping			
Lost items			

(continued)

TABLE 2.1 *(continued)*

Distraction	Yes (Y) No (N)	Controllable (C) Uncontrollable (U)	Solutions
Worries/Stress			
Family			
Socializing/Friends			
Multitasking			
Illness, self or others			
Work schedule			
Pleasure reading			

What did you learn about yourself, the distractions that get in your way, and some ideas for taking control? What choices are you willing to make to maximize your time?

RETENTION STRATEGY ❯
Evaluating specific goals is a way of inviting students to think again about their purposes for being in college. The more focused they are on a meaningful purpose, the more likely they are to persist.

SETTING PRIORITIES

As you work to overcome procrastination and limit distractions, think about how to **prioritize**, which means putting your tasks, goals, and values in order of importance. (Below, we'll discuss strategies to avoid becoming overextended, which goes hand in hand with setting priorities.) Ask yourself which goals are most important, but also which ones are most urgent. For example, studying in order to get a good grade on tomorrow's test might have to take priority over attending a job fair today, or completing an assignment that is due tomorrow might have to take priority over driving your friend somewhere.

However, don't ignore long-term goals in order to meet short-term goals. With good time management, you can study during the week prior to the test so that you can attend the job fair, too. Skilled time managers often establish priorities by maintaining a term calendar and to-do lists on which they rank the items in order of importance to determine schedules and deadlines for each task.

From the beginning of the term, plan your work on term papers and major projects that might not be due for several weeks or even months. Consult with a tutor or a more experienced student to help you break large assignments down into smaller steps, such as choosing a topic, doing research, creating an outline, or writing a first draft. Once you have entered your future commitments in a term planner and

isthisyou?

Time Flies

Do you find yourself wondering where your time has gone at the end of a long day? Are you aware of how you spend your time when you're not in class, or does this time just seem to vanish? Of all the time-management strategies presented in this chapter, developing an awareness of how you spend your time might be the most important. Using a day planner or your smart phone, develop an "ideal" hour-by-hour schedule that covers the next week. At the end of each day, go back and check to see if you used your time as planned. If not, make sure your projections were realistic, adjust them if necessary, and then try some of the strategies presented in this chapter to improve your ability to control the way you spend your time.

Set Priorities Like the Pros

Professional coaches help their teams thrive by setting effective priorities, whether it's making a plan for the next play, for the whole game, or for an entire season. In setting your own priorities, take a lesson from these coaches: Prioritize your long-term plans while making sensible play-by-play decisions every day.

Jeff Gross/Getty Images

decided how your time will be spent each week, create your to-do list, which is especially handy for last-minute reminders. A to-do list helps you keep track of errands to run, appointments to make, and anything else you might forget. You can keep this list on your cell phone or tablet, in a notebook, or on a bulletin board in your room. Use your to-do list to keep track of all the tasks you need to remember, not just academics. Consider developing a system for prioritizing the items on your list: using different colors of ink for different groups of tasks; highlighting the most important assignments; marking items with one, two, or three stars; or adding letters A, B, C, and so on to indicate which tasks are most important (Figure 2.4).

IN CLASS ❯ Ask students to discuss the importance of a to-do list. Why is a list important in time management? What experiences have students had with to-do lists? You can share your own experiences with such lists.

FIGURE 2.4 ❯ To-Do List

You can keep a to-do list on a mobile device, in a notebook, or on a bulletin board. Use it to keep track of all the tasks you need to remember, not just academics. Consider adding Saturday and Sunday as these are productive days for many busy people. As you complete a task, cross it off your list. Enjoy the satisfaction of each accomplishment.

THIS WEEK	COLLEGE	WORK	PERSONAL
Monday	Schedule a math tutoring session	Meet with the department chair about my schedule	Make a haircut appointment
Tuesday	Make appointment with Prof. Velez to discuss paper topic		Order birthday gift for dad
Wednesday	Meet my history study group at 4:00 p.m.	Work in department, 9:00 a.m.–noon	
Thursday	Finish English essay		Pick up dry cleaning
Friday		Work in department, 9:00 a.m.–noon	Make eye appointment

Find a Balance

Another aspect of setting priorities while in college is finding a way to balance your academic schedule with the rest of your life. Social and extracurricular activities (for instance, participating in a club, writing for the college newspaper, attending special lectures, concerts, athletic events, or theater performances) are important parts of the college experience. Time spent alone and time spent thinking are also essential to your overall well-being.

Don't Overextend Yourself

Being **overextended**, or having too much to do given the resources available to you, is a primary source of stress for college students. Determine what a realistic workload is for you, but note that this can vary significantly from one person to another, and only you can determine what is realistic. Although being involved in social and family life is very important, don't allow your academic work to take a backseat to other time commitments. Take on only what you can handle. Learn to say *no,* as this is an effective time-management strategy! Say no to requests that will prevent you from meeting your academic goals. Remember that even if you can find the time for extra tasks, you may not be able to find the energy.

If you are feeling stressed, assess your time commitments and let go of one or more. If you choose to drop a course, make sure you do so before the drop deadline so that you won't have a low grade on your permanent record. If you receive financial aid, keep in mind that you must be registered for a minimum number of credit hours to maintain your current level of financial aid. Read more about financial aid in the chapter on managing money.

Hang On

It's important to find a balance between your studies, work, family, exercise, and other responsibilities so you do not overextend yourself. Keep your goals and priorities in mind, and avoid an event like this one the day before an exam!

© Jessica Rinaldi/Reuters/Corbis

Stay Focused

Many students of all ages question their decision to attend college and sometimes feel overwhelmed by the additional responsibilities it brings. Some first-year students, especially recent high school graduates, might temporarily forget their main purposes for coming to college and spend their first term of college engaging in a wide array of new experiences.

Allowing yourself a little time to adjust to college is OK within limits, but you don't want to spend the next four or five years trying to make up for poor decisions made early in your college career, such as skipping class and not taking your assignments seriously. Such decisions can lead to a low grade point average (GPA) and the threat of academic probation or, worse, academic dismissal.

A great way to focus and to keep your priorities on track is to finish what *needs* to be done before you move from work to pleasure. From time to time, you will have competing responsibilities; for example, you might have to work additional hours at your job when you need additional time to study

IN CLASS ❯ Have pairs of students discuss their "perfect life" ten years from now. What goals do they need to set now to achieve their dreams?

Work Study

Did you know that the majority of college students have jobs? If you need to work, try to find a job that is flexible and allows you to study during down-time. Use every available minute to stay up to date with your classwork.
Courtesy of Sue McDermott Barlow

for an exam. In cases like these, talk to the people involved, including your instructors and your employer, to see how you can manage the conflict.

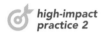

high-impact practice 2

your turn   Write and Reflect

What Are Your Priorities?

List your current priorities, and assign a value to each on a scale of 1–5 with 1 as most important and 5 as least important. Write a short paper about why you consider some things more important than others. Think about whether your personal priorities support your goals for college success.

_____   _____
_____   _____
_____   _____
_____   _____
_____   _____

APPRECIATING THE VALUE OF TIME

Time is a valuable resource, perhaps your most valuable resource. You've likely heard the expression "Time is money." Just as you don't want to waste your money, you shouldn't waste your time or the time of others. Did you ever make an appointment with someone who either forgot the

Getting from Here to There

College students have the responsibility to get themselves to class on time and must plan transportation carefully, whether walking, driving, bicycling, ride-sharing, taking public transportation, or using another method of getting from place to place. If you have an emergency situation that causes you to run late, talk to your instructor. He or she will understand a real emergency and help you make up work you missed.

wong yu liang/Shutterstock

appointment entirely or was very late? How did you feel? Were you upset or disappointed because the person wasted your time? Most of us have experienced the frustration of having someone else disrespect our time. In college, if you repeatedly arrive late for class or leave early, you are breaking the basic rules of politeness and showing a lack of respect for your instructors and your classmates.

Punctuality, or being on time, is expected in college, work, and elsewhere in our society. Being strictly on time may be a difficult adjustment for you if you grew up in a home or culture that is more flexible in its approach to time, but it is important to recognize the value of punctuality. Although you should not have to alter your cultural identity to succeed in college, you must be aware of the expectations that instructors typically have for students.

Here are a few basic guidelines for respectful behavior in class and in other interactions with instructors:

- Get to class on time. This means you need to get enough sleep at night so that you can wake up at a time that allows you to arrive in class early enough to take off your coat, shuffle through your backpack, and have your completed assignments and notebooks ready to go by the time the class starts.
- Be on time for scheduled appointments, such as during office hours.
- Avoid behaviors that show a lack of respect for both the instructor and other students, such as leaving class to answer your cell phone. Similarly, texting, doing homework for another class, falling asleep, or talking (even whispering) during a lecture are all considered rude.
- Make transportation plans in advance, and have a backup plan.

Not only is time management important for you, but it is also a way in which you show respect for your coworkers, friends, family, college instructors, and yourself. Can you think of the number of times you may have been late (one of the symptoms of procrastination) this week alone? Think back and then take the quiz shown here in Table 2.2:

TABLE 2.2

Situation	Number of Times This Week
How many times were you late to class?	
How many times were you late for appointments/dates?	
How many times were you late for work, a car-pool, or another job and/or responsibility?	
How many times were you so late returning an e-mail, phone call, or text that a problem resulted from this lateness?	
How many times were you late paying a bill or mailing any important document?	
How many times were you late getting to bed or waking up?	
TOTAL	

Did the total number of times you were late surprise you? Two to five incidences of being late in a week is fairly normal. Everyone is late sometimes. Being late more than eight times this week might indicate that you are avoiding situations and tasks that are unpleasant for you. Or maybe you find it difficult to wait for other people, and so you would rather have others wait for you. Try and think of lateness from the other person's perspective. Getting more organized might help if you find that you don't have enough hours in the day to get everything done the way you think it should be. Position yourself for success and develop a reputation for being dependable!

Creating a Workable Class Schedule

Building your class schedule so that it works for you is part of using your valuable time wisely. If you live on campus, you might want to create a schedule that situates you near a dining hall at mealtimes or allows you to spend breaks between classes at the library. Alternatively, you might need breaks in your schedule for relaxation, catching up with friends, or spending time in a student lounge, college union, or campus center. You might want to avoid returning to your residence hall to take a nap between classes if the result is that you could feel lethargic or oversleep and miss later classes. Also, if you attend a large university, be sure to allow adequate time to get from one class to another.

Scheduling Your Classes in Blocks

One option for building a class schedule is using blocks of time when you can schedule several classes in a row, back-to-back, without any breaks. If you're a commuter student or if you must carry a heavy workload to afford going to school, you might prefer block scheduling, which allows you to cut travel time by attending school one or two days a week. Block scheduling might also provide more flexibility if you have to schedule a job or family commitments.

Scheduling classes in blocks, however, can also have significant drawbacks. When all your classes are scheduled in a block of time, you run several risks. If you become ill on a class day, you could fall behind in all your classes. You might also become fatigued from sitting in class after class. When one class immediately follows another, it will be difficult for you to have a last-minute study period immediately before a test because you will be attending another class and are likely to have no more than a 15-minute break in between. Finally, remember that if you take back-to-back classes, you might have several exams scheduled for the same day. Scheduling classes in blocks might work better if you have the option of attending lectures at alternative times in case you are absent, if you alternate classes with free periods, and if you seek out instructors who are flexible with due dates for assignments.

If your classes are offered at more than one time of day or more than one day a week, you will find it easier to design a schedule that works best for you. Often, however, you will be forced to take a class at an inconvenient time because that's the only time the class is offered. Remember that any schedule you develop will have pros and cons, but with advance planning, you can make the most of your in-class and out-of-class time.

your turn | Work Together

Scheduling Your Classes

In a small group or with a partner, share your current schedule and explain what you like or dislike about it. If your current schedule is not working well, discuss why that might be and identify changes you can make for the next term.

checklist for success

Time Management

- **Make sure that you set clear priorities for the way you spend your time.** All your time doesn't have to be spent studying, but remember that your instructors will expect you to study two hours out of class for each hour in class.

- **Get organized by using a calendar or planner.** Choose either an electronic or a paper calendar. Your campus bookstore will have a campus-specific version. Your calendar can help you allocate time in the present for completing large assignments that are due in the future.

- **Create and use daily paper or electronic to-do lists.** Crossing off those tasks you have completed will give you a real sense of satisfaction.

- **Quickly identify and address common time-management problems you are having before they spiral out of control.** Be aware of problems with procrastination, distractions, overscheduling, and motivation. As you notice them happening, take stock and make changes. If any of these issues becomes a serious problem, seek help from your campus counseling center.

- **Remember the relationship between time and respect.** Be aware of how others might perceive your behavior. If you disregard formal or informal appointments or if you are consistently late for class, you are showing a lack of respect for others even if that's not your intent.

- **Think about your course schedule.** As you plan for next term, try to schedule your classes in a way that works best for you, given your other obligations.

REFLECT ON CHOICES

high-impact practice 2

College presents you with choices. One of them is whether you are going to pay close attention to how you spend your time. If you choose to neglect the issue of time management, you will risk losing a resource that you can never re-cover and sabotaging your chances for success in college. Did any of the time-management tips in this chapter appeal to you? If so, which ones? Do you still have questions about time management? If so, what are they? Write about these choices and questions in a journal entry or readily accessible file. Revisit these questions throughout your first-year experience.

APPLY WHAT YOU'VE LEARNED

Now that you have read and discussed this chapter, consider how you can apply what you have learned to your academic and personal life. The following prompts will help you reflect on chapter material and its relevance to you both now and in the future.

1. Review the procrastination section of this chapter. Think of one upcoming assignment in any of your current classes and describe how you can avoid waiting until the last min-ute to get it done. Break down the assignment and list each step it will take to complete the assignment. Give yourself a due date for each step and a due date for completing the assignment.

2. After reading about effective time-management strategies, consider how you manage your own time. If you were grading your current set of time-management skills, what grade (A, B, C, or lower) would you give yourself? Why? What is your biggest impedi-ment to becoming a more effective time manager?

USE YOUR RESOURCES

> **Academic Skills Center**   Your campus academic skills center offers more than just assistance in studying for exams. Head here for time-management advice specific to you. For instance, if you are struggling with manag-ing the process of writing a paper, talk with a writing tutor about how to break the process into manageable steps, and create a timetable for those steps so you can meet course dead-lines. If you are an online student, communi-cate with your instructors and other online students about how to manage time in an online environment.

> **Counseling Center**   Make an appointment at your campus counseling office if your time-management problems involve emotional issues.

> **Your Academic Adviser or Counselor**   If you have a good relationship with your academic adviser, ask him or her for time-management advice or for a referral to another person on campus.

> **Office for Commuter Students**   If you com-mute back and forth to campus, visit the office for commuter students to see what kinds of suggestions they offer about transportation to and from campus. You may be able to reduce the amount of time you spend in transit.

> **Your Peer Leader**   Peer leaders in college success classes are selected for their wisdom and experience. Talk to your peer leader about how he or she has developed time-management strategies.

> **A Fellow Student**   Don't overlook your closest resources! If you feel your time slipping away, ask a friend who is a good student for advice.

 LaunchPad

LaunchPad for *Your College Experience* is a great resource. Go online to master concepts using the LearningCurve study tool and much more. **macmillanhighered.com/gardner12e**

3
EMOTIONAL INTELLIGENCE

YOU WILL EXPLORE

What emotional intelligence is all about

Emotional intelligence in everyday life: motivation, resilience, establishing balance, prioritizing, and anger management

Developing emotional intelligence in college

How emotions influence success

Ways to improve your emotional intelligence

⚐ High-impact practices 2 (writing) and 3 (collaboration)

Gustavo Mejia, 20

Business Administration major
South Texas College

" **Going to college is not only about enjoying success and accomplishments, but also about persevering when things get difficult or go wrong.** "

When he was growing up in Turmero, Venezuela, Gus Mejia's family always encouraged him to attend college. "I see college as the path to the future," he says, "one that will help me build a better life for my family." Gus began college at Sinclair Community College in Dayton, Ohio, where he took classes full-time while working two days a week at his uncle's restaurant. He quickly learned a few things that helped him succeed. "As an international student, I left important parts of my life behind when I made the decision to go to college, such as family and my country. Being alone for almost a year taught me how important it is to have a positive attitude and an optimistic spirit."

This realization didn't come without hard work and practice. One of the most important things Gus had to learn during his first year of college was how to deal with the stress of managing college, work, and living in a new environment, and Gus figured out that having a good sense of his own emotional intelligence helped. Being aware of how these stresses affected him emotionally helped him better understand how to deal with difficult situations and kept him from reacting negatively during times of stress. Emotional intelligence has also played a big role in Gus's favorite class (so far): organizational behavior, where he had to learn how to work with other students, no matter what their customs and beliefs. "I liked this class not only because it related directly to my major," he says, "but also because it taught me to communicate with others. Being able to work

efficiently with different people from different backgrounds is very valuable."

Gus decided to begin the transfer process last year. Transferring to South Texas College represented a new beginning for him, one that came with its own fair share of challenges that he had to face with a clear head. Some of the credits for his classes—such as English literature, as well as courses on Microsoft Excel and PowerPoint—did not transfer because they weren't part of the business curriculum at his new college. Gus had to learn all the requirements for transferring, including admission tests, and be sure to meet them to make the transition as smooth as possible. His one piece of advice for other first-year students: Don't give up. "Going to college is not only about enjoying success and accomplishments, but also about persevering when things get difficult or go wrong," he says.

Gus had the ability to understand himself and others and to get along with people in a new environment. He was also able to manage time well, get things done, and anticipate potential problems before they occurred. Gus's problems with transferring to a new college are not uncommon, but he was able to deal with them without letting them become a barrier to his success. Why do some individuals struggle to handle stressful situations while others, like Gus, seem to handle them with ease? Although we tend to think of these abilities as inborn personality traits that can't be changed, social skills and stress-management skills really can be learned and improved.

P articularly in the first year of college, some students who have the ability to succeed academically can have difficulty establishing positive relationships with others, dealing with pressure, or making wise decisions. Other students exude optimism and happiness and seem to adapt to their new environment without any trouble. The difference between the two types of students lies not in their academic talent but in their emotional intelligence (EI), or their ability to recognize and manage moods, feelings, and attitudes. A growing body of evidence shows a clear connection between students' EI and whether they stay in college.

As you read this chapter, you will develop an understanding of EI, and you will learn how to use it to become a more successful student and person. You will begin to look at yourself and others through an EI lens, observe the behaviors that help people succeed, get to know yourself better, and learn to examine your feelings before you act. Then, as you read each subsequent chapter in this book, try to apply what you have learned about EI and think about how it might relate to the behaviors of successful college students. You can't always control the challenges and frustrations of life, but with practice, you *can* control how you respond to them.

WHAT IS EMOTIONAL INTELLIGENCE?

Emotional intelligence is the ability to recognize, understand, use, and manage emotions—moods, feelings, and attitudes. There are many competing theories about EI, some of them complex. While experts vary in their definitions and models, all agree that emotions are real, can be changed for the better, and have a profound impact on whether a person is successful.

In the simplest terms, emotional intelligence consists of two general abilities:

1. *Understanding emotions* involves the capacity to monitor and label your feelings accurately (nervousness, happiness, anger, relief, and so forth) and to determine why you feel the way you do. It also involves predicting how others might feel in a given situation. Emotions contain information, and the ability to understand and think about that information plays an important role in behavior.

2. *Managing emotions* involves the ability to modify and even improve feelings. At times, you need to stay open to your feelings, learn from them, and use them to take appropriate action. At other times, it is better to disengage from an emotion and return to it later. Anger, for example, can lead you to act in negative or antisocial ways; used positively, however, anger can help you overcome adversity, bias, and injustice.

The first key step in learning to control your emotions and use them in productive ways is to understand that you and your emotions are not one

Emotional Intelligence Questionnaire

Your daily life gives you many opportunities to take a hard look at how you handle emotions. Here are some questions that can help you begin thinking about your own EI.

1. What do you do when you are under stress?

    a. I tend to deal with it calmly and rationally.
    b. I get upset, but it usually blows over quickly.
    c. I get upset but keep it to myself.

2. My friends would say that:

    a. I play, but only after I get my work done.
    b. I am ready for fun anytime.
    c. I hardly ever go out.

3. When something changes at the last minute:

    a. I easily adapt.
    b. I get frustrated.
    c. I don't care, since I don't really expect things to happen according to plan.

4. My friends would say that:

    a. I am sensitive to their concerns.
    b. I spend too much time worrying about other people's needs.
    c. I don't like to deal with other people's petty problems.

5. When I have a problem to solve, such as having too many assignments due at the end of the week:

    a. I write down a list of the tasks I must complete, come up with a plan indicating specifically what I can accomplish and what I cannot, and follow my plan.
    b. I am very optimistic about getting things done and just dig right in and get to work.
    c. I get a little frazzled. Usually I get a number of things done and then push aside the things I can't do.

Review your responses. a responses indicate that you probably have a good basis for strong EI. **b** responses indicate that you may have some strengths and some challenges in your EI. **c** responses indicate that your success in life and in school could be negatively affected by your EI.

and the same. You can stand apart from and observe your emotions; you are separate from them. Whatever your emotions at any given moment, you might be using them to filter your perception of a situation by magnifying all the negative details and filtering out all positive aspects—without realizing that you're doing this. You might even pick out a single pleasant or unpleasant detail and dwell on it exclusively so that your vision of reality becomes distorted. If you are feeling sad, you might view the world in a certain way, while if you are feeling happy, you are likely to interpret the same events differently.

Another important step in becoming more emotionally intelligent is developing an awareness of how your emotions affect you. When you start paying attention to emotions instead of ignoring them, you will have a better emotional understanding of different situations, and therefore be able to respond to these situations more appropriately. You can learn not only how to cope with life's pressures and demands, but also how to harness your knowledge of the way you feel, which can lead to more effective problem solving, reasoning, decision making, and creative endeavors.

A number of sophisticated tools can be used to assess emotional intelligence, or you can take the short questionnaire on the previous page to begin thinking about it. Even without a formal test, you can take a number of steps to get in touch with your own EI. You'll have to dig deep inside yourself and be willing to be honest about how you really think and how you really behave. This process can take time, and that's fine. Think of your EI as a work in progress.

---

yourturn Stay Motivated

Overcoming Tough Challenges

Think about a challenge you have experienced in college that made you want to throw in the towel. How did that challenge affect your overall motivation for doing well in college? What lessons did you learn from the experience, and how can you use those lessons in the future to maintain your motivation?

EMOTIONAL INTELLIGENCE IN EVERYDAY LIFE

You have already used your emotional intelligence in your life experiences. For example, you graduated from high school and are making the transition to college. The decision to attend college might have involved evaluating the reputation and characteristics of different colleges or universities and the opportunities they offered. But if you had been planning to attend a particular college your whole life, you might have filtered your college-choice experience through your emotional attachment to one place. If you made campus visits, how did you react to hearing information that concerned or excited you, exploring the different buildings, or

Truth in Fiction

The 2012 film *Silver Linings Playbook*, which stars Bradley Cooper, Jennifer Lawrence, and Robert DeNiro, explores issues of mental illness, anger management, family, and new beginnings. If you have seen the film, discuss how the characters attempt to handle their emotions. What works? What doesn't work? What other movies, TV shows, or novels can you think of that feature characters with emotional issues? What can you learn from such fictional accounts?

meeting staff, faculty, or other students? What impact did your emotions have on your final decision?

Naming and labeling emotions, in addition to focusing on related experiences, strengthens emotional intelligence skills. For instance, new college students often face the fear of social rejection. You might feel ignored or rejected by students you have met before. The feeling of rejection can even cause a physical reaction—your face might feel hot and you might even feel slightly sick to your stomach. If you can acknowledge and name what you are feeling, you will be less likely to be controlled by it. You will be in a better place to confront the fear by walking up to the students, introducing yourself again, and perhaps asking to join them.

Hearing something emotional often triggers our own emotional reaction. For instance, how would you react if a close friend said she had been sexually assaulted? Could you be empathetic and helpful, or would your own emotional reaction cause you to barrage her with questions about where she had been, what she had been wearing, and whether she had been drinking? These accusations could impede your friend's recovery and make her even more vulnerable. As you work to develop your emotional intelligence, you'll need to consider how to use logic rather than your own emotional reactions to evaluate a situation and be helpful to others.

Motivation

Most college students have many responsibilities, and it can be hard to stay motivated when you have too much to do. Positive feedback can help, and it's important to realize that this can come from within—motivating yourself is a big part of being emotionally intelligent. Draw from past positive experiences to propel yourself through a current challenge. Consider how conquering a challenge provides an example to others. What positive outcomes will result? Being emotionally intelligent also means knowing when you need some distance from a challenge or project. Identify the experiences that have motivated you in the past and call on them when you do not feel motivated to persevere.

Resilience

Resilience is another important component of emotional intelligence. As you learned in Chapter 1, being resilient means that you are optimistic and tough in the face of adversity. You remain positive even when you are faced with negative circumstances. While you're in college, you might receive an "F" on a paper, have trouble making connections with others in class, or lose a student government election. Such experiences might cause you to question whether you should be in college at all. Resilient students, though, look past negative experiences, learn from them, and try again. What can you do to improve your grade on your next paper? Perhaps you didn't allow yourself enough time to do the proper research. How can you feel more comfortable in your classes? Maybe it would help to join a study group. Why were you passed over for the student government office that you wanted? Consider the possibility that you may need to show a greater commitment to campus governance issues. Developing coping mechanisms and life skills leads to resilience. You were born with the ability to be resilient—it's up to you to let your resilience emerge and to embrace it.

Balance and Priority Management

You will find that it is difficult to balance the many, and often competing, aspects of your life when you are in college. Finding balance goes beyond taking care of obligations—it extends to your mental and physical health, which relates directly to wellness, a topic we'll discuss later in this book. Using healthy emotional intelligence to prioritize involves applying time-management techniques to how you handle your obligations. For instance, create a to-do list and review it regularly. If you know that packing your lunch and workout clothes in the evening will save you time in the morning, make that a priority and pack the night before. And schedule your day to make time for everything that is important to you, such as exercise, eating a healthy diet, talking to your friends, and studying. With more balance in your day comes greater confidence. Consider what happens when you fail to prioritize or use your time-management strategies. Does the stress lead to emotional reactions that then lead to negative consequences? Paying attention to these kinds of issues and making changes when needed are all part of developing a stronger emotional intelligence.

Anger Management

Humans experience a wide range of emotions and moods. On one hand, we can be very generous and positive, and on the other hand, we can lash out in anger. Anger management is an EI skill that is important to develop. Anger can hurt others and can harm your mental and physical health. You may even know someone who uses their anger to manipulate and control others.

Upside of Anger

Since the 1960s, college students have used their anger about political, social, and campus-specific issues (like tuition increases) in positive ways through organized demonstrations. Such demonstrations have influenced major actions in U.S. history, such as President Richard Nixon's decision to resign, and President Lyndon B. Johnson's decision to end the Vietnam War. What issues would "bring students to the barricades" today?

AP Photo/Cathleen Allison

In spite of the problems it creates, anger does not always result in negative consequences. Psychologists see anger as a primary, natural, and mature emotion that has value for human survival because it can mobilize us to take corrective action or to stand up for what is right.

How do you use anger? Are you in control of how you express this emotion, or does your anger occasionally control you?

isthisyou?

Older than Average

Are you an older student, maybe in your thirties or forties, who is back in college? As an adult, you probably have a great deal of life experience in dealing with tough times. You might have real strengths in emotional intelligence that you have developed at work, at home, or with your family, but you may also have some areas that you need to improve. How are you using your skills to stand up for yourself and negotiate with others as you face the challenges of college? Using your existing strengths and skills in college could allow you to be a role model for others. You might want to give some advice to younger students who seem to be struggling with the day-to-day interactions that are part of college life and help those students find ways to be more adaptable, resilient, and assertive.

DEVELOPING EMOTIONAL INTELLIGENCE

As you get to know yourself, you might find that engaging in deep personal reflection makes you feel vulnerable. But as you reflect more on your own attitudes and behavior and learn why you have the emotions that you do, you'll improve your emotional intelligence. Living on your own, studying unfamiliar subjects, and interacting with new and diverse people all challenge your EI skills and force you to step outside of your comfort zone. Your first year of college is especially critical and affords you a significant opportunity to grow as a person.

Identifying Competencies: Looking at the Research

Emotional intelligence includes many capabilities and skills that influence a person's ability to cope with life's pressures and demands. Reuven Bar-On, a professor at the University of Texas at Austin and a world-renowned EI expert, developed a model that demonstrates how categories of emotional intelligence directly affect general mood and lead to effective performance (see Figure 3.1).

IN CLASS ❯ Ask your students to think about the contexts within the college experience in which they could practice developing EI competencies. The idea is for students to see how college is an environment that can help them develop more fully. For example, one competency describes "interpersonal skills." What kinds of college activities, settings, and circumstances could help students develop these skills?

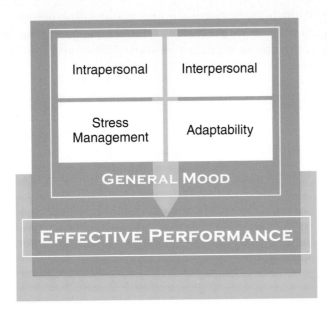

FIGURE 3.1 ❯
Bar-On Model of Emotional Intelligence

Let's look more closely at the fifteen specific skills and competencies that Bar-On has identified as the pieces that make up a person's emotional intelligence.[1] They are similar to the pieces of a jigsaw puzzle—once you've put them all together, you will begin to see yourself and others more clearly.

Intrapersonal Skills. This first category relates to both how well you know and like yourself, and how effectively you can do the things you need to do to stay happy. Understanding yourself and why you think and act as you do is the glue that holds all of the EI competencies together. This category is made up of five specific competencies:

1. **Emotional self-awareness.** Knowing how and why you feel the way you do.
2. **Assertiveness.** Standing up for yourself when necessary without being too aggressive.
3. **Independence.** Making important decisions on your own without having to get everyone's opinion.
4. **Self-regard.** Liking yourself in spite of your flaws (and we all have them).
5. **Self-actualization.** Being satisfied and comfortable with your achievements.

PEER LEADERS ❯ Ask the students in your class to review the fifteen EI competencies, select their strongest and weakest competencies, and write them anonymously on slips of paper, identifying each as a personal strength or weakness. Tally the results to see which weaknesses and strengths are most common in your class. Facilitate a class discussion to generate ideas to address the most common weaknesses.

---

[1] Adapted from Bar-On EQ-i Technical Manual © 1997, 1999, 2000 Multi-Health Systems, Inc. Toronto, Canada.

Interpersonal Skills. Recent studies have shown that people with extensive support networks are generally happier and tend to enjoy longer, healthier lives. Your ability to build relationships and get along with other people depends on the competencies that form the basis for the interpersonal skills category:

- **Empathy.** Making an effort to understand another person's situation or point of view.
- **Social responsibility.** Establishing a personal link with a group or community and cooperating with its other members in working toward shared goals.
- **Interpersonal relationships.** Seeking out and maintaining healthy and mutually beneficial relationships, such as friendships, professional networks, family connections, mentoring relationships, and romantic partnerships.

Adaptability. Things change. Adaptability—the ability to adjust your thinking and behavior when faced with new or unexpected situations—helps you cope and ensures that you'll do well in life, no matter what the challenges. This category includes three key competencies:

- **Reality testing.** Ensuring that your feelings are appropriate by checking them against external, objective criteria.
- **Flexibility.** Adapting and adjusting your emotions, viewpoints, and actions as situations change.
- **Problem solving.** Approaching challenges step by step and not giving up in the face of obstacles.

high-impact practice 3

HIGH-IMPACT PRACTICE > This Your Turn exercise will give your students a chance to practice collaboration—a key to better learning—and to share what they observe by watching TV shows about emotional intelligence.

IN CLASS > Point students to the Wellness chapter for an overview of specific stress-management techniques.

PEER LEADERS > Ask students to role-play stressful or difficult situations that they may encounter in college. For example, you can use the case studies in the Instructor's Manual, or you can use a stressful scenario from your own college experience. Ask students to react to and discuss the situations.

your turn Work Together

Observing Emotional Intelligence

Working with one or two other students, agree to watch at least one TV show during the coming week—a situation comedy, drama, or even a cable news program. Each group member can watch the same show or a different show. Take brief notes on how the fictional or nonfictional characters handle their emotions, especially in stressful situations. How many of the fifteen EI competencies were represented—either positively or negatively—in the shows you watched? During next week's class, discuss what you saw and what you learned.

Stress Management. In college, at work, and at home, now and in the future, you'll face what can seem like never-ending pressures and demands. Managing the resulting stress depends on two skills:

- **Stress tolerance.** Recognizing the causes of stress and responding in appropriate ways, so you can stay strong under pressure.
- **Impulse control.** Thinking carefully about potential consequences before you act, and delaying gratification for the sake of achieving long-term goals.

"The key to stress management is knowing
how to vent your frustration."

GLASBERGEN

Don't Blow Your Top

There are good ways and bad ways to vent frustration. Having it out with another person or eating a gallon of ice cream are poor strategies. Going for a walk or run, doing yoga, or "talking it out" with someone you trust, however, will help you deal with the frustrations that are common to college life without making things worse.

© Randy Glasbergen

Overall Mood. It might sound sappy, but having a positive attitude really does improve your chances of doing well. Bar-On emphasizes the importance of two emotions in particular:

- **Optimism.** Looking on the bright side of any problem or difficulty and being confident that things will work out for the best.
- **Happiness.** Being satisfied with yourself, with others, and with your situation in general. It makes sense: If you feel good about yourself and manage your emotions, you can expect to get along with others and enjoy a happy, successful life.

Knowledge of self is strongly connected to respect for others and their way of life. If you don't understand yourself and why you do the things you do, it can be difficult for you to understand others. What's more, if you don't like yourself, you can hardly expect others to like you.

HIGH-IMPACT PRACTICE ❯ Ask students to write down their top ten stressors. Then break students into small groups and have them reach a consensus on the top stressors for first-year college students. Finally, have each group share its list with the rest of the class. How different are the lists? How similar are they? What does that suggest?

yourturn Make Good Choices

Act Instead of React

Your emotional reactions, whether positive or negative, affect your interactions with other people. Pretend that you are your own therapist. In what kinds of situations have you had "knee-jerk" reactions when you've reacted with defensiveness, anger, sadness, annoyance, resentment, or humiliation? Take a step back and "process" these reactions. Think about what you said or did in response to your feelings, and why. Then talk with a trusted friend or classmate about how you reacted and whether you could have chosen to act differently. What can you do to take control and make good choices the next time you are faced with a potentially volatile situation?

Accentuate the Positive

You probably know people who always find the negative in any situation. Constantly focusing on what's missing or what's not perfect will likely make you the kind of person whom others avoid. Practice looking on the bright side.

marekuliasz/Shutterstock

HOW EMOTIONS INFLUENCE SUCCESS

Emotions are strongly tied to physical and psychological well-being. For example, some studies have suggested that cancer patients who have strong EI live longer than those with weak EI. People who are aware of the needs of others tend to be happier than people who are not. An extensive study done at the University of Pennsylvania found that the best athletes succeed in part because they're extremely optimistic. A number of studies link strong EI skills to college success in particular. Studies indicate that emotionally intelligent students get higher grades. Researchers looked at students' grade point averages at the end of their first year of college. Students who had tested high for intrapersonal skills, stress tolerance, and adaptability when they entered in the fall did better academically than those who had lower overall EI test scores. Here are a few other highlights of those studies:

- **Motivation:** Motivation is one of the most important attributes that college students can have. Figuring out what actually does motivate anyone is complex, but striving to find out and nurture these motivations is the goal.
- **Resilience:** We discussed resilience above—stronger emotional intelligence leads to greater resilience. Students with healthy emotional intelligence might act proactively by asking instructors for feedback on projects, papers, and tests, participating in classroom discussions, and joining study groups. Students with unhealthy EI are likely to struggle academically, panic before taking tests, have trouble concentrating on coursework, and engage in risky behaviors such as alcohol and drug abuse in an effort to cope. Dr. Richard Kadison, a former director of mental health services at Harvard University, noted that "the emotional well-being of students goes hand in hand with their academic development. If they're not doing well emotionally, they are not going to reach their academic potential."[2]
- **Persistence:** Some college students develop persistence in spite of the obstacles and challenges during their college experience. Persistent students make forward progress through challenging situations, even if progress is slow.
- **Delaying gratification:** Research has shown that students who can delay gratification tend to do better overall. Impulse control leads to achievement. A study conducted in the 1970s looked at the case of will-power in children. It is referred to as the Stanford Marshmallow Study.[3] The study observed children's behavior when they were left alone at a table with a marshmallow. They were told that they could have a second marshmallow if they waited 15 minutes before eating

IN CLASS › A component of "impulse control" is "delaying gratification." Divide the class into small groups and ask them to discuss this concept and how it relates to children, college students, and adults in today's society. When is it OK for us to get what we want immediately? When are we better off practicing delayed gratification?

---

[2]Richard Kadison and Theresa Foy DiGeronimo, *College of the Overwhelmed: The Campus Mental Health Crisis and What to Do about It* (San Francisco: Jossey-Bass, 2004), 156.

[3]Walter Mischel, et al., "Delay of Gratification in Children," *Science,* 244, no. 4907 (1989): 933–38.

the first one. Fourteen years later, the children who had immediately eaten their marshmallow were more likely to experience significant stress, irritability, and an inability to focus on goals. The children who had waited to eat their marshmallow scored an average of 210 points higher on the SAT; had more confidence, better concentration, and reliability; held better-paying jobs; and reported being more satisfied with life.

Healthy EI and the First-Year Seminar

Healthy EI contributes to overall academic success, positive professional and romantic relationships, and overall career development and satisfaction. EI skills can be enhanced in a first-year seminar. In one study conducted in Australia and another conducted separately in the United States, researchers found that college students enrolled in a first-year seminar who demonstrated good EI skills were more likely to do better in college than students who did not exhibit those skills.

You can get by in college without strong EI, but you might miss out on the full range and depth of competencies and skills that can help you succeed in your chosen field and have a fulfilling and meaningful life.

IN CLASS > Ask students to think about this course, its content, and its in-class activities. What have they been doing in this class—and what could they do more of—that might help them develop their EI skills?

RETENTION STRATEGY > Students who are easily frustrated and make impulsive decisions may give up on college. Encourage any student who expresses the wish to drop out or transfer to have a one-on-one discussion with you or a counselor before taking that step.

HOW TO IMPROVE YOUR EMOTIONAL INTELLIGENCE

Developing your EI is an important step toward getting the full benefit of a college education. Think about how you cope with emotional stress. Do you often give up because something is just too hard or because you can't figure it out? Do you take responsibility for what you do, or do you blame others if you fail? How can you communicate effectively if you are not assertive or if you are overly aggressive? If you're inflexible, how can you solve problems, get along with coworkers and family members, or learn from other people's points of view?

The good news is that you *can* improve your EI. It might not be easy—old habits are hard to change—but it can definitely be done. Here are some suggestions:

1. **Identify your strengths and weaknesses.** Take a hard look at yourself, and consider how you respond to situations. Most people have trouble evaluating their own behaviors realistically, so ask someone you trust and respect for insight.
2. **Set realistic goals.** As you identify areas of emotional intelligence that you would like to improve, be as specific as possible. Instead of deciding to be more assertive, for example, focus on a specific issue that is giving you trouble.
3. **Formulate a plan.** With a particular goal in mind, identify a series of steps you could take to achieve the goal, and define the results that would indicate success.
4. **Check your progress on a regular basis.** Continually re-evaluate whether or not you have met your goals, and adjust your strategy as needed.

techtip

USE BLOGS AND TWITTER

Everyone is an expert at something. Web sites like WordPress, Twitter, and Blogger give people space to write about or otherwise produce information that they know something about. Many of the most frequently used news Web sites and social networking sites get information that is sent—or "fed"—to them from someone's blog.

Twitter is a microblogging site. It's called "microblogging" because you can only write a maximum of 140 characters per message, or "tweet." Get off the sidelines and into the world of microblogging. It doesn't take much time to post to Twitter because of its 140-character limit. Twitter also allows you to follow the tweets of people, events, and organizations that interest you.

The Problem

You've heard people talk about blogs and Twitter, but you don't know why you'd join or what you'd do with them.

The Fix *Dive in!*

How to Do It

Research areas that you find interesting on blogging sites like wordpress.com, blogger.com, technorati.com, or alltop.com, or create a Twitter account.

Add the WordPress, Blogger, or Twitter app to your phone or tablet. This will allow you to keep up-to-date on information you find interesting and will get you in the habit of commenting, liking, responding, and posting so that you develop your "digital self" as a professional.

Participate in a network of people who share your interests. While you are in college, connect with people who are experts in your professional or personal areas of interest. Follow their posts to get advice and understand what people are talking about. You can also create a blog yourself and have other people follow your journey.

Sports/Entertainment: You can use Twitter or a blog to keep up with your favorite actors, bands, and sports teams. Some tweet about projects they're working on, some tweet political commentary, and others just share great jokes.

Education: Authors tweet or blog about their books and often engage in conversations with their readers.

Professionals and scholars in many fields share links to news articles, book reviews, Web sites, and videos related to their careers and areas of study.

Job-hunting: Many career Web sites have Twitter accounts and blogs. Following the official Twitter feed of a company you want to work for can lead to instant notifications of new job opportunities and give you the chance to get your résumé ready.

Community involvement: One amazing feature of Twitter is that it allows for real-time global conversations on important issues. Twitter was a key component in the Arab Spring of 2011–2012, a period that saw dozens of political demonstrations and revolutionary movements across the Arab world.

EXTRA STYLE POINTS: Create an online professional self that shows how fun or interesting or creative or compassionate you really are. A word of caution: Think about what you reveal about your emotional intelligence by what you post, and think about what you can tell about others' emotional intelligence by their posts.

It's important not to try to improve everything at once. Instead, identify specific EI competencies that you can define and describe, and then set measurable goals for change. Don't expect success overnight. Remember that it took you a while to develop your specific approach to life, and changing it will take commitment and practice.

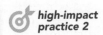

your turn   Write and Reflect

Thinking Ahead

Write a description of yourself as a successful person ten years after you graduate. What kinds of skills will you have? Don't just focus on your degree or a job description; include the EI competencies that help explain why you have become successful.

high-impact practice 2

HIGH-IMPACT PRACTICE ❯ This writing exercise gives your students another opportunity to practice and improve their writing. Remember that writing is a high-impact key to learning.

checklist for success

Emotional Intelligence

- **What is emotional intelligence?** Define the most significant abilities of EI and reflect on your connection to those abilities.

- **Be aware of how your emotions affect the way you react to difficult or frustrating situations.** Some key aspects of EI include motivation, resilience, balance, and anger management. Use your awareness to try to control your negative reactions before you get into a potentially frustrating situation.

- **Identify how you develop EI in college.** What can you learn from other students? Think about the most significant ways you have developed since you started college.

- **Evaluate your EI skills through assessment.** As a student, use assessments as tools to gauge where you are in terms of your development. This is how you improve.

- **Learn and then practice EI improvement strategies such as** identifying your strengths and weaknesses, setting realistic goals, formulating a plan, and checking your progress on a regular basis.

- **If you aren't satisfied with your emotional reactions, make an appointment at the campus counseling center to discuss your feelings and get help.** Counselors can help you monitor and understand your emotional responses in a confidential setting.

3 buildyourexperience

REFLECT ON CHOICES

high-impact practice 2 This chapter offers several opportunities for self-reflection and writing in an effort to encourage you to identify and improve your EI skills. What goals can you set to improve your emotional intelligence, and what strategies did you get from this chapter that can help? Consider situations that you will confront in the coming weeks and months. What choices can you make that involve emotional intelligence? What skills will you use? Reflect on these choices and questions in a journal entry or readily accessible file. Revisit these questions throughout your first-year experience.

APPLY WHAT YOU'VE LEARNED

Now that you have read and discussed this chapter, consider how you can apply what you have learned to your everyday life, both academically and personally. The following prompts will help you reflect on the chapter material and its relevance to you, both now and in the future.

1. Managing stress is an important skill in college, and balancing priorities is a component of emotional intelligence. Take a look through your course syllabi and make a list of assignments, exams, and important dates. Do any of your assignments or exams seem to cluster around the same time in the term? Can you anticipate times when you might be especially likely to get stressed? What can you do in advance to avoid becoming overwhelmed and overstressed?

2. College life offers many opportunities to meet new people and develop a new support network, but finding friends and mentors you can trust is not always easy. What steps have you taken so far to meet new people and build a network of support in college? How can these experiences help you develop your emotional intelligence?

USE YOUR RESOURCES

> **Academic Advising Center**
> Academic advisers are trained to help you deal with the stress of taking certain courses or planning your degree program.

> **Your College Counseling Center**
> Counselors who work in these centers have special training in stress management, anger management, conflict resolution, and other behavioral issues.

> **Health or Wellness Center**
> If personal problems are affecting your overall health—your sleep, diet, or ability to concentrate—visit your campus health center and talk to a health professional about strategies to deal with these issues.

> **Special Workshops that Focus on Personal Emotional Issues** Be alert for any workshops offered at your institution or in the local community that would help you improve your overall emotional intelligence.

> **Disability Services**
> If you are a student with a physical or learning disability that causes additional emotional problems for you, the office of disability services may be your best source of support.

> **Adult Student Services**
> Professionals in this office have special training in helping nontraditional students manage the social, personal, and emotional challenges that often arise when adults return to college.

> **Your Peer Leader**
> Your peer leader can be a sounding board for you if you are having problems with relationships, stress, anger, or any other personal issues. He or she can also refer you to an appropriate office for additional support.

LaunchPad

LaunchPad for *Your College Experience* is a great resource. Go online to master concepts using the LearningCurve study tool and much more. macmillanhighered.com/gardner12e

4

HOW YOU LEARN

YOU WILL EXPLORE

Tools for measuring your learning style

Strategies for handling a mismatch between how you learn best and how you are being taught

How to understand and recognize a learning disability

♂ High-impact practices 2 (writing), 3 (collaboration), and 6 (learning communities)

© eurobanks/Shutterstock

Daniel Graham, 24

Computer Science major
Northeastern Illinois University

> " **Apply your learning style to your everyday life. Eventually you will learn in a different, smarter, and more efficient way.** "

Although he tells us, "I didn't have much knowledge of learning styles before I started college," Daniel Graham from Northeastern Illinois University in Chicago enrolled in the college success seminar in his first term. There, he took a learning-styles inventory called the VARK and learned that he's both a kinesthetic learner, which means that he learns by doing, and a read/write learner, which means that he learns by reading and writing down material from class. Since then, he has been able to employ numerous strategies that apply specifically to his form of multimodal learning to help him succeed in class. He does things like rewriting terms and concepts in his own words so that he better understands what they mean, and he uses note cards to help him memorize. He says that knowing his learning style has improved his performance. "When I take notes, I read them silently on note cards and continue to return to them so I can memorize the meaning," he says.

It's not surprising that Daniel is also a kinesthetic learner, as he spends ten to fifteen hours a week working in his family home-remodeling business. "A hands-on approach has my name written all over it. I like being able to use my hands and express myself, and I like being able to figure things out just by playing with them for a bit." He translates this hands-on approach to learning by using tactics like taking practice exams until he feels ready for the real exam.

Daniel chose to begin higher education at Northeastern because it was close to home and because he learned from former Northeastern students that he would receive lots of one-on-one attention there. When Daniel enrolled, he took advantage of the TRiO program, which helps prepare students for college success through advising services and extra tutoring. All that work paid off: After completing his bachelor's degree, Daniel plans to transfer to the University of Illinois at Chicago to pursue a master's degree in computer information systems. Daniel plans to finish his master's and then explore job opportunities. He ultimately hopes to be working in computer science or finance, and he plans to continue to rely on his learning styles: "Apply your learning style to your everyday life. Eventually you will learn in a different, smarter, and more efficient way."

Have you ever thought about how you learn? If not, it would probably help to think about this topic now that you are in college. People learn differently. This is hardly a new idea, but if you want to do well in college, it is important that you become aware of how you learn. Maybe you have trouble paying attention to a long lecture, or maybe listening is the way you learn best. You might love classroom discussion, or you might consider hearing what other students have to say in class a big waste of time. You have developed your learning style or preference over time because of your personal characteristics and experiences. Even if you didn't exactly choose your preference for the way you learn best, you can choose to learn how to adapt to multiple styles of classroom instruction.

Perhaps you have not thought about it, but college instructors have their own styles of teaching and communicating. Those different styles will be evident in the way that courses are organized and taught. Your preferred style of learning might not match up with the teaching methods in some of your courses. Many instructors lecture almost exclusively; others use lots of visual aids, such as PowerPoint or Prezi presentations, charts, graphs, and pictures. In science courses, you will conduct experiments or go on field trips where you can observe or touch what you are studying. In dance, theater, or physical education courses, learning takes place in both your body and your mind. And in almost all courses, you'll learn by reading both textbooks and other materials. Some instructors are friendly, warm, and obviously enjoy all aspects of teaching; others seem to want little interaction with students.

This chapter will first help you understand how you learn best, and then help you think of ways in which you can create a link between your learning style and the expectations of each of your courses and instructors. This chapter will also explore learning disabilities, which are common among college students. You will learn how to recognize them and what to do if you or someone you know has a learning disability.

While the concept of learning may seem simple, educational researchers have discovered that not everyone learns in the same way. Not only do we have different learning styles, we also have unique preferences for the speed at which we learn, the mode of learning (online or face to face), and whether we learn better alone or in a group. Your college or university may offer courses that run four to six weeks or "flipped" classes in which you learn material on your own before class and spend class time in discussion groups or working problems.

If your college success course is linked with one or more other courses so that you share other classes with the same group of students, you are in a learning community. About 50 percent of U.S. colleges and universities offer learning communities in the first year. Being in a learning community will help you learn in a different way by emphasizing the connections between different courses. This experience will also help you develop stronger relationships with other students in the linked classes.

IN CLASS > Ask students to discuss why it is important for new college students to understand how they learn best. Do they understand what is meant by the term *learning style?*

IN CLASS > Ask students to think about the ways that faculty members approach teaching. Are there different styles of teaching? What is the relationship between teaching and learning?

RETENTION STRATEGY > The most important aspect of retention is giving students the tools they need for successful academic learning, because academic learning is the outcome that colleges prize the most. At the beginning of the chapter, ask students to brainstorm ways that each learning style supports student success.

HIGH-IMPACT PRACTICE > If your college success course is part of a learning community, perhaps even a residential learning community, you will want to help your students understand how the learning community experience can be a high-impact practice. Be alert to varying definitions of the term "learning community." Some institutions use the term to define a more generic notion of "learning in community." The definition used in this chapter specifically describes a linked or paired course structure.

 **high-impact practice 6**

RETENTION STRATEGY ➤ While it would be ideal if all college students liked their instructors and the content of their courses, the reality is that they will have to go beyond the concept of liking or disliking and adapt to a variety of teaching styles and academic materials.

LEARNING STYLES AND THE TOOLS USED FOR MEASURING THEM

Learning styles are particular preferences for learning that are unique to each individual. For example, one person might prefer to read instructional materials to understand how something works, whereas another might prefer to use a "hands-on" approach. There are many ways of thinking about and describing learning styles. Some learning styles will make a lot of sense to you; others might seem confusing at first. Some learning style theories are very simple, and some are complex. You will notice at least a little overlap between the different theories and tools; using more than one of them might help you do a better job of discovering your own learning style. If you are interested in reading more about learning styles, the library and your campus learning center will have many resources on this topic.

Learning happens all the time, especially in a college or university setting. Some, but not all, of what students learn happens in the classroom, organized by an instructor or other students. If you had been a student in the Middle Ages (500 AD–1500 AD), your instructor, most likely a monk, would have taught you entirely through lecture. Only a few handwritten books existed at that time, and if you wanted a book, you would most likely have had to write it yourself, if you even knew how to write. The invention of the printing press (credited to Johannes Gutenberg in 1440) and the availability of books made reading another option for learning. Even today, listening and reading remain the primary learning methods students are expected to use in college.

Over time, however, instructors have realized that not all students learn best through listening and reading. New technology offers visual tools such as PowerPoint, graphics, video, and online resources that help many students learn. And we also know that powerful learning results when students take charge of their own learning through "experiential," kinesthetic, or hands-on methods.

The VARK Learning-Styles Inventory

The VARK is a sixteen-item questionnaire that focuses on how learners prefer to use their senses (hearing, seeing, writing, reading, experiencing) to learn. The acronym VARK stands for "Visual," "Aural," "Read/Write," and "Kinesthetic." As you read through the following descriptions, see which ones ring true to how you learn.

- **Visual** learners prefer to learn information through charts, graphs, symbols, and

is**this**you?

Disappointed in My Classes

Have you found that some of your classes aren't as interesting and engaging as you expected? Is one of the problems a mismatch between the way you like to learn and the instructor's teaching method? Perhaps you're a visual learner but are forced to sit through mostly lecture classes, or perhaps you really don't enjoy working with others even though your chemistry course requires you to complete lab assignments with a partner. This chapter will help you understand your own learning style and adapt it to any classroom situation.

other visual means. If you can most easily remember data that is presented in graphic form or in a picture, map, or video, you are a visual learner.

- **Aural** learners prefer to hear information and discuss it with friends, classmates, or instructors. If talking about information from lectures or textbooks helps you remember it, you are an aural learner.
- **Read/Write** learners prefer to learn information through words on a printed page. During a test, if you can sometimes visualize where information appears in the textbook, you are a read/write learner.
- **Kinesthetic** learners prefer to learn through experience and practice, whether simulated or real. They often learn through their sense of touch. Recopying or typing notes helps them remember the material. They also learn better when their bodies are in motion, whether participating in sports, dancing, or working out. If you are a kinesthetic learner, you may find that even your sense of taste or smell contributes to your learning process.

Two or three of these modes probably describe your preferred ways of learning better than the others. At the college level, faculty members tend to share information primarily via lecture and the textbook, but many students like to learn through visual and interactive means. This difference creates a mismatch between learning and teaching styles. Is this a problem? Not necessarily, if you know how to handle such a mismatch. Later in this chapter you'll learn strategies to adapt lecture material and the text to your preferred modes of learning. First, though, to determine your learning style(s) according to the VARK, respond to the questionnaire.

The VARK Questionnaire, Version 7.1

This questionnaire is designed to tell you about your preferences for how you work with information. Choose answers that explain your preference(s). Check the box next to those items. For each question, select *as many boxes as apply to you*. If none of the response options applies to you, leave the item blank. (You can also take the VARK questionnaire online at **vark-learn.com/english/page .asp?p=questionnaire.**)

1. You are helping someone who wants to go to your airport, the center of town, or railway station. You would:

☐ a. go with her.
☐ b. tell her the directions.
☐ c. write down the directions.
☐ d. draw, or show her a map, or give her a map.

2. A Web site has a video showing how to make a special graph. There is a person speaking, some lists and words describing what to do, and some diagrams. You would learn most from:

☐ a. seeing the diagrams.
☐ b. listening.
☐ c. reading the words.
☐ d. watching the actions.

3. You are planning a vacation for a group. You want some feedback from them about the plan. You would:

☐ a. describe some of the highlights they will experience.
☐ b. use a map to show them the places.
☐ c. give them a copy of the printed itinerary.
☐ d. phone, text, or e-mail them.

4. You are going to cook something as a special treat. You would:

☐ a. cook something you know without the need for instructions.
☐ b. ask friends for suggestions.
☐ c. look on the Internet or in some cookbooks for ideas from the pictures.
☐ d. use a good recipe.

5. A group of tourists wants to learn about the parks or wildlife reserves in your area. You would:

☐ a. talk about, or arrange a talk for them, about parks or wildlife reserves.

☐ b. show them maps and Internet pictures.
☐ c. take them to a park or wildlife reserve and walk with them.
☐ d. give them a book or pamphlets about the parks or wildlife reserves.

6. You are about to purchase a digital camera or mobile phone. Other than price, what would most influence your decision?

☐ a. trying or testing it
☐ b. reading the details or checking its features online
☐ c. it is a modern design and looks good
☐ d. the salesperson talking about its features

7. Remember a time when you learned how to do something new. Avoid choosing a physical skill (e.g., riding a bike). You learned best by:

☐ a. watching a demonstration.
☐ b. listening to somebody explaining it and asking questions.
☐ c. diagrams, maps, and charts—visual clues.
☐ d. written instructions (e.g., a manual or book).

8. You have a problem with your heart. You would prefer that the doctor:

☐ a. give you something to read to explain what was wrong.
☐ b. use a plastic model to show what was wrong.
☐ c. describe what was wrong.
☐ d. show you a diagram of what was wrong.

9. You want to learn a new program, skill, or game on a computer. You would:

☐ a. read the written instructions that came with the program.

b. talk with people who know about the program.

c. use the controls or keyboard.

d. follow the diagrams in the book that came with it.

10. You like Web sites that have:

a. things you can click on, shift, or try.

b. interesting design and visual features.

c. interesting written descriptions, lists, and explanations.

d. audio channels where you can hear music, radio programs, or interviews.

11. Other than price, what would most influence your decision to buy a new nonfiction book?

a. the way it looks is appealing

b. quickly reading parts of it

c. a friend talks about it and recommends it

d. it has real-life stories, experiences, and examples

12. You are using a book, CD, or Web site to learn how to take photos with your new digital camera. You would like to have:

a. a chance to ask questions and talk about the camera and its features.

b. clear written instructions with lists and bullet points about what to do.

c. diagrams showing the camera and what each part does.

d. many examples of good and poor photos and how to improve them.

13. You prefer a teacher or a presenter who uses:

a. demonstrations, models, or practical sessions.

b. questions and answers, talk, group discussion, or guest speakers.

c. handouts, books, or readings.

d. diagrams, charts, or graphs.

14. You have finished a competition or test and would like some feedback:

a. using examples from what you have done.

b. using a written description of your results.

c. from somebody who talks it through with you.

d. using graphs showing what you achieved.

15. You are going to order food at a restaurant or café. You would:

a. choose something that you have had there before.

b. listen to the waiter or ask friends to recommend choices.

c. choose from the descriptions in the menu.

d. look at what others are eating or look at pictures of each dish.

16. You have to make an important speech at a conference or special occasion. You would:

a. make diagrams or get graphs to help explain things.

b. write a few key words and practice saying your speech over and over.

c. write out your speech and learn from reading it over several times.

d. gather many examples and stories to make the talk real and practical.

Scoring the VARK.

Now you will match up each one of the boxes you selected with a category from the VARK Questionnaire using the following scoring chart. Circle the letter (V, A, R, or K) that corresponds to each one of your responses (A, B, C, or D). For example, if you marked both B and C for question 3, circle both the V and R in the third row.

Responses to Question 3:	A	B	C	D
VARK letter	K	Ⓥ	Ⓡ	A

Count the number of each of the VARK letters you have circled to get your score for each VARK.

Scoring Chart

Question	A Category	B Category	C Category	D Category
1	K	A	R	V
2	V	A	R	K
3	K	V	R	A
4	K	A	V	R
5	A	V	K	R
6	K	R	V	A
7	K	A	V	R
8	R	K	A	V
9	R	A	K	V
10	K	V	R	A
11	V	R	A	K
12	A	R	V	K
13	K	A	R	V
14	K	R	A	V
15	K	A	R	V
16	V	A	R	K

Total number of **V**s circled = ____   Total number of **A**s circled = ____
Total number of **R**s circled = ____   Total number of **K**s circled = ____

Because you could choose more than one answer for each question, the scoring is not a simple matter of counting. It's like four stepping stones across water. Enter your scores **from highest to lowest** on the stones in the figure, with their V, A, R, and K labels.

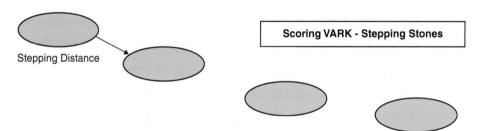

Stepping Distance

Scoring VARK - Stepping Stones

Your stepping distance comes from this table:

The total of my four VARK scores is	My stepping distance is
16–21	1
22–27	2
28–32	3
More than 32	4

Follow these steps to establish your preferences:

1. Your first preference is always your highest score. Check that first stone as one of your preferences.

2. Now subtract your second highest score from your first. If that figure is larger than your stepping distance, you have a single preference. Otherwise, check this stone as another preference and continue with step 3.

3. Subtract your third score from your second one. If that figure is larger than your stepping distance, you have a strong preference for two learning styles (bimodal). If not, check your third stone as a preference and continue with step 4.

4. Last, subtract your fourth score from your third one. If that figure is larger than your stepping distance, you have a strong preference for three learning styles (trimodal). Otherwise, check your fourth stone as a preference, and you have all four modes as your preferences! You may also find that you prefer the four learning styles equally.

Note: If you are bimodal or trimodal or you have checked all four modes as your preferences, you are *multimodal* in your VARK preferences.

IN CLASS › After the students have completed the VARK inventory, discuss the model. Take a poll to determine the variety of learning styles among the class. What does this variety mean for the dynamics of the class?

HIGH-IMPACT PRACTICE › Ask students to write a short paper on what they learned after completing and scoring the VARK Questionnaire. This brief writing assignment will help students reflect on the value of understanding their own learning preferences.

---

your turn   Work Together

Sharing Different Approaches to Learning

Did you know what type of learner you were before taking the VARK? Find one or two other students in your class with different learning styles. Share thoughts on strategies you are using to study in all your classes, referring to the examples in Table 4.1. What strategies are working for everyone in the group?

high-impact practice 3

HIGH-IMPACT PRACTICE › This collaborative exercise can help students share study strategies across multiple learning styles. Collaboration will help them remember and apply what they learn.

Use VARK Results to Study More Effectively

How can knowing your VARK score help you do better in your college classes? The following table offers suggestions for using learning styles to

TABLE 4.1 › Study Strategies by Learning Style

Visual	Aural	Read/Write	Kinesthetic
Underline or highlight your notes.	Talk with others to verify the accuracy of your lecture notes.	Write and rewrite your notes.	Use all your senses in learning: sight, touch, taste, smell, and hearing.
Use symbols, charts, or graphs to display your notes.	Put your notes on audiotape, or audiotape class lectures.	Read your notes silently.	Supplement your notes with real-world examples.
Use color to highlight important concepts.	Read your notes out loud; ask yourself questions and speak your answers.	Organize diagrams or flowcharts into statements.	Move and gesture while you are reading or speaking your notes.
Create a graphic representation of your notes (e.g., a mind map) and redraw it from memory.		Write imaginary exam questions and respond in writing.	

develop your own study strategies. Consider also how online course management systems (see this chapter's Tech Tip) provide opportunities for different types of learners to connect with the material they are studying.

The Kolb Inventory of Learning Styles

RETENTION STRATEGY ❯
Consider telling your students about research that shows that the learning-style preferences of most students do *not* align with the learning/teaching-style preferences of most faculty members. Specifically, students tend to prefer hands-on experiential learning, while some instructors tend to prefer teaching through lectures. By explaining this reality, you can get your students thinking about how they can adapt to these differences. If students can adjust, they are more likely to be successful, and hence retained.

The Kolb Inventory of Learning Styles is a widely used and referenced learning model that is more complex than the VARK Inventory. While the VARK Inventory investigates how learners prefer to use their senses in learning, the Kolb Inventory focuses on the abilities we need to develop so we can learn. This inventory, developed in the 1980s by David Kolb, is based on a four-stage cycle of learning (see Figure 4.1 below).

According to Kolb, effective learners need four kinds of abilities:

1. *Concrete experience* abilities, which allow them to be receptive to others and open to other people's feelings and specific experiences. An example of this type of ability is learning from and empathizing with others.
2. *Reflective observation* abilities, which help learners reflect on their experiences from many perspectives. An example of this type of ability is remaining impartial while considering a situation from a number of different points of view.
3. *Abstract conceptualization* abilities, which help learners integrate observations into logically sound theories. An example of this type of ability is analyzing ideas intellectually and systematically.
4. *Active experimentation* abilities, which enable learners to make decisions, solve problems, and test what they have learned in new situations. An example of this type of ability is being ready to move quickly from thinking to action.

Kolb's Inventory of Learning Styles measures differences along two basic dimensions that represent opposite styles of learning. The first dimension is *abstract-concrete,* and the second is *active-reflective.* See Figure 4.1 below to visualize how these opposing characteristics combine to create four discrete groups of learners: *divergers, assimilators, convergers,* and *accommodators.*

Doing well in college will require you to adopt some behaviors that are characteristic of each of these four learning styles. Some of them might be uncomfortable for you, but that discomfort will indicate that

FIGURE 4.1 ❯ Kolb's Four-Stage Cycle of Learning

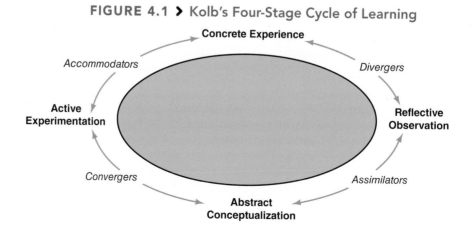

you're growing, stretching, and not relying on the learning style that might be easiest or most natural for you.

If you are a diverger, you are adept at reflecting on situations from many viewpoints. You excel at brainstorming, and you're imaginative, people-oriented, and sometimes emotional. On the downside, you sometimes have difficulty making decisions. Divergers tend to major in the humanities or social sciences.

If you are an assimilator, you like to think about abstract concepts. You are comfortable in classes where the instructor lectures about theoretical ideas without relating the lectures to real-world situations. Assimilators often major in math, physics, or chemistry.

If you are a converger, you like the world of ideas and theories, but you are also good at thinking about how to apply those theories to real-world, practical situations. You differ from divergers in your preference for tasks and problems rather than social and interpersonal issues. Convergers tend to choose health-related and engineering majors.

If you are an accommodator, you prefer hands-on learning. You are skilled at making things happen, and you rely on your intuition. You like people, but you can be pushy and impatient at times, and you might use trial and error, rather than logic, to solve problems. Accommodators often major in business, especially in marketing or sales.[1]

---

your turn   Stay Motivated

Where Are You on the Cycle of Learning?

On the basis of the descriptions we have provided here, where do you see yourself in the Kolb Inventory? Are you more like a diverger, assimilator, converger, or accommodator? Do you sometimes feel forced to engage in behaviors that are uncomfortable for you? Is it hard to be motivated when you want hands-on experience but find that some courses require you to consider abstract theories, or when you want to use your imagination but find you must come up with concrete answers? Choose to adopt behaviors that are characteristic of each of Kolb's learning styles. Don't let some initial discomfort hamper your motivation.

The Myers-Briggs Type Indicator

One of the best-known and most widely used personality inventories that can also be used to describe learning styles is the Myers-Briggs Type Indicator, or MBTI.[2] Whereas the VARK measures your preferences for using your senses to learn and the Kolb Inventory focuses on learning abilities, the MBTI investigates basic personality characteristics and how they relate to human interaction and learning. The MBTI was created by Isabel Briggs Myers and her mother, Katharine Cook Briggs. The inventory identifies and measures psychological types as developed in the personality theory of Carl Gustav Jung, the great twentieth-century psychoanalyst. The MBTI

An online bibliography listing almost eight thousand known studies on the MBTI is available at **capt.org**. For instructors in any academic specialty, workshops (including online workshops) to train and qualify you to give the MBTI are available from several reputable organizations listed on the Myers & Briggs Foundation Web site (**myersbriggs.org**).

IN CLASS ❯ Ask students their thoughts about an inventory that claims to measure personality types. Ask for student volunteers to do an Internet search on the Myers-Briggs Type Inventory and share their findings in class.

---

[1]Adapted from *The Modern American College: Responding to the New Realities of Diverse Students and a Changing Society*/Chickering. Copyright © 1981. Reprinted with permission of John Wiley & Sons, Inc.

[2]Isabel Briggs Myers, *Introduction to Type,* 6th ed. (Mountain View, CA: CPP, 1998).

IN CLASS > Develop a lesson on the Myers-Briggs types. Explain how the letters are used. Ask someone on campus who has experience with the Myers-Briggs assessment to assist you or come talk to your class.

is given to several million people around the world each year. Employers often use this test to give employees insight into how they perceive the world, make decisions, and get along with other people. Many first-year seminar or college success courses also include a focus on the MBTI because it provides a good way to begin a dialogue about human interaction and how personality types affect learning.

All the psychological types described by the MBTI are normal and healthy. There is no good or bad or right or wrong; people are simply different. When you complete the MBTI, your score represents your "psychological type," or the combination of your preferences on four different scales. These scales measure how you take in information and how you then make decisions or come to conclusions about that information. Each preference has a one-letter abbreviation. The four letters together make up your type. Although this book doesn't include the actual survey, you will find a description of the basic MBTI types below. Based on these scales, you can be any combination of these eight types.

high-impact practice 2

HIGH-IMPACT PRACTICE > If you require students in your class to make frequent entries in a journal, you are providing them with an intensive, but nonthreatening, writing experience. Be sure to provide some feedback on the content of these journal entries.

---

your turn   Write and Reflect

Discerning the Extraverts from the Introverts in Your Life

Read the following descriptions of extraverts and introverts. Make a list of your friends and family members, and indicate with an "E" or an "I" which are extraverts and which are introverts. How about you? Which type describes you best? Would you like to be different from the way you are? Reflect on these questions in a journal entry.

Extraversion (E) versus Introversion (I): The Inner or Outer World. The E-I preference indicates whether you direct your energy and attention primarily toward the outer world of people, events, and things or the inner world of thoughts, feelings, and reflections. Personality characteristics of extraverts and introverts are summarized here:

Extraverts	Introverts
Outgoing, gregarious, talkative (may talk too much)	Shy, reflective; careful listeners
People of action (may act before they think)	Consider actions deeply (may think too long before acting or neglect to act at all)
Energized by people and activity	Refreshed by quiet and privacy
Good communicators and leaders	Less likely to voice their opinions; often viewed as unaware of people and situations around them

Sensing (S) versus Intuition (N): Facts or Ideas.

The S-N preference indicates how you perceive the world and take in information: directly, through your five senses, or indirectly, by using your intuition. Personality characteristics of sensing and intuitive types are summarized here:

Sensing Types	Intuitive Types
Interested above all in the facts, what they can be sure of; dislike unnecessary complication; prefer practicing skills they already know	Fascinated by concepts and big ideas; prefer learning new skills over those already mastered
Relatively traditional and conventional	Original, creative, and nontraditional
Practical, factual, realistic, and down-to-earth	Innovative but sometimes impractical; need inspiration and meaning; prefer to look to the future rather than at the present
Accurate, precise, and effective with routine and details; sometimes miss the "forest" for the "trees"	May exaggerate facts unknowingly; dislike routine and details; work in bursts of energy

Thinking (T) versus Feeling (F): Logic or Values.

The T-F preference indicates how you prefer to make your decisions: through logical, rational analysis or through your subjective values, likes, and dislikes. Personality characteristics of thinking types and feeling types are summarized here:

Thinking Types	Feeling Types
Logical, rational, analytical, and critical	Warm, empathetic, and sympathetic
Relatively impersonal and objective in making decisions, less swayed by feelings and emotions; sometimes surprised and puzzled by others' feelings	Need and value harmony; often distressed or distracted by argument and conflict; reluctant to tackle unpleasant interpersonal tasks
Need and value fairness; can deal with interpersonal disharmony	Need and value kindness and harmony
Fair, logical, and just; firm and assertive	Facilitate cooperation and goodwill in others; sometimes unable to be assertive when appropriate
May seem cold, insensitive, and overly blunt and hurtful in their criticisms	Occasionally illogical, emotionally demanding, and unaffected by objective reason and evidence

It is inappropriate, unethical, and illegal to use the MBTI as a screening device to decide whether or not to hire an applicant for a job or admit someone to an educational program. The proper use of the MBTI is to help people identify satisfying career specialties for themselves.

PEER LEADERS ❯ As a peer leader, you have probably had some introduction to the Myers-Briggs Type Indicator. If not, visit your counseling or career center for a quick introduction. Facilitate a class discussion on the advantages or disadvantages of being one type or another. Stress how all types include characteristics that are valuable in college and in the workplace. Students will quickly be able to "assign" types to themselves, their friends, and family members. Remind them that all types have value both in and after college.

IN CLASS ❯ If your students have taken the MBTI, arrange the chairs or desks in a circle or square, beginning with the most "sensing" students and progressing to the most "intuitive" students as you circle around the group. Arrange students by MBTI type as much as possible so that students are next to people with whom they feel naturally comfortable and can quickly make friends. Note that they are sitting opposite, and are thus most likely to speak and listen to, people whose viewpoints are quite different from theirs. It might sound odd, but it really works!

FYI ❯ Myers's *Introduction to Type* is the only full-length book on psychological type. It is richly informative and requires no prior training in psychology. Our favorite brief discussion is *Introduction to Type in Organizations*, 3rd ed., by Sandra Krebs Hirsh and Jean M. Kummerow (Mountain View, CA: CPP, 2012).

Judging (J) versus Perceiving (P): Organization or Adaptability. The J-P preference indicates how you characteristically approach the outside world: by making decisions and judgments or by observing and perceiving instead. Personality characteristics of judging and perceiving types are summarized here:

Judging Types	Perceiving Types
Orderly, organized, punctual, and tidy	Spontaneous and flexible
In control of their own world and sphere of influence	Adapt to their world rather than try to control it; comfortable dealing with changes and unexpected developments
Quick decision makers; like to make and follow plans	Slow to make decisions; prefer a wait-and-see approach
Sometimes judgmental and prone to jump to conclusions or make decisions without enough information; have trouble changing plans	Tendency toward serious procrastination and juggling too many things at once without finishing anything; sometimes messy and disorganized

To learn more about these personality types and to access a questionnaire to find out more about your type, visit the Myers & Briggs Foundation at **myersbriggs.org/my-mbti-personality-type/take-the-mbti-instrument.** Remember that while some Myers-Briggs personality types may be particularly advantageous in certain situations, no one type is inherently superior to another. Be alert to both the positive and negative effects your type might have on your success in college.

Multiple Intelligences

IN CLASS > Present students with some criticisms and some praise of Howard Gardner's work. Then organize a debate on the topic of multiple intelligences.

Another way of measuring how we learn is the theory of **multiple intelligences,** which suggests that all human beings have at least eight different types of intelligence. This theory was developed in 1983 by Dr. Howard Gardner, a professor of education at Harvard University. Gardner's theory is based on the idea that the traditional definition of human intelligence is very limited. Gardner argues that students should be encouraged to develop the abilities they have, and that evaluation should measure all forms of intelligence.

 **high-impact practice 2**

HIGH-IMPACT PRACTICE > The ongoing debate about Howard Gardner's theory can be an opportunity for your students to write a longer paper (up to five pages) in which they take a position for or against Gardner's theory and use existing scholarship or research to support their views.

> **your turn**   Write and Reflect
>
> **Is There Really More than One Type of Intelligence?**
> Do a Google search for the phrase *multiple intelligences debate*. Write a one-page paper that describes different opinions about Howard Gardner's theory. Do you agree with the theory? Why or why not?

Gardner's work is controversial because it questions our traditional definitions of intelligence. According to Gardner's theory,

all human beings have at least eight different types of intelligence, as follows:

1. A **verbal/linguistic** learner likes to read, write, and tell stories, and is good at memorizing information.
2. A **logical/mathematical** learner likes to work with numbers and is good at problem solving and logical processes.
3. A **visual/spatial** learner likes to draw and play with machines and is good at puzzles and reading maps and charts.
4. A **bodily/kinesthetic** learner likes to move around and is good at sports, dance, and acting.
5. A **musical/rhythmic** learner likes to sing and play an instrument and is good at remembering melodies and noticing pitches and rhythms.
6. An **interpersonal** learner likes to have many friends and is good at understanding people, leading others, and mediating conflicts.
7. **Intrapersonal** learners like to work alone, understand themselves well, and are original thinkers.
8. A **naturalistic** learner likes to be outside and is good at preservation, conservation, and organizing a living area.

Where do you think you see yourself? In your opinion, which of these eight intelligences best describes you? As you think of your friends and family, what kinds of intelligences do you think they have? Verify your assumptions about the intelligences of friends and family members by taking the Multiple Intelligences Inventory together. Were there any surprises or were your assumptions confirmed?

Multiple Intelligences Inventory

Put a check mark next to all the items within each intelligence that apply to you.

Verbal/Linguistic Intelligence

_____ I enjoy telling stories and jokes.

_____ I enjoy word games (e.g., Scrabble and puzzles).

_____ I am a good speller (most of the time).

_____ I like talking and writing about my ideas.

_____ If something breaks and won't work, I read the instruction book before I try to fix it.

_____ When I work with others in a group presentation, I prefer to do the writing and library research.

Logical/Mathematical Intelligence

_____ I really enjoy my math class.

_____ I like to find out how things work.

_____ I enjoy computer and math games.

_____ I love playing chess, checkers, or Monopoly.

_____ If something breaks and won't work, I look at the pieces and try to figure out how it works.

Visual/Spatial Intelligence

_____ I prefer a map to written directions.

_____ I enjoy hobbies such as photography.

_____ I like to doodle on paper whenever I can.

_____ In a magazine, I prefer looking at the pictures rather than reading the text.

_____ If something breaks and won't work, I tend to study the diagram of how it works.

Bodily/Kinesthetic Intelligence

_____ My favorite class is gym because I like sports.

_____ When looking at things, I like touching them.

_____ I use a lot of body movements when talking.

_____ I tend to tap my fingers or play with my pencil during class.

_____ If something breaks and won't work, I tend to play with the pieces to try to fit them together.

Musical/Rhythmic Intelligence

_____ I enjoy listening to CDs and the radio.

_____ I like to sing.

_____ I like to have music playing when doing homework or studying.

_____ I can remember the melodies of many songs.

_____ If something breaks and won't work, I tend to tap my fingers to a beat while I figure it out.

Interpersonal Intelligence

_____ I get along well with others.

_____ I have several very close friends.

_____ I like working with others in groups.

_____ Friends ask my advice because I seem to be a natural leader.

_____ If something breaks and won't work, I try to find someone who can help me.

Intrapersonal Intelligence

_____ I like to work alone without anyone bothering me.

_____ I don't like crowds.

_____ I know my own strengths and weaknesses.

_____ I find that I am strong-willed, independent, and don't follow the crowd.

_____ If something breaks and won't work, I wonder whether it's worth fixing.

Naturalist Intelligence

_____ I am keenly aware of my surroundings and of what goes on around me.

_____ I like to collect things like rocks, sports cards, and stamps.

_____ I like to get away from the city and enjoy nature.

_____ I enjoy learning the names of living things in the environment, such as flowers and trees.

_____ If something breaks and won't work, I look around me to see what I can find to fix the problem.

Review your responses. Now, count up the check marks for each intelligence, and write the total for each intelligence here. Your score for each intelligence will be a number between 1 and 6:

TOTAL SCORE

_____ Verbal/Linguistic

_____ Logical/Mathematical

_____ Visual/Spatial

_____ Bodily/Kinesthetic

_____ Musical/Rhythmic

_____ Interpersonal

_____ Intrapersonal

_____ Naturalist

Your scores of 3 or more will help you to get a sense of your own multiple intelligences.

Depending on your background and age, some intelligences are likely to be more developed than others. Now that you know where your intelligences are, you can work to strengthen the other intelligences that you do not use as often. How do college courses measure ways in which you are intelligent? Where do they fall short? Looking to the future, you can use your intelligences to help you choose a major, choose activities, and investigate career options. This information will help you appreciate your own unique abilities, and also those of others.

Source: Greg Gay and Gary Hams, "The Multiple Intelligences Inventory." Copyright © Learning Disabilities Resource Community, www.ldrc.ca. Reprinted by permission of the authors.

WHEN LEARNING STYLES AND TEACHING STYLES CONFLICT

Do you enjoy listening to lectures, or do you find yourself gazing out the window or dozing? When your instructor assigns a group discussion, what is your immediate reaction? Do you dislike talking with other students, or is that the way you learn best? How do you react to lab sessions when you have to conduct an actual experiment? Is it an activity you look forward to, or one you dread? Each of these learning situations appeals to some students more than others, but each is inevitably going to be part of your college experience. Your college or university has intentionally designed courses for you to have the opportunity to listen to professors who are experts in their field, to interact with other students in structured groups, and to learn through doing. Because they are all important components of your college education, it's important for you to make the most of each situation.

    Instructors tend to teach in ways that fit their _own_ particular styles of learning, which might surprise you. So an instructor who learns best in a read/write mode or aural mode will probably just lecture and give the class little opportunity for either interaction or visual and kinesthetic learning. But an instructor who prefers a more interactive, hands-on environment will likely involve students in discussion and learning through experience.

    When you recognize a mismatch between how you best learn and how you are being taught, it is important that you take control of your

RETENTION STRATEGY **>**
Retention is connected to how well students can engage with faculty. A good predictor of first-year persistence is out-of-class interaction between students and faculty.

techtip

CORRELATE ONLINE LEARNING WITH YOUR LEARNING STYLE

Do you like the idea of taking an online class? Maybe that would be a good fit for your work or family schedule. Maybe it would be easier than looking for a parking space on campus. But would you still learn, even if you don't go to a class meeting?

First, consider your learning style:

- If you like the thought of a two-hour lecture where you mostly listen to someone talking, chances are you're an **auditory learner**.
- If you're a **visual learner**, you want to see charts, graphs, and videos.
- If you are a **hands-on learner**, you thrive when engaged in an activity and working with others.

Many colleges and universities use an online learning management system (LMS) for online learning. An LMS is a Web site that helps you connect with the material you're studying—as well as with your instructors and classmates. There is something for every learning style in the LMS environment.

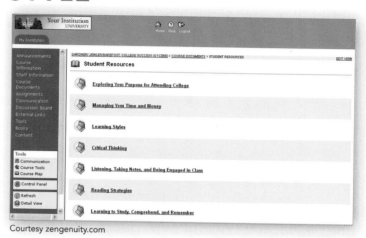

Courtesy zengenuity.com

The Problem

You have some idea about how you learn best, but you don't really understand what an LMS is or how to use one.

The Fix

Understand your learning style and what kind of learning environment will work best for you.

How to Do It

Explore your school's LMS. Be open-minded and patient with yourself. Find out if there is an orientation seminar or video you can watch; you can ask your instructors or visit the student learning center.

- Take online surveys to understand your learning style. Here are two sites to try: edutopia .org/multiple-intelligences-learning-styles-quiz and vark-learn.com.

An LMS offers lots of ways to connect with your instructors, classmates, and material. It lets you keep track of your grades and assignments, and offers a digital drop box where you can submit your work. It can also offer a lot of fun things, such as online discussion forums and interactive group projects where you can sketch ideas on whiteboards that other students can view, or even collaborate on written assignments in real time. Some platforms have videos, recorded lectures, or even your instructor's lecture notes.

1. If you're an auditory learner, you'll love audio recordings. Read your notes and textbook aloud

back to yourself.) Consider listening to audiobooks and joining a study group for discussions. Another tip: Listen to videos once and then play them back with your eyes closed.

2. If you're a visual learner, you'll love videos, pictures, maps, and graphs. Whenever you take notes, illustrate them, playing up key points with colored highlighters, pictures, or symbols. You can also create your own graphs or charts.

3. If you're a hands-on learner, you'll love labs, group projects, and fieldwork. Be sure to take notes and read things aloud as you study. Build models or spreadsheets. Take a field trip with others or even by yourself.

IS IT FOR YOU?

Now that you know what kind of learner you are and something about your college's LMS:

- Are you disciplined enough to work independently?
- Would you miss interacting with your instructor or classmates if you didn't attend classes?

You need to know yourself because learning is really

learning process. Use Table 4.2 as a guide to identify these mismatches and discover strategies for how to handle them. Don't depend on the instructor or the classroom environment to give you everything you need to maximize your learning. Employ your own preferences, talents, and abilities to develop many different ways to study and retain information. For instance, if you don't like listening to a lecture, you will want to sit close to the front of the classroom to reduce distractions. You might also want to record the lecture (with the instructor's permission) so that you can listen to it again. Look back through this chapter to remind yourself of the ways that you can use your own learning styles to be more successful in any class you take.

PEER LEADERS ❯ Facilitate a class discussion about teaching/learning style differences. Use your own experience to help students understand how you overcame the challenge of a particular kind of course.

TABLE 4.2 ❯ Using the VARK to Adapt

Try to use the VARK to figure out how your instructors teach their classes. List your classes, your instructors' teaching styles, and then your learning style. Do they match? If not, list a strategy you can use to adapt.

My Classes	Teaching Style	My Learning Style	Match: Yes or No?
Example: *Psychology*	*Uses PowerPoints with her lecture so: Visual and Auditory*	*I am kinesthetic and visual.*	*No, but I can ride a stationary bike while looking over my notes.*

LEARNING DISABILITIES

While everyone has a learning style, some people have a **learning disability,** a general term that covers a wide variety of specific learning problems resulting from neurological disorders that can make it difficult to acquire certain academic and social skills. Learning disabilities are very common in students of all ages.

Learning disabilities are usually recognized and diagnosed in grade school, but some students can successfully compensate for a learning problem, perhaps without realizing that's what it is, and reach the first year of college without having been properly diagnosed or assisted. Learning disabilities can show up as specific difficulties with spoken and written language, coordination, self-control, or attention. Such difficulties can impede the ability to read, write, or do math. The term *learning disability* covers a

"As we start a new school year, Mr. Smith, I just want you to know that I'm an Abstract-Sequential learner and trust that you'll conduct yourself accordingly!"

broad range of possible causes, symptoms, treatments, and outcomes. Therefore, it is difficult to diagnose a learning disability or pinpoint its cause. The types of learning disabilities that most commonly affect college students are attention disorders that affect the development of academic skills, including reading, writing, and mathematics.

You might know someone who has been diagnosed with a learning disability, such as dyslexia, which is a reading disability that occurs when the brain does not properly recognize and process certain symbols, or attention deficit disorder, which affects concentration and focus. It is also possible that you have a special learning need and are not aware of it. This section seeks to increase your self-awareness and your knowledge about such challenges to learning. You will learn more about common types of learning disabilities, how to recognize them, and what to do if you or someone you know has a learning disability.

Attention Disorders

Attention disorders are common in children, adolescents, and adults. Some students who have attention disorders appear to daydream excessively, and once you do get their attention, they can be easily distracted. Individuals with attention deficit disorder (ADD) or attention deficit hyperactivity disorder (ADHD) often have trouble organizing tasks or completing their work. They don't seem to listen to or follow directions, and their work might be messy or appear careless. Although they are not strictly classified as learning disabilities, ADD and ADHD can seriously interfere with academic performance, leading some educators to classify them with other learning disabilities.[4]

---

[4]Adapted from Sharyn Neuwirth, *Learning Disabilities* (Darby, PA: National Institute of Mental Health, 1993), 9–10.

If you have trouble paying attention or getting organized, you won't really know whether you have ADD or ADHD until you are evaluated. Check out resources on campus or in the community. After you have been evaluated, follow the advice you get, which might or might not mean taking medication. If you receive a prescription for medication, be sure to take it according to your physician's directions. You can also improve your focus through your own behavioral choices, whether or not you have an attention disorder. The Web site for the National Institute of Mental Health offers the following suggestions for adults with attention disorders:

> A professional counselor or therapist can help an adult with ADHD learn how to organize his or her life with tools such as a large calendar or date book, lists, reminder notes, and by assigning a special place for keys, bills, and paperwork. Large tasks can be broken down into smaller, more manageable steps so that completing each part of the task provides a sense of accomplishment.[5]

Cognitive Learning Disabilities

Other learning disabilities are related to cognitive skills. Dyslexia, for example, is a common developmental reading disorder. Though a person can have problems with any of the tasks involved in reading, scientists have found that a significant number of people with dyslexia share an inability to distinguish or separate the sounds in spoken words. For instance, people with dyslexia sometimes have difficulty assigning the appropriate sounds to individual letters or to letters that have been combined to form words. Reading is more than recognizing words, however. If the brain is unable to form images or relate new ideas to those stored in memory, the reader can't understand or remember the new concepts. So other types of reading disabilities can appear when the focus of reading shifts from word identification to comprehension.[6]

Writing involves several brain areas and functions as well. The brain networks for vocabulary, grammar, hand movement, and memory must all be in good working order. A developmental writing disorder might result from problems in any of these areas. Someone who can't distinguish the sequence of sounds in a word will often have problems with spelling. People with writing disabilities, particularly expressive language disorders (the inability to express oneself using accurate language or sentence structure), are often unable to write complete, grammatical sentences.[7]

A student with a developmental arithmetic disorder will have difficulty recognizing numbers and symbols, memorizing facts such as multiplication tables, and understanding abstract concepts such as place value and fractions.[8]

---

[5]"Attention Deficit Hyperactivity Disorder." U.S. Department of Health and Human Services, National Institutes of Health, NIH Publication No. 12-3572, p. 17 (Revised 2012). www.nimh.nih.gov/health/publications/attention-deficit-hyperactivity-disorder/index.shtml, accessed September 3, 2014.

[6]Ibid.

[7]Ibid.

[8]Ibid.

The following questions may help you determine whether you or some-one you know should be screened for a possible learning disability:

Do you perform poorly on tests, even when you feel that you have stud-ied and are capable of performing better?

Do you have trouble spelling words?

Do you work harder than your classmates at basic reading and writing?

Do your instructors point out inconsistencies in your classroom perfor-mance, such as answering questions correctly in class but incorrectly on a written test?

Do you have a really short attention span, or do your family members or instructors say that you do things without thinking?

Although responding *yes* to any of these questions does not mean that you have a disability, your campus learning center or the office for student disability services can help you address any potential problems and devise ways for you to learn more effectively.

If you have a documented learning disability, make sure to notify the office of student disability services at your college or university to receive reasonable accommodations, as required by law. Reasonable accommodations might include use of a computer during some exams, readers for tests, in-class note-takers, extra time for assignments and tests, or the use of audio textbooks, depending on your needs and the type of disability you have.

Anyone who is diagnosed with a learning disability is in good company. According to national data, between 15 and 20 percent of Americans have a learning disability. Pop star Jewel, National Football League host and former player Terry Bradshaw, actor Patrick Dempsey, and CNN news anchor Anderson Cooper are just a few of the famous and successful peo-ple who have diagnosed learning disabilities. Here is a final important message: A learning disability is a learning *difference*, but is in no way related to intelligence. Having a learning disability is not a sign that you are stupid. In fact, some of the most intelligent individuals in human his-tory have had a learning disability.

IN CLASS ❯ Share information on where students should go for help on campus if they have a learning disability, or if they think they might have one and want to be evaluated.

yourturn   Make Good Choices

Accept the Challenge to Do Your Best, No Matter What!

Although you generally won't be able to select courses and instructors based on your learning style, you can choose how to handle yourself in each class. Think about your courses this term and look at how you filled in Table 4.2. Which classes are challenging you because of the way the instructors teach? If you are using an instructor's teaching style as an excuse for your poor performance, you are making a choice that may affect your overall college success. Your college or university has plenty of resources available to help you. Seek them out and choose to get the assistance you need to do your best.

checklist **for** success

How You Learn

- ☐ **Take a learning-styles inventory, either in this chapter or at your campus learning or counseling center(s).** See if the results might explain, at least in part, your level of performance in each class you are taking this term.

- ☐ **Learn about and accept your unique learning preferences.** Make a special note of your strengths, in terms of those things you learn well and easily. See if those skills could be applied to other learning situations.

- ☐ **Adapt your learning style to the teaching styles of your professors.** Consider talking to your professors about how you might best be able to adapt to their teaching strategies.

- ☐ **Use your learning style to develop study strategies that work best for you.** You can walk, talk, read, listen, or even dance while you are learning.

- ☐ **If you need help with making the best use of your learning style, visit your learning center.** Consider taking some courses in the social and behavioral sciences, which could help you better understand how people learn.

- ☐ **If you think you might have a learning disability, go to your campus learning center and ask for a diagnostic assessment so that you can develop successful coping strategies.** Make sure to ask for a personal interpretation and follow-up counseling or tutoring.

4 buildyourexperience

REFLECT ON CHOICES

high-impact practice 2 This chapter has introduced you to the ways people prefer to learn from their environment. The choice of what to do with that information is up to you. Successful college students learn to adapt to teaching styles that they may not prefer. They know what they have to do to be successful learners, they set goals, and they monitor their progress toward their goals. In a journal entry or readily accessible file, reflect on and write about what you have learned about learning styles and learning disabilities in this chapter and how you can apply the chapter information and strategies in college and in your career. Revisit and build upon your observations throughout your first-year experience.

APPLY WHAT YOU'VE LEARNED

Now that you have read and discussed this chapter, consider how you can apply what you have learned to your academic life and your personal life. The following prompts will help you reflect on chapter material and its relevance to you both now and in the future.

1. It is almost certain that you will find yourself in a class where your learning style conflicts with your instructor's preferred style of teaching. After reading this chapter, describe what you can do to take control and make the most of your strongest learning preferences.

2. It is important to understand various learning styles in the context of education, but it is also important to understand how learning preferences affect career choices. Considering your own learning styles, what might be the best careers for you? Why?

USE YOUR RESOURCES

> **Campus Learning Center or Center for Students with Disabilities**
Whether you are an online or on-campus student, a recent high school graduate, or someone who is older, your college or university will have resources to help students learn more about learning styles or to diagnose a learning disability.

> **Your Instructors or Your Peer Leader**
To gather information about the support services your campus has to offer, talk to your first-year seminar instructor or instructors in education or psychology, who have a strong interest in the processes of learning. You'll find that your peer leader can also steer you in the right direction. If you *are* a peer leader, make sure you have a working knowledge of the learning styles covered in this chapter.

> **Campus Library**
A great deal of published information is available that describes how we learn. A campus librarian can help you locate books and online resources on learning styles and learning disabilities.

> **Social Media**
You will find groups on Facebook (**facebook.com**) that were created by students who have learning disabilities or ADHD. Connect with other students with learning disabilities at your college or university or at other institutions. If you have been diagnosed with a learning disability, the members of these groups can offer support and help you seek out appropriate resources to be successful in college.

 LaunchPad

PART TWO
PREPARING TO LEARN

Phase4Studios/
Shutterstock

5 THINKING IN COLLEGE

Student Goals

- Understand what college-level thinking involves
- Learn how to become a critical thinker
- Develop an appreciation for Bloom's taxonomy and how it relates to critical thinking

Chris Schmidt/
Getty Images

6 READING TO LEARN

Student Goals

- Apply the four steps in active reading: previewing, marking, reading with concentration, and reviewing
- Develop strategies for reading textbooks across different subject areas
- Improve and monitor your reading

wavebreakmedia/
Shutterstock

7 GETTING THE MOST FROM CLASS

Student Goals

- Understand the benefits to your learning that result from being engaged in class
- Learn ways to prepare before class
- Appreciate the value of participating in class by listening critically and speaking up
- Know how to assess and improve your note-taking skills and how to use your notes to be engaged in learning

Ammentorp Photography/
Shutterstock

8 STUDYING

Student Goals

- Learn how to make good choices for better concentration and efficient studying
- Understand how memory works and become familiar with myths about memory
- Gain skills to improve your memory

9 TEST TAKING

Student Goals

- Prepare yourself for tests and exams physically, emotionally, and academically
- Learn strategies for taking different types of tests and handling various question types
- Recognize the symptoms of test anxiety and gain strategies to overcome it
- Understand what cheating is and how to avoid it and learn guidelines for maintaining academic honesty

10 INFORMATION LITERACY AND COMMUNICATION

Student Goals

- Understand what it means to be information literate
- Learn how to choose a research topic, narrow it down, and research it
- Know how to use your college library with assistance from librarians
- Apply the guidelines for evaluating sources
- Gain an understanding of how to move from research to writing and use each step of the writing process
- Learn the guidelines for successful public speaking

5
THINKING IN COLLEGE

YOU WILL EXPLORE

What college-level thinking involves

How to become a critical thinker

Bloom's taxonomy and how it relates to critical thinking

High-impact practices 2 (writing), 3 (collaboration), and 4 (diversity)

Alyssa Manning, 18

Psychology major
The University of North Carolina at Charlotte

> " Thinking for ourselves and coming up with new conclusions will be really helpful when we enter the workforce. "

As a psychology student at the University of North Carolina at Charlotte (UNC Charlotte), Alyssa Manning understands the importance of thinking skills both inside and outside the classroom. When Alyssa arrived on campus last fall, she learned that she would be living in the international residence hall with students from all over the world. She quickly learned that interacting with people who don't know anyone else in the United States and who have different customs, study habits, and food presented some welcome challenges and tested her thinking skills. "Some of the questions the international students ask about America make me think in a different way because I never think about my own country in that way." One way she has been able to reach out to the students she lives with is by joining an international student organization, which helps bring new international students to campus and get them settled into campus life.

Alyssa grew up in Philadelphia and decided to attend UNC Charlotte because she was interested in the research opportunities available to her as an undergraduate psychology major. The beautiful campus and location in Charlotte didn't hurt either! So far, her favorite class has been social psychology. She has found good thinking skills to be essential to succeeding in all her classes. "Professors will give you a lot of facts and general information, but they expect you to be able to relate all the information and come up with your own conclusions. Thinking for ourselves and coming up with new conclusions will be really helpful when we enter the workforce," she says.

After Alyssa graduates, she's open to new experiences and opportunities, but she hopes to continue on to graduate school. As an aspiring psychiatrist, she says that "thinking skills will help a lot when dealing with cases and needing to diagnose disorders and develop treatment plans. They will also be helpful in clinical settings." Her advice to other first-year students? Look for ways to recognize problems and come up with unique solutions.

 **LaunchPad**

To access the LearningCurve study tool, video activities, and more, go to LaunchPad for *Your College Experience.* macmillanhighered.com /gardner12e

Learning to think—using the mind to produce ideas, opinions, decisions, and memories—is part of normal human development. Just as our bodies grow, so does our ability to think logically and rationally about abstract concepts. The Nobel-prize-winning economist, Daniel Kahneman, describes two types of thinking: "fast thinking" and "slow thinking." He characterizes fast thinking as automatic, emotional, stereotypic, and subconscious; this type of thinking is certainly appropriate in some circumstances. Slow thinking takes more effort, more conscious attention, and is more logical, rational, and deep.[1] By improving your slower and more logical thinking abilities and strategies, you will become a better learner and problem solver.

---

[1]Daniel Kahneman, *Thinking, Fast and Slow*, (New York: Farrar, Straus and Giroux, 2013).

The concept of "critical thinking" might not be new to you; you have probably heard the term before. Here we define **critical thinking** as the thoughtful consideration of the information, ideas, observations, and arguments that you encounter. In essence, critical thinking is a search for truth. It is similar to slow thinking as described by Kahneman, but it also emphasizes the importance of analyzing and evaluating information to guide belief and action—this is the kind of thinking you will do in college, and it's what this chapter is all about. We will explain how developing and applying your critical-thinking skills can make the search for answers a worthwhile and stimulating adventure.

COLLEGE-LEVEL THINKING: HIGHER AND DEEPER

In college, the level of thinking that your instructors expect from you exceeds that which you did in high school, both in terms of the questions that are asked and the answers that are expected. For instance, if a high school teacher asked, "What are the three branches of the U.S. government?" he or she would ask you to give the one right answer: "legislative, executive, and judicial." A college instructor, on the other hand, might ask, "Under what circumstances might conflicts arise among the three branches of government, and what do the circumstances and the conflicts reveal about the democratic process?" There is no simple, quick, or single acceptable answer to the second question—that's the point of higher education. Questions that suggest complex answers engage you in the process of deep thinking. The shift to this higher or deeper level of thinking can be an adjustment—it might even catch you off guard and cause you some stress.

One step toward deep and critical thinking is becoming comfortable with uncertainty. In college, it's important to challenge assumptions and conclusions, even those presented by so-called experts. Rather than just

RETENTION STRATEGY › One thing that keeps students motivated to stay in college is engaging in learning that they think is relevant to improving their employment options. This chapter focuses on how to develop a skill that is highly sought by employers—critical thinking!

IN CLASS › Critical thinking is one of the most important concepts in this book. Point out the relationship between this concept and your institution's mission statement on its Web site or catalog. Discuss the college mission statement to help your students understand your institution's educational goals; tie in the meaning of a liberal education as appropriate. You might want to point out that most employers value the ability to think critically more than they value specific content knowledge.

taking in information, studying it, and then recalling it for a test, in college you'll go far beyond these skills and gain the ability and the confidence to arrive at your own conclusions—to think for yourself. Educational researchers describe this process as "constructing" knowledge for yourself rather than merely "receiving" knowledge from others. Courses in every discipline will encourage you to ask questions, sort through competing information and ideas, form well-reasoned opinions, and defend them.

It is natural to feel frustrated by answers that are neither entirely wrong nor right, yet the complicated questions are usually the ones that are the most interesting and worthy of study. Working out the answers can be both intellectually exciting and personally rewarding.

Problem Solving in and out of Class

College will give you experience in decision making and problem solving—processes that are linked to your abilities to use logical thinking processes, to weigh evidence, and to formulate conclusions. Your success both in college and in your future life will depend on how well you make decisions and solve problems. Here are some examples of situations commonly encountered in college that will call upon these skills:

- Deciding how to allocate your research and writing time when you have two papers due on the same day
- Finding a way to ask your roommate to compromise on a suitable lights-out time because you're not getting the sleep you need
- Mapping out how to incorporate time for exercising into your busy schedule in order to maintain a healthy fitness level and avoid weight gain
- Deciding whether to go home on the weekends or stay on campus to study and participate in campus events
- Understanding the advantages and disadvantages of the variety of readily available information sources, including Facebook, Twitter feeds, CNN, *USA Today*, *The New York Times*, the *Onion*, and your school newspaper.

In addition to these situations, which provide opportunities for you to flex your problem-solving muscles on a more personal level, the college years also represent a time in your life when you get to know yourself. You will begin to develop your own positions on societal and political issues, learn more about what is important to you, and develop into a contributing citizen of your country and also the world.

In college, you'll be exposed to ideas and often-conflicting opinions about contemporary issues such as same-sex marriage, U.S. military operations, global human rights, animal rights, comprehensive sex education, food safety, the state of public education in the U.S., student loan debt and loan forgiveness, and economic inequality. The list goes on and on. Before accepting any opinion on any issue as "the truth," look for evidence that supports different positions on these debates. In fact, look for opportunities to participate in such debates. In most colleges, these opportunities abound.

Making a Choice between Slow and Fast Thinking

At the start of the chapter, we introduced the concepts of slow and fast thinking. While fast thinking has its place, improving your slower and more logical thinking abilities will allow you to become a better learner. But you might notice that some people seem to do no real thinking at all, or at least no thinking of their own.

IN CLASS > Ask students why some people do not think for themselves, instead relying on others to think for them.

People who do not develop their thinking skills often make spur-of-the-moment decisions based on what seems easiest, results in the least conflict, or conforms to preconceived notions. You probably know a lot of people like that—who do not think critically, depend on others to think for them, and assume that what they believe is true simply because they wish, hope, or feel that it is true. You might also know people who like things just because they are popular, and still others whose beliefs may be based on what they heard growing up, without ever examining the underlying assumptions that support those beliefs. As you might have noticed, the followers, the wishful believers, and the rigid thinkers tend not to have much control over their lives or to have any real power in business or society.

The slow thinkers, those who use critical-thinking skills, are different. They examine problems, ask questions, suggest new answers that challenge the existing situation, discover new information, question authorities and traditional beliefs, make independent judgments, and develop creative solutions. Being a good critical thinker does not mean that you are "critical" or negative in your dealings with others. Rather, the term refers to thoughtful consideration of the information, ideas, and arguments that you encounter. When employers say they want workers who can find reliable information, analyze it, organize it, draw conclusions from it, and present it convincingly to others, that means they want employees who are good critical thinkers.

Whatever else you do in college, make it a point to develop and sharpen your critical-thinking skills. You won't become a great critical thinker overnight. With practice, however, you can learn how to tell if information is truthful and accurate. Thinking critically—mastering slow thinking—will help you make better decisions, come up with fresh solutions to difficult problems, and communicate your ideas effectively.

---

your turn   Make Good Choices

If You Had a "Do-Over"

Think about a past problem or difficult situation you were unsuccessful in solving. If you could go back in time, how would you choose to solve the problem to get the outcome you desire? What would you do differently? What different choices would you make? Could you more deliberately use slow thinking in approaching the situation?

Rate Your Critical-Thinking Skills

It will be interesting to see how your critical-thinking skills change over the next few weeks and months. Given where you are currently, rate yourself as a "critical" thinker. At the end of the term, return to this table, and see how much you've changed.

Circle the number that best fits you in each of the critical situations described below.

Critical Situations	Never				Sometimes				Always	
In class, I ask lots of questions when I don't understand.	1	2	3	4	5	6	7	8	9	10
If I don't agree with what the group decides is the correct answer, I challenge the group opinion.	1	2	3	4	5	6	7	8	9	10
I believe there are many solutions to a problem.	1	2	3	4	5	6	7	8	9	10
I admire those people in history who challenged what was believed at the time, such as "the earth is flat."	1	2	3	4	5	6	7	8	9	10
I make an effort to listen to both sides of an argument before deciding which way I will go.	1	2	3	4	5	6	7	8	9	10
I ask lots of people's opinions about a political candidate before making up my mind.	1	2	3	4	5	6	7	8	9	10
I am not afraid to change my belief system if I learn something new.	1	2	3	4	5	6	7	8	9	10
Authority figures do not intimidate me.	1	2	3	4	5	6	7	8	9	10

The more 7–10 scores you have circled, the more likely it is that you use your critical-thinking skills often. The lower scores indicate that you may not use critical-thinking skills very often, or that you use them only during certain activities.

high-impact practice 3

IN CLASS ❯ Discuss the value of collaborative thinking as it applies to critical thinking, especially in the area of creative brainstorming.

HIGH-IMPACT PRACTICE ❯ The findings about the link between collaboration and critical thinking are an important reason that student collaboration is found to be a high-impact educational practice.

Collaboration

One way to become a better critical thinker is to practice with other people. By getting feedback from others, you can see the possible flaws in your own position or approach. Whether debating an issue in a political science class or making a dress in a fashion design class, appreciate how people bring their own life experiences, personal taste, knowledge, and expertise to the table. Most questions do not have clear-cut answers, and there are often several ways of approaching any task. Getting input from others can help make your finished product a masterpiece.

Researchers who study thinking of elementary school students, high school students, and college students find that critical thinking and collaboration go hand in hand. Students at all levels are more likely to exercise their critical-thinking abilities when they are confronted by the experiences and opinions of others. Having more than one student involved in the learning process generates a greater number of ideas than one person can generate alone. People think more clearly when they talk as well as listen, which is a very good reason to participate actively in your classes. Creative brainstorming and group discussion encourage original thought. These habits also teach participants to consider alternative points of view carefully and to express and defend their own ideas clearly. As a group negotiates ideas and learns to agree on the most reliable concepts, it moves closer to a conclusive solution.

As you leave college and enter the working world, you will find that collaboration—not only with people in your work setting but also with others around the globe—is essential to almost any career you may pursue. Whether in person or through electronic communication, teamwork improves your ability to think critically.

HIGH-IMPACT PRACTICE ❯ This paragraph will provide your students with both a rationale for the value of collaboration in learning and a clear statement on why collaboration is a high-impact practice in college.

RETENTION STRATEGY ❯ By definition, you can't collaborate alone; you collaborate with another person or with others in a group. There is much good research reporting a positive correlation between students who have study partners or join study groups and their retention in college. Urging students to participate in groups not only teaches collaboration but also fosters retention.

Creativity

Our society is full of creative individuals who think outside the box, challenge the status quo, or simply ask questions that others are not asking. Many have achieved fame by using their thinking skills and actions to change our world. Even a single thought can have a ripple effect that leads to major progress. As you move through your other first-year courses such as sociology, psychology, history, or technology, you will learn about people who have used their creative-thinking abilities to become world changers in their academic areas.

Below are some critical thinkers of our past and present. Some might surprise you. What contributions to our world did each of these individuals make, and how do these contributions continue to affect our lives?

- **Abraham Lincoln** When we think of great leaders, Lincoln often comes to mind. Lincoln was able to think about the relationship between national policy and human rights in new and different ways. By working slowly and deliberately, Lincoln changed American laws and began a long process toward guaranteeing equal rights for all U.S. citizens—a journey that culminated in the civil rights legislation of the 1960s.
- **Martin Luther King Jr.** King could be considered one of the greatest activists of all time. When segregation ruled in the South, he contributed to the civil rights movement by voicing his concerns and presenting his dream of a different world. He created opportunities for change in many unfair societal policies and practices.
- **Twitter creators Jack Dorsey, Evan Williams, Biz Stone, and Noah Glass** Twitter was created in 2006 as a social networking and microblogging site to enhance communication around the world through hashtag statements that are limited to 140 characters each. In spite of early public resistance, the site quickly gained popularity and changed our way of communicating in times of national and international crisis due to its ability to disseminate information to millions of people instantly.
- **Steve Jobs** As an innovative and dynamic thinker, Jobs shaped the way our society viewed technology and digital capabilities. He persevered with passion, even through tough times, such as when he was ousted from his position as the head of Apple.

- **Lady Gaga** Pushing her artistic expression through fashion and activism, Lady Gaga projects an androgynous identity that challenges gender expectations and voices her belief in equality for all individuals.
- **Your instructors** You may not know it yet, but many of your instructors have conducted and written about cutting-edge research in their respective fields. Some may have even written textbooks that you are currently using in class!

---

yourturn Stay Motivated

Follow the Examples of Others

People who make a difference in their communities, nation, or the world stay motivated. They don't quit, even when they experience tough times. What other people in our world today—religious leaders, politicians, scientists, athletes, or entrepreneurs—have maintained their motivation and achieved major successes within their spheres of influence? What can you learn from them about what it means to stay motivated?

BECOMING A CRITICAL THINKER

As you've read, a high-priority goal in college is to develop strong thinking and decision-making skills. Not only will you develop your own competence and confidence, you will contribute to the larger society by helping solve community and national problems.

Asking Questions

The first step of thinking at a deeper level, of true critical thinking, is to be curious. This involves asking questions. Instead of accepting statements and claims at face value, question them. Here are a few suggestions:

- When you come across an idea or a statement that you consider interesting, confusing, or suspicious, first ask yourself what it means.
- Do you fully understand what is being said, or do you need to pause and think to make sense of the idea?
- Do you agree with the statement? Why or why not?
- Can the statement or idea be interpreted in more than one way?

Don't stop there.

- Ask whether you can trust the person or group making a particular claim, and ask whether there is enough evidence to back up that claim (more on this later).
- Ask who might agree or disagree and why.
- Ask how a new concept relates to what you already know.
- Think about where you might find more information about the subject, and what you could do with what you learn.

- Ask yourself about the effects of accepting a new idea as truth.
  - Will you have to change or give up what you have believed in for a long time?
  - Will it require you to do something differently?
  - Will it be necessary to examine the issue further?
  - Should you try to bring other people around to a new way of thinking?

© Randy Glasbergen.
www.glasbergen.com

WATER
99¢

LO-CARB
WATER
$2.99

GLASBERGEN

Considering Multiple Points of View and Drawing Conclusions

Before you draw any conclusions about the validity of information or opinions, it's important to consider more than one point of view. College reading assignments might deliberately expose you to conflicting arguments and theories about a subject, or you might encounter differences of opinion as you do research for a project. Your own belief system will influence how you interpret information, just as others' belief systems and points of view might influence how they present information. For example, consider your own ideas about the issue of K–12 education in the United States. American citizens, politicians, and others often voice opinions on options such as charter, private, and public schools. What kind of pre-college education do *you* think is best, and *why* do you hold this viewpoint?

The more ideas you consider, the more sophisticated your thinking will become. Ultimately, you will discover not only that it is okay to change your mind but also that a willingness to do so is the mark of a reasonable, educated person. Considering multiple points of view means synthesizing material, evaluating information and resources that might contradict each other or offer multiple points of view on a topic, and then honoring those differences. After considering multiple viewpoints and drawing

IN CLASS > Ask whether students have been told that once they make up their minds, they have to stick with their decisions. If so, who told them that? Under what circumstances? Why does it make more sense to be able to change your mind if you believe that you have a better solution? Suggest that they think about these questions with reference to how U.S. presidents make—or unmake—major policy decisions.

conclusions, the next step is to develop your own viewpoint based on cred-ible evidence and facts, while staying true to your values and beliefs. Crit-ical thinking is the process you go through in deciding how to align your experience and value system with your viewpoint.

This process isn't necessarily a matter of figuring out the right idea. Depending on the goals of the activity, the "right" idea might simply be the one that you think is the most fun or the most practical, or it might be a new idea of your own creation.

Drawing conclusions based on your consideration of many opinions and other types of evidence involves looking at the outcome of your inquiry in a more demanding, critical way. If you are looking for solutions to a problem, which ones seem most promising after you have conducted an exhaustive search for materials? If you have found new evidence, what does that new evidence show? Do your original beliefs hold up in the face of new evidence? Do they need to be modified? Which notions should be abandoned? Most important, consider what you would need to do or say to persuade someone else that your ideas are valid. Thoughtful conclusions are the most useful when you can share them with others.

 **high-impact practice 3**

HIGH-IMPACT PRACTICE ❯ This "Work Together" exercise will help your students dig deeply for evidence that would support or reject this position. By working together, students can challenge each other to go beyond personal opinion and learn about the implications of the First Amendment.

> **your turn** Work Together
>
> **Moving from Opinion to Logical Conclusion**
>
> Imagine that your state has just approved a license plate design incorporating a cross and the slogan, "I Believe." Almost immediately, a number of organizations begin protesting that this license plate is a violation of the First Amendment of the U.S. Constitution. Work with a small group of other students in your class and decide whether you agree or disagree with the state's action. Ask all members of the group to set aside their personal opinions and try to reach the best conclusion using solid evidence.

Making Arguments

IN CLASS ❯ Select a topic on which there are differences of opinion. The topic could relate to your institution, your community, your state, or the nation. One possibility would be the legalization of marijuana. Divide the class into two teams and schedule a debate on this topic. Some of the group members could be assigned to do background research, and some could be assigned to debate the issue. After the debate, ask class members to critique the arguments presented and determine which group presented the strongest case in support of its position.

What does the word *argument* mean to you? If you're like most people, the first image it conjures up might be an ugly fight you had with a friend, a yelling match you witnessed on the street, or a heated disagreement between family members. True, such unpleasant confrontations are argu-ments, but the word also refers to a calm, reasoned effort to persuade someone of the value of an idea.

When you think of it this way, you'll quickly recognize that arguments are central to academic study, work, and life in general. Scholarly articles, business memos, and requests for spending money all have something in common: The effective ones make a general claim, provide reasons to sup-port it, and back up those reasons with evidence. That's what argument is.

It's important to consider multiple points of view, or arguments, in tackling new ideas and complex questions, but arguments are not all equally valid. Good critical thinking involves analyzing assumptions that might have been omitted and scrutinizing the quality of the evidence used to support a claim. Whether examining an argument or making one, a good critical thinker is careful to ensure that ideas are presented in an understandable, logical way.

Challenging Assumptions and Beliefs

To some extent, it's unavoidable to have beliefs based on gut feelings or blind acceptance of something you've heard or read. However, some assumptions should be examined more thoughtfully, especially if they will influence an important decision or serve as the foundation for an argument.

We develop an understanding of information based on our value systems and how we view the world. Our family backgrounds influence these views, opinions, and assumptions. College is a time to challenge those assumptions and beliefs and to think critically about ideas we have always had.

Well-meaning people will often disagree. It's important to listen to both sides of an argument before making up your mind. If you follow the guidelines in this chapter, we can't promise that your classes will be easier or that you'll solve major problems, but you will be better equipped to handle them. You will have the skills to use critical thinking to figure things out instead of depending purely on how you feel or what you've heard. As you listen to a lecture, debate, or political argument about what is in the public's best interest, try to predict where it is heading and why. Ask yourself whether you have enough information to justify your own position.

FYI ❯ Sharing examples from personal experience should help students generate their own examples and feel comfortable sharing them.

Examining Evidence

Another important part of thinking critically is checking that the evidence supporting an argument—whether someone else's or your own—is of the highest possible quality. To do that, simply ask a few questions about the argument as you consider it:

- What general idea am I being asked to accept?
- Are good and sufficient reasons given to support the overall claim?
- Are those reasons backed up with evidence in the form of facts, statistics, and quotations?
- Does the evidence support the conclusions?
- Is the argument based on logical reasoning, or does it appeal mainly to emotions?
- Do I recognize any questionable assumptions?

- Can I think of any counterarguments, and if so, what facts can I muster as proof?
- What do I know about the person or organization making the argument?
- What credible sources can I find to support the information?

If you have evaluated the evidence used in support of a claim and are still not certain of its quality, it's best to keep looking for more evidence. Drawing on questionable evidence for an argument has a tendency to backfire. In most cases, a little persistence will help you find better sources.

Recognizing and Avoiding Faulty Reasoning

Although logical reasoning is essential to solving any problem, whether simple or complex, you need to go one step further to make sure that an argument hasn't been compromised by faulty reasoning. Here are some of the most common missteps—referred to as logical fallacies or flaws in reasoning—that people make in their use of logic:

- **Attacking the person.** Arguing against other people's positions or attacking their arguments is perfectly acceptable. Going after their

Logic That Just Doesn't Fly

This cartoon presents an obvious example of faulty reasoning. Some conversations or arguments tend to include reasoning like this. Can you think of a similarly illogical leap that someone used in an argument with you? Did you use critical thinking to counter it, or did your emotions get the best of you?

© Randy Glasbergen

PENGUINS ARE BLACK AND WHITE.
SOME OLD TV SHOWS ARE BLACK AND WHITE.
THEREFORE, SOME PENGUINS ARE OLD TV SHOWS.

GLASBERGEN

Logic: another thing that penguins aren't very good at.

personalities, however, is not OK. Any argument that resorts to personal attack ("Why should we believe a cheater?") is unworthy of consideration.

- **Begging.** "Please, officer, don't give me a ticket! If you do, I'll lose my license, and I have five little children to feed, and I won't be able to feed them if I can't drive my truck." None of the driver's statements offer any evidence, in any legal sense, as to why she shouldn't be given a ticket. Pleading *might* work if the officer is feeling generous, but an appeal to facts and reason would be more effective: "I fed the meter, but it didn't register the coins. Since the machine is broken, I'm sure you'll agree that I don't deserve a ticket."

- **Appealing to false authority.** Citing authorities, such as experts in a field or the opinions of qualified researchers, can offer valuable support for an argument. However, a claim based on the authority of someone whose expertise is questionable relies on the appearance of authority rather than on real evidence. We see examples of false authority all the time in advertising: Sports stars who are not doctors, dieticians, or nutritionists urge us to eat a certain brand of food; famous actors and singers who are not dermatologists extol the medical benefits of a costly remedy for acne.

- **Jumping on a bandwagon.** Sometimes we are more likely to believe something that many others also believe. Even the most widely accepted truths can turn out to be wrong, however. At one time, nearly everyone believed that the world was flat, until someone came up with evidence to the contrary.

- **Assuming that something is true because it hasn't been proven false.** If you go to a bookstore or look online, you'll find dozens of books detailing close encounters with flying saucers and extraterrestrial beings. These books describe the people who had such encounters as beyond reproach in their integrity and sanity. Because critics could not disprove the claims of the witnesses, the events are said to have actually occurred. Even in science, few things are ever proved completely false, but evidence can be discredited.

- **Falling victim to false cause.** Frequently, we make the assumption that just because one event followed another, the first event must have caused the second. This reasoning is the basis for many superstitions. The ancient Chinese once believed that they could make the sun reappear after an eclipse by striking a large gong, because they knew that on a previous occasion the sun had reappeared after a large gong had been struck. Most effects, however, are usually the result of a complex web of causes. Don't be satisfied with easy before-and-after claims; they are rarely correct.

- **Making hasty generalizations.** If someone selected a green marble from a barrel containing a hundred marbles, you wouldn't assume that the next marble drawn from the barrel would also be green. After all, you know nothing about the colors of the ninety-nine marbles still in the barrel. However, if you were given fifty draws from the barrel, and each draw produced a green marble after the barrel had been shaken thoroughly, you would be more willing to conclude that the next marble drawn would be green, too. Reaching a conclusion based on the opinion of one source is like assuming that all the marbles in the barrel are green after pulling out only one marble.

- **Slippery slope.** "If we allow tuition to increase, the next thing we know, it will be $20,000 per term." Such an argument is an example of "slippery slope" thinking. Fallacies like these can slip into even the most careful reasoning. One false claim can derail an entire argument, so be on the lookout for weak logic in what you read and write. Never forget that accurate reasoning is a key factor in succeeding in college and in life.

 *high-impact practice 2*

HIGH-IMPACT PRACTICE > When students reflect and write about their occasional temptation to use a logical fallacy to support their position, they will have a deeper understanding of this content and will be less likely to resort to this strategy in the future.

> **yourturn** Write and Reflect
>
> **Tempted to Use a Logical Fallacy?**
>
> Have you ever used a logical fallacy to justify decisions you have made? In looking back, did your flawed argument convince anyone that you were right? Why or why not? Describe your experiences in a journal entry.

APPLYING BLOOM'S TAXONOMY

Benjamin Bloom, a professor of education at the University of Chicago during the second half of the twentieth century, worked with a group of other researchers to design a system of classifying goals for the learning process. This system is known as Bloom's taxonomy, and it is now used at all levels of education to define and describe the process that students use to understand and think critically about what they are learning.

IN CLASS > Ask students which of these six levels they have been asked to use in their classes so far this term. Prompt them to provide specific examples.

RETENTION STRATEGY > While this taxonomy may initially appear daunting to your students, assure them that as they become successful in college, this is how they will think and learn. Urge them to concentrate initially on the lower levels, and explain that they will gradually build their skill levels with more college experience.

Bloom's Six Levels of Learning

Bloom identified six levels of learning, as represented in Figure 5.1. The higher the level, the more critical thinking it requires. Bloom's taxonomy is used in developing curricula, textbooks, learning management systems, and other academic work. You have been using the levels of Bloom's taxonomy throughout your education, perhaps without being aware of it.

Bloom's Taxonomy and the First Year of College

As you progress through your first year of college, you will notice that your level of comprehension and reflection begin to deepen as you engage with material and apply it to your experience in order to retain and synthesize it. If you pay close attention, you will discover that Bloom's taxonomy is often the framework that college instructors use to design classroom activities and out-of-class assignments. No matter what the topic is, this framework will help move you to deeper understanding and an ability to apply what you learn to other situations and concepts. Now we'll take a closer look at Bloom's taxonomy and then we'll take a concept you're likely to encounter in your first year of college—diversity—and match your cognitive development of the concept to Bloom's taxonomy.

IN CLASS > As your students finish reading the chapter, ask for their thoughts on the meaning and the significance of critical thinking.

FIGURE 5.1 ❯ The Six Levels of Learning of Bloom's Taxonomy

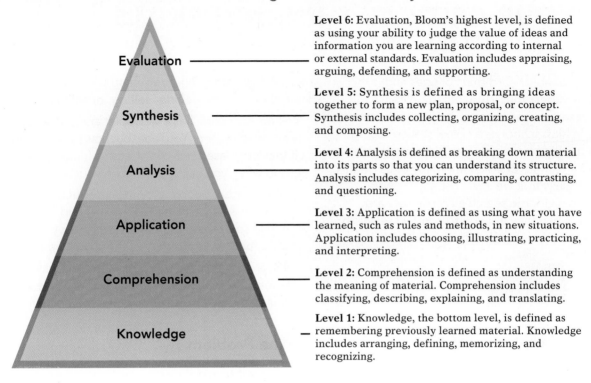

Level 6: Evaluation, Bloom's highest level, is defined as using your ability to judge the value of ideas and information you are learning according to internal or external standards. Evaluation includes appraising, arguing, defending, and supporting.

Level 5: Synthesis is defined as bringing ideas together to form a new plan, proposal, or concept. Synthesis includes collecting, organizing, creating, and composing.

Level 4: Analysis is defined as breaking down material into its parts so that you can understand its structure. Analysis includes categorizing, comparing, contrasting, and questioning.

Level 3: Application is defined as using what you have learned, such as rules and methods, in new situations. Application includes choosing, illustrating, practicing, and interpreting.

Level 2: Comprehension is defined as understanding the meaning of material. Comprehension includes classifying, describing, explaining, and translating.

Level 1: Knowledge, the bottom level, is defined as remembering previously learned material. Knowledge includes arranging, defining, memorizing, and recognizing.

Concept: Diversity

high-impact practices 2, 4

Level 1 (Knowledge) Read a dictionary definition of the word *diversity*.

Level 2 (Comprehension) Explain the concept of diversity to another student without reading the dictionary definition.

Level 3 (Application) Write about all the types of human diversity that exist within the student body at your college or university and possible categories of human diversity that are not represented there.

Level 4 (Analysis) Conduct two separate analyses. The first analysis will be why your institution has large numbers of certain types of students. The second analysis will be why your institution has small numbers of other types of students.

Level 5 (Synthesis) Write a paper that combines your findings in Level 4 and hypothesizes what components of your college or university culture either attract or repel certain students.

Level 6 (Evaluation) In your paper, evaluate the institution's "diversity profile" and argue for or against change in the way your campus supports diversity.

USE YOUR CRITICAL-THINKING SKILLS IN CONDUCTING RESEARCH

You have probably heard that colleges and universities expect their students to be able to conduct research when they write papers or create projects. In high school or a casual setting, doing research usually means going to a search engine like Google, Yahoo, or Ask.com. Many of us do this so automatically that we say, "Let me 'Google' that." But is a Google search all professors are looking for when they ask you to conduct research? How else could you conduct research?

Internet searches will help you find people basically doing three things: **yelling**, **selling**, or **telling**.

Yelling: Someone has a viewpoint and puts it forward on Blogger or YouTube, but how do you know if they are biased or a member of a fringe or hate group when you use their video in your project?

Selling: Often, people promote products or services in a way that makes them sound like credible sources of information when they are really simply trying to get you to buy something.

Telling: These places and people actually have credible information that you find informative and useful, but how can you verify their credibility?

The Problem

You need to conduct research for a paper, but you're not sure how to evaluate the types of information found on the Internet.

The Fix

Use a critical-thinking system to conduct your research.

Rommel Canlas/Shutterstock

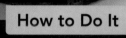

How to Do It

Start with good questions. If you are researching a topic, such as "marijuana legalization," generate some questions you have about that subject rather than just going to Google and typing "marijuana" into the search box:

- What is the history of marijuana use in the U.S.
- Why was it made illegal in the first place?
- Where has it been legalized and why?
- What have been some of the positive and negative outcomes of making it legal?

Generating questions will save you time by clarifying what you need to know, so you will recognize useful results and ignore the ones that won't help you.

Go to the library. Show the reference librarians your list of questions. They can help you fine-tune them and will recommend good places to find answers.

Use databases. Your school pays for research databases, which collect a variety of credible, scholarly research. When you use research databases, you can be sure that the information is reliable, and you can refine your search terms to produce 20 or 30 returns, as opposed to 20 or 30 million. Most databases are

available online with login information that your college can provide, so you can use them anytime from home or on your laptop.

Use a variety of locations to confirm information. When you see the same information in a variety of credible sources, you can start to trust its accuracy. *Remember that there are still good sources of information in print form that are not available online.*

Consider the quality of the information. Where did it come from? Who said it and why? How current is it? Has anything major happened in this area since this information was published?

EXTRA STYLE POINTS: Get in the habit of reading (not just watching) a variety of information sources. If you get news only from TV or links on Facebook, you will miss important stories. Remember this: Professionals need to be up to date in their areas of expertise, but they also must understand larger current events happening in the world around them. You must have broad knowledge in order to place your professional knowledge in context.

checklist for success

Thinking in College

☐ **Make sure that you understand what kind of thinking you will develop in college.** If you are not clear, discuss it with the instructor of this course, another instructor, or a staff member in the learning center.

☐ **Find ways to express your imagination and curiosity, and practice asking questions.** If you have the impulse to raise a question, don't stifle yourself. College is the perfect venue for self-expression and exploration.

☐ **Challenge your own and others' assumptions that are not supported by evidence.** To help you better understand someone's position on a given issue, practice asking for additional information in a calm, polite manner that does not reject his or her ideas.

☐ **During class lectures, presentations, and discussions, practice thinking about the subjects being discussed from multiple points of view.** Start with the view that you would most naturally take toward the matter at hand. Then, force yourself to imagine what questions might be raised by someone who doesn't see the issue the same way you do.

☐ **Draw your own conclusions and explain to others what evidence you considered that led you to these positions.** Don't assume that anyone automatically understands why you reached your conclusions.

☐ **Seek out opportunities for collaboration.** Join study groups or class project teams so you can collaborate with other students. When you are a member of a team, volunteer for roles that challenge you. That is how you will really experience significant gains in learning and development.

☐ **Learn to identify false claims in commercials and political arguments.** Then look for the same faulty reasoning in people's comments you hear each day.

☐ **Practice critical thinking, not only in your academic work, but also in your everyday interactions with friends and family.** Your environment both in and out of college will give you lots of opportunities to become a better critical thinker.

5 buildyourexperience

REFLECT ON CHOICES

high-impact practice 2 | This chapter has introduced you to critical thinking—the kind of thinking you will be expected to do in college. Reflect on what you have learned and how you would explain college-level thinking to someone else. Create a written summary of your ideas.

APPLY WHAT YOU'VE LEARNED

Consider how you can apply what you have learned to your academic and personal life. The following prompts will help you reflect on chapter material and its relevance to you both now and in the future.

1. After reading this chapter, think of professions (for example, health care, engineering, marketing) for which problem solving and thinking outside the box are necessary. Choose one career and describe why you think critical thinking is a necessary and valuable skill for that job.

2. In your opinion, is it harder to think critically than to base your arguments on how you feel about a topic? Why or why not? What are the advantages of finding answers based on your feelings versus based on problem solving and evidence? How might you use both approaches in seeking answers to questions?

USE YOUR RESOURCES

> **Logic Courses**
> If you are interested in learning more about critical thinking and how to apply critical-thinking skills, check out the introductory course in logic offered by your college's philosophy department. It might be the single best course designed to teach you critical-thinking skills, and nearly all colleges and universities offer such a course. Also, talk with a philosophy or logic instructor about in-class and out-of-class opportunities on your campus. A major in either area might be right for you.

> **Argument Courses and Critical-Thinking Courses**
> Does your institution offer either an argument or a critical-thinking course? Check your campus catalog to see what you can find. Such courses will help you develop the ability to formulate logical arguments and avoid such pitfalls as logical fallacies.

> **Debating Skills**
> Some of the very best thinkers developed debating skills during college. Go to either your student activities office or your department of speech and drama to find out whether your campus has a debate club or team. Debating can be fun, and chances are you will meet some interesting student thinkers that way.

> ***12 Angry Men* by Reginald Rose (New York: Penguin Classics, 2006)**
> This reprint of the original teleplay, which was written in 1954, was made into a film in 1958. Read the teleplay or watch the movie version of this stirring courtroom drama that pits twelve jurors against one another as they argue the outcome of a murder trial in which the defendant is a teenage boy. Although critical thinking is needed to arrive at the truth, all the jurors except one use noncritical arguments to arrive at a guilty verdict. The analysis of that one holdout, however, produces a remarkable change in their attitudes.

> **Bloom's Taxonomy**
> Florida International University provides a helpful resource about understanding and using Bloom's taxonomy at **online.fiu.edu/faculty/resources/bloomstaxonomy**.

> **Evaluating Resources**
> Ithaca College provides a guide to using critical-thinking skills to evaluate resources you'll encounter when doing research in college at **ithacalibrary.com/sp/subjects/evalres**.

 LaunchPad

LaunchPad for *Your College Experience* is a great resource. Go online to master concepts using the LearningCurve study tool and much more. macmillanhighered.com/gardner12e

6
READING TO LEARN

YOU WILL EXPLORE

The four steps in active reading: previewing, marking, reading with concentration, and reviewing

How to apply strategies for reading textbooks across different subject areas

Ways to improve and monitor your reading

⌖ High-impact practices 2 (writing) and 3 (collaboration)

Intellistudies/Shutterstock

Keira Sharma, 18

Communications major
Sam Houston State University

" **While my habits have worked well for me, students should get to know their own learning habits and find a reading method that works best for them.** "

Keira Sharma was born in Texas and then spent most of her childhood in Baton Rouge, Louisiana, where she learned study habits that have helped throughout her education. Just before high school, her family moved back to Texas. She decided to go to Sam Houston State University after visiting the campus and speaking with faculty and current students in the communications program. In addition, she thought that the campus was beautiful, and she liked the community. Last, it put her only an hour away from her family.

As someone who loves to learn, Keira came to college with some strategies in place. "There is definitely a lot more reading involved in college than in high school," she says. "However, the good thing is that professors give out syllabi that detail when readings will be due, so you can plan accordingly." Like many first-year students, she also had to learn to balance the amount of reading required. "I had to get used to measuring how long it took to read, and then manage my time accordingly."

Many of the other strategies Keira employs revolve around good time management and organization. "Learning how to juggle all other coursework, meals, a social life, and sleep can be difficult, but it is possible. I mostly organize my time in order of priorities, usually based on due dates and how much time it takes to do [the assignment]," she says. Keira explains that once she starts reading, "I usually write down headings within the chapter as I go to keep me guided in the right direction and so that I know what the main point of upcoming sections will be. I then read through and write down any important dates, names, words, or anything that better explains the concept or explains it in a different way. This way I have multiple views on the subject that further enhance my understanding. It also doesn't hurt to reread sections and go over notes." She adds an important note: "While my habits have worked well for me, students should get to know their own learning habits and find a reading method that works best for them."

Keira also has some simple advice for other first-year students: "As much work as college is and as overwhelming as it can feel sometimes, *don't stress too much*. College is one of the best times of life. Enjoy it!"

LaunchPad

To access the LearningCurve study tool, video activities, and more, go to LaunchPad for *Your College Experience*. macmillanhighered.com /gardner12e

As Keira mentions, reading college textbooks is more challenging than reading high school texts or reading for pleasure. College texts are loaded with concepts, terms, and complex information that you are expected to learn on your own in a short period of time. To accomplish it all, you will find it helpful to learn and use the active reading strategies in this chapter. They are intended to help you get the most out of your college reading. This chapter will also explore different strategies you can use when reading textbooks across the academic disciplines. These strategies include building your overall vocabulary and increasing your familiarity with terms that are unique to your particular field of study. Choose to make your textbook reading something you do every day. Reading in small chunks will help you concentrate and will increase your comprehension.

Depending on how much reading you did before coming to college—reading for pleasure, for your classes, or for work—you might find that reading is your favorite or least favorite way to learn. When you completed the VARK learning styles inventory in the chapter "How You Learn," you determined your preferences about reading and writing as a learning strategy. Even if reading *isn't* your favorite thing to do, it is absolutely essential to doing well in college and at work—no matter your major or profession.

A PLAN FOR ACTIVE READING

Active reading involves using strategies, such as highlighting and taking notes, that help you stay focused. Active reading is different from reading for pleasure, which doesn't require you to do anything while you are reading. By choosing active rather than passive reading, you will increase your focus and concentration, understand more of what you read, and prepare more effectively for tests and exams.

These are the four active reading steps designed to help you read college textbooks:

1. Previewing
2. Marking
3. Reading with concentration
4. Reviewing

your turn Work Together

Comparing Textbook Reading Strategies

With a group of your classmates, share which of these four steps you always, sometimes, or never do. Have one member of the group keep a tally and report results to the class. Are there steps that almost everyone avoids? If so, discuss the reasons why.

Previewing

Previewing involves taking a first look at your assigned reading before you really tackle the content. Think of previewing as browsing in a newly remodeled store. You locate the pharmacy and grocery areas. You get a feel for the locations of the men's, women's, and children's clothing departments; housewares; and electronics. You pinpoint the restrooms and checkout areas. You get a sense for where things are in relation to each other and compared to where they used to be. You identify where to find the items that you buy most often, whether they are diapers, milk, school supplies, or prescriptions. You get oriented.

Previewing a chapter in your textbook or other assigned reading is similar. The purpose is to get the big picture, to understand the main ideas covered in what you are about to read and how those ideas connect both with what you already know and with the material the instructor covers in class. Here's how you do it:

- Begin by reading the title of the chapter. Ask yourself: What do I already know about this subject?
- Next, quickly read through the learning objectives, if the chapter has them, or the introductory paragraphs. **Learning objectives** are the main ideas or skills that students are expected to learn from reading the chapter.
- Then turn to the end of the chapter and read the summary, if there is one. A **summary** highlights the most important ideas in the chapter.
- Finally, take a few minutes to skim the chapter, looking at the headings, subheadings, key terms, tables, and figures. You should also look at the end-of-chapter exercises.

As you preview, note how many pages the chapter contains. It's a good idea to decide in advance how many pages you can reasonably expect to cover in your first study session. This can help build your concentration as you work toward your goal of reading a specific number of pages. Before long, you'll know how many pages are practical for you to read in one sitting.

Previewing might require some time up front, but it will save you time later. As you preview the text material, look for connections between the text and the related lecture material. Remember the related terms and concepts in your notes from the lecture. Use these strategies to warm up. Ask yourself: Why am I reading this? What do I want to know?

Keep in mind that different types of textbooks can require more or less time to read. For example, depending on your interests and previous knowledge, you might be able to read a psychology text more quickly than a biology text that includes many scientific words that might be unfamiliar to you. Ask for help from your instructor, another student, or a tutor at your institution's learning assistance center.

Mapping. **Mapping** is a preview strategy in which you draw a wheel or branching structure to show relationships between main ideas and secondary ideas and how different concepts and terms fit together; it also helps you make connections to what you already know about the subject (see Figure 6.1). Mapping the chapter during the previewing process provides a visual guide for how different chapter ideas work together. Because many students identify themselves as visual learners, visual mapping is an excellent learning tool, not only for reading, but also for test preparation.

In the wheel structure, place the central idea of the chapter in the circle. The central idea should be in the chapter introduction; it might even be in the chapter title. Place secondary ideas on the lines connected to the circle, and place offshoots of those ideas on the lines attached to the main lines. In the branching map, the main idea goes at the top, followed by supporting ideas on the second tier, and so forth. Fill in the title first. Then, as you skim the chapter, use the headings and subheadings to fill in the key ideas.

FIGURE 6.1 › Wheel and Branching Maps

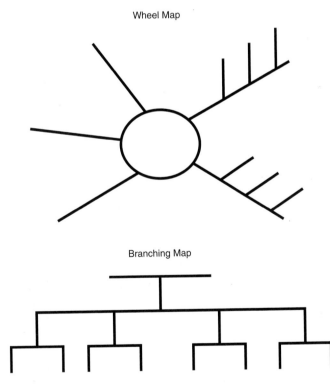

Wheel Map

Branching Map

Outlining or Listing. Perhaps you are more of a read/write learner than a visual learner and prefer a more step-by-step visual image. If so, consider making an outline of the headings and subheadings in the chapter. You can usually identify the text's main topics, subtopics, and specific terms within each subtopic by the size of the print. Notice, also, that the different levels

RETENTION STRATEGY › This is another occasion to remind your students of the positive correlation between seeking assistance and academic success in college. Also, point out that, disproportionately, it is the students who are already performing well who make the most use of such learning centers. The key idea here is to stress that these centers are not for dummies! They are for all students, and the best students use them.

OUTSIDE CLASS › After discussing how to map a chapter, have students map a chapter from a textbook they're using in another course.

IN CLASS › Have students bring the maps to class for sharing.

PEER LEADERS › As a peer leader, you can teach by example. Students will be interested in seeing whatever methods you use to identify important topics in the readings. If you create maps, bring them to class. If you prefer outlines, lists, or other methods, share these with your students.

of headings in a textbook look different. In a textbook, headings are designed to show relationships among topics and subtopics covered within a section. Flip through this textbook to see how the headings are designed. See a sample outline of this chapter in Figure 6.2 below. (Review the chapter "Getting the Most from Class" for more on outlining.)

To save time when you are outlining, don't write full sentences. Rather, include clear explanations of new technical terms and symbols. Pay special attention to topics that the instructor covered in class. If you aren't sure whether your outlines contain too much or too little detail, compare them with the outlines your classmates or members of your study group have made. You can also ask your instructor to check your outlines

FIGURE 6.2 ❯ Sample Outline

Here is how an outline of the first section of this chapter might look.

I. Active Reading

   A. Previewing
      1. Mapping
      2. Alternatives to Mapping
         a. Outlines
         b. Lists
         c. Chunking
         d. Flash cards
   B. Marking textbooks—Read and think BEFORE
      1. Underlining
      2. Highlighting
      3. Annotating (Margin notes)
   C. Reviewing—Each week, review
      1. Notes
      2. Study questions
      3. Annotations
      4. Flash cards
      5. Visual maps
      6. Outlines
   D. Reading with concentration—Use suggestions like
      1. Find proper location
      2. Turn off electronic devices
      3. Set aside blocks of time with breaks
      4. Set study goals

during office hours. In preparing for a test, review your chapter outlines so you can see how everything fits together.

Another previewing technique is listing. A list can be effective when you are dealing with a text that introduces many new terms and their definitions. Set up the list with the terms in the left column, and fill in definitions, descriptions, and examples on the right as you read or reread. Divide the terms on your list into groups of five, seven, or nine, and leave white space between the clusters so that you can visualize each group in your mind. This practice is known as **chunking**. Research has shown that we learn material best when it is presented in chunks of five, seven, or nine.

Creating Flash Cards. **Flash cards** are like portable test questions—you write a question or term on the front of a small card and the answer or definition on the back. In a course that requires you to memorize dates, like American history, you might write a key date on one side of the card and the event that correlates to that date on the other. To study chemistry, you would write a chemical formula on one side and the ionic compound on the other. You might use flash cards to learn vocabulary words or practice simple sentences for a language course. (See Figure 6.3.) Creating the cards from your readings and using them to prepare for exams are great ways to retain information, and they are especially helpful for visual and kinesthetic learners. Some apps, such as Flashcardlet and Chegg Flashcards, enable you to create flash cards on your electronic devices.

FIGURE 6.3 > Examples of Flash Cards

Strategies for Marking Your Textbook

After completing your preview, you are ready to read the text actively. With your map, outline, list, or flash cards to guide you, mark the sections that are most important. To avoid marking too much or marking the wrong information, first read without using your pencil or highlighter. This means you should read the text *at least* twice.

Marking is an active reading strategy that helps you focus and concentrate as you read. When you mark your textbook, you underline, highlight, or make margin notes or annotations. **Annotations** are notes or remarks about a piece of writing. Figure 6.4 provides an example of each method:

FIGURE 6.4 ❯ Examples of Marking

Using a combination of highlighting, underlining, and margin notes, the reader has made the content of this page easy to review. Without reading the text, review the highlighted words and phrases and the margin notes to see how much information you can gather from them. Then read the text itself. Does the markup serve as a study aid? Does it cover the essential points? Would you have marked this page any differently? Why or why not? Source: Adapted from *Discovering Psychology*, 6th ed., p. 534, by D. H. Hockenbury and S. E. Hockenbury. Copyright © 2013 by Worth Publishers. Used with permission.

CULTURE AND HUMAN BEHAVIOR

The Stress of Adapting to a New Culture

differences affecting cultural stress

Refugees, immigrants, and even international students are often unprepared for the dramatically different values, language, food, customs, and climate that await them in their new land. The process of changing one's values and customs as a result of contact with another culture is referred to as *acculturation*. **Acculturative stress** is the stress that results from the pressure of adapting to a new culture (Sam & Berry, 2010).

acceptance of new culture reduces stress

also speaking new language, education, & social support

Many factors can influence the degree of acculturative stress that a person experiences. For example, when the new society accepts ethnic and cultural diversity, acculturative stress is reduced (Mana & others, 2009). The transition is also eased when the person has some familiarity with the new language and customs, advanced education, and social support from friends, family members, and cultural associations (Schwartz & others, 2010). Acculturative stress is also lower if the new culture is similar to the culture of origin.

how attitudes affect stress

Cross-cultural psychologist John Berry (2003, 2006) has found that a person's attitudes are important in determining how much acculturative stress is experienced (Sam & Berry, 2010). When people encounter a new cultural environment, they are faced with two questions: (1) Should I seek positive relations with the dominant society? (2) Is my original cultural identity of value to me, and should I try to maintain it?

4 patterns of acculturation

The answers produce one of four possible patterns of acculturation: integration, assimilation, separation, or marginalization (see the diagram). Each pattern represents a different way of coping with the stress of adapting to a new culture (Berry, 1994, 2003). 1 *Integrated* individuals continue to value their original cultural customs but also seek to become part of the dominant society. They embrace a *bicultural* identity (Hunyh & others, 2011). Biculturalism is associated with higher self-esteem and lower levels of depression, anxiety, and stress, suggesting that the bicultural identity may be the most adaptive acculturation pattern (Schwartz & others, 2010). The successfully integrated individual's level of acculturative stress will be low (Lee, 2010).

2 * *Assimilated* individuals give up their old cultural identity and try to become part of the new society. They adopt the customs and social values of the new environment, and abandon their original cultural traditions.

possible rejection by both cultures

Assimilation usually involves a moderate level of stress, partly because it involves a psychological loss—one's previous cultural identity. People who follow this pattern also face the possibility of being rejected either by members of the majority culture or by members of their original culture (Schwartz & others, 2010). The

Acculturative Stress Acculturative stress can be reduced when immigrants learn the language and customs of their newly adopted home. Here, two friends, one from China, one from Cuba, help each other in an English class in Miami, Florida.

process of learning new behaviors and suppressing old behaviors can also be moderately stressful.

3 *Individuals who follow the pattern of *separation* maintain their cultural identity and avoid contact with the new culture. They may refuse to learn the new language, live in a neighborhood that is primarily populated by others of the same ethnic background, and socialize only with members of their own ethnic group.

*separation may be self-imposed or discriminating

In some cases, separation is not voluntary, but is due to the dominant society's unwillingness to accept the new immigrants. Thus, it can be the result of discrimination. Whether voluntary or involuntary, the level of acculturative stress associated with separation tends to be high.

higher stress with separation

4 *Finally, the *marginalized* person lacks cultural and psychological contact with *both* his traditional cultural group and the culture of his new society. By taking the path of marginalization, he lost the important features of his traditional culture but has not replaced them with a new cultural identity.

Although rare, the path of marginalization is associated with the greatest degree of acculturative stress. Marginalized individuals are stuck in an unresolved conflict between their traditional culture and the new society, and may feel as if they don't really belong anywhere. Fortunately, only a small percentage of immigrants fall into this category (Schwartz & others, 2010).

*marginalized = higher level of stress

Question 1:
Should I seek positive relations with the dominant society?

Question 2: Is my original cultural identity of value to me, and should I try to maintain it?		Yes	No
	Yes	Integration	Separation
	No	Assimilation	Marginalization

Patterns of Adapting to a New Culture
According to cross-cultural psychologist John Berry, there are four basic patterns of adapting to a new culture (Sam & Berry, 2010). Which pattern is followed depends on how the person responds to the two key questions shown.

No matter what method you prefer, remember these important guidelines:

1. **Read before you mark.** Finish reading a section before you decide which are the most important ideas and concepts.

2. **Think before you mark.** When you read a text for the first time, everything can seem important. After you complete a section, reflect on it to identify the key ideas. Ask yourself: What are the most important ideas? What terms has the instructor emphasized in class? What will I see on the test? Knowing the likely answers to these questions can help you avoid marking too much material. On a practical note, if you find that you have made mistakes in how you have highlighted or that your textbooks were already highlighted by another student, use a different color highlighter.

3. **Take notes along with marking.** If you only make notes or underline in your textbook, you will have to read all the pages again. Rather than relying on marking alone, consider taking notes as you read. You can add your notes to the map, outline, list, or flash cards that you created while previewing the text. These methods are also more practical if you intend to review with a friend or study group. One more step in the note-taking process—putting your notes in your own words—will help you learn the material. When you rewrite your notes in your own words, you are not only predicting exam questions but also evaluating whether you can answer them.

A few words of caution about marking: For some students, highlighting or underlining is actually a form of procrastination and can lead to a false sense of security—just noting what's most important doesn't mean you've learned the material. Some students highlight or underline nearly everything they read, which does more harm than good. Remember, highlights and underlines are intended to pull your eye to key words and important facts. You won't be able to identify important concepts quickly if they're lost in a sea of color or lines. Ask yourself whether highlighting or underlining helps you take a more active role in your learning process. If not, you might want to try a different technique, such as making margin notes or annotations.

Reading with Concentration

Students often have trouble concentrating or understanding the content when they read textbooks. This is normal, and many factors contribute to this problem: the time of day, your energy level, your interest in the material, and your study location.

IN CLASS > Students might complain that a marked book won't get a high buyback price when the course is over. As an exercise in values, ask them to consider which they value more: a few bucks or a better grade. Ask them to check buyback policies at local bookstores to find out how much of the book's value they will lose by marking their books.

IN CLASS > Divide the class into groups of four students. In each group, ask students to choose two or more of the tips for building concentration and understanding. Ask them to practice these tactics over the next few days and report on what worked, what did not work, and why.

HIGH-IMPACT PRACTICE ▶ As part of their ongoing journal, this writing exercise will help students monitor their own reading behavior and reflect more deeply on it.

your turn   Write and Reflect

Improving Your Powers of Concentration

The next time you are reading a textbook, monitor your ability to concentrate. Check your watch when you begin and check it again when your mind begins to wander. How many minutes did you concentrate on your reading? Write a journal entry listing some strategies to keep your mind from wandering.

Consider these suggestions and decide which would help you improve your reading ability:

- **Find a quiet place to study.** Choose a room or location away from traffic and distracting noises, such as the campus information commons. Avoid studying in your bed because your body is conditioned to go to sleep there.
- **Mute or turn off your electronic devices.** Store your cell phone in your book bag or some other place where you aren't tempted to check it. If you are reading on a device like a laptop or tablet, download what you need and disconnect from Wi-Fi so that you aren't tempted to e-mail, chat, or check social media sites.
- **Read in blocks of time, with short breaks in between.** Some students can read for 50 minutes, while others may find that a 50-minute reading period is too long. By reading in small blocks of time throughout the day instead of cramming in all your reading at the end of the day, you should be able to process material more easily.
- **Set goals for your study period.** A realistic goal might be "I will read twenty pages of my psychology text in the next 50 minutes." Reward yourself with a 10-minute break after each 50-minute study period.
- **Engage in physical activity during breaks.** If you have trouble concentrating or staying awake, take a quick walk around the library or down the hall. Stretch or take some deep breaths, and think positively about your study goals. Then go back to studying.
- **Actively engage with the material.** Write study questions in the margins, take notes, or recite key ideas. Reread confusing parts of the text, and make a note to ask your instructor for clarification on any material that remains unclear.
- **Focus on the important portions of the text.** Pay attention to the first and last sentences of paragraphs and to words in italics or bold type.
- **Understand the words.** Use the text's glossary or a dictionary to define unfamiliar terms.
- **Use organizers as you read.** Have the maps, outlines, lists, or flash cards you created during your preview available as you read, and add to them as you go. The next page shows an example of an organizer to use when you are reading; you can use it to organize a chapter you are currently reading in this or any other class.

IN CLASS ▶ Explain that maps, outlines, lists, and flash cards might also include students' reactions to the material or questions they need to ask in class.

Date:	Title:
Textbook:	Chapter:

What is the overall idea of the reading?	
What is the main idea of each major section of the reading?	Section 1: Section 2: Section 3:
What are the **supporting ideas** presented in the reading? Examples? Statistics? Any reference to research?	1. 4. 2. 5. 3.
What are the key terms and what do they mean?	
What are the conclusions from the reading?	
What are two or three things that I remember after reading?	1. 2. 3.

Reviewing

The final step in active textbook reading is reviewing. **Reviewing** involves looking through your assigned reading again. Many students expect to be able to read through their text material once and remember the ideas four, six, or even twelve weeks later when it's time for their exam. More realistically, you will need to include regular reviews in your study process. Your notes, study questions, margin notes and annotations, flash cards, visual maps, or outlines will prove very useful during the reviewing process. Your study goal should be to review the material from each chapter every week. Here are some strategies:

- Consider ways to use your senses to review.
- Recite aloud.
- Tick off each item on a list on your fingers.
- Post diagrams, maps, or outlines around your living space so that you will see them often and will likely be able to visualize them while taking the test.

Mark and Review

Marking the text and reviewing carefully are among the best approaches to getting more from your reading. These strategies seem to be good enough for George Clooney. Are they good enough for you?

Michael Buckner/Getty Images for American Foundation for Equal Rights

STRATEGIES FOR READING TEXTBOOKS

As you begin to read, be sure to learn more about the textbook and its author by reading the sections at the beginning of the book, such as the preface, foreword, introduction, and the author's biographical sketch. The **preface**, which is a brief overview near the beginning of a book, is usually written by the author(s) and will tell you why they wrote the book and what material the book covers. It will also explain the book's organizational structure and give insight into the author's viewpoint—all of which can help you see the relationships among the facts presented and comprehend the ideas discussed throughout the book. Reading the preface can come in handy if you are feeling a little lost at different points in the term. The preface often lays out the tools available in each chapter to guide you through the content, so if you find yourself struggling with the reading, be sure you go back and read this section.

The **foreword** is often an endorsement of the book written by someone other than the author. Some books have an additional **introduction** that describes the book's overall organization and its contents, often chapter by chapter. Some textbooks include study questions at the end of each chapter. Take time to read and respond to these questions, whether or not your instructor requires you to do so.

---

your turn Stay Motivated

Do ALL the Required Reading

Some first-year students, especially those who have trouble managing their time, believe that they can skip some of the required reading and still get good grades on tests and exams. The best students, however, will tell you that this isn't a smart strategy. Instructors assign readings because they believe they're important to your understanding, and concepts and details in the readings will be on the tests. Maintain your motivation to do well by reading all the materials assigned by your instructors.

All Textbooks Are Not Created Equal

Textbooks in different **disciplines**—areas of academic study—can differ in their organization and style of writing. Some may be easier to understand than others, but don't give up if the reading level is challenging.

Math and science texts are filled with graphs and figures that you will need to understand in order to grasp the content and the classroom lectures. They are also likely to have less text and more practice exercises than other textbooks. If you have trouble reading and understanding any of your textbooks, get help from your instructor or your college's learning center.

Textbooks cover a lot of material in a limited space, and they won't necessarily provide all the information you want to know about a topic. If you find yourself interested in a particular topic, go to the **primary sources**—the original research or documents on that subject. You'll find those sources referenced in almost all textbooks, either at the end of each chapter or at the back of the book.

You can also refer to other related sources that make the text more interesting and easier to understand. Your instructors might use the textbook only to supplement their lectures. Some instructors expect you to read the textbook carefully, while others are much more concerned that you understand broad concepts that come primarily from their lectures. Ask your instructors what the tests will cover and what types of questions will be used.

Finally, not all textbooks are written in the same way. Some are better designed and written than others. If your textbook seems disorganized or hard to understand, let your instructor know your opinion. Other students likely feel the same way. Your instructor might spend some class time explaining the text, and he or she can meet with you during office hours to help you with the material.

isthisyou?

The Challenge of Being "First"

Are you the first person in your family to go to college? If so, you are in good company. Many "first-generation" students attend colleges and universities today. Make sure that you understand the rules and regulations and the unique higher-education terminology at your institution. If you or your family members feel lost or confused, talk to your college success instructor and ask about what services are available for first-generation students. Also, remember that some of our nation's most successful individuals were the first in their families to attend and graduate from college.

Math Texts

While the previous suggestions about textbook reading apply across the board, mathematics textbooks present some special challenges because they usually have lots of symbols and few words. Each statement and every line in the solution of a problem needs to be considered and processed slowly. Typically, the author presents the material through definitions, theorems, and sample problems. As you read, pay special attention to definitions. Learning all the terms that relate to a new topic is the first step toward understanding.

Math texts usually include derivations of formulas and proofs of theorems. You must understand and be able to apply the formulas and theorems, but unless your course has a particularly theoretical emphasis, you are less likely to be responsible for all the proofs. So if you get lost in the proof of a theorem, go to the next item in the section. When you come to a sample problem, it's time to get busy. Pick up a pencil and paper, and work through the problem in the book. Then cover the solution and think through the problem on your own.

Of course, the exercises in each section are the most important part of any math textbook. A large portion of the time you devote to a math course will be spent completing these assigned exercises. It is absolutely necessary to work out these exercises before the next class, whether or not your instructor collects the work. Success in mathematics requires regular practice, and students who keep up with their math homework, either by working alone or in groups, perform better than students who don't, particularly when they include in their study groups other students who have more advanced math skills.

After you complete the assignment, skim through the other exercises in the problem set. Reading the unassigned problems will increase your comprehension. Finally, talk through the material to yourself, and be sure your focus is on understanding the problem and its solution, not on memorization. Memorizing something might help you remember how to work through one problem, but it does not help you learn the steps involved so that you can use them to solve other, similar problems.

high-impact practice 3

HIGH-IMPACT PRACTICE ❯ This group exercise can be the beginning of a math study group that meets frequently. Group study, especially in math, correlates with better grades and a greater understanding of math concepts.

IN CLASS ❯ Ask a reading specialist from your campus developmental skills center or learning assistance center to come to class to provide tips on how to approach a science textbook.

your turn Work Together

Tackle Math as a Team

In a small group, discuss with classmates two or three of your challenges in learning from your math textbooks. Find students who are taking the same math course, share some strategies that you use to study the material for this course, and consider forming a study group.

Science Texts

Your approach to your science textbook will depend somewhat on whether you are studying a math-based science, such as physics, or a text-based science, such as biology. In either case, you need to become familiar with the overall format of the book. Review the table of contents and the **glossary** (a list of key words and their definitions), and check the material in the **appendixes** (supplemental materials at the end of the book). There you will find lists of physical constants, unit conversions, and various charts and tables. Many physics and chemistry books also include a mini-review of the math you will need in those science courses. (See Figure 6.5.)

Notice the organization of each chapter, and pay special attention to graphs, charts, and boxes. The amount of technical detail might seem overwhelming. Remember that textbook authors take great care to present material in a logical format, and they include tools to guide you through the material. Chapter-opening learning objectives and end-of-chapter summaries can be useful to study both before and after reading the chapter. You will usually find answers to selected problems in the back of the book. Use the answer key or the student solutions manual to make sure that you're solving problems and answering questions accurately.

FIGURE 6.5 › Reading Science Textbooks

This page from an allied-health-themed chemistry textbook includes abbreviations you'd need to know for dosages, practice exercises, and a formula for calculating medicine dosages. If you need help with any of your textbooks, ask your instructor or classmates. Source: Excerpt from page 23 of *Essentials of General, Organic, and Biochemistry*, 2nd ed., by Denise Guinn. Copyright © 2012 by W. H. Freeman. Used by permission.

PRACTICE EXERCISES

23 Using the conversions on page 12, convert the following units into calories:
   a. 5.79 kcal   **b.** 48.8 J
24 How many joules are there in 2.45 cal?
25 How many joules are there in 2,720 Calories, the amount of energy the average person consumes in a day?

Dosage Calculations

For some medicines prescribed for patients, the dosage must be adjusted according to the patient's weight. This is especially true when administering medicine to children. For example, a dosage of "8.0 mg of tetracycline per kilogram body weight daily" is a dosage based on the weight of the patient. A patient's weight is often given in pounds, yet many drug handbooks give the dosage per kilogram body weight of the patient. Therefore, to calculate the correct amount of medicine to give the patient, you must first convert the patient's weight from pounds into kilograms with an English-metric conversion, using Table 1-3.

It is important to recognize that the dosage is itself a conversion factor between the mass or volume of the medicine and the weight of the patient. Whenever you see the word *per*, it means *in every* and can be expressed as a ratio or fraction where *per* represents a division operation (divided by). For example, 60 miles *per* hour can be written as the ratio 60 mi/1 hr. Similarly, a dosage of 8.0 mg *per* kg body weight can be expressed as the fraction 8.0 mg/1 kg. Hence, dosage *is* a conversion factor:

$$\frac{8 \text{ mg}}{1 \text{ kg}} \quad \text{or} \quad \frac{1 \text{ kg}}{8 \text{ mg}}$$

Dimensional analysis is used to solve dosage calculations by multiplying the patient's weight by the appropriate English-metric conversion factor and then multiplying by the dosage conversion factor, as shown in the following worked exercise.

> Some common abbreviations indicating the frequency with which a medication should be administered include *q.d.* and *b.i.d.*, derived from the Latin meaning administered "daily" and "twice daily," respectively. If the medicine is prescribed for two times daily or four times daily, divide your final answer by two or four to determine how much to give the patient at each administration.

WORKED EXERCISE Dosage Calculations

1-19 Tetracycline elixir, an antibiotic, is ordered at a dosage of 8.0 mg per kilogram of body weight q.d. for a child weighing 52 lb. How many milligrams of tetracycline elixir should be given to this child daily?

Solution
Step 1: Identify the conversions. Since the dosage is given based on a patient's weight in kilograms, an English-to-metric conversion must be performed. From Table 1-3 this is 1.000 kg = 2.205 lb. The dosage itself is already a conversion factor.
Step 2: Express each conversion as two possible conversion factors. The English-to-metric conversion factors for the patient's weight are

$$\frac{1 \text{ kg}}{2.205 \text{ lb}} \quad \text{or} \quad \frac{2.205 \text{ lb}}{1 \text{ kg}}$$

The dosage *is* a conversion factor between the mass of medicine in milligrams and the weight of the patient in kilograms:

$$\frac{8.0 \text{ mg}}{1 \text{ kg}} \quad \text{or} \quad \frac{1 \text{ kg}}{8.0 \text{ mg}}$$

IN CLASS > Explain that a large percentage of students have difficulty with introductory science and mathematics courses such as calculus, physics, and organic chemistry. Discuss why doing well in introductory courses is especially critical for some majors.

As you begin an assigned section in a science text, skim the material quickly to gain a general idea of the topic and to familiarize yourself with any new vocabulary and technical symbols. Then look over the end-of-chapter problems so that you'll know what to look for in your detailed reading of the chapter. State a specific goal: "I'm going to learn about recent developments in plate tectonics," or "I'm going to distinguish between mitosis and meiosis," or "Tonight I'm going to focus on the topics in this chapter that were stressed in class."

Should you underline and highlight, or should you outline the material in your science textbooks? You might decide to underline or highlight for a subject such as anatomy, which involves a lot of memorization. In most sciences, however, it is best to outline the text chapters.

Social Sciences and Humanities Texts

Many of the suggestions that apply to science textbooks also apply to reading in the **social sciences** (academic disciplines that examine human aspects of the world, such as sociology, psychology, anthropology, economics, political science, and history). Social science textbooks are filled with special terms that are specific to a particular field of study. (See Figure 6.6.) These texts also describe research and theory building and contain references to many primary sources. Your social science texts might also describe differences in opinions or perspectives. Social scientists do not all agree on any one issue, and you might be introduced to a number of ongoing debates about particular topics. In fact, your reading can become more interesting if you seek out differing opinions on an issue. You might have to go beyond your course textbook, but your library is a good source of various viewpoints about ongoing controversies.

Textbooks in the **humanities** (branches of knowledge that investigate human beings, their culture, and their self-expression, such as philosophy, religion, literature, music, and art) provide facts, examples, opinions, and original material such as stories or essays. You will often be asked to react to your reading by identifying central themes or characters.

---

yourturn Make Good Choices

Buy Your Course Materials

Textbooks are expensive, and it may be tempting to think that you can borrow one from another student, find the text in the library, or even do well in the course without having access to the textbook. No one will force you to purchase your textbooks—it's really up to you. To succeed in college, however, it's critically important that you choose to buy them and do all the assigned reading. Read the Tech Tip in this chapter for information on the benefits of e-books and for help in evaluating whether these are a good option for you.

FIGURE 6.6 ❯ Social Science Textbook Page

Strategies for reading and note taking should change depending on what kind of textbook you are reading. When reading a social science textbook, such as the economics book shown here, you can see how a section is broken into subsections. Headings help guide you through the content. A table is included with examples that illustrate what is being discussed and help you understand the material. Source: From *Core Economics*, 3rd ed., by Eric Chiang. Copyright © 2014 by Eric Chiang. Used by permission of Worth Publishers.

Determinants of Elasticity

Price elasticity of demand measures how sensitive sales are to price changes. But what determines elasticity itself? The four basic determinants of a product's elasticity of demand are (1) the availability of substitute products, (2) the percentage of income or household budget spent on the product, (3) the difference between luxuries and necessities, and (4) the time period being examined.

Substitutability The more close substitutes, or possible alternatives, a product has, the easier it is for consumers to switch to a competing product and the more elastic the demand. For many people, beef and chicken are substitutes, as are competing brands of cola, such as Coke and Pepsi. All have relatively elastic demands. Conversely, if a product has few close substitutes, such as insulin for diabetics or tobacco for heavy smokers, its elasticity of demand tends to be lower.

Proportion of Income Spent on a Product A second determinant of elasticity is the proportion (percentage) of household income spent on a product. In general, the smaller the percent of household income spent on a product, the lower the elasticity of demand. For example, you probably spend little of your income on salt, or on cinnamon or other spices. As a result, a hefty increase in the price of salt, say 25%, would not affect your salt consumption because the impact on your budget would be tiny. But if a product represents a significant part of household spending, elasticity of demand tends to be greater, or more elastic. A 10% increase in your rent upon renewing your lease, for example, would put a large dent in your budget, significantly reducing your purchasing power for many other products. Such a rent increase would likely lead you to look around earnestly for a less expensive apartment.

Luxuries Versus Necessities The third determinant of elasticity is whether the good is considered a luxury or a necessity. Luxuries tend to have demands that are more elastic than those of necessities. Necessities such as food, electricity, and health care are more important to everyday living, and quantity demanded does not change significantly when prices rise. Luxuries such as trips to Hawaii, yachts, and designer watches, on the other hand, can be given up when prices rise.

Time Period The fourth determinant of elasticity is the time period under consideration. When consumers have some time to adjust their consumption patterns, the elasticity of demand becomes more elastic. When they have little time to adjust, the elasticity of demand tends to be more inelastic. Thus, as we saw earlier, when gasoline prices rise suddenly, most consumers cannot immediately change their transportation patterns, therefore gasoline sales do not drop significantly. However, as gas prices continue to remain high, we see shifts in consumer behavior, to which automakers respond by producing smaller, more fuel-efficient cars.

Table 1 provides a sampling of estimates of elasticities for specific products. As we might expect, medical prescriptions and taxi service have relatively inelastic price elasticities of demand, while foreign travel and restaurant meals have relatively elastic demands.

Selected Estimates of Price Elasticities of Demand					TABLE 1
Inelastic		**Roughly Unitary Elastic**		**Elastic**	
Salt	0.1	Movies	0.9	Shrimp	1.3
Gasoline (short run)	0.2	Shoes	0.9	Furniture	1.5
Cigarettes	0.2	Tires	1.0	Commuter rail service (long run)	1.6
Medical care	0.3	Private education	1.1	Restaurant meals	2.3
Medical prescriptions	0.3	Automobiles	1.2	Air travel	2.4
Pesticides	0.4			Fresh vegetables	2.5
Taxi service	0.6			Foreign travel	4.0

Source: Compiled from numerous studies reporting estimates for price elasticity of demand.

EMBRACE THE E-BOOK

In college we have textbooks, workbooks, and notebooks. While textbook publishers continue to make traditional books available, the same content is increasingly available in digital formats. In most courses today, students are required to access some course material digitally. For students who are used to buying or renting printed books from the college bookstore, this can be confusing.

© W2 Photography/Corbis

The Problem

You have heard about electronic books that are alternatives to traditional textbooks, but you aren't sure what device to buy to read e-books. You really want to know the advantages and disadvantages that an e-book has when compared to a traditional book.

The Fix

Explore different platforms that deliver e-book content, and discover how reading with a digital reader differs from (and can even be better than) reading traditional books.

How to Do It

Go to the library. Many libraries have tablets of different kinds. Ask a librarian to download a book in a variety of formats for you, so you can try different tablets out before choosing one to buy.

Try the different media available. E-books give you access to the pages of the text, as well as video, audio, and Web content.

PROS OF E-BOOKS

- Digital reading devices are eminently portable and can hold thousands of books.
- E-books save trees, can be bought without shipping costs, and have a low carbon footprint.
- E-readers let you buy books online from anywhere with Web access, and you can start reading within minutes.
- You can type notes in an e-book as well as highlight passages and copy and paste sections.
- You can print out pages simply by hooking the device up to your printer.
- You can access many e-books for free from the public library; you can even use the British Library's Online Gallery to peruse some of the world's oldest and rarest books.
- Some e-books come with bonus audio, video, or animation features.
- Many digital reading devices accept audio books and can read to you aloud.
- The backlit screen means that you can read in bed with the light off, without disturbing anyone.
- You can adjust the size of the text.

- Some e-readers have a built-in dictionary. Others link to reference Web sites like Google or Wikipedia when a Wi-Fi or 3G connection is available.
- E-books are searchable and even sharable.

CONS OF E-BOOKS

- Digital reading devices are expensive, can break if you drop them, and are more likely to be stolen than books.
- Looking at a screen can cause some eye fatigue.
- It's harder to flip through pages of an e-book than a printed book.
- If you have limited or temporary access to e-books for your courses, your access will expire after the academic term. But you can keep the print textbooks you buy and build your own library.

GOOD TO KNOW

Some electronic readers are no-frills, basic models designed to replicate the experience of reading a paper book. Others offer Web browsers, video, music, and thousands of free and for-purchase apps. Because most are Web-enabled, you can use them for other things like listening to music or audio books, checking e-mail, creating presentations, and writing papers. This increased functionality might be distracting but can also make you more productive.

EXTRA STYLE POINTS: Price your textbooks in both the print and digital formats. Factoring in the cost of the e-reader, which format is cheaper?

Supplementary Material

Whether or not your instructor requires you to read material in addition to the textbook, you will learn more about a topic if you go to some of the primary and supplementary sources that are referenced in each chapter of your text. These sources can be journal articles, research papers, or original essays, and they can be found online or in your library. Reading the original source material will give you more detail than most textbooks do.

Many of these sources were originally written for other instructors or researchers, so they often refer to concepts that are familiar to other scholars, but not necessarily to first-year college students. If you are reading a journal article that describes a theory or research study, one technique for easier understanding is to read the article backwards—from the end to the beginning. Read the article's conclusion and discussion sections first, and then go back to see how the author performed the experiment or formed the ideas. In almost all scholarly journals, articles are introduced by an **abstract**, which is a paragraph-length summary of the article's methods and major findings. Reading the abstract is a quick way to get the main points of a research article before you start reading it. As you're reading research articles, always ask yourself: So what? Was the research important to what we know about the topic, or, in your opinion, was it unnecessary?

IMPROVING YOUR READING

With effort, you *can* improve your reading. Remember to be flexible and to adjust *how* you read depending on *what* you are reading. Here are a few suggestions:

- Evaluate the importance and difficulty of the assigned readings, and adjust your reading style and the time you set aside to do the reading. How you read your math textbook is different than how you read your psychology textbook. When reading your math textbook, you should have a notebook to record your solutions to the problems. When you read your psychology textbook, you should highlight the important ideas or make margin notes.
- Connect one important idea to another by asking yourself: Why am I reading this? Where does this fit in? Writing summaries and preparing notes and outlines can help you connect ideas across chapters.
- When the textbook material is exactly the same as the lecture material, you can save time by concentrating mainly on one or the other.

It takes a planned approach to read and understand textbook materials and other assigned readings and to remember what you have read.

OUTSIDE CLASS > Encourage students to use the learning center's reading resources to help them improve their reading rate and master various methods for remembering material. Consider taking them to the center for a trial visit.

IN CLASS ❯ Ask students to practice this method of monitoring with a study partner. Ask them to share what they learn with the rest of the class.

Monitoring Your Reading

You can monitor your comprehension while reading textbooks by asking yourself: Do I understand this? If not, stop and reread the material. Look up words that are not clear. Try to clarify the main points and how they relate to one another.

Another way to check that you understand what you are reading is to try to recite the material aloud, either to yourself or to your study partner. Using a study group to monitor your comprehension gives you immediate feedback and is highly motivating. After you have read with concentration from the first section of the chapter, proceed to each subsequent section until you have finished the chapter.

After you have completed each section and before you move on to the next section, ask again: What are the key ideas? What will I see on the test? At the end of each section, try to guess what information the author will present in the next section.

Developing Your Vocabulary

Textbooks are full of new words and terms. A **vocabulary** is a set of words in a particular language or field of knowledge. As you become familiar with the vocabulary of an academic field, reading the texts related to that field becomes easier.

If words are such a basic and essential component of our knowledge, what is the best way to learn them? The following are some basic vocabulary-building strategies:

- **Notice and write down unfamiliar terms while you preview a text.** Consider making a flash card for each term or making a list of terms.
- **Think about the context when you come across challenging words.** See whether you can guess the meaning of an unfamiliar term by using the words around it.
- **Consider a word's parts.** If context by itself is not enough to help you guess the meaning of an unfamiliar word, try analyzing the term to discover its root (or base part) and any prefixes (parts that come before the root) or suffixes (parts that follow the root). For example, *transport* has the root *port,* which means "carry," and the prefix *trans,* which means "across." Together the word means "carry across" or "carry from one place to another." Knowing the meaning of prefixes and suffixes can be very helpful. For example, *anti* means "against," and *pro* means "for."
- **Use the glossary of the text or a dictionary.** Textbook publishers carefully compile glossaries to help students learn the vocabulary of a given discipline. If the text has no glossary, have a dictionary on hand. If a given word has more than one definition, search for the meaning that fits your text. The online Merriam-Webster's Dictionary (**merriam-webster.com**) is especially helpful for college students.
- **Use new words in your writing and speaking.** If you use a new word a few times, you'll soon know it. In addition, any flash cards you have created will come in handy for reviewing the definitions of new words at exam time.

| **your turn** | Write and Reflect |

Building Your Vocabulary

Choose a chapter in this or another textbook. As you read it, list the words that are new to you or that you don't understand. Using a dictionary, write out the definition of each word, and then write a short paragraph using the word in an appropriate context. Set a goal to add at least one new word a week to your personal vocabulary.

What to Do When You Fall Behind on Your Reading

From time to time, life might get in the way of doing your assigned readings on time. You may get sick or have to take care of a sick family member, you may have to work extra hours, or you may have a personal problem that prevents you from concentrating on your courses for a short time. Unfortunately, some students procrastinate and think they can catch up. That is a myth. The less you read and do your assignments, the harder you will have to work to make up for lost time.

A Marathon, Not a Sprint

If you fall behind in your reading, you're not alone—many students do. Remember that your studies are more like a marathon than a sprint; you should take time to catch up, but do so at a steady pace. Do your assigned readings, study with others, get help, and do not give up!

© Jerome Prevost/TempSport/Corbis

If you try to stay on schedule with your assigned readings but fall behind, do not panic. Here are some suggestions for getting back on track:

- **Add one or two hours a day to your study time to go back and read the material that you missed.** In particular, take advantage of every spare moment to read; for example, read during your lunch hour at work, while you are waiting for public transportation, or in the waiting room at the doctor's office.
- **Join a study group.** If everyone in the group reads a section of the assigned chapter and shares and discusses his or her notes, summaries, or outlines with the group, you can cover the content more quickly.
- **Ask for help.** Visit your college learning center to work with a tutor who can help you with difficult concepts in the textbook.
- **Talk to your instructor.** Ask for extra time to make up your assignments if you have fallen behind for a valid reason such as sickness or dealing with a personal problem. Most instructors are willing to make a one-time exception to help students catch up.
- **Do not give up.** You may have to work harder for a short period of time, but you will soon get caught up.

If English Is Not Your First Language

The English language is one of the most difficult languages to learn. Words are often spelled differently from the way they sound, and the language is full of **idioms**—phrases that cannot be understood from the individual meanings of the words. For example, if your instructor tells you to "hit the books," she does not mean for you to physically pound your texts with your fist, but rather to study hard.

If you are learning English and are having trouble reading your texts, don't give up. Reading slowly and reading the material more than once can help you improve your comprehension. Make sure that you have two good dictionaries—one in English and one that links English with your primary language—and look up every key word you don't know. Be sure to practice thinking, writing, and speaking in English, and take advantage of your college's services. Your campus might have English as a second language (ESL) tutoring and workshops. Ask your adviser or your first-year seminar instructor to help you find out where those services are offered on your campus.

checklist for success

Reading to Learn

☐ **Be sure to practice the four steps of active reading: previewing, marking, reading with concentration, and reviewing.** If you practice these steps, you will understand and retain more of what you read.

☐ **Take your course textbooks seriously.** They contain essential information you'll be expected to learn and understand. Never try to "get by" without the text.

☐ **Remember that not all textbooks are the same.** They vary by subject area and style of writing. Some may be easier to comprehend than others, but don't give up if the reading level is challenging.

☐ **Learn and practice the different techniques suggested in this chapter for reading and understanding texts on different subjects.** Which texts are easiest for you to understand? Which are the hardest? Why?

☐ **In addition to the textbook, be sure to read all supplemental assigned reading material.** Also, try to find additional materials to take your reading beyond what is required. The more you read, the more you will understand, and the better your performance will be.

☐ **As you read, be sure to take notes on the material.** Indicate in your notes what specific ideas you need help in understanding.

☐ **Get help with difficult material before too much time elapses.** College courses use sequential material that builds on previous material. You will need to master the material as you go along.

☐ **Discuss difficult readings in study groups.** Explain to one another what you do and don't understand.

☐ **Find out what kind of assistance your campus offers to increase reading comprehension and speed.** Check out your learning and counseling centers for free workshops. Even faculty and staff sometimes take advantage of these services. Most everyone wants to improve reading speed and comprehension.

☐ **Use reading to build your vocabulary.** Learning new words is a critical learning skill and outcome of college. The more words you know, the more you'll understand, and your grades will show it.

REFLECT ON CHOICES

In this chapter you have learned that reading textbooks is an essential part of being a successful student. The choice of how to approach your reading is up to you. Reflect on the strategies that have been suggested, list those that you already use, and make a separate list of those you want to try in the future.

APPLY WHAT YOU HAVE LEARNED

Now that you have read and discussed this chapter, consider how you can apply what you have learned to your academic life and your personal life. The following prompts will help you reflect on the chapter material and its relevance to you both now and in the future.

1. Choose a reading assignment for one of your upcoming classes. After previewing the material, begin reading until you reach a major heading or until you have read at least a page or two. Now stop and write down what you remember from the material. Go back and review what you read. Were you able to remember all the main ideas?

2. It is easy to say that there is not enough time in the day to get everything done, especially when you're faced with a long reading assignment. Your future depends on how well you do in college, however. Challenge yourself not to use that excuse. How can you modify your daily activities to make time for reading?

USE YOUR RESOURCES

> **Learning Assistance Center**
Find out about your campus's learning assistance center and any reading assistance that is available there. Most centers are staffed by full-time professionals and student tutors. Both the best students and struggling students use learning centers.

> **Peer Leaders**
Your peer leader is a great source of information on campus resources and the availability of tutoring. Ask him or her for suggestions about where you can go for help with your reading and comprehension.

> **Fellow Students**
Your best help can come from a fellow student. Look for the best students, those who appear to be the most serious and conscientious. Hire a tutor if you can, or join a study group. You are much more likely to be successful.

> **College or University Online Resources**
Dartmouth College offers "Active Reading: Comprehension and Rate" at **dartmouth .edu/~acskills/success/reading.html**. Mount Saint Vincent University in Canada offers "Reading Textbooks Effectively" at **msvu.ca/en/home /studentservices/academicadvisingsupport /studyskills/readingtextbookseffectively.aspx**, and Niagara University's Office for Academic Support offers "21 Tips for Better Textbook Reading" at **niagara.edu/oas-21-tips**.

LaunchPad

LaunchPad for *Your College Experience* is a great resource. Go online to master concepts using the LearningCurve study tool and much more. macmillanhighered.com/gardner12e

7

GETTING THE MOST FROM CLASS

YOU WILL EXPLORE

Benefits to your learning that result from being engaged in class

Ways to prepare before class

Why you should participate in class by listening critically and speaking up

Methods for assessing and improving your note-taking skills and how to use your notes to be engaged in learning

⚙ High-impact practices 2 (writing) and 3 (collaboration)

Dillon Watts, 19

History major
Sacramento State University

> ❝ Taking notes should never be a substitute for paying attention and understanding the deeper elements of lectures and verbal discourse. ❞

Dillon Watts grew up in Sacramento, California. After graduating from high school, he attended Sacramento City College for one year and then transferred to Sacramento State University. In reflecting on his experience in college classes so far, he says, "Most of the time the questions you have are questions that will help the whole class. Everyone in the class benefits from an instructor's answer." He points out, however, that no one appreciates a student asking questions just for the participation points or to show off. "I always try to be direct and simple when asking questions so that the class can get direct and simple answers," Dillon says.

This same no-nonsense attitude is also present in the way he prepares for class. He explains, "I just make sure to be there on time, every time, and to stay until the class is over. I make an effort to pay attention, and I'm careful to write down key points of the lecture. I also do all the assigned reading, and I find it pretty easy to maintain good grades."

"In a class with lots of information, I take notes really well. Sometimes it makes it harder to actually pay attention to concepts, but it certainly pays off for tests and such. In less formal classes such as speech or ethics, which are very idea-heavy, I tend to not take notes that much or even at all. Taking notes should never be a substitute for paying attention and understanding the deeper elements of lectures and verbal discourse," he says.

Dillon plans to get a master's degree at Stanford, Berkeley, or another California school. In ten years he hopes to be a journalist or a philosophy or history instructor. He also hopes to put his class-participation skills to good use. "It is my dream to take part in debates and public speeches," he says. His advice to other first-year students: "Do your best. Try to get as much as you can out of your classes and to do your best, whether or not you feel like it. It always pays off in the end."

 **LaunchPad**

To access the LearningCurve study tool, video activities, and more, go to LaunchPad for *Your College Experience.*
macmillanhighered.com/gardner12e

IN CLASS ❯ Let students know that many test questions on college exams are drawn from class lectures, not textbooks. Ask your students how many of their current courses are lecture-based and how many are discussion-based.

Dillon's advice is sound when you consider that in order to earn high grades in any college class you take, you'll need to master certain skills such as listening, taking notes, and being engaged in learning. Engagement in learning means that you take an active role in your classes by attending, listening critically, asking questions, contributing to discussions, and providing answers. These active-learning behaviors will enhance your ability to understand abstract ideas, find new possibilities, organize those ideas, and recall the material once the class is over, resulting in strong performance on exams, as many exam questions are based on material covered in class lectures and discussions.

This chapter shows you several note-taking methods. Choose the one that works best for you. Because writing down everything the instructor

assess your strengths

Students who are engaged in college life, both in and out of class, practice many of the behaviors that are reviewed in this chapter. What about you? Were you engaged in classes and activities in high school? Which were your favorites and why? Most students find that engagement makes them more enthusiastic and actually increases their learning. As you begin to read this chapter, consider your strengths in the area of engagement.

set goals

What are your most important objectives in learning the material in this chapter? Do you have a good method of note taking? Do you devote time and energy to academic work by attending class and studying out of class? Use this chapter to help you develop strategies and goals that relate to engagement in learning. Do all the assigned reading and warm up for each class session so you can see how being prepared for class makes a difference. Consider scheduling visits with your instructors during their office hours to show them your notes from recent classes and ensure that you are writing down the most important points.

says is probably not possible and because you might need some help to determine which are the most important ideas presented, ask questions in class and become comfortable reviewing your notes with your instructor, either after class or during office hours. You might consider making an audio recording of the lecture and discussion, if you have the instructor's permission. Reviewing your notes with a tutor, someone from your campus learning center, a friend from class, or in a study group can also help you clarify your understanding of a lecture's most important points.

RETENTION STRATEGY ❯ Share with students that one of their textbook's authors was failing all his courses in his first year of college until he learned how to take notes. For him, note taking was the single most important study technique he learned in college.

BECOME ENGAGED IN LEARNING

RETENTION STRATEGY ❯ Engaged students are more likely to be retained! That's why it's worth your effort in class to encourage and monitor student engagement.

Engaged students are those who are fully involved with the college experience and spend the time and energy necessary to learn, both in and out of class. Engaged learners who have good listening and note-taking skills get the most out of college.

You can learn by listening to a lecture, and you can better understand that lecture by considering what the information presented means to you. Practice the techniques of **active learning** by talking with others, asking questions in class, studying in groups, and seeking out information beyond the lecture material and required reading. Explore other information sources in the library or on the Internet. Think about how the material relates to your own life or experience. For instance, what you learn in a psychology class might help you recognize patterns of behavior in your own family, or the material presented in a sociology class may shed light on the group dynamics in a team or group to which you belong. When you are actively engaged in learning, you will not

Stay Engaged

Students of all kinds benefit from active learning strategies, whether in arts and sciences courses or professional training situations, like the one in which these military cadets are engaged.

Yana Paskova/For *The Washington Post* via Getty Images

only learn the material in your notes and textbooks, but you will also build valuable skills that you can apply to college, work, and your personal life, such as:

- **Working with others.** Learning to work with others is one of the most important skills you can develop for success in college and your career.
- **Improving your thinking, listening, writing, and speaking skills.** These are the primary skills that define a college-educated person.
- **Functioning independently and teaching yourself.** Your first year of college will help you become an **independent learner.** Independent learners are self-motivated and do not always wait for an instructor to point them in the right direction.
- **Managing your time.** Time management sounds easy, but it is a challenge for almost all students, regardless of their academic abilities.
- **Gaining sensitivity to cultural differences.** The world we live in requires all of us to develop our own knowledge about, and respect for, cultures that are different from our own.

Engagement in learning requires your full and active participation in the learning process. Your instructors will set the stage and provide valuable information, but it's up to you to do the rest. For instance, if you disagree with what your instructor says, politely share your opinion. Most instructors will listen. They might still disagree with you, but they might also appreciate your efforts to think independently.

Not all instructors teach in a way that includes active learning. Ask your friends to recommend instructors who encourage students to participate in class, work in groups, explore materials independently, and otherwise engage fully in learning.

RETENTION STRATEGY ❯ Point out that these are the same skills that employers look for in job candidates. Most students attend college in hopes of getting a good job, so this point can help increase their motivation to become more engaged in learning.

PEER LEADERS ❯ Discuss with your students your own experience in openly disagreeing with an instructor. Consider role-playing respectful and disrespectful ways to disagree. Be honest about the risks and benefits of this behavior.

IN CLASS ❯ The fact that students and instructors will disagree at times could be used to generate an interesting class discussion. You might also discuss likely differences between first-year seminar instructors (you!) and other instructors.

PREPARE FOR CLASS

Have you ever noticed how easy it is to learn the words of a song? It's easier to remember song lyrics than other kinds of information because songs follow a tune, have a beat, and often relate to things in our personal lives. It is easier to remember new information if you can connect it to what you already know. In your first-year classes, you'll listen to and read material that might seem hard to understand. Beginning on the first day of class, you will be more likely to remember what you hear and read if you try to link it to something you have already learned or experienced.

Preparing for class is a very important first step toward success. Here are some strategies that will help you begin listening, learning, and remembering before each class session:

1. **Do the assigned reading.** Doing the assigned reading before class will help you understand new terms, listen better, and pick out the most important information when taking notes in class. Some instructors assign readings during class; others expect you to follow the **syllabus** (course outline) to keep up with the assigned readings. As you read, take good notes (more on note taking later in this chapter). In books you own, **annotate** (add explanatory notes in the margins), highlight, or underline key points. In books you do not own, such as library books, make a photocopy of the pages and then annotate or highlight the photocopies.

2. **Pay careful attention to your course syllabus.** The syllabus you receive at the start of each course will include the course requirements, your instructor's expectations, and how the course will be graded. Instructors expect students to understand and follow the syllabus with few or no reminders. You might find that this is a key difference between college and high school.

3. **Make use of additional materials provided by the instructors.** Many instructors post lecture outlines or notes in the course management system (CMS) before class. Download and print these materials for easy use during class. CMS materials often provide hints about the topics that the instructor considers most important; they can also create an organizational structure for taking notes.

4. **Warm up for class.** Review chapter introductions and summaries that refer to related sections in your text, and quickly review your notes from the previous class period. This prepares you to pay attention, understand, and remember.

5. **Get organized.** Decide how you want to take notes. If you handwrite your notes, using three-ring binders can help you organize them, as you can punch holes in syllabi and other course handouts and keep them with your class notes. You might want to buy notebook paper with a large left-hand margin, so that you can annotate your lecture notes (more on this later in the chapter). You can also download and print blank notebook paper from several free Web sites.

    If you take notes on a laptop or tablet, keep your files organized in separate folders for each of your classes, and make sure that the file name of each document includes the date and topic of the class. See the Tech Tip in this chapter for more information on using electronic devices to take effective notes.

IN CLASS ❯ Remind students that information that is mentioned both in class lectures and discussions and in the reading material is more likely to be included on tests and exams.

IN CLASS ❯ Before you start class, remind students to do the warm-up exercise. Ask them to identify the main points covered in the last session as they review their notes.

PARTICIPATE IN CLASS

FYI ❯ If at all possible, try to use an electronic-response system like Poll Everywhere in this course; that way, all students can participate using their smartphones, laptops, or tablets via wireless Internet access.

OUTSIDE CLASS ❯ The literature on the advantages of active learning is extensive. Ask students to research the topic of active learning using library and Internet resources. Ask each student to bring in one documented benefit of active learning from their research.

PEER LEADERS ❯ Let students know that one way to become an active learner is to look for opportunities to link in-class and out-of-class learning. Help your students find opportunities at your institution to link abstract learning with concrete experience. For example, students might link what they've learned in a psychology course to behavior they've observed in a student club or organization, or they might connect what they've learned in English composition class with their experience writing for the student newspaper.

IN CLASS ❯ As an experiment, tell your students not to take notes, but instead to listen for the main points as you give a five-minute lecture. Next, ask them to write down those main points and, working in small groups, compare their notes with those of other students. Finally, ask each group to report to the class.

IN CLASS ❯ Remind students that because instructors believe that what they say in class is important, they are likely to test students on this material.

Learning is not like watching sports; it's like playing a sport. To play a sport—and not just watch it—you have to participate. Participation is the heart of **active learning**. To really learn, you must listen carefully, talk about what you are learning, write about it, connect it to past experiences, and make what you learn part of yourself. When you participate in class, whether to answer a question or to ask a question of your own, you are more likely to remember the information discussed than if you listen passively to someone else.

Listen Critically and with an Open Mind

Listening in class is different from listening to a TV show, listening to a friend, or even listening during a meeting. In such everyday activities, you might not be required to remember or use the information you hear. Knowing how to listen in class can help you get more out of what you hear, understand better what you have heard, and save time. Here are some suggestions:

1. **Be ready for the message.** Prepare yourself to hear, to listen, and to receive the message. If you have done the assigned reading, you will already know details from the text, so you can focus your notes on key concepts from the lecture. You will also notice information that the text does not cover, and you will be prepared to pay closer attention when the instructor presents new material.

2. **Listen to the main concepts and central ideas, not just to facts and figures.** Although facts are important, they will be easier to remember and will make more sense when you can place them within concepts, themes, and ideas.

3. **Listen for new ideas.** Even if you are an expert on a topic, you can still learn something new. Do not assume that college instructors will present the same information you learned in a similar course in high school. Even if you listen to the same lecture multiple times, if you pay attention, you will be able to pick out and learn new information each time. As an engaged student, make a note of questions in your mind as you listen, but save the judgments for later.

4. **Repeat mentally.** Words can go in one ear and out the other unless you make an effort to remember them. Think about what you hear, and say it silently in your own words. If you cannot translate the information into your own words, ask the instructor for more explanation.

5. **Decide whether what you have heard is unimportant, somewhat important, or very important.** While most of what your instructors say and do in class is important, occasionally they may make comments or tell stories that are only somewhat related to the class material, or may not be related at all. If an instructor's comment is really unrelated to the focus of the class, you don't need to write it down. If it's very important, make it a major point in your notes by highlighting or underlining it, or use it as a major topic in your

outline if that's the method you use for taking notes. If it's somewhat important, try to relate it to a very important topic by writing it down as a part of that topic.

6. **Keep an open mind.** Every class holds the promise of letting you discover new ideas and uncover different opinions. Some instructors might intentionally present information that challenges your ideas and values. College is supposed to teach you to think in new ways and train you to provide support for your own beliefs. Instructors want you to think for yourself; they don't necessarily expect you to agree with everything they or your classmates say. However, if you want people to respect your values and ideas, you must show respect for theirs by listening to what they say with an open mind.

7. **Ask questions.** Early in the term, determine whether your instructor wants you to ask questions during the lecture. Some instructors prefer that students ask their questions after the lecture, during separate discussion sections, labs, or office hours. If your instructor answers questions when students ask them, speak up if you did not hear or understand what was said. Ask for explanations immediately, if possible; other students are likely to have the same questions. If you can't hear another student's question or response, ask him or her to repeat the question.

8. **Sort, organize, and categorize.** When you listen, try to match what you are hearing with what you already know. Take an active role in deciding how best to remember what you are learning. If you find yourself daydreaming during a lecture, quickly refocus your thoughts on the topic and actively take notes. After class or during your instructor's next office hours, ask him or her to help you fill in any gaps in your notes.

Speak Up

Naturally, you will be more likely to participate in a class when the instructor emphasizes class discussion, calls on students by name, shows signs of approval and interest, and avoids criticizing students for an incorrect answer. Often, answers you and other students offer may not be quite correct, but they can lead to new perspectives on a topic.

Whether you are in a large or a small class, you might be nervous about asking a question, fearing you will make a fool of yourself. However, it is likely that other students have the same question but are too nervous to ask. If so, they may thank you silently or even aloud! Many instructors set time aside to answer questions in class, so to take full advantage of these opportunities, try using the techniques listed on the next page.

IN CLASS > Speaking in public is one of the most common human fears. Ask students to brainstorm with one another on how to overcome this fear.

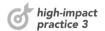
HIGH-IMPACT PRACTICE ❯ This activity is another opportunity for students to learn from each other and improve their in-class learning by working in a group.

FYI ❯ Sitting up front is especially important for students who are easily distracted by other students.

Hands Up!

Participating in class not only helps you learn but also shows your instructor that you're interested and engaged. You may be anxious the first time you raise your hand, but you may quickly find that participating in class raises your interest and enjoyment.

Jonathan Stark

---

your turn Work Together

Do You Ask Questions in Class?

Think about the number of times during the past week you have raised your hand in class to ask a question. How many times has it been? Do you ask questions frequently, or is this something you avoid? Make a list of the reasons you either do or don't ask questions in class. Would asking more questions help you earn better grades? Be prepared to share your reflections with a small group. Did you hear anything from your peers that encourages you to participate more in class?

1. **Take a seat as close to the front as possible and keep your eyes on the instructor.** Sitting close to the front can help you concentrate better and avoid distractions from other students. It will also make it easier to maintain eye contact with your instructors.

2. **Focus on the lecture and class discussions.** Avoid distractions. Sit away from friends who can distract you, do not engage in side conversations, and turn off all electronic devices that you are not using for class.

3. **Raise your hand when you don't understand something.** If you don't understand something, you have a right to ask for an explanation. Never worry that you're asking a stupid question. Don't let embarrassment or shyness stop you. The instructor might answer you immediately, ask you to wait until later in the class, or throw your question to the rest of the class. In each case, you benefit in several ways. The instructor will get to know you, other students will get to know you, and you will learn from both the instructor and your classmates. But don't overdo it, or you'll risk disrupting class. Office hours provide the perfect opportunity for following up on class lectures.

4. **Speak up in class.** Ask a question or volunteer to answer a question or make a comment. This becomes easier every time you do it, and you will be more likely to remember what happens in class if you are an active participant.

5. **When the instructor calls on you to answer a question, don't bluff.** If you know the answer, give it. If you're not certain, begin with, "I think . . . , but I'm not sure I have it all correct." If you don't know, just say so.

6. **If you have recently read a book or article that is relevant to the class topic, bring it in.** Use it either to ask questions about the topic or to provide information that was not covered in class.

TAKE EFFECTIVE NOTES

What are effective notes? They are notes that cover all the important points of the lecture or reading material without being too detailed or too limited. Most important, effective notes prepare you to do well on quizzes and exams. They also help you understand and remember concepts and facts. Becoming an effective note-taker takes time and practice, but this skill will help you improve your learning and your grades in the first year of college and beyond.

---

your turn Make Good Choices

Going Back in Time

Think back to high school. Did you choose to save any of your high school notes? Do you remember the note-taking method you used? If you have an old notebook, look at the way you took notes in high school and think about whether this method works for you now. Is it time to choose a better method of taking notes? Consider this question as you learn about different note-taking formats.

Note-Taking Formats

You can make class time more productive by using your listening skills to take effective notes, but first you have to decide on one of the following four commonly used formats for note taking: the Cornell, outline, paragraph, and list formats. Any format can work as long as you use it consistently.

IN CLASS ❯ If you saved any of your college notebooks and if you think that you were a good note-taker, bring an old notebook into class and pass it around to your students. They will get a kick out of this.

RETENTION STRATEGY ❯ Although no direct research links note taking and retention, it is one of the critical skills that can determine academic success and, therefore, the likelihood that students will persist. Note taking is a skill that few students learn in high school because high school classes have less lecturing than college classes.

Serious Business

The importance of developing good note-taking skills cannot be overstated. Carefully read about different note-taking formats presented on the next several pages, study the examples carefully, and try out each one. Find the format that works best for you. Use it to its fullest, and you're on your way to college success.

wavebreakmedia/Shutterstock

FIGURE 7.1 › Note Taking in the Cornell Format

	Psychology 101, 1/27/16
	Theories of Personality
Personality	*Personality trait = "durable disposition to*
trait: define	*behave in a particular way in a variety of*
	situations"
Big 5: Name +	*Big 5-McCrae + Costa- (1)extroversion,*
describe them	*(or positive emotionality)=outgoing,*
	sociable, friendly, upbeat, assertive; (2)
	neuroticism=anxious, hostile, self-
	conscious, insecure, vulnerable;
	(3)openness to experience=curiosity,
	flexibility, imaginative; (4)
	agreeableness=sympathetic, trusting,
	cooperative, modest;
	(5)conscientiousness=diligent,
	disciplined, well organized,
	punctual, dependable
	Psychodynamic Theories-focus on
	unconscious forces
Psychodynamic	*Freud-psychoanalysis-3 components of*
Theories: Who?	*personality-(1)id=primitive, instinctive,*
	operates according to pleasure principle
3 components of	*(immediate gratification);*
personality: name	*(2)ego=decision-making component,*
and describe	*operates according to reality principle*
	(delay gratification until appropriate);
	(3)superego=moral component, social
	standards, right + wrong
	3 levels of awareness-(1) conscious=what
3 levels of	*one is aware of at a particular moment;*
awareness: name	*(2)preconscious=material just below*
and describe	*surface, easily retrieved;*
	(3)unconscious=thoughts, memories, +
	desires well below surface, but have great
	influence on behavior

Cornell Format. Using the **Cornell format,** one of the best-known methods for organizing notes, you create a "recall" column on each page of your notebook or your document by drawing a vertical line about 2 to 3 inches from the left border (see Figure 7.1). As you take notes during class—whether writing down or typing ideas, making lists, or using an outline or paragraph format—write only in the wider column on the right; leave the left-hand recall column blank. You will use the recall column to write down or type the main ideas and important details for tests and exams as you go through your notes, which you should do as soon as possible after class, preferably within an hour or two. Many students have found the recall column to be an important part of note taking, one that becomes an effective study tool for tests and exams.

FIGURE 7.2 › Note Taking in the Outline Format

Psychology 101, 1/27/16: Theories of Personality

I.   Personality trait = "durable disposition to behave in a
     particular way in a variety of situations"
II. Big 5-McCrae + Costa
     A. Extroversion (or positive emotionality)=outgoing,
        sociable, friendly, upbeat, assertive
     B. Neuroticism=anxious, hostile, self-conscious,
        insecure, vulnerable
     C. Openness to experience=curiosity, flexibility,
        imaginative
     D. Agreeableness=sympathetic, trusting, cooperative,
        modest
     E. Conscientiousness=diligent, disciplined, well
        organized, punctual, dependable
III. Psychodynamic Theories-focus on unconscious forces--
     Freud—psychoanalysis
     A. 3 components of personality
        1. Id=primitive, instinctive, operates according to
           pleasure principle (immediate gratification)
        2. Ego=decision-making component, operates
           according to reality principle (delay
           gratification until appropriate)
        3. Superego=moral component, social standards,
           right + wrong
     B. 3 levels of awareness
        1. Conscious=what one is aware of at a particular
           moment
        2. Preconscious=material just below surface, easily
           retrieved
        3. Unconscious=thoughts, memories, + desires well
           below surface, but have great influence on
           behavior

Outline Format. Some students find that an **outline** is the best way for them to organize their notes. In a formal outline, Roman numerals (I, II, III, etc.) mark the main ideas. Other ideas relating to each main idea are marked by uppercase letters (A, B, C, etc.). Arabic numerals (1, 2, 3, etc.) and lowercase letters (a, b, c, etc.) mark related ideas in descending order of importance or detail. Using the outline format allows you to add details, definitions, examples, applications, and explanations (see Figure 7.2).

IN CLASS › Discuss the kinds of courses and topics that might be difficult to outline. Ask students how they might supplement regular note taking in these situations.

FIGURE 7.3 › Note Taking in the Paragraph Format

Psychology 101, 1/27/16: Theories of Personality

A personality trait is a "durable disposition to behave in a particular way in a variety of situations"

Big 5: According to McCrae + Costa most personality traits derive from just 5 higher-order traits: extroversion (or positive emotionality), which is outgoing, sociable, friendly, upbeat, assertive; neuroticism, which means anxious, hostile, self-conscious, insecure, vulnerable; openness to experience characterized by curiosity, flexibility, imaginative; agreeableness, which is sympathetic, trusting, cooperative, modest; and conscientiousness means diligent, disciplined, well organized, punctual, dependable

Psychodynamic Theories: Focus on unconscious forces

Freud, father of psychoanalysis, believed in 3 components of personality: id, the primitive, instinctive, operates according to pleasure principle (immediate gratification); ego, the decision-making component, operates according to reality principle (delay gratification until appropriate); and superego, the moral component, social standards, right + wrong

Freud also thought there are 3 levels of awareness: conscious, what one is aware of at a particular moment; preconscious, the material just below surface, easily retrieved; and unconscious, the thoughts, memories, + desires well below surface, but have great influence on behavior

IN CLASS › Lecture to the class and ask students to take notes. Give them an additional five minutes to revise and complete their notes. Collect and review their notes, or prepare a handout for taking notes and using a recall column.

Paragraph Format. When you take notes while you read, you might decide to write **summary paragraphs**—two or three sentences that sum up a larger section of material (see Figure 7.3). This method might not work well for class notes because it's difficult to summarize a topic until your instructor has covered it completely. By the end of the lecture, you might have forgotten critical information.

FIGURE 7.4 › Note Taking in the List Format

> *Psychology 101, 1/27/16: Theories of Personality*
>
> - *A personality trait is a "durable disposition to behave in a particular way in a variety of situations"*
> - *Big 5: According to McCrae + Costa most personality traits derive from just 5 higher-order traits*
>   - *extroversion, (or positive emotionality)=outgoing, sociable, friendly, upbeat, assertive*
>   - *neuroticism=anxious, hostile, self-conscious, insecure, vulnerable*
>   - *openness to experience=curiosity, flexibility, imaginative*
>   - *agreeableness=sympathetic, trusting, cooperative, modest*
>   - *conscientiousness=diligent, disciplined, well organized, punctual, dependable*
> - *Psychodynamic Theories: Focus on unconscious forces*
> - *Freud, father of psychoanalysis, believed in 3 components of personality*
>   - *id=primitive, instinctive, operates according to pleasure principle (immediate gratification)*
>   - *ego=decision-making component, operates according to reality principle (delay gratification until appropriate)*
>   - *superego=moral component, social standards, right + wrong*
> - *Freud also thought there are 3 levels of awareness*
>   - *conscious=what one is aware of at a particular moment*
>   - *preconscious=material just below surface, easily retrieved*
>   - *unconscious=thoughts, memories, + desires well below surface, but have great influence on behavior*

List Format. The list format can be effective in taking notes on terms and definitions, facts, or sequences, such as the body's digestive system (see Figure 7.4). It is easy to use lists in combination with the Cornell format, with key terms on the left and their definitions and explanations on the right.

Note-Taking Techniques

Whatever note-taking format you choose, follow these important steps:

1. **Identify the main ideas.** The first principle of effective note taking is to identify and write down the most important ideas around which the lecture is built. Although supporting details are important as well, focus your note taking on the main ideas. These ideas can be buried in details, statistics, examples, or problems, but you will need to identify and record them for further study. Some instructors announce the purpose of a lecture or offer an outline of main ideas, followed by details. Other instructors develop PowerPoint presentations. If your instructor makes such materials available on a

Web site prior to class, you can print them out and take notes on the outline or next to the PowerPoint slides during the lecture. Some instructors change their tone of voice or repeat themselves for each key idea. Some ask questions or provide an opportunity for discussion. If an instructor says something more than once, chances are it is important. Ask yourself, "What does my instructor want me to know at the end of today's class?"

2. **Don't try to write down everything.** Some first-year students try to do just that. They stop being thinkers and become just note-takers. As you take notes, leave spaces so that you can fill in additional details that you might have missed during class but remember or read about later. Take the time to review and complete your notes as soon as you can after class. Once you have decided on a format for taking notes, you might also want to develop your own system of abbreviations. For example, you might write "inst" instead of "institution" or "eval" instead of "evaluation." Just make sure you will be able to understand your abbreviations when it's time to review.

3. **Don't be thrown by a disorganized lecturer.** When a lecture is disorganized, it's your job to try to organize the material presented into general and specific points. When information is missing, you will need to indicate in your notes where the gaps are. After the lecture, review the reading material, ask your classmates to fill in these gaps, or ask your instructor for help. Some instructors have regular office hours for student appointments, while others are willing to spend time after class answering students' questions. However, it is amazing how few students use these opportunities for one-on-one instruction. The questions you ask might help your instructor realize which parts of the lecture need more attention or repetition.

FYI ❯ New college students do not yet understand how courses are sequential and build on each other. Explain to them how saving their notes and textbooks can help them in later courses.

4. **Keep your notes and supplementary materials for each course separate.** Whether you use folders, binders, or some combination, label your materials with the course number and name. Before class, label and date the paper you will use to take notes; after class, organize your notes chronologically. In your folder or binder, create separate tabbed sections for homework, lab assignments, graded and returned tests, and other materials. If you take notes electronically, you should create separate files and folders for each class, with specific names and dates. You can create a folder for each course and add subfolders for notes, assignments, and projects within each folder.

5. **Download notes, outlines, diagrams, charts, and graphs from the CMS site and bring them to class.** You might be able to save yourself a lot of time during class if you do not have to copy graphs and diagrams while the instructor is talking. Instead, you can focus on the ideas being presented while adding labels and notes to the printouts.

6. **If handouts are distributed in class, label them and place them near your notes.** Buy a portable three-hole punch, and use it to add handouts to your binder or folder as you review your notes each day.

your turn   Write and Reflect

What Note-Taking Method Works Best for You?

Over the next week, try a variety of note-taking methods, such as the Cornell format, the outline format, and a random format where you write down what you think is important in no particular order. Then compare your notes and decide which format you like best—which is easiest for you and which helps you the most when you study and prepare for tests. Write a short essay describing your experience using these methods.

Taking Notes in Nonlecture Courses. Always be ready to change your note-taking methods based on the situation. Group discussion is a popular way to teach in college because it engages students in active participation. On your campus, you might also have courses with **Supplemental Instruction (SI)** opportunities, which allow students to discuss the information covered in class lectures and discussions outside of class.

How do you keep a record of what's happening in such classes? Let's assume that you are taking notes on a problem-solving group assignment. You would begin your notes by writing down the problem that the group is being asked to solve. As the group discussion continues, you would list the solutions that are offered. These would be your main ideas. The important details might include the pros and cons of each viewpoint or suggested solution. The important thing to remember when taking notes in non-lecture courses is that you need to record the information presented by your classmates as well as the information presented by your instructor, and you need to consider all reasonable ideas, even those that differ from your own.

When a course has separate lecture and discussion sessions, you will need to understand how the discussion sessions relate to and supplement the lectures. If the material covered in the discussion session differs from what was covered in the lecture, you might need to ask for help in organizing your notes. When similar topics are covered, you can combine your lecture and discussion notes so that you have full coverage of each topic.

How you organize the notes you take in a class discussion session depends on the purpose or form of the discussion. It usually makes sense to begin with a list of the issues or topics under discussion. Another approach is to list the questions raised for discussion. If the discussion explores reasons for and against a particular argument, divide your notes into columns or sections for each set of reasons. When different views are presented in discussion, record all the ideas. Your instructor might ask you to compare your own opinions to those of other students and explain why and how you formed those opinions.

Taking Notes in Science and Mathematics Courses. Many mathematics and science courses build on one another from term to term and from year to year. When you take notes in these courses, you will likely need to go back to them in the future. For example, when taking organic

techtip

TAKE BETTER NOTES IN BETTER WAYS

Studies have shown that people remember only half of what they hear, which is a major reason to take notes during lectures. Solid note taking will help you distill key concepts and make it easier to study for tests. Note taking also engages the brain in a process known as rehearsal. Writing things down is important for you to start the process of creating your own way of understanding the materials.

The Problem

You don't take good notes because you aren't sure what is important. You have access to technology, but aren't sure how to use it to take notes.

The Fix

Along with making use of the note-taking formats presented in this chapter, use your smart phone, tablet, or laptop to save information and create tools that will help you study.

© Erik Isakson/Tetra Images

How to Do It

1. Microsoft Word is great for most classes. To highlight main ideas, you can bold or underline text, change the size and color, highlight whole sections, and insert text boxes or charts. You can make bullet points or outlines and insert comments. As you review your notes, you can cut and paste to make things more coherent. You can also create a folder for each class so you can find everything you need easily.
2. Microsoft Excel is especially good for any class that involves calculations or financial statements. You can embed messages in the cells of a spreadsheet to explain calculations. (The notes will appear whenever you hover your cursor over that cell.)
3. Microsoft PowerPoint can be invaluable for visual learners. Instead of creating one giant, potentially confusing Word file, you can make a slideshow with a new slide for each key point. Some instructors also post the slides that they plan to use in class before class begins. You can write notes on printouts of the slides, or download them and add your notes in PowerPoint.

Some Cool Apps for Note Taking and Reviewing:
- Pocket (iOS and Android) allows you to store and review written content from your phone.
- Evernote (iOS and Android) lets you take a picture of handwritten or printed notes—or anything else you want to recall later—then you can file content and search it by keyword later.

- CamScanner (iOS and Android) allows you to photograph, scan, and store notes.
- Scan Edit (iOS) lets you scan any document and convert it into a PDF, saving time and money.
- Tiny Tap (iOS) lets you create multiple-choice quizzes that you can take as practice and share with other students.
- StudyBlue (iOS, Android, and Web Apps) allows you to make amazing-looking flash cards.

EXTRA STYLE POINTS: No matter what program or app you use, some rules always apply:
- Write down main points using phrases or key terms instead of long sentences.
- Date your notes; keep them in order and in one place; save files using filenames with the course number, name, and date of the class; and back up everything.
- Keep a pen and paper handy for sketching graphs and diagrams.
- If you find it hard to keep up, keep practicing your listening and typing skills. Consider a typing class, program, or app to learn how to type properly.
- If you prefer a spiral notebook and a ballpoint pen, that's OK; these formats are tried and true.
- Practice teaching others what you learned in class. You can also learn note-taking strategies from your peers.

chemistry, you might need to review the notes you took in earlier chemistry courses. This can be particularly important if some time has passed since you completed your last related course, such as after a summer or winter break.

Taking notes in math and science courses can be different from taking notes in other classes. The following tips can help:

- Write down any equations, formulas, diagrams, charts, graphs, and definitions that the instructor puts on the board or screen.
- Write the instructor's words as precisely as possible. Technical terms often have exact meanings that cannot be changed.
- Use standard symbols, abbreviations, and scientific notation.
- Write down all worked problems and examples step by step. The steps are often necessary in answering exam questions. Actively engage in solving the problem yourself as it is being solved during class. Be sure that you can follow the logic and understand the sequence of steps. If you have questions you cannot ask during the lecture, write them down in your notes so that you can ask them in a discussion session, in the lab, or during the instructor's office hours.
- Consider taking your notes in pencil or erasable pen. You might need to make changes if you are copying long equations while trying to pay attention to the instructor. You want to keep your notes as neat as possible. Later, you can use colored ink to add other details.
- Listen carefully to other students' questions and the instructor's answers. Take notes on the discussion and during question-and-answer periods.
- Use asterisks, exclamation points, question marks, or symbols of your own to highlight both important points in your notes and questions that you need to come back to when you review.
- Refer to the textbook after class; the text might contain better diagrams and other visual representations than you can draw while taking notes in class. If they are not provided in handouts or on the instructor's Web site, you might even want to scan or photocopy diagrams from the text and include them with your notes in your binder.
- Keep your binders for math and science courses until you graduate (or even longer if you are planning to go to graduate or professional school). They will serve as good review materials for later classes in math and science. In some cases, these notes can also be helpful in the workplace.

Using Technology to Take Notes.
While some students use laptops, tablets, or other mobile devices for note taking, others prefer taking notes by hand so that they can easily circle important items or copy equations or diagrams while they are being presented. If you handwrite your notes, entering them on a computer after class for review purposes might be helpful, especially if you are a kinesthetic learner who prefers to learn through experience and practice. After class, you can also cut and paste diagrams and other visuals into your notes and print a copy, since a printout might be neater and easier to read than notes you wrote by hand.

IN CLASS > In the Hawaiian language, the words for *teaching* and *learning* are the same. Ask students: How can someone teach and learn at the same time?

IN CLASS ❯ Ask how many students use laptops to take notes during class. Have these students discuss the advantages and drawbacks of taking notes this way. Ask how they use their notes to study for exams. Encourage students to ask advanced students these questions, or invite guest speakers to share their experiences with note taking in class.

IN CLASS ❯ To demonstrate how easy it is to forget information, ask students to think back to a lecture from the previous day and then write down as many main ideas and supporting details as they can remember.

Some students—especially aural learners, who prefer to hear information—find it is advantageous to record lectures. But if you record, don't become passive; listen actively. Students with specific types of learning disabilities might be urged to record lectures or use the services of note-takers, who type on a laptop while the student views the notes on a separate screen.

Review Your Notes

Unless we take steps to remember it, we forget much of the information we receive within the first twenty-four hours; in fact, the decline of memory over time is known as the **forgetting curve**. So if you do not review your notes almost immediately after class, it can be difficult to remember the material later. In two weeks, you will have forgotten up to 70 percent of it! Forgetting can be a serious problem when you are expected to learn and remember many different facts, figures, concepts, and relationships for a number of classes.

Immediate reviewing will help your overall understanding as well as your ability to remember important details during exams. Use the following three strategies:

1. **Write down the main ideas.** For five or ten minutes, quickly review your notes and select key words or phrases. Fill in the details you still remember but missed writing down during class. You might also want to ask your instructor or a classmate to quickly look at your notes to see if you have covered the major ideas.
2. **Repeat your ideas out loud.** Repeat a brief version of what you learned from the class either to yourself or to someone else. For many, the best way to learn something is to teach it to others. You will understand something better and remember it longer if you try to explain it in your own words. This helps you discover your own reactions and find the gaps in your understanding of the material. Asking and answering questions in class can also provide you with the feedback you need to make sure that your understanding is accurate.
3. **Review your notes from the previous class just before the next class session.** As you sit in class the next time it meets, waiting for the instructor to begin, use the time to quickly review your notes from the previous class session. This will prepare you for the lecture that is about to begin and help you to ask questions about material from the earlier lecture that was not clear to you.

What if you have three classes in a row and no time to study between them? Repeat the information as soon as possible after class. Review the most recent class first. Never delay doing this; if you do, it will take you longer to review, select main ideas, and repeat the ideas. With practice, you can complete the review of your main ideas from your notes quickly, perhaps between classes, during lunch, or while waiting for or riding the bus.

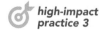 *high-impact practice 3*

Compare Notes

Comparing notes with other students in a study group, SI session, or learning community has a number of benefits: You will probably take better notes when you know that someone else will see them, you can tell whether

your notes are as clear and organized as those of other students, and you can use your comparisons to see whether you agree on what the most important points are.

Take turns testing each other on what you have learned. This will help you predict exam questions and find out if you can answer them. In addition to sharing specific information from the class, you can also share tips on how you take and organize your notes. You might get new ideas that will help your overall learning.

Be aware, however, that merely copying another student's notes, no matter how good those notes are, does not benefit you as much as comparing notes. If you had to be absent from a class because of illness or a family emergency, it's fine to look at another student's notes to see what you missed, but just rewriting those notes might not help you learn the material. Instead, summarize the other student's notes in your own words to enhance your understanding of the important points.

Class Notes and Homework

Once you have reviewed your notes, you can use them to complete homework assignments. Follow these steps:

1. **Do a warm-up for your homework.** Before doing the assignment, look through your notes again. Use a separate sheet of paper to rework examples, problems, or exercises. If there is related assigned material in the textbook, review it. Go back to the examples. Try to respond to the questions or complete the problems without looking at the answers or solutions. Keep in mind that it can help to go back through your course notes, reorganize them, highlight the important items, and create new notes that let you connect with the material.

IN CLASS ❯ Talk about comparing notes for the purpose of learning versus plagiarism and cheating. Emphasize that sharing notes can be good practice for retaining information, but it can be counterproductive when students rely on someone else's notes because they missed class or failed to take good notes themselves.

RETENTION STRATEGY ❯ Suggest that students compare their notes with those of successful students from previous first-year seminars. Remember: The greatest impact on students is the experience of other students. Advanced students can help retain beginning students.

OUTSIDE CLASS ❯ Ask students to practice these steps and report the results to the rest of the class, or have them write about the results in a journal or a blog.

2. **Do any assigned problems, and answer any assigned questions.** When you start doing your homework, read each question or problem and ask: What am I supposed to find or find out? What is most important? What is not that important? Read each problem several times, and state it in your own words. Solve the problem without referring to your notes or the text, as though you were taking a test. In this way, you will test your knowledge and know whether you are prepared for exams.

3. **Don't give up too soon.** Start your homework with the hardest subject first while you are most energetic. When you face a problem or question that you cannot easily solve or answer, move on only after you have tried long enough. After you have completed the whole assignment, come back to any problems or questions that you could not solve or answer. Try once more, and then take a break. You might need to think about a particularly difficult problem for several hours or even days. Inspiration might come when you are waiting at a stoplight or just before you fall asleep.

4. **Complete your work.** When you finish an assignment, talk to yourself about what you learned from it. Think about how the problems and questions were different from one another, which strategies were successful, and what form the answers took. Be sure to review any material you have not mastered. Ask for help from the instructor, a classmate, a study group, the campus learning center, or a tutor to learn how to answer questions that stumped you.

FYI ❯ After reviewing this chapter's suggestions on getting the most out of class, remind students where they can go on campus or at their college's Web site to get help with these strategies. Tell them that it is the most successful students who are most likely to seek such assistance, and that such actions correlate with higher probabilities for retention and graduation.

---

your turn   Stay Motivated

Use What You Have Learned

Now that you've read these suggestions about taking notes and studying for class, which ideas are you motivated to implement in your own note taking? Come to class ready to explain which ideas appeal to you most and why.

---

checklist for success

Getting the Most from Class

☐ **Practice the behaviors of engagement.** These behaviors include listening attentively, taking notes, and contributing to class discussion. Engagement also means participating in out-of-class activities without being "required" to do so.

☐ **Seek out professors who practice "active" teaching.** Ask other students, your seminar instructor, and your adviser to suggest the most engaging professors.

☐ **Prepare for class before class; it is one of the simplest and most important things you can do.** Read your notes from the previous class and do the assigned readings.

☐ **Go to class.** A huge part of success is simply showing up. You have no chance of becoming engaged in learning if you're not there.

☐ **Identify the different types of note taking covered in this chapter and decide which one(s) might work best for you.** Compare your notes with those of another good student to make sure that you are covering the most important points.

☐ **As you review your notes before each class, make a list of any questions you have and ask both fellow students and your instructor for help.** Don't wait until just before the exam to try to find answers to your questions.

REFLECT ON CHOICES

high-impact practice 2 | This chapter offers several options for effective note taking. Before you make a choice to try a new note-taking format, think back on those we suggested: Cornell, outline, paragraph, and list. Which one is most similar to the method you currently use, and which is most different? Reread the material, and do a brief written comparison of the recommended formats. Which do you think is most complex, which would be the easiest to use, and, given your learning style, which format would help you best understand and remember the material?

APPLY WHAT YOU HAVE LEARNED

Now that you have read and discussed this chapter, consider how you can apply what you have learned to your academic life and your personal life. The following prompts will help you reflect on the chapter material and how you can use it both now and in the future.

1. What is your least engaging class—the one in which the instructor does not encourage you to engage in active learning? Think of some ways you could make this class more engaging, such as asking questions or doing extra reading on the class material. Make a list of your ideas and share it with your college success instructor. He or she might have other ideas to suggest to you.

2. This chapter makes the point that it is easier to learn and remember new material when you can connect it to something you already know or have experienced. Which of your first-year classes connects most directly to something you learned in the past or something that happened to you? Write a brief paper in which you describe these connections.

USE YOUR RESOURCES

> **Learning Assistance Center**
Almost every campus has a learning assistance center, and this chapter's topic is one of their specialties. More and more, the best students—and good students who want to be better students—use learning centers as much as students who are having academic difficulties. Services at learning centers are offered by both full-time professionals and highly skilled student tutors.

> **Fellow College Students**
Often, the best help we can get comes from those who are closest to us: fellow students. Keep an eye out in your classes, residence hall, co-curricular groups, and other places for the most serious, purposeful, and directed students. They are the ones to seek out. Find a tutor. Join a study group. Students who do these things are the ones most likely to stay in college and be successful. It does not diminish you in any way to seek assistance from your peers.

> **Computer Center**
If you need help using Word, Excel, PowerPoint, or electronic note-taking systems, visit the computer center on your campus.

> **Math Center**
Your college may have a special center that provides help for math courses. If you are having difficulty figuring out what kind of notes to take in math classes, visit this center to ask for assistance.

> **Disabled Student Services**
Your institution's office of disabled student services can help arrange for a note-taker if you cannot take notes because of a documented disability.

> **Toastmasters International**
This organization offers public speaking tips at **toastmasters.org**. When you feel more confident about speaking in public, you will participate more in class. Find additional guidelines for speaking in class at **school-for-champions .com/grades/speaking.htm**.

 LaunchPad

LaunchPad for *Your College Experience* is a great resource. Go online to master concepts using the LearningCurve study tool and much more. **macmillanhighered.com/gardner12e**

Ammentorp Photography/Shutterstock

8
STUDYING

YOU WILL EXPLORE

Ways to concentrate and study more effectively

How memory works and myths about memory

Skills to improve your memory

⌖ High-impact practices 2 (writing) and 3 (collaboration)

Joe Miranda, 19

Engineering major
Spokane Falls Community College

> " **Two of the biggest challenges of making the transition from high school to college were learning time management and study skills.** "

Early in high school, Joe Miranda did well enough in his classes to be able to play basketball and football. He hoped to be a college athlete, but then a knee injury derailed those plans. In his senior year of high school in Spokane, Washington, one of Joe's teachers recommended that he look into engineering as a profession. Joe had always been interested in math and science, but he hadn't done much planning for college. He researched different careers and types of engineering and found that environmental engineering excited him. Then he researched programs close to home.

Joe plans to complete his associate's degree in pre-engineering at Spokane Falls Community College (SFCC) and then transfer to Washington State University. SFCC has a six-quarter pre-engineering program intended to prepare students for transfer to a four-year engineering college in their junior year. When he was in high school, Joe didn't take the college-prep courses he needed to enter the engineering program at SFCC right away. As a result, he is taking lower-level college courses that will allow him to ramp up to higher-level courses like calculus and advanced chemistry, which he'll need in order to transfer. Joe knows all his time and effort will be worth it. "I found a great tutor at the learning center on campus who is helping me keep up the good grades I am getting," he says.

Joe is good at math and science, but that doesn't mean his transition to college was easy. "In high school," he says, "my studying habits were slim to none. I was the type of high school student who was able to pass a test just from listening and from what I remembered from class."

At SFCC, Joe had to change some of his study habits when he found that he wasn't able to remember everything the instructors required him to learn. "Two of the biggest challenges in making the transition from high school to college were learning time management and study skills," Joe says. He notes that, compared with high school, his college classes go twice as fast and instructors expect students to do a lot more work on their own. One of the first steps Joe took to adjust his study habits was to stop setting aside huge blocks of unstructured study time. "I learned that studying for more than four hours straight is not the best for me. I need to study for an hour, take a half hour break, and then study another hour. I realized that after an hour, I had trouble remembering things." By taking breaks to eat, exercise, or watch TV, Joe knows that he's giving his brain time to process information.

His one piece of advice to other first-year students? "The first year is going to be the hardest because it's so different," he says. "Just push through it. You'll find that it all starts making sense."

 LaunchPad

To access the LearningCurve study tool, video activities, and more, go to LaunchPad for *Your College Experience.*
macmillanhighered.com
/gardner12e

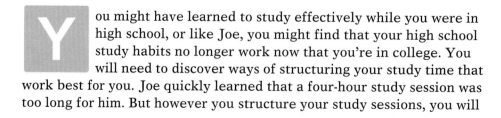

You might have learned to study effectively while you were in high school, or like Joe, you might find that your high school study habits no longer work now that you're in college. You will need to discover ways of structuring your study time that work best for you. Joe quickly learned that a four-hour study session was too long for him. But however you structure your study sessions, you will need to allocate regular times each week to review course material, do assigned reading, and keep up with your homework. Occasionally, you will also want to do additional (unassigned) reading and investigate particular topics that interest you, as these are strategies that will help you retain knowledge.

Studying, comprehending, and remembering are essential to getting the most from your college experience. Although many students think that the only reason to study is to do well on exams, a far more important reason is to learn and understand course information. If you study to increase your understanding, you are more likely to remember and apply what you learn, not only to tests, but also to future courses and to life beyond college.

This chapter considers two related topics: concentration and memory. It begins with the role of concentration in studying—if you cannot concentrate, you'll find it next to impossible to remember anything. Next, the chapter offers a number of tools to help you make the best use of your study time. It concludes with a thorough discussion of what memory is, how it works, and how you can improve your memory.

RETENTION STRATEGY ❯ One reason first-year seminars are correlated with retention is that they focus on the study skills essential for college success. Even if your students tell you they have heard it before, remind them that college-level study skills are different from high-school-level skills. If you don't feel comfortable teaching study skills, find someone on your campus who can be a resource person for you, perhaps starting with staff in the learning assistance center, or a faculty member who teaches developmental studies.

is this you?

Making A's without Studying

Were you a straight-A student in high school who spent almost no time studying? In the first few weeks of college, maybe you went to class and listened, and you read through the assigned material on time. But you never took notes, reviewed your reading, or spent extra time preparing for tests and exams. You believed that your brainpower would carry you through college, just like it did in high school. But your first round of college exams gave you a horrible shock: You got a C in your easiest course, three D's, and an F. You quickly realized that something had to change. Clearly in college you can't coast effortlessly like you did in high school. This chapter will help you develop systematic strategies for studying that will help you pull up your grades before the end of the term.

STUDYING IN COLLEGE: MAKING CHOICES AND CONCENTRATING

Learning new material takes a lot of effort on your part. You must concentrate on what you hear and read. This might sound simple, but considering all the responsibilities that college students must balance, the opportunity to concentrate and really focus on what you're learning and studying can be hard to come by. Understanding how to maximize your ability to concentrate through what you do and where you do it is a good place to start.

Making a few changes in your behavior and in your environment will allow you to concentrate better and remember more. With concentration, you'll probably need fewer hours to study because you will use your time more efficiently. What are you willing to do to make this happen? Working through the following exercise, you'll begin to navigate some tough choices.

Tough Choices	Your Answer: Yes or No?
Are you willing to do assigned reading before you come to class?	
Are you willing to find a place away from home, either on campus or elsewhere, for quiet study?	
Are you willing to turn off your cell phone while you read?	
Are you willing to turn off distracting music or TV while you are studying?	
Are you willing to sit in a spot in class where you can see and hear better?	
Are you willing to go over your notes after class to revise or rewrite them?	
Are you willing to form study groups or work with partners?	
Are you willing to reduce stress through exercise, sleep, or meditation?	
Are you willing to take a few minutes on the weekend to organize the week ahead?	
Are you willing to study for tests four or five days in advance?	

Attending a college or university is a major responsibility, one you shouldn't take lightly. It is a lot of work, but it also offers you a lot of opportunities. For most people, a college degree is a pathway to a better, more fulfilling life. As a college learner, you may need to make different choices about how you manage your time and your study environment. Depending on your past study habits, some of these choices may not be easy. You may find that you have to invest more time in reading and reviewing, and that you have to study in groups with other students. Behaviors such as these can have a direct, positive impact on your ability to remember and learn the information you will need in the months and years ahead.

With these realities in mind, what did you learn about yourself from answering the questions in the exercise on the previous page? Think especially about the questions to which you answered "no." Which of these are you willing or unwilling to change right now? Remember: Changing behaviors that disrupt your ability to get the most out of college, both in and out of the classroom, will save you a lot of headaches in the future.

---

your turn Write and Reflect

Are You Able to Concentrate?

The next time that you read a textbook, monitor your ability to concentrate. Check your watch when you begin, and check it again when your mind begins to wander. How many minutes did you concentrate on your reading? List some strategies to keep your mind from wandering. Write a journal entry containing ideas you have heard that you think will work well for you.

high-impact practice 2

HIGH-IMPACT PRACTICE ❯ This exercise gives students another opportunity to write briefly about their academic strengths and weaknesses. The more students think and write about themselves, the more effectively they will be able to understand their strengths and alter behaviors that threaten to get in the way of their college goals.

HOW MEMORY WORKS

Learning experts describe two different processes involved in memory (see Table 8.1). The first is **short-term memory**, which is defined as how many items you are able to understand and remember at one time. After less than 30 seconds—and sometimes much faster—you will forget the information stored in your short-term memory unless you take action either to keep that information in short-term memory or to move it to long-term memory.

Although short-term memory is significantly limited, it has a number of uses. It serves as an immediate holding tank for information, some of which you might not need for long. It helps you maintain a reasonable attention span so that you can keep track of topics mentioned in conversation, and it also enables you to stay on task with the goals you are pursuing at any given moment. But even these simple functions of short-term memory fail on occasion. If you are interrupted in any way, by a ringing phone or someone asking a question, you might find that your attention suffers and that you have to start over to reconstruct the contents of your short-term memory.

IN CLASS ❯ Ask students why they think that the authors included material in this textbook about memory. Is memory related to learning and academic success? Why or why not? Can memory be improved? If so, how?

The second memory process is also important for college success. **Long-term memory**, the capacity to retain and recall information over the long term, from hours to years, can be divided into three categories:

- *Procedural memory* deals with knowing how to do something, such as solving a mathematical problem or driving a car. You use your procedural memory when you ride a bicycle, even if you haven't ridden one in years; when you cook a meal that you know how to prepare without using a recipe; or when you send a text message.
- *Semantic memory* involves facts and meanings without regard to where and when you learned those things. Your semantic memory is used when you remember word meanings or important dates, such as your mother's birthday.
- *Episodic memory* deals with particular events, their time, and their place. You use episodic memory when you remember events in your life—a vacation, your first day of school, or the moment your child was born. Some people can recall not only the event, but also the very time and place the event happened. For others, although the event stands out, the time and place are harder to remember.

TABLE 8.1

Short-Term Memory	Long-Term Memory
Stores information for about 30 seconds.	Can be described in three ways:
Can handle from five to nine chunks of information at one time.	Procedural—remembering how to do something
Information is either forgotten or moved to long-term memory.	Semantic—remembering facts and meanings
	Episodic—remembering events, including their time and place

IN CLASS › Remind students of the difference between memorization and learning. Explain that once they have mastered important concepts, using memory techniques will be an easy way to file facts for future use.

Connecting Memory to Deep Learning

Multitasking has become a fact of life for many of us, but research summarized on the Web site of the American Psychological Association[1] shows that trying to do several tasks at once can make it harder to remember the most important things. It is hard to focus on anything for long if your life is full of daily distractions and competing responsibilities—school, work, commuting, and family responsibilities—or if you're not getting the sleep you need. Have you ever had the experience of walking into a room with a specific task in mind and immediately forgetting what that task was? You were probably interrupted, either by your own thoughts or by someone or something else. Or have you ever felt the panic that comes when your mind goes blank during a test, even though you studied hard and knew the material? If you spent all night studying, lack of sleep may have raised your stress level, causing you to forget what you worked hard to learn. Such experiences happen to most people at one time or another.

---

[1]www.apa.org/research/action/multitask.aspx.

To do well in college and in life, it's important that you improve your ability to remember what you read, hear, and experience. Concentration is a key element of learning and is so deeply connected to memory that you can't really have one without the other.

The benefits of having a good memory are obvious. In college, your memory will help you retain information and earn excellent grades on tests. After college, the ability to remember important details—names, dates, and appointments—will save you energy and time, and will prevent a lot of embarrassment.

Most memory strategies tend to focus on helping you remember bits and pieces of knowledge: names, dates, numbers, vocabulary words, formulas, and so on. However, if you know the date when the Civil War began and the name of the fort where the first shots were fired but you don't know why the Civil War was fought or how it affected history, you're missing the point of a college education. College is a time to develop **deep learning**, which involves understanding the why and how behind the details. So while remembering specific facts is necessary, to do well in college and in your career, you will need to understand major themes and ideas. You will also need to improve your ability to think deeply about what you're learning. For more on the sorts of thinking skills you need to develop in college, see the chapters on "Information Literacy and Communication" and "Thinking in College."

---

your turn   Stay Motivated

The Fun of Improving Your Memory

What might motivate you to improve your memory? Do your friends complain that you keep forgetting the times you had planned to meet? Have you forgotten the due date for a paper, or have you forgotten your mother's birthday? If you want to develop a better memory, try some fun strategies for memory improvement. For example, many memory games are available that you can play for a few minutes every day; some of them can be accessed online or on your mobile device. Check out these free apps: Brain Workout for Android or Music Game for iPhone.

Myths about Memory

To understand how to improve your memory, let's first look at what we know about how memory works. Although scientists keep learning new things about how our brains function, author Kenneth Higbee[2] suggests some myths about memory, some of which you might have heard, and

IN CLASS > Assign groups of students to read and discuss the myths about memory. Which of these myths do most students believe are true? Why?

---

[2]Kenneth L. Higbee, *Your Memory: How It Works and How to Improve It*, 2nd rev. ed. (New York: Marlowe, 2001).

techtip

USE THE CLOUD

Most of us have created files on computers. We usually store them on the computer's internal hard drive or on a removable drive, such as a thumb or flash drive. But colleges are moving away from allowing students to store data on their student accounts, so moving from computer to computer when you are working can present a problem. Also, if you don't have the latest word processing or presentation software on your own computer, it might be difficult to use files for your classes that were created in these software programs.

Cloud computing allows you to use the Internet as a storage device. Some sites even have pared-down versions of word processing, spreadsheet, and presentation software that you can use for free.

Another great advantage of cloud computing is the ability to share your files or folders with others. You can create a personal digital library and decide who gets to check out what file. It also tracks the changes that you and others have made to a file and keeps you from having multiple different versions if you are sharing the file with a group.

The Problem

You store your class files on a drive or laptop that you don't always have with you. How can you access your files anytime you need?

The Fix

Save your files to the cloud and have access to them from any Internet-connected device.

Pixsooz/Shutterstock

How to Do It

Sign up for a free account from a cloud storage site. These sites allow you to save files to an online location. You'll have your own private, password-protected storage space. Cloud storage is great for collaboration because you can choose to share all or some of your files with your classmates and friends. Here are four sites with free storage.

1. *Dropbox* (dropbox.com) is probably the best known cloud storage site. Users get 2 GB of free storage. You can upgrade to up to 500 GB for a monthly fee, or earn more storage space by referring others to the site. Dropbox has both a Web interface that you can access from any computer and a downloadable client that you can save to your computer. (A client is a piece of hardware or software that accesses a service made available by a server.) This client makes Dropbox look like any other folder on your computer, but when you add files to it, Dropbox actually adds them to your online folder. Dropbox is available as a stand-alone app on iPhone, iPad, and Android devices, and it works with other document-editing apps for

2. *Google Drive* (drive.google.com) allows users to store and share documents up to 5 GB. A great feature of Google Drive is that you can edit documents in real time with others. If you're writing a group paper, all your coauthors can view and edit the same document simultaneously. There is even a chat window so you can talk to each other while editing. Like Dropbox, Google Drive is available as a stand-alone app, and it integrates well with iPhone, iPad, and Android apps. If you have a Gmail account, you already have an account for Google Drive.

3. *MediaFire* (mediafire.com) lets you work collaboratively and access your files using stand-alone apps on iPhone, iPad, and Android devices. Its key feature is 50 GB of free storage space.

4. *Microsoft OneDrive* uses the Microsoft Office Suite and allows you to create, store, and share files. It comes with 15 GB of free space, but you can expand that space for a fee. It also has a free, stand-alone app for smart phones or tablets. If you have a Hotmail account, you can

some you might even believe. Here are five of these memory myths and what experts say about them:

1. **Myth:** Some people have bad memories.
   Reality: Although the memory ability you are born with is different from that of others, nearly everyone can improve his or her ability to remember and recall. Improving your concentration will benefit your ability to remember!

2. **Myth:** Some people have photographic memories.
   Reality: Some individuals have truly exceptional memories, but these abilities result more often from learned strategies, interest, and practice than from the natural ability to remember.

3. **Myth:** Memory benefits from long hours of practice.
   Reality: Experts believe that practice often improves memory, but they argue that the way you practice is more important than how long you practice.

4. **Myth:** Remembering too much can clutter your mind.
   Reality: For all practical purposes, the storage capacity of your memory is unlimited. In fact, the more you learn about a particular topic, the easier it is to learn even more. How you organize the information is more important than the quantity of the information.

5. **Myth:** People use only 10 percent of their brain power.
   Reality: No one knows exactly how much of our brain's resources we actually tap. However, most researchers believe that we all have far more mental ability than we actually use.

IMPROVING YOUR MEMORY

Just as you can use strategies to improve your ability to concentrate, you can also improve your ability to store information in your brain for future use. Psychologists and learning specialists have developed a number of strategies you can use when studying. Some of these strategies might be new to you, but others will be familiar.

Have you ever had to memorize a speech or lines from a play? How you remember the lines might depend on your learning style. If you're an aural learner, you might decide to record your lines, along with those of other characters, and listen to them on tape. If you're a visual learner, you might remember best by visualizing where your lines appear in the script. If you learn best by reading, you might simply read the script over and over. If you're a kinesthetic learner, you might need to walk or move as you read the script.

Although knowing specific words will help, remembering concepts and ideas can be much more important. To store such ideas in your mind, ask yourself these questions as you review your notes and textbook material:

1. What is the basic idea in what I'm reading?
2. Why does the idea make sense? Is it logical?

3. How does this idea connect to other ideas in the material or to experiences in my life?
4. What are some possible arguments against the idea?

To prepare for an exam that will cover large amounts of material, you need to reduce your notes and text pages into manageable study units. Review your materials with these questions in mind: Is this one of the key ideas in the chapter or unit? Will I see this on the test? Five study tools in particular can help you remember what you have learned: review sheets, mind maps, flash cards, summaries, and mnemonics.

Review Sheets

Use your notes to develop **review sheets**—lists of key terms and ideas that you need to remember. If you're using the Cornell format to take notes, you'll make these lists in the recall column. Also be sure to use your lecture notes to test yourself or others on the information presented in class.

Mind Maps

A **mind map** (see Figure 8.1 on the next page) is essentially a visual review sheet that shows the relationships between ideas; its visual patterns provide you with clues to jog your memory. Because they are visual, mind maps help many students—particularly English language learners—remember information more easily.

An Elephant (Almost) Never Forgets

Although elephants apparently do have pretty good memories, they're like the rest of us in that they occasionally forget. Work to develop your memory by using the specific strategies in this chapter. One of the most important strategies you can use is considering the big-picture context behind bits and pieces of information.

© Shannon Burns

"Is this the memory seminar?"

FIGURE 8.1 > Sample Mind Map

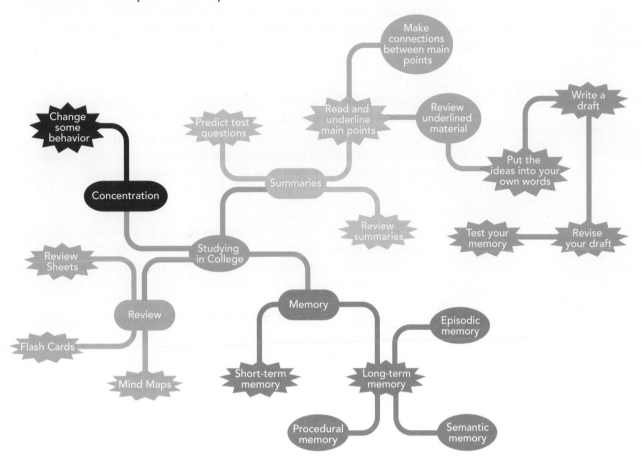

To create a mind map, start with a main idea and place it in the center. Then add major categories that branch out from the center. To these branches, add pieces of related information to form clusters. You can use different shapes and/or colors to show the relationships among the various pieces of information. You can find many apps for creating mind maps on your computer or mobile device. Figure 8.1 shows a mind map of this chapter, created by using an app called Total Recall. Other mind-map apps include MindMeister and SimpleMind.

Flash Cards

Just as you can create flash cards during the process of active reading, you can also use them as a tool for improving your memory. Flash cards—with a question, term, or piece of information on one side and the answer, definition, or explanation on the other—can serve as memory aids. One of the advantages of flash cards is that you can keep them in your backpack or jacket, or on your mobile device. Then you can look at them anywhere, even when you don't have enough time to take out your notebook to study.

Flash cards can help you make good use of time that might otherwise be wasted, such as time spent on the bus or waiting for a friend. Flash cards are excellent tools for improving your vocabulary, especially if you are learning English as a second language. See the "Reading to Learn" chapter for more information about creating and using flash cards.

Summaries

OUTSIDE CLASS › Have students write a summary of this chapter by following the outlined steps on this page. Ask students to discuss the differences between the mind map and the summary. Which tool is more helpful to them? Why?

An immediate benefit of writing summaries of class topics is that they can help you answer short-answer and essay questions successfully. They also allow you to see connections between ideas and help you identify major and minor details. By summarizing the main ideas and putting them into your own words, you will be able to remember information better. Here's how you can create a good summary in preparation for taking a test:

1. **Read the assigned material, your class notes, or your instructor's presentation slides.** Underline or mark the main ideas as you go, make explanatory notes or comments about the material, or make an outline on a separate sheet of paper. Predict test questions based on your active reading.
2. **Make connections between main points and key supporting details.** Reread to identify each main point and its supporting evidence. Create an outline in the process.
3. **Review underlined material.** Put those ideas into your own words in a logical order.
4. **Write your ideas in a draft.** In the first sentence, state the purpose of your summary. Follow this statement with each main point and its supporting ideas. See how much of the draft you can develop from memory without relying on your notes.
5. **Review your draft.** Read it over, adding missing details or other information.
6. **Test your memory.** Put your draft away, and try to repeat the contents of the summary out loud to yourself or to a study partner who can let you know whether you have forgotten anything.
7. **Schedule time to review your summary and double-check your memory shortly before the test.** You might want to do this with a partner, but some students prefer to review alone. Some instructors might be willing to help you with this process and give you feedback on your summaries.

PEER LEADERS › How good is your memory? Be candid with the students in your class about any challenges you have had remembering course information. Tell them about your particular memory strategies, such as your note-taking method, visual methods such as mind maps, and mnemonics.

high-impact practice 3

HIGH-IMPACT PRACTICE › When students who share the same learning style work together on memory strategies, they will inevitably come up with new ideas they can share with each other.

---

yourturn Work Together

Using Learning Styles to Study and Remember

With your instructor's help, identify other students in your class who share your learning style. Get together to brainstorm strategies for remembering material for exams using your learning style, and keep track of the most helpful ideas.

Mnemonics

Mnemonics (pronounced "ne-MON-iks") are different methods or tricks to help you remember information. Mnemonics tend to fall into four basic categories:

1. **Acronyms.** Acronyms, which are new words created from the first letters of several words, can be helpful in remembering. The names of the Great Lakes can be more easily recalled by remembering the word *HOMES* for **H**uron, **O**ntario, **M**ichigan, **E**rie, and **S**uperior.

2. **Acrostics.** An acrostic is a verse in which certain letters of each word or line form a message. Many piano students were taught the notes on the treble clef lines (E, G, B, D, F) by remembering the acrostic "**E**very **G**ood **B**oy **D**eserves **F**udge." Many students are taught the following to remember the planets of our solar system: **M**y **V**ery **E**xcellent **M**other **J**ust **S**erved **U**s **N**achos (**M**ercury, **V**enus, **E**arth, **M**ars, **J**upiter, **S**aturn, **U**ranus, **N**eptune).

3. **Rhymes or songs.** Do you remember learning "Thirty days hath September, April, June, and November. All the rest have thirty-one, excepting February alone. It has twenty-eight days' time, but in leap years twenty-nine"? If so, you were using a mnemonic rhyming technique to remember the number of days in each month.

4. **Visualization.** You can use visualization to connect a word or concept with a visual image. The more ridiculous the image, the more likely you are to remember the word or concept. For example, if you want to remember the name of George Washington, you may think of a person you know by the name of George. You should then picture that person washing a ton of dishes. Now every time you think of the first president of the United States, you see George washing a ton of dishes.[3]

---

your turn   Make Good Choices

Choose Review Methods That Work for You

This chapter has offered several strategies for reviewing material before you take a test or exam, including review sheets, mind maps, flash cards, summaries, and mnemonics. Some of these strategies might work better for certain subject areas. For instance, mnemonics and flash cards will help when you have to remember definitions or other specific bits of information. Review sheets, mind maps, and summaries work more effectively when you need to understand broad concepts. When you begin studying for your next test, let the type of test and the material it will cover help you choose the best study method.

---

[3]Example from Jim Somchai, "Memory and Visualization," EzineArticles.com, ezinearticles.com/?Memory-and-Visualization&id=569553.

Mnemonics are a sort of mental filing system that provide a way of organizing material. They probably aren't needed if what you are studying is logical and organized, but they can be really useful when material doesn't have a pattern of its own. Although using mnemonics can be helpful in remembering information, it takes time to think up rhymes, associations, or visual images that have limited use when you need to analyze or explain the material in depth.

STUDYING TO UNDERSTAND AND REMEMBER

Studying will help you accomplish two goals: understanding and remembering. While memory is a necessary tool for learning, what's most important is that you study to develop a deep understanding of course information. When you really comprehend what you are learning, you will be able to place names, dates, and specific facts in context. You will also be able to exercise your critical-thinking abilities.

Here are some methods that might be useful when you're trying to remember detailed information:

- **Pay attention and avoid distractions.** This suggestion is the most basic, but the most important. If you're sitting in class thinking about everything except what the professor is saying, or if you're reading and you find that your mind is wandering, you're wasting your time. Force yourself to focus. Review your responses to the questions posed in the exercise you completed earlier in this chapter about what you're willing to do to improve your concentration.
- **Be confident that you can improve your memory.** Recall successes from the past when you learned things that you didn't think you could or would remember. Choose memory improvement strategies that best fit your preferred learning styles: aural, visual, read/write, or kinesthetic. Identify the courses where you can make the best use of each memory strategy.
- **Overlearn the material.** Once you think you understand the material you're studying, go over it again to make sure that you'll remember it for a long time. Test yourself, or ask someone else to test you. Repeat what you're trying to remember out loud and in your own words.
- **Explain the material to another person.**
- **Make studying a part of your daily routine.** Don't allow days to go by when you don't open a book or work on course assignments. Make studying a daily habit!
- **Check the Internet.** If you're having trouble remembering what you have learned, Google a key word and try to find interesting details that will engage you in learning more about the subject. Many first-year courses cover such a large amount of material that you might miss some interesting details unless you look for them yourself. As your interest increases, so will your memory about the topic. Make sure to check multiple online sources.

- **Go beyond memorizing words and focus on understanding and then remembering the big concepts and ideas.** Keep asking yourself questions like: What is the main point here? Is there a big idea? Whenever you begin a course, review the syllabus, talk with someone who has already taken the course, and take a brief look at all the reading assignments. Having the big picture will help you understand and remember the details of what you're learning. For example, the big picture for a first-year college success class is to give students the knowledge and strategies to be successful in college.

- **Look for connections between your life and what's going on in the content of your courses.** College courses might seem unrelated to you and your goals, but if you look more carefully, you'll find many connections between course material and your daily life. Seeing those connections will make your courses more interesting and will help you remember what you're learning. For example, if you're taking a sociology class and studying marriage and the family, think about how your own family experiences relate to those described in your readings or in the lectures.

- **Get organized.** If your desk or your computer is organized, you won't waste time trying to remember where you put a particular document or what name you gave to a file. And as you rewrite your notes, putting them in an order that makes sense to you (for example, by topic or by date) will help you learn and remember them.

PEER LEADERS › One of the factors that prevents some students from becoming more organized is the time it takes to get started. Share how you organize your life, your time, and your work or living space. Let students know if staying organized is a challenge for you, and how you work to overcome that challenge.

high-impact practice 3

HIGH-IMPACT PRACTICE › By collaborating with other students and a peer leader, your students will better understand the benefits of getting organized.

---

your turn Work Together

Is It Worth the Time and Effort to Get Organized?

With a small group of your classmates, share how organized you are in your living space and on your computer. Is your living space more or less organized than your laptop, desktop, or iPad? Do group members think that being organized is important? How does being disorganized affect time management? Work with your peer leader to come up with strategies to be more organized. Keep track of the initial time you spend getting organized, and the time you save over a two- or three-week period by being more organized.

- **Reduce the stress in your life.** Many college students experience stress because they have to juggle college, work, and family life. Stress-reducing habits, such as eating well and getting enough exercise and sleep, are especially important for college students (see the "Wellness" chapter for strategies). Remember, too, that your college probably has a counseling center or health center where you can seek help in dealing with whatever might be causing stress in your daily life.

IN CLASS › Have students discuss how stress can affect memory. What experiences have they had when stress caused memory problems? Ask for a student volunteer to research whether or not your counseling center offers any kind of anxiety- or stress-management workshops, and have that student report to the class.

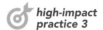
Work Together

One way to enhance your memory is to study with others. Each of you can check specific facts and details and share the strategies you use to remember them. You can also motivate and support one another.

Digital Vision/Getty Images

IN CLASS > Offer to help students form study groups. Make sure that each group includes both strong students and those who need help.

IN CLASS > Divide the class into groups and ask students to brainstorm the pros and cons of study groups. Have each group report to the class. Ask the class to offer suggestions on how to create and maintain effective study groups.

RETENTION STRATEGY > Explain that research has discovered that students who seek assistance from others in college are more likely to be successful.

- **Collaborate.** In your first year of college, join a group of students who study together. Your instructors or the college learning center can help you organize study groups. Study groups can meet throughout the term or can get together only to review for midterm or final exams.
- **Get a tutor.** Tutoring is not just for students who are failing. Often the best students ask for help to make sure that they understand course material. Most tutors are students, and at most community colleges, tutoring services are free.

As you learned in this chapter, memory and concentration play very important roles in achieving success in college because they help you understand, remember, and deeply learn the material so that you can apply that learning to your career and life.

checklist for success

Studying

▢ **Make studying a part of your daily routine.** Don't allow days to go by when you don't crack a book or keep up with course assignments.

▢ **Manage your study time wisely.** Create a schedule that will allow you to prepare for exams and complete course assignments on time. Be aware of "crunch times" when you might have several exams or papers due at once. Create some flexibility in your schedule to allow for unexpected distractions.

▢ **Collaborate.** One of the most effective ways to study is in a group with other students.

▢ **Be confident that you can improve your memory.** Remind yourself occasionally of things you have learned in the past that you didn't think you could or would remember.

▢ **Choose the memory improvement strategies that best fit your preferred learning style(s): aural, visual, read/write, or kinesthetic.** Identify the courses where you can make the best use of each memory strategy.

▢ **Go beyond simply trying to memorize words, and focus on trying to understand and remember the big concepts and ideas.** Keep asking yourself: What is the main point here? Is there a big idea? Am I getting it?

▢ **Be alert for external distractions.** Choose a place to study where you can concentrate, and allow yourself uninterrupted time to focus on the material you are studying.

▢ **Get a tutor.** Tutoring is not just for students who are failing. Often the best students seek assistance to ensure that they fully understand course material. Most tutors are students, and most campus tutoring services are free.

REFLECT ON CHOICES

high-impact practice 2 Reflect on what you have learned about college success in this chapter and how you will apply the chapter information or strategies in college and in your career. Without opening your book, write a brief paper summarizing what you learned in this chapter. Then go back to the chapter subheadings to see what you remembered and what you might have forgotten. Which of the strategies presented in this chapter were already familiar to you, and which new ones will you choose to adopt?

APPLY WHAT YOU HAVE LEARNED

Now that you have read and discussed this chapter, consider how you can apply what you have learned to your academic life and your personal life. The following prompts will help you reflect on the chapter material and its relevance to you both now and in the future.

1. Give mnemonics a try. Choose a set of class notes that you need to study for an upcoming quiz or exam. As you study, pick one concept and create your own acronym, acrostic, rhyme, song, or visualization to help you remember.

2. The way that students study in high school is often very different from the way they need to study in college. It can be difficult to adapt to new ways of doing things. Write a one-page paper describing how you studied in high school and how you can improve on those habits to do well in college.

USE YOUR RESOURCES

> **Learning Assistance Center**
  Here, staff can help you develop effective memory strategies. Pay a visit and ask about specific workshops or one-on-one assistance with memory.

> **Peers and Your Peer Leader**
  Ask fellow students and your peer leader to share their own tips for improving memory.

> **Your Instructor**
  Ask your instructor if there is someone on your campus who is an expert on memory strategies. If so, make an appointment to meet that person.

> **The Library**
  Your college or university library will have many books on the topic of memory. Some were written by researchers for the research community, but others were written for people like you. Download or check out a book on memory to see what you can learn. Here are some good options: Tony Buzan, *Use Your Perfect Memory*, 3rd ed., (New York: Penguin Books, 1991); Kenneth L. Higbee, *Your Memory: How It Works and How to Improve It*, 2nd ed., (New York: Marlowe, 2001); Harry Lorayne, *Super Memory, Super Student: How to Raise Your Grades in 30 Days* (Boston: Little, Brown, 1990). Ask your college librarian to help you identify some helpful online resources as well, such as this site that offers memorization techniques, maintained by the Alamo Community College District: **alamo.edu/memory**.

 LaunchPad

LaunchPad for *Your College Experience* is a great resource. Go online to master concepts using the LearningCurve study tool and much more. macmillanhighered.com/gardner12e

9
TEST TAKING

YOU WILL EXPLORE

Ways to prepare for exams physically, emotionally, and academically

Tips for test taking

Strategies for taking different types of tests and handling various question types

How to overcome test anxiety

What cheating is, how to avoid it, and how to maintain academic honesty

⚙ High-impact practices 2 (writing) and 3 (collaboration)

Nicole Bradley, 24

Nursing major
University of Washington

❝ The first step to improving my test-taking abilities was changing my attitude about my 'academic self.' ❞

Nicole Bradley grew up all over the country, moving with her parents as part of a military family. "My parents were young and adventurous and willing to move wherever the military sent them," she says. At age sixteen, she landed in Bothell, Washington, near Seattle, and was able to finish high school. Soon after her graduation, Nicole gave birth to a son and found herself working to support herself and her child. For a while, college was the furthest thing from her mind, but eventually she realized that she wanted more for her son—and for herself. "Ultimately, being a single mother is what motivates me, not only to provide a better life for both of us, but also to set an example that was not always set for me," she explains.

Part of going to college and raising a family involves finding that ever-elusive work-life balance in areas such as preparing for tests. Nicole always thought that she just wasn't good at taking tests or learning, so she usually finished in the middle of the pack on tests and exams. "The first step to improving my test-taking abilities," she says, "was

changing my attitude about my 'academic self.'" Once Nicole worked to improve her attitude, she began looking at the test-preparation strategies that worked best for her. One thing she figured out was that note taking was integral to a good performance on tests. "I found that I remember things best by relating them to things that I already know," she says. Now she knows to take careful notes during class, underline key terms, and make additional marginal notes so that when she gets home, she can create associations to help with memory. She also knows that her brain works best when the rest of her body is well cared for and has plenty of rest, good food, exercise, and often meditation and relaxation. "It works better than cram studying, and I get a lot more out of my courses and do better on my exams," she explains.

As with many things in life, Nicole realizes that with test taking, you sometimes have to get it wrong before you get it right. Her advice to other first-year students? "Go back over the questions you got wrong on a test and try to figure out what you got wrong and why."

LaunchPad

To access the LearningCurve study tool, video activities, and more, go to LaunchPad for *Your College Experience.* macmillanhighered.com /gardner12e

Tests and exams are the primary ways that instructors will evaluate your learning. In general, tests are shorter than exams and will count less toward your overall course grade. A course might have only a final exam, or it might have a midterm and a final. These exams generally take two or more hours to complete and comprise a major component of your final grade in a course.

You can prepare for tests and exams in many ways. Sometimes you'll have to recall names, dates, and other specific bits of information. Many instructors, especially in courses such as literature and history, will also expect you to have a good overall understanding of the subject matter. Even in math and science courses, your instructors want you not only to remember the correct theory, formula, or equation, but also to understand

Victorpr/Shutterstock

and apply what you have learned. Knowing your preferred learning style, managing your time and energy, and using the study and memory strategies discussed in previous chapters will help you prepare for any kind of test or exam you face. This chapter provides you with several strategies to prepare for and take tests and exams successfully, describes types of tests and test questions you may encounter, and includes tips for managing test anxiety and maintaining academic honesty.

GETTING READY . . .

Believe it or not, you actually began preparing for tests on the first day of the term. Your lecture notes, assigned readings, and homework are all part of that preparation. As you get closer to the test day, you should know how much additional time you will need for review, what material the test will cover, and what format the test will take. It is very important to double-check the exam dates on the syllabus for each of your classes, as in Figure 9.1 on the next page, and to incorporate these dates into your overall plans for time management—for example, in your daily and weekly to-do lists.

Prepare for Test Taking

Tests are usually a major portion of your grade in college, so proper preparation for them is essential. Of course you need to understand the material, but there are many ways you can prepare for exams in addition to your regular study routines.

Find Out about the Test. Ask your instructor about the test format, how long the test will last, and how it will be graded. Find out the types of questions and the content that will be covered. Talk with your instructor to clarify any misunderstandings you might have about your reading or lecture notes. If you have a part-time instructor who does not have office hours, try to talk to him or her before or after class. Some instructors might let you view copies of old exams so that you can see the types of questions they use. Never miss the last class before an exam; your instructor might take part or all of that class session to summarize and review valuable information.

RETENTION STRATEGY > Many of us tell our students that learning is more important than grades. We should acknowledge, however, that grades do matter. First-year students who have earned A's and B's in high school may be shocked to see their first C, D, or worse. The material in this chapter will help students do their best to earn good grades, but make sure that you also encourage them not to give up on college if they receive a disappointing grade on a particular test or exam.

IN CLASS > Ask students what they know about midterm and final exam periods. Why do colleges set these times aside for examinations?

IN CLASS > Have your students check their schedules, and make sure that they have written down all their exam dates for each of their classes.

IN CLASS > Most college instructors would agree that essay exams measure learning far better than objective tests do. Explain why so many objective tests are given (e.g., large classes, easier to grade). Why do students need to alter their study methods according to the type of exam?

FIGURE 9.1 > Exam Schedule from Sample Course Syllabus

History 111, US History to 1865
Fall 2016

Examinations
Note: In this course, most of your exams will be on Fridays,
except for the Wednesday before Thanksgiving and the final.
This is to give you a full week to study for the exam and
permit me to grade them over the weekend and return the
exams to you on Monday. I believe in using a variety of
types of measurements. In addition to those scheduled
below, I reserve the right to give you unannounced quizzes
on daily reading assignments. Also, current events are fair
game on any exam! Midterm and final exams will be
cumulative (on all material since beginning of the course).
Other exams cover all classroom material and all readings
covered since the prior exam. The schedule is as follows:

Friday, 9/9: Objective type

Friday, 9/23: Essay type

Friday, 10/14: Midterm: essay and objective

Friday, 11/4: Objective

Wednesday, 11/16: Essay

Tuesday, 12/20: Final exam: essay and objective

RETENTION STRATEGY > Your
efforts to get students to learn
more about different types
of tests and what they might
cover provides another chance
for you to urge students
to take advantage of your
institution's academic support
opportunities. Supplemental
Instruction (SI) is a highly
validated strategy for doing
this. If your institution doesn't
offer SI, then an alternative
is for your learning center
personnel to advise students
about testing procedures in
any given course.

Design an Exam Plan. Use information about the test as you design an
exam-preparation plan. Create a schedule that will give you time to review
for the exam without waiting until the night before. Develop a to-do list of
the major steps you need to take to be ready, and schedule review dates. Be
sure that your schedule is flexible enough to allow for unexpected distrac-
tions or emergencies. If you are able to schedule your study sessions over
several days, your mind will continue to process the information between
study sessions, which will help you during the test. Be sure you have read
and learned all the material one week before the exam. That way, you can
use the week before the exam to review. In that final week, set aside several
one-hour blocks for review, and make specific notes on what you plan to do
during each hour. Also, let your friends and family know when you have
important exams coming up and how that will affect your time with them.

Use Online Quizzing.
Many textbooks have related Web sites that offer a number of study tools such as flash cards, videos, or online quizzing. Ask your instructors about these sites, and also check the preface of your textbooks for information on accessing these sites. You might also use Google to find them.

Join a Study Group.
As mentioned in previous chapters, joining a study group is one of the best ways to prepare for exams. Group members can share different views of the most important topics to review, quiz one another on facts and concepts, and gain support from other serious students. Some instructors will provide time in class for the formation of study groups, or you might choose to approach classmates on your own. You can always ask your instructor, academic adviser, or the college's tutoring or learning center professionals to help you find other interested students and decide on guidelines for the group. Study groups can meet throughout the term, or they can just review for midterms or final exams. Group members should prepare questions or discussion points before the group meets. If your study group decides to meet just before exams, allow enough time to share notes and ideas.

Talk to Other Students.
Other students, especially those who have previously taken a course you are currently taking from the same instructor, may be able to give you a good idea of what to expect on tests and exams. If your college is small, you shouldn't have any trouble finding students who have taken the same courses you are taking now. If you're at a large college, your instructor may be able to suggest a former student who could serve as a tutor. But keep in mind that your instructor might decide to take a different approach in your class than he or she did in past classes.

Get a Tutor.
Most colleges and universities offer free tutoring services. Ask your academic adviser, counselor, or college learning center staff members about arranging for tutoring. Keep in mind that some of the best

high-impact practice 3

HIGH-IMPACT PRACTICE ❯
Study groups are among the most powerful and well-researched collaborative strategies to improve student learning, especially in math and science.

RETENTION STRATEGY ❯
You can enhance student retention by facilitating meetings between your current students and your successful former students.

Strength in Numbers
Study groups can meet anytime, but studying and reviewing with others in your class can be most helpful just before and just after a test or exam.

students seek out tutoring, not just students who are struggling. Most students who receive tutoring are successful in their courses. Many learning centers employ student tutors who have done well in the same courses you are taking. These students might have some good advice on how to prepare for tests given by particular instructors. If you earn good grades in a specific course, you could eventually become a tutor and be paid for your services. Serving as a tutor also deepens your own learning and helps you become more successful in your major.

Prepare for Math and Science Exams

Math and science exams often require additional—and sometimes different—preparation techniques. Here are some suggestions for doing well on these exams:

- Do your homework regularly even if it is not graded, and do all the assigned problems. As you do your homework, write out your work as carefully and clearly as you will be expected to on your tests. This practice will allow you to use your homework as a review for the test. Figure 9.2 shows a page from a textbook with practice problems.
- Attend each class, always be on time, and stay for the entire class. Many instructors use the first few minutes of class to review homework, and others may end the class by telling you what will be on the test.
- Build a review guide throughout the term. As you begin your homework each day, write out a problem from each homework section in a notebook that you use solely to review material for that course. Then when you need to review for your exam, you can come back to this notebook to make sure you have a representative problem from each section you've studied.
- Throughout the term, keep a list of definitions or important formulas and put them on flash cards. Review several of them as part of every study session. Another technique is to post the formulas and definitions in your living space—on the bathroom wall, around your computer work area, or on the door of the microwave. Seeing this information frequently will help you keep it in your mind.

If these strategies don't seem to help you, ask a tutor to give you a few practice exams so you can review your responses together.

Prepare Physically

Keeping your body healthy is another key part of preparing yourself for quizzes, tests, and exams. The following strategies will help you prepare physically:

- **Maintain your regular sleep routine.** To do well on exams, you will need to be alert so that you can think clearly, and you are more likely to be alert when you are well rested. Last-minute, late-night cramming does not allow you to get sufficient sleep, so it isn't an effective study strategy. Most students need seven to eight hours of sleep the night before the exam.

IN CLASS > Have your students fill out an anonymous survey that asks how many hours of sleep they get each night, how much exercise they get each week, what kinds of foods they are most likely to eat, and what their overall levels of energy and concentration are. Compile and discuss the results. A staff member from the health and wellness center can be invited to class for this discussion.

IN CLASS > Ask the class how often they have crammed in a last-minute review of their notes just before a test is to begin. Tell the class that last-minute cramming usually will not improve a test score. It is better to prepare early and try to relax before the test starts.

FIGURE 9.2 ❯ Solving Practice Problems

Completing plenty of practice problems, like the ones shown here, is a great way to study for math and science classes. So try your hand at all the problems provided in your textbook—even those that your instructor hasn't assigned—and check out Web sites offering such problems. Source: Excerpt from page 315, COMAP, *For All Practical Purposes: Mathematical Literacy in Today's World*, 9th ed. Copyright © 2013 by W. H. Freeman. Used by permission.

(c) What is the probability that 5 cards drawn at random from a 52-card deck will yield a royal flush?

■ **30.** Biblical permutations: The King James Version of the Old Testament has its 39 books canonized in a different order than the Hebrew Bible does. What mathematical expression would yield the number of possible orders of these 39 books? Is this number larger than you expected?

8.4 Continuous Probability Models

31. Generate two random real numbers between 0 and 1 and take their sum. The sum can take any value between 0 and 2. The density curve is the shaded triangle shown in Figure 8.13.

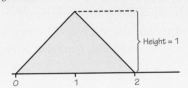

Figure 8.13 The density curve for the sum of two random numbers, for Exercise 31.

(a) Verify by geometry that the area under this curve is 1.
(b) What is the probability that the sum is less than 1? (Sketch the density curve, shade the area that represents the probability, and then find that area. Do this for part (c) as well.)
(c) What is the probability that the sum is less than 0.5?

32. Suppose two data values are each rounded to the nearest whole number. Make a density curve for the sum of the two roundoff errors (assuming each error has a continuous uniform distribution).

33. On the TV show *The Price Is Right*, the "Range Game" involves a contestant being told that the suggested retail price of a prize lies between two numbers that are $600 apart. The contestant has one chance to position a red window with a span of $150 that will contain the price. On one episode, the price of a piano is between $8900 and $9500. If we assume a uniform continuous distribution (i.e., that all prices within the $600 interval are equally likely), what is the probability that the contestant will be successful?

8.5 The Mean and Standard Deviation of a Probability Model

34. You have a campus errand that will take only 15 minutes. The only parking space anywhere nearby is a faculty-only space, which is checked by campus police about once every hour. If you're caught, the fine is $25.

(a) Give the probability model for the money that you may or may not have to pay.
(b) What's the expected value of the money that you will pay for your unauthorized parking?

35. Exercise 15 gives a probability model for the grade of a randomly chosen student in Statistics 101 at North Carolina State University, using the 4-point scale. What is the mean grade in this course? What is the standard deviation of the grades?

36. In Exercise 14, you gave a probability model for the intelligence of a character in a role-playing game. What is the mean intelligence for these characters?

37. Exercise 16 gives probability models for the number of rooms in owner-occupied and rented housing units. Find the mean number of rooms for each type of housing. Make probability histograms for the two models and mark the mean on each histogram. You see that the means describe an important difference between the two models: Owner-occupied units tend to have more rooms.

38. Typographical and spelling errors can be either "nonword errors" or "word errors." A nonword error is not a real word, as when "the" is typed as "teh." A word error is a real word, but not the right word, as when "lose" is typed as "loose." When undergraduates write a 250-word essay (without spell-checking), the number of nonword errors has this probability model:

Errors	0	1	2	3	4
Probability	0.1	0.2	0.3	0.3	0.1

The number of word errors has this model:

Errors	0	1	2	3
Probability	0.4	0.3	0.2	0.1

(a) What is the mean number of nonword errors in an essay?
(b) What is the mean number of word errors in an essay?
(c) How does the difference between the means describe the difference between the two models?

39. Find (and explain how you found) the mean for:

(a) the continuous probability model in Exercise 31.
(b) the probability model in Exercise 32.

■ **40.** The idea of insurance is that we all face risks that are unlikely but carry a high cost. Think of a fire destroying your home. Insurance spreads the risk: We all pay a small amount, and the insurance policy pays a large amount to those few of us whose homes burn down. An insurance

- **Follow your regular exercise program.** Exercise is a positive way to relieve stress and to give yourself a much-needed break from long hours of studying.
- **Eat right.** Eat a light breakfast before a morning exam, and avoid greasy or acidic foods that might upset your stomach. Limit the amount of caffeinated beverages you drink on exam day because caffeine can make you jittery. Choose fruits, vegetables, and other foods that are high in energy-rich complex carbohydrates. Avoid eating sweets before an exam; the immediate energy boost they create can be quickly followed by a loss of energy and alertness. Ask the instructor whether you may bring a bottle of water with you to the exam.

Prepare Emotionally

Just as physical preparation is important, so is preparing your attitude and your emotions. You'll benefit by paying attention to the following ideas:

- **Know the material.** If you have given yourself enough time to review, you will enter the classroom confident that you are in control. Study by testing yourself or quizzing others in a study group so that you will be sure you really know the information.
- **Practice relaxing.** Some students experience test anxiety, which can lead to upset stomachs, sweaty palms, racing hearts, and other unpleasant physical symptoms. The section on test anxiety later in this chapter includes an anxiety quiz; if that quiz reveals that test anxiety is a problem for you, consult your counseling center about relaxation techniques. Some campus learning centers also provide workshops on reducing test anxiety.
- **Use positive self-talk.** Instead of telling yourself, "I never do well on math tests" or "I'll never be able to learn all the information for my history essay exam," make positive statements, such as "I have always attended class, done my homework, and passed the quizzes. Now I'm ready to do well on the test!"

> **your turn** Stay Motivated
>
> **Avoid Becoming Discouraged**
>
> Are you sometimes down on yourself when you've performed poorly on a test or exam? Does your disappointment negatively affect your motivation to do well in a particular course or in college? Remember that a positive attitude, plus a clear plan for improvement, will both help you stay motivated to do your best and make you more resilient. Believe in your ability to overcome the temporary stumbling blocks that are part of everyone's college experience.

TIPS FOR TEST TAKING

Throughout your college career, you will take tests in many different formats, in many subject areas, and with many different types of questions. It may surprise you to find that your first-year tests are likely to be more challenging than those in later years because, as a new student, you are still developing your college test-taking skills. The following test-taking tips apply to any test situation.

IN CLASS > Remind students that many errors on tests, especially those that require problem solving, occur when a student does not read or follow directions. Ask students whether failing to follow directions has ever resulted in a poor test score for them. How does test anxiety relate to reading and following directions?

1. **Write your name on the test.** Usually you will have to write your name on a test booklet or answer sheet. Some instructors, however, may require you to fill in your student ID number.
2. **Look over the whole test and stay calm.** Carefully read all the directions before beginning the test so that you understand what to do.

Ask the instructor or exam monitor for clarification if you don't understand something. Be confident. Don't panic. Answer one question at a time.

3. **Make the best use of your time.** Quickly review the entire test and decide how much time you will spend on each section. Be aware of the point values of different sections of the test. If some questions are worth more points than others, you need to spend more of your time answering them.

4. **Jot down idea starters before the test.** Check with your instructor ahead of time to be sure that it is OK to write some last-minute notes on the test or on scrap paper. If so, then before you even look at the test questions, turn the test paper over and take a moment to write down the formulas, definitions, or major ideas you have been studying. This will help you go into the test with confidence and knowledge, and your notes will provide quick access to the information you may need throughout the test.

5. **Answer the easy questions first.** Expect that you won't completely understand some questions. Make a note to come back to them later. If different sections have different types of questions (such as multiple-choice, short-answer, and essay questions), first finish the types of questions that are easiest for you to answer. Be sure to leave enough time for any essays.

6. **If you feel yourself starting to panic or go blank, stop whatever you are doing.** Take a deep breath, and remind yourself that you will be OK and you do know the material and can do well on this test. If necessary, go to another section of the test and come back later to the item that triggered your anxiety.

7. **Try to answer each question, even if you can only provide a partial answer.** You may not be able to answer all the questions fully; provide as much information as you can remember. Particularly for math and science test questions, you may get some credit for writing down equations and descriptions of how to solve the problems even if you cannot fully work them out or if you run out of time before you finish them.

8. **If you finish early, don't leave immediately.** Stay and check your work for errors. Reread the directions one last time.

TYPES OF TESTS

While you are in college, you will take many different types of tests. Some may be used in specific subjects such as English or math; others can be used in any class you might take. This section discusses the different test types and presents helpful tips for succeeding on each one.

Problem-Solving Tests

In science, mathematics, engineering, and statistics courses, some tests will require you to solve problems and show all the steps that led to the solution. Even if you know a shortcut, it is important to document how you got from step A to step B. For these tests, you must also be careful to avoid errors in your scientific notation. A misplaced sign, parenthesis, or bracket can make all the difference.

If you are allowed to use a calculator during the exam, it is important to check that your input is accurate. The calculator does what you tell it to, and if you miss a zero or a negative sign, the calculator will not give you the correct answer to the problem.

Read all directions carefully. Whenever possible, after you complete the problem, work it in reverse to check your solution. Also check to make sure that your solution makes sense. You can't have negative bushels of apples, for example, or a fraction of a person, or a correlation less than negative 1 or greater than 1.

Machine-Scored Tests

For some tests, you may have to enter your answers on a Scantron form. The instructor will feed those forms into a machine that scans the answers and prints out your score. When taking any test, especially a machine-scored test, carefully follow the directions. In addition to your name, be sure to provide all other necessary information on the answer sheet. Each time you fill in an answer, make sure that the number on the answer sheet corresponds to the number of the item on the test.

Although scoring machines have become more sophisticated over time, they might still misread stray marks or incomplete bubbles on your answer sheet. When a machine-scored test is returned to you, check your answer sheet against the scoring key, if one is provided, to make sure that you receive credit for all the questions you answered correctly.

Example of a Scantron Answer Sheet

Each time you fill in a Scantron answer sheet, make sure that the number on the answer sheet corresponds to the number of the item on the test, and make sure that all bubbles are filled in completely.

Vixit/Shutterstock

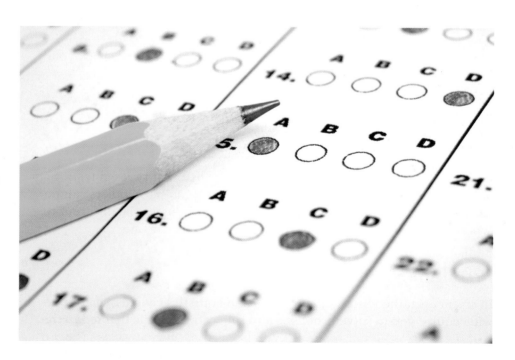

Computerized Tests

Computerized tests are often taken in a computer lab or testing center and are usually *not* administered online. (Read this chapter's Tech Tip about *online* tests.) Computerized tests and test questions can be significantly different from one another depending on the kind of test, the academic subject, and whether the test was written by the instructor, a textbook company, or another source. Be sure to take advantage of any practice test opportunities to get a better sense of what these tests and test questions will be like. Often they are timed, as is the case with most computerized placement tests. The more experience you have with computerized tests, the more comfortable you will be taking them, which is true with the other test types.

Some multiple-choice computerized tests allow you to scroll through all the questions, while others only allow you to see one question at a time. Some computerized tests might not allow you to return to questions you've already completed to double-check your answers.

For computerized tests in math and other subjects that require you to solve problems, be sure to check each answer before you submit it. Also, know in advance whether you are allowed to use additional materials, such as a calculator or scratch paper, for working the problems.

Laboratory Tests

In many science courses, you will have laboratory tests that require you to move from one lab station to the next to solve problems, identify parts of models or specimens, or explain chemical reactions. To prepare for lab tests, always attend your labs, take good notes, and study your lab notebook carefully before the test.

You might also have lab tests in foreign language courses that can include both oral and written sections. Work with a partner or study group to prepare for oral exams. Have group members ask one another questions that require the use of key vocabulary words.

Open-Book and Open-Notes Tests

Although you may like the idea of being able to refer to your book or notes during an exam, open-book and open-note tests are usually harder than other tests, not easier. You won't really have time to read whole passages during an open-book exam. Study as completely as you would for any other test, and do not be fooled into thinking that you don't need to know the material. The best way to prepare for an open-book test is to study as you would for any other test. But as you prepare, you can develop a list of topics and the page numbers where they are covered in your text or in your lecture notes. Type a three-column grid (or use an Excel spreadsheet) with your list of topics in alphabetical order in the first column and corresponding pages from your textbook and lecture notebook in the second and third columns so that you can refer to them quickly when necessary.

During the test, keep an eye on the time. Don't waste time looking up information in your text or notes if you are sure of your answers. Instead, wait until you have finished the test, and then, if you have extra time, go back and look up answers and make any necessary changes.

IN CLASS > Ask students to think about the challenges of an open-book or open-note test. As an exercise, give the class an open-book test and ask them to work together in groups to complete the test. Then ask them which techniques worked and which did not.

your concentration, you will be glad to have the outline to help you regain your focus. If you find that you are running out of time and cannot complete an essay question, provide an outline of key ideas at the very least. Instructors usually assign points on the basis of your coverage of the main topics from the material. That means you will usually earn more points by responding briefly to all parts of the question than by addressing just one part of the question in detail. You might receive some credit for your outline even if you cannot finish the essay.

4. **Write concise, organized answers.** Some students answer essay questions by quickly writing down everything they know on the topic. Long answers are not necessarily good answers. Answers that are too general, unfocused, or disorganized may not earn high scores.

5. **Know the key task words in essay questions.** Being familiar with key task words that appear in an essay question will help you frame your answer more specifically. Table 9.1 lists common key task words. If your instructor allows you to do so, consider circling or underlining key words in the question so that you are sure of how to organize your answer.

IN CLASS > Divide the class into groups of four to five. Ask each group to prepare several potential essay questions from their notes, using the key task words you have assigned to them.

TABLE 9.1 › Key Task Words in Essay Questions

Analyze	Break the whole topic into parts to explain it better; show how the parts work together to produce the overall pattern.
Compare	Identify similarities in ideas, events, or objects. Don't just describe the elements; state how they are alike.
Contrast	Identify the differences between ideas, events, or objects. Don't just describe the ideas; state how they are different.
Criticize/Critique	Judge something; give your opinion. Criticism can be positive, negative, or mixed. A critique should generally include your own judgments (supported by evidence) and those of experts who agree with you.
Define	Give the meaning of a word or expression.
Describe	Give more information about a topic.
Discuss	Give broad statements backed up by detailed information. Discussion often includes identifying the important questions related to an issue and trying to answer these questions.
Evaluate	Discuss the strengths and weaknesses of an idea or a position. When you evaluate, you stress the idea of how well something meets a certain standard.
Explain	Clarify a statement. Explanations generally focus on why or how something has come about.
Justify	Argue in support of a decision or conclusion by showing evidence or reasons that support the argument. Try to support your argument with both logical and concrete examples.
Narrate	Relate a series of events in the order they occurred, as you do when you tell a story.
Outline	Present a series of main points in order. Some instructors want a formal outline with numbers and letters.
Summarize	Give information in brief form, without examples and details. A summary is short but covers all the important points.

Multiple-Choice Questions

Multiple-choice questions provide a number of possible answers, often between three and five. The answer choices are usually numbered (1, 2, 3, 4, . . .) or lettered (a, b, c, d, . . .), and the test taker is supposed to select the correct or the best one. Preparing for multiple-choice tests requires you to actively review all of the material that has been covered for a specific period, such as a week or a month. Reviewing flash cards, summary sheets, mind maps, or the recall column in your lecture notes is a good way to review large amounts of material efficiently.

Look for particular cues and quirks that multiple-choice questions include. Take extra care when choosing the answer to questions that contain words such as *not, except, all,* and *but.* Also read each answer choice carefully; be suspicious of choices that use words such as *always, never,* and *only.* These choices are often (but not always) incorrect. Often the correct answer is the option that is the most comprehensive.

In some multiple-choice questions, the first part of the question is an incomplete sentence called the stem, and the answer choices complete the sentence. In these questions, any answer choices that do not fit the grammar of the stem correctly are usually wrong. For example, in Figure 9.3, "Margaret Mead was an" is the stem. Which of the four answer options does not grammatically fit the stem, and can therefore be ruled out?

IN CLASS > Tell students that when answering multiple-choice questions, the first answer that comes to mind is usually the correct one. In general, students should try not to second-guess themselves.

FIGURE 9.3 > Example of a Multiple-Choice Question

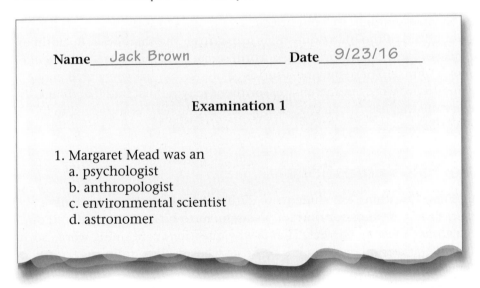

Name __Jack Brown_____ Date __9/23/16__

Examination 1

1. Margaret Mead was an
   a. psychologist
   b. anthropologist
   c. environmental scientist
   d. astronomer

To avoid becoming confused by answer choices that sound alike, predict your own answer to the question before reading the options. Then choose the answer that best matches your prediction.

If you are totally confused by a question, place a check mark in the margin and come back to it later. Sometimes a question later in the exam may provide a clue to the answer of the question you are unsure about. If you have absolutely no idea, look for an answer that at least has some pieces of information. If there is no penalty for guessing, fill in an answer for every question, even if it is just a guess. If there is a penalty for guessing, don't just choose an answer at random; leaving the answer blank might be a wiser choice. Finally, always go back, if you have time at the end, and double-check that you chose the right answer for the right question, especially if you are using a Scantron form.

high-impact
practice 3

HIGH-IMPACT PRACTICE ▸ This group activity will help your students reflect on the exams they will take during the first term of college. As they discuss these exams, they may be surprised to learn that student exam preferences are not always the same.

> **your turn**   Work Together
>
> ### Is One Type of Exam Better than Another?
>
> Many college instructors do not give essay exams in first-year courses, and instead use multiple-choice questions. With a small group of other students, discuss the kind of learning that multiple-choice exams measure, and the kind of learning they miss. Which type of exam do students in the group prefer? Share your reactions and ideas with the whole class.

Fill-in-the-Blank Questions

Fill-in-the-blank questions consist of a phrase, sentence, or paragraph with a blank space indicating where the student should provide the missing word or words. In many ways, preparing to answer fill-in-the-blank questions is similar to getting ready to answer multiple-choice items, but fill-in-the-blank questions can be harder because you do not have a choice of possible answers right in front of you.

Not all fill-in-the-blank questions are written the same way. Sometimes the answers will consist of a single word; sometimes the instructor is looking for a phrase. There may be a series of blanks to give you a clue about the number of words in the answer, or there may be just one long blank. If you are unsure, ask the instructor whether the answer is supposed to be one word or more.

True/False Questions

True/False questions ask students to determine whether a statement is correct or not. Remember that for a statement to be true, every detail of the sentence must be correct. That is why questions containing words such as *always, never,* and *only* tend to be false, whereas less definite terms such as *often* and *frequently* suggest the statement might be true. Read through the entire exam to see whether information in one question will help you answer another. Do not begin to second-guess what you know or doubt your answers just because a sequence of questions appears to be all true or all false.

Matching Questions

Matching questions are set up with terms in one column and descriptions or definitions in the other, and you must match the proper term with its definition. Before matching any items, review all of the terms and descriptions. Then match the terms you are sure of. As you do so, cross out both the term and its description, and use the process of elimination to help you answer the remaining items. To prepare for matching questions, try using flash cards and lists that you create from the recall column in your notes.

OVERCOMING TEST ANXIETY

Test anxiety takes many different forms. Part of dealing with test anxiety is understanding why it happens and identifying its symptoms. Whatever the reason for test anxiety, you should know that it is common among college students.

Test anxiety has many causes. It can be the result of the pressure that students put on themselves to succeed. Some stress connected with taking exams is natural and can motivate you to perform better. However, when students put too much pressure on themselves or set unrealistic goals, the result can be stress that is no longer motivating. The expectations of parents, a spouse or partner, friends, and other people who are close to you can also create test anxiety.

Finally, some test anxiety is caused by lack of preparation. The awareness that you are not prepared, that you have fallen behind on assigned reading, homework, or other academic commitments, is usually the source of anxiety. Procrastination can also be a big problem because if you do poorly on the first test in a course, you will be under even more pressure to do well on other tests to pull up your course grade. This situation becomes even more difficult if the units of the course are cumulative—that is, if they build on one another, as in math and foreign languages—or if the final exam includes all the material that has been covered throughout the course.

Some test anxiety comes from a negative prior experience. Forgetting past failures can be a challenge; however, the past is not the present. If you carefully follow the strategies in this chapter, you are likely to do well on future tests. Remember that a little anxiety is OK, but if you find that anxiety is getting in the way of your performance on tests and exams, be sure to ask for help from your college counseling center.

Ace the Test—Any Type of Test

No matter what type of test you are taking, read each question carefully so that you have the best chance of selecting the right answer. And remember, when you take a machine-scored test, one of the simplest and most important steps you can take is to make sure you match the questions with your answer sheet numbers.
© fStop/Alamy

IN CLASS > Ask students to share their experiences with test anxiety. Discuss the underlying causes of test anxiety.

IN CLASS > Invite a student development counselor or other staff member who has experience helping students with test anxiety. Ask this person to your class to share his or her expertise and provide practical ways to control test anxiety. Also tell students about any free workshops on anxiety-management techniques offered by your college's counseling center. Tell your students that being anxious about taking tests is normal, not a sign of weakness or illness.

Symptoms of Test Anxiety

Test anxiety can manifest itself in many ways. Some students feel it on the very first day of class. Other students begin showing symptoms of test anxiety when it's time to start studying for a test. Others do not get nervous until the night before the test or the morning of an exam day. And some students experience symptoms only while they are actually taking a test.

Symptoms of test anxiety can include:

- butterflies in the stomach
- queasiness
- nausea
- headaches
- an increased heart rate
- hyperventilation, which is unusually deep or rapid breathing as a result of anxiety
- shaking, sweating, or muscle cramps
- "going blank" during the exam and being unable to remember information

Test anxiety can undermine the success of any college student, no matter how intelligent, motivated, and prepared. That is why it is important to seek help from your college's counseling service or another professional if you think that you have severe test anxiety. If you are not sure where to go for help, ask your adviser or counselor, but seek help promptly! If your symptoms are so severe that you become physically ill (with headaches, hyperventilation, or vomiting), you should also consult your physician or campus health center.

Types of Test Anxiety

Students who experience test anxiety don't necessarily feel it in all testing situations. For example, you might do fine on classroom tests but feel anxious during standardized examinations such as a college placement test. One reason such standardized tests can create anxiety is that they can change your future. One way of dealing with this type of test anxiety is to ask yourself: What is the worst that can happen? Remember that no matter what the result, it is not the end of the world. How you do on standardized tests might limit some of your options, but going into these tests with a negative attitude will certainly not improve your chances for success.

Test anxiety can often be subject-specific. For example, some students have anxiety about taking math tests. It is important to understand the differences between anxiety that arises from the subject itself and general test anxiety. Perhaps subject-specific test anxiety relates to old beliefs about yourself, such as "I'm no good at math" or "I can't write well." Now is the time to try some positive self-talk and realize that by preparing well, you can be successful even in your hardest courses. If the problem continues, talk to a counselor to learn about strategies that can help you deal with such fears. Take the following test anxiety quiz to find out more about how you feel before taking tests.

IN CLASS > Share your personal experiences with test anxiety. What memories do you have, particularly with high-stakes tests such as the SAT or ACT?

OUTSIDE CLASS > Have students do an Internet search on test anxiety. Claude Steele, a professor at Stanford University, researched student performance on high-stakes exams and found that one of the major barriers to the achievement of blacks, women, and other underrepresented groups is a phenomenon he calls "stereotype threat," the threat of being viewed through the lens of a negative stereotype or the fear of doing something that would inadvertently confirm that stereotype (**pbs.org/wgbh /pages/frontline/shows/sats /interviews/steele.html**). A team of interested students can research Steele's work.

IN CLASS > Have the group make a class presentation on what they learned from their Internet research on test anxiety.

Test Anxiety Quiz

Do you experience feelings of test anxiety? Read each of the following questions and consider your responses. If your answer to a question is "yes," place a check mark in the box. If your answer is "no," leave the box blank.

Mental

☐ Do you have trouble focusing and find that your mind easily wanders while studying the material or during the test itself?

☐ During the test, does every noise bother you—sounds from outside the classroom or sounds from other people?

☐ Do you often "blank out" when you see the test?

☐ Do you remember answers to questions only after the test is over?

Physical

☐ Do you get the feeling of butterflies, nausea, or pain in your stomach?

☐ Do you develop headaches before or during the test?

☐ Do you feel like your heart is racing, that you have trouble breathing, or that your pulse is irregular?

☐ Do you have difficulty sitting still, are you tense, or are you unable to get comfortable?

Emotional

☐ Are you more sensitive and more likely to lose patience with a roommate or friend before the test?

☐ Do you feel pressure to succeed, either from yourself or from your family or friends?

☐ Do you toss and turn the night before the test?

☐ Do you fear the worst—that you will fail the class or flunk out of college because of the test?

Personal Habits

☐ Do you often stay up late studying the night before a test?

☐ Do you have a personal history of failure in taking certain types of tests (essay, math, etc.)?

☐ Do you drink more than your usual amount of caffeine or forget to eat breakfast before a test?

☐ Do you avoid studying until right before a test, choosing to do other activities that are less important because you don't want to think about the test?

See the following for your Test Anxiety Reflection Score.

TEST ANXIETY REFLECTION SCORE

How many items did you check? Count your total, and then see what level of test anxiety you experience.

13–16 Severe: You may want to see if your college counseling center offers individual sessions to provide strategies for dealing with test anxiety. You have already paid for this service through your student fees, so if you have this level of anxiety, take advantage of help that is available for you.

9–12 Moderate: You may want to see if your counseling center offers a seminar on anxiety-prevention strategies. Such seminars are usually offered around midterms or just before final exams. Take the opportunity to do something valuable for yourself!

5–8 Mild: Be aware of what situations—whether it is certain types of classes or particular test formats—might cause anxiety and disrupt your academic success. If you discover a weakness, address it now before it is too late.

1–4 Slight: Almost everyone has some form of anxiety before tests, and it actually can be beneficial! In small doses, stress can improve your performance, so consider yourself lucky.

Bouncing Back from a Bad Grade

You bombed a test, and now you are feeling hopeless and unsure about how to do better. First, know that a bad grade is not the end of the world. Almost every student performs poorly at some point in college. Don't let one D or F get you down. Use the opportunity to build your resilience—to become stronger and show your tough spirit. One way to bounce back from disappointment is to take control of the situation. Talk to the course instructor, work to understand what went wrong, and develop a strategy for improvement. That strategy might be finding a tutor, meeting on a regular basis with your instructor, or working with a learning center professional who can help you improve your skills in reading, studying, remembering, and preparing for tests. Your college success instructor can help you decide what first steps you need to take to improve your academic performance.

CHEATING

Imagine what our world would be like if researchers reported fake results that were then used to develop new machines or medical treatments, or to build bridges, airplanes, or subway systems. Fortunately, few researchers falsify their findings; most follow the rules of academic honesty. That honesty is a foundation of higher education, and activities that jeopardize it can damage everyone: your country, your community, your college or university, your classmates, and yourself.

What Is Cheating?

Different colleges define *cheating* in different ways. Some include the following activities in their definition of cheating: looking over a classmate's shoulder for an answer, using a calculator when it is not permitted, obtaining or discussing an exam or individual questions from an exam without permission, copying someone else's lab notes, purchasing term papers over the Internet, watching the video instead of reading the book, and copying computer files. Whatever your college's rules about cheating, it's essential that you follow them.

Many schools do not allow certain activities, in addition to lying or cheating. Here are some examples of prohibited behaviors:

- intentionally inventing information or results
- submitting the same piece of academic work, such as a research paper, for credit in more than one course
- giving your exam answers to another student to copy during an exam or before that exam is given to another class

IN CLASS › Academic honesty is a serious issue. Review the types of misconduct and discuss the effect of the Internet on academic honesty. Bring in your campus's academic honesty policy for the class to discuss.

OUTSIDE CLASS › Ask the class to collect information about their college's definition of cheating, as well as the policies for addressing infractions of its rules about lying and cheating. Discuss their findings in class.

- bribing anyone in exchange for any kind of academic advantage
- helping or trying to help another student commit a dishonest act

Why Students Cheat and the Consequences of Cheating

Students mainly cheat when they believe they cannot do well on their own. Some college students developed a habit of cheating in high school or even earlier, and do not trust their own ability to succeed in classes. Other students simply don't know the rules. For example, some students incorrectly think that buying a term paper isn't cheating. Some think that using a test file (a collection of actual tests from previous terms) is fair behavior.

Cultural and college differences may cause some students to cheat. In other countries and at some U.S. colleges, students are encouraged to review past exams as practice exercises. Some student government associations or student social organizations maintain test files for use by students. Some colleges permit sharing answers and information for homework and other assignments with friends. Make sure you know the policy at your college.

Pressure from others—family, peers, and instructors—might cause some students to consider cheating. And there is no doubt that we live in a competitive society, where winning can trump all other values. But in truth, grades are nothing if you cheat to earn them. Even if your grades help you get a job, it is what you have actually learned that will help you keep that job and be promoted. If you haven't learned what you need to know, you won't be ready to work in your chosen field.

Sometimes lack of preparation will cause students to cheat. Perhaps they tell themselves that they aren't really dishonest and that cheating just "one time" won't matter. But if you cheat one time, you're more likely to do it again.

PEER LEADERS ❯ As a peer leader, you can help new students develop a clearer understanding of what is or is not considered cheating at your institution and how students can avoid all forms of academic dishonesty. Pull examples from your own experience to discuss misunderstandings students might have about the specific rules on your campus.

PEER LEADERS ❯ Write a one-page case study from your own or someone else's experience that presents a dilemma related to academic honesty. While it's OK to look for fictional case studies—there are many on the Internet—this instructional method is more powerful when the case is based on a real-life situation, especially one in which there is no clear right or wrong answer. Ask your instructor for feedback on your case study before presenting it to the class.

Stop! Thief!

When students sit close to each other while taking a test, they may be tempted to let their eyes wander to someone else's answers. Don't let this happen to you. Cheating is the same as stealing. Also, don't offer to share your work or make it easy for other students to copy your work. Reduce temptation by covering your answer sheet.

Jonathan Stark

Cheating in college is not uncommon, and researchers have found that first-year students are more likely to cheat than other students are. Although you might see some students who seem to be getting away with cheating, such behaviors can have severe and life-changing results. In some cases, students who have cheated on exams have been suspended or expelled, and graduates have had their college degrees revoked.

Here are some steps you can take to reduce the likelihood of problems with academic honesty.

1. **Know the rules.** Learn the academic code for your college by going to its Web site or checking the student handbook.
2. **Set clear boundaries.** Refuse when others ask you to help them cheat. This might be hard to do, but you must say no. Leave your cell phone in your book bag; instructors are often suspicious when they see students looking at their cell phones during an exam.
3. **Improve time management.** Be well prepared for all quizzes, exams, projects, and papers.
4. **Seek help.** Find out where you can get help with study skills, time management, and test taking. If your skills are in good shape but the content of the course is too hard, consult your instructor, join a study group, or visit your campus learning center or tutorial service.
5. **Withdraw from the course.** Your college has a policy about dropping courses and a deadline to drop without penalty. You might decide to drop a course that's giving you trouble. Some students choose to withdraw from all classes and take time off before returning to school if they find themselves in over their heads or if a long illness, a family crisis, or something else has caused them to fall behind. But before withdrawing, you should ask about college policies in terms of financial aid and other scholarship programs. See your adviser or counselor before you decide to withdraw.
6. **Reexamine goals.** Stick to your own realistic goals instead of giving in to pressure from family members or friends to achieve impossibly high standards. You might also feel pressure to enter a particular career or profession that doesn't interest you. If that happens, sit down with counseling or career services professionals or your academic adviser and explore your options.

FYI ❯ This simple point illustrates how many of the suggestions and topics of this book are closely interconnected. In this case, learning time-management skills will help students avoid getting into a time bind that might lead them to consider cheating.

FYI ❯ This simple but important issue brings us back to a key point from the beginning of the course about getting students to focus on their purposes for being in college in the first place. There is instructional and learning value to circling back to and repeating these very important points.

your**turn** Make Good Choices

Understand Academic Integrity

Sometimes students are confused about what constitutes dishonest behavior in their college classrooms. There are some actions that are on the line between cheating and being honest. Do you think it is acceptable to get answers from another student who took an exam you're about to take earlier in the term or in a prior term? What do you believe your instructors think? If you're not sure, ask your instructors how they view such behavior.

checklist **for** success

Test Taking

☐ **Learn as much as you can about the type of test you will be taking.** You will study differently for an essay exam than you will for a multiple-choice test.

☐ **Realize that you started preparing for test taking the very first day of the course.** Make the most of the first class sessions of the term—they are the most important ones *not* to miss. If you skip class, you are behind on your test preparation from day one.

☐ **Prepare yourself physically through proper sleep, diet, and exercise.** These behaviors are as important as studying the actual material. You may not control what is on the exams, but you can control your physical readiness to do your best.

☐ **Prepare yourself emotionally by being relaxed and confident.** Confidence comes from the knowledge that you have prepared well and know the material.

☐ **If you experience moderate to severe test anxiety, seek help from your counseling center.** Professionals can help you deal with this problem.

☐ **Develop a systematic plan of preparation for every test.** Be specific about when you are going to study, for how long, and what material you will cover.

☐ **Join a study group and participate conscientiously and regularly.** Students who join study groups perform better on tests. It's a habit you should practice.

☐ **Never cheat or plagiarize.** Experience the satisfaction that comes from learning and doing your own work and from knowing that you don't have to worry about getting caught or using material that may be incorrect.

☐ **Make sure that you understand what constitutes cheating and plagiarism on your campus so that you don't inadvertently do either.** If you are not clear about policies, ask your instructors or the professionals in your campus learning center or writing center.

REFLECT ON CHOICES

high-impact practice 2 | Test taking is an inevitable part of college life. But you can choose how you are going to prepare for tests, deal with any test anxiety you might feel, and pay attention to your grades and instructor feedback. Reflect on your biggest problem in taking tests. Is it with certain types of tests or all of them? Is it related to certain subjects or any subject? Write a brief summary of strategies you have learned in this chapter to deal with this problem.

APPLY WHAT YOU HAVE LEARNED

Now that you have read and discussed this chapter, consider how you can apply what you have learned to your academic and personal life. The following prompts will help you reflect on the chapter material and its relevance to you both now and in the future.

1. Identify your next upcoming test or exam. What time of day is it scheduled, and what type of test will it be? What strategies have you read about in this chapter that will help you prepare for and take this test?

2. Is there one course you are taking this term that you find especially difficult? If you are anxious about taking tests in that class, adopt a positive self-message to help you stay focused. It could be a favorite quote or even something as simple as "I know I can do it!"

USE YOUR RESOURCES

> **Learning Center**
Before you take your first tests, locate your campus's learning center. Almost every campus has one, and helping students study for tests is one of its specialties. The best students, good students who want to be the best students, and students with academic difficulties use learning centers and tutoring services.

These services are offered by both full-time professionals and highly skilled student tutors, and they are usually free. If you are an online student, there may be a special learning center that focuses on helping you do your best in online courses.

> **Counseling Services**
College and university counseling centers offer a wide array of services, including workshops and individual or group counseling for test anxiety. Sometimes these services are also offered by the campus health center. Ask your first-year seminar instructor where you can find counseling services on your campus. If you are an adult student, you may be very anxious about your first tests. Seek out services designed specifically for adults.

> **Fellow College Students and Peer Leaders**
Often the best help we can get is the closest to us. Keep an eye out in your classes, residence hall, and extracurricular activities for the best students, those who appear to be the most serious, purposeful, and directed. Find a tutor. Join a study group. Talk with your peer leader. Students who do these things are much more likely to be successful than those who do not.

> **College and University Exam Preparation Resources**
A wealth of helpful resources is available from many institutions. For instance, Florida Atlantic University's Center for Learning and Student Success (CLASS) offers a list of tips to help you prepare for exams: **fau.edu/CLASS /success/keys_to_success.php.** The State University of New York offers some excellent strategies for exam preparation: **blog.suny.edu/2013 /12/scientifically-the-best-ways-to-prepare-for -final-exams.** And here is some exam preparation advice from the University of Leicester in England: **le.ac.uk/offices/ssds/healthy-living -for-students/preparation-for-exams.**

LaunchPad

LaunchPad for *Your College Experience* is a great resource. Go online to master concepts using the LearningCurve study tool and much more. macmillanhighered.com/gardner12e

10
INFORMATION LITERACY AND COMMUNICATION

YOU WILL EXPLORE

What it means to be information literate

How to choose a topic, narrow it down, and research it

How to use your college or university library and get help from librarians

Strategies for evaluating sources

How to move from research to writing and effectively use all steps in the writing process

Guidelines for effective public speaking

High-impact practices 2 (writing) and 3 (collaboration)

Analee Bracero, 26

Criminal Justice major
Montclair State University

Start researching the topic you will be writing about as soon as possible.

When Analee was looking into going to college, she found that Montclair State University in New Jersey had everything she wanted: affordability, online courses, and a variety of student clubs. The college also has a good library that allows her to conduct research and write papers while on campus.

Analee grew up in a small town in Puerto Rico where she attended high school, completed a certificate program in medical office billing and coding, and then worked for a few years. When she decided that she wanted to change careers, she realized a degree in criminal justice was just what she needed. "I intend to join a law enforcement agency," she says. "My goal is to join the FBI as a behavior analyst."

Now that she is in college, Analee has had to develop a number of strategies to help her write well-researched papers that are very different from those she wrote in high school. "In high school, they didn't emphasize how important it was to include your opinions," she says. "In college, they

want you to research your work, cite as many sources as you can, think about your topic, and form opinions. It is very different for me." She tells us that her best strategy is to start early and prepare to write, rewrite, and edit the same material a few times before handing it in for a grade. "Start researching the topic you will be writing about as soon as possible," she advises. "Every day, look for more data and take additional notes. That way you can prevent procrastination and reduce your stress when it's time to put the research together on the paper."

Analee does most of her research online, where information is at her fingertips. She is careful about checking the validity of material she finds on the Web, especially on sites like Wikipedia. "I use Wikipedia and other online encyclopedias to start learning about a topic," she explains, "but I rely on other sources for writing my paper and carefully check any information I pull from the Web to ensure accuracy." She can access the databases she needs from her laptop or at the library.

To access the LearningCurve study tool, video activities, and more, go to LaunchPad for *Your College Experience.* macmillanhighered.com /gardner12e

A s Analee's story illustrates, developing the skills to locate and use information will increase your ability to keep up with what is going on in the world, participate in activities that interest you, and succeed in college, career, and community. The research skills you learn and use as a student will serve you well as a successful professional in whatever career you choose. Whether you're a student of nursing, political science, or business, one of your main tasks in college is to manage information. In a few years, as a nurse, lawyer, or accountant, one of your main tasks will be the same: to manage and present information for your employers and clients. All colleges and many companies provide libraries for this purpose.

Finding information and using it involves more than operating a computer or browsing the bookshelves. To make sense of the enormous amount of information at your fingertips in a reasonable amount of time, you'll need to develop a few key research and information-literacy skills.

INFORMATION LITERACY

Information literacy is the ability to find, interpret, and use information to meet your needs. It includes computer literacy, media literacy, and cultural literacy:

- **Computer literacy** is the ability to use electronic tools to conduct searches and to communicate and present to others the information you have found and analyzed. This ability involves using different computer programs, digital video and audio tools, and social media.
- **Media literacy** is the ability to think deeply about what you see and read through both the content and context of television, film, advertising, radio, magazines, books, and the Internet.
- **Cultural literacy** is knowing what has gone on and is going on around you. You have to understand the difference between the American Civil War and the Revolutionary War, U2 and YouTube, and Eminem and M&Ms so that you can keep up with everyday conversation and with your college reading material.

Information matters. It helps people make good choices. The choices people make often determine their success in careers, their happiness as friends and family members, and their well-being as citizens of our planet.

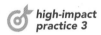

your **turn**   Work Together

Information Literacy—A Survival Skill?

Brainstorm with a group of classmates and make a list of the components of "information literacy." How many separate components did your group identify? This chapter asserts that information literacy is the premier survival skill for the modern world. Does your group agree? Why or why not? Share your group's ideas with others in the class.

Learning to Be Information Literate

People are amazed at the amount of information available to them everywhere, especially online. Many think that because they checked out some links they found on a search engine, they are informed or can easily become informed. Most of us, though, are unprepared for the number of available sources and the amount of information that we can find at the press of a button. What can we do about information overload? To become an informed and successful user of information, keep three basic goals in mind.

1. **Know how to find the information you need.** Once you have figured out where to look for information, you'll need to ask good questions and learn how to search information systems, such as the Internet, libraries, and databases. You'll also want to get to know your college librarians, who can help you ask questions, decide what sources you need to investigate, and find the information you need.

2. **Learn how to interpret the information you find.** It is important to find information, but it is even more important to make sense of that information. What does the information mean? Have you selected a source you can understand? Is the information correct? Can the source be trusted?

3. **Have a purpose for collecting information and then do something with it once you have it.** Even the best information won't do much good if you don't know what to do with it. True, sometimes you'll hunt down a fact simply to satisfy your own curiosity, but more often, you'll communicate what you've learned to someone else. First you should decide how to put your findings into an appropriate format, such as a research paper for a class or a presentation at a meeting. Then you need to decide what you want to accomplish. Will you use the information to make a decision, solve a problem, share an idea, prove a point, or something else?

In this chapter, we'll explore ways to work toward each of these goals.

What's Research—and What's Not?

In the past, you might have completed assignments that required you to find a book, journal article, or Web page related to a particular topic. While finding information is an essential part of research, it's just one step, not the end of the road. Research is not just copying a paragraph from a book or putting together bits and pieces of information without adding any of your own comments. In fact, such behavior could easily be considered plagiarism, a form of cheating that could result in a failing grade or worse. (Plagiarism is discussed later in this chapter.) At the very least, repeating information or ideas without thinking about or interpreting them puts you at risk of careless use of old, incorrect, or biased resources.

Research is a process of steps used to collect and analyze information to increase understanding of a topic or issue. Those steps include asking questions, collecting and analyzing data related to those questions, and presenting one or more answers. Good research is information literacy in action. If your instructor asks you to select and report on a topic, you might search for information about it, find a dozen sources, evaluate them, interpret them, discard a few, organize the ones you wish to keep, select related portions, write a paper or presentation that cites your sources, write an introduction that explains what you have done, draw some conclusions of your own, and submit the results. That's research. The conclusion that you make based on your research is new information!

IN CLASS > These days, many students confuse retrieval for research. Be sure to push them further. Emphasize the importance of evaluating, analyzing, and using information effectively, and consider giving assignments designed to have them truly benefit from working with a librarian.

RETENTION STRATEGY > Ask your students to research the topics of "college student success" or "college student retention." Encourage them to explore videos on college student success. Students are more likely to take their college success course seriously if they know there is credibility in what your institution is doing.

CHOOSING, NARROWING, AND RESEARCHING A TOPIC

Assignments that require the use of library materials can take many forms and will be a part of most of your classes. We'll consider several ways to search for information later in the chapter. Before you start searching, however, you need to have an idea of what you're looking for.

Choosing a topic is often the most difficult part of a research project. Even if an instructor assigns a general topic, you'll need to narrow it down to a particular aspect that interests you enough to research it. Imagine, for example, that you have been assigned to write a research paper on the topic of global warming. What steps should you take? Your first job is to get an overview of your topic. You can begin by conducting a Google search. Once you've found some basic information to guide you toward an understanding of your topic, you have a decision to make: What aspects of the subject will you research? Soon after you start researching your topic, you may realize that it is really large (for example, simply typing "global warming" into Google will return millions of hits) and that it includes many related subtopics.

You can use this new information to create keywords. A **keyword** is a word or phrase that tells an online search tool what you're looking for. You can create a list of keywords by brainstorming different terms and subtopics within your general topic. For example, for the topic "global warming," keywords may include "climate change," "greenhouse effect," "ozone layer," "smog," or "carbon emissions." Even those terms will generate a large number of hits, and you will probably need to narrow your search several times.

OUTSIDE CLASS > Create an assignment that shows students how important it is to narrow their research topics. They can also ask a librarian for help and practice keyword searches, as described later in the chapter.

What you want are twelve or so focused and highly relevant hits that you can use to write a well-organized essay. Begin by figuring out what you already know and what you would like to learn more about. Perhaps you know a little about global warming's causes and effects, and you're curious about its impacts on animals and plants. In that case, you might decide on a two-part topic: impacts on animals, impacts on plants. By consulting a few general sources, you'll find that you can narrow a broad topic to something that interests you and is a manageable size. You may end up focusing on the impact of global warming on one particular animal or plant in one specific geographical area.

If you are having trouble coming up with keywords, you can begin your research in an encyclopedia. Encyclopedias provide general overviews of topics. They can help you understand the basics of a concept or event, but you will need to use other resources for most college-level research projects. An encyclopedia is a great place to start your research, but not a good place to end it.

You have probably used an encyclopedia recently—you may use one all the time without thinking about it: Wikipedia. A *wiki* is a type of Web site that allows many different people to edit its content. This means that information on wikis can be constantly changing. Wikipedia is controversial in college work. Many instructors feel that the information on Wikipedia cannot be guaranteed to be reliable because anyone can change it; they instead want students to use sources that have gone through a formal editing and reviewing process. Your instructors might even forbid Wikipedia; if so, avoid it altogether. Even if an instructor permits the use of Wikipedia, it's best to use it only as a *starting point* for your research. Do not plan on citing Wikipedia in your final paper. Rather, check the references at the bottom of Wikipedia pages, or otherwise verify claims made at Wikipedia in another trustworthy source.

Even with an understanding of various types of sources, it can be difficult to determine exactly what you need for your assignment. Figure 10.1 provides an overview of when to use different common research sources and gives examples of what you'll find in each source.

USING THE LIBRARY

Whenever you have research to do for a class, your job, or your personal life, visit a library. We can't stress this enough. Although the Internet is loaded with billions of pages of information, don't be fooled into thinking

FIGURE 10.1 ▶ Using Common Research Sources

This information time line helps identify when and how to use each type of source, whether for classwork or for your personal life.

INFORMATION TIME LINE		
Source	**When to access information**	**What it offers**
Newspapers (print and online)	Daily/hourly after an event	Primary-source, firsthand discussions of a current event, and of what happened at the time of the event; short articles
Magazines	Weekly/monthly after an event	Analysis by a journalist or reporter of an event days or weeks after it occurred; longer articles than in newspapers; informally credits sources; might include more interviews or research as well as historical context
Scholarly articles	Months after an event	In-depth analyses of issues; research-based scientific studies with formally credited sources, written and reviewed by experts; contains graphs, tables, and charts
Books	Months/years after an event	A comprehensive overview of a topic with broad and in-depth analyses

it will serve all of your needs. For one thing, you'll have to sort through a lot of junk to find your way to good-quality online sources. More important, if you limit yourself to the Web, you'll miss out on some of the best materials. Although we often think that everything is electronic and can be found through a computer, a great deal of valuable information is still stored in traditional print formats and in your college library database.

Get to the Library

How often do you go to your campus library? Beyond having a library tour, have you explored this important academic resource? Although information is available from many sources, the most reliable resource will be a professional librarian, who can guide you to relevant books, articles, and online information.

Blend Images-Hill Street Studios/ Getty Images

IN CLASS > Share information with your students on the rich research resources available in your campus library. Have your students select a method—phone, e-mail, or in person—to contact a librarian and ask a question. Follow up with a short discussion about their experiences in contacting a librarian.

OUTSIDE CLASS > Many librarians will be glad to host a visit from you and your class. Provide the librarian with a copy of your assignment, and he or she will talk your students through the research process. Have a conversation with the librarian beforehand to ensure that he or she covers the topics you consider necessary for the assignment.

Every library has books, journals, and a great number of items in electronic databases that aren't available on public Web sites. Librarians at your college work with your instructors to determine the kinds of materials that support their teaching. Librarians carefully select well-respected and credible resources with you and your research in mind. Most libraries also have several other types of collections, such as government documents, microfilm, rare books, manuscripts, dissertations, fine art, photographs, historical documents, maps, music, and films, including archival and documentary productions. A key component of being information literate is determining the kinds of sources you need to satisfy your research questions.

A college library is far more than a document warehouse, however. For starters, most campus libraries have Web sites and apps that offer lots of help to students. Some provide guidelines on writing research papers, conducting online searches, or navigating the **stacks**—the area of a library where most of the books are shelved.

Of course, no one library can possibly own everything you might need or have enough copies of each item to satisfy demand, so groups of libraries share their materials with each other. If your college library does not have a journal or book that looks promising for your project, or if the item you need is checked out, you can use **interlibrary loan**, a service that allows you to request an item at no charge from another library at a different college or university. The request process is simple, and the librarians can help you get started.

If it is difficult for you to go to your college library because of commuting, family, work challenges, time constraints, or because you are an online student who lives far from campus, you will still have off-campus, online access to library materials through a school-provided ID and password. You can also have online chats with librarians who can help you in real time. To learn more, check your library's Web site, or e-mail or phone the reference desk. Be sure to use the handouts and guides that are available at the reference desk or online. You will also find tutorials and virtual tours that will help you become familiar with the collections, services, and spaces available at your library.

The 20-Minute Rule

If you have been working hard trying to locate information for a research project for 20 minutes and haven't found what you need, stop and ask a librarian for help. Let the librarian know what searches you've tried, and he or she will be able to help you figure out new strategies to get to the books, articles, and other sources you need. In addition, the librarian can help you develop strategies to improve your research and writing skills. Doing research without a librarian is like driving cross-country without a map or GPS—technically, you can do it, but you will get lost along the way and you may not get to your destination on time. Get to know at least one librarian as your go-to expert. College librarians are dedicated to helping students like you.

Scholarly Articles and Journals

Many college-level research projects will require you to use articles from **scholarly journals**, collections of original, peer-reviewed research articles written by experts or researchers in a particular academic

discipline. Examples are the *Journal of Educational Research* and the *Social Psychology Quarterly*. The term **peer-reviewed** means that other experts in the field read and evaluate the articles in the journal before they are published. You might find that some of your instructors use the terms *peer-reviewed* or *academic* to refer to scholarly articles or journals. Be sure to clarify what your instructor expects of your sources before you begin your research.

Scholarly articles focus on a specific idea or question and do not usually provide a general overview of a topic. For example, for the topic of climate change, you might find scholarly articles that compare temperature data over a certain period, analyze the effects of pollution, or explore public and political conversations on the topic. Scholarly articles always include a reference list that contains other sources related to the topic; you may find those sources useful in finding other relevant articles.

The most popular way to find scholarly articles is to use an online **database**, an organized and searchable set of information often categorized by subject areas. Some databases are specific to one subject, like chemistry, while others include articles from many different disciplines. Many libraries have dozens, if not hundreds, of databases. It can be difficult to figure out which ones you should use, but your librarian can help you determine which databases are best for your research.

When you use a database, you can easily add filters to ensure that your results include scholarly articles only, and you can clearly see who the authors are. Your database search should result in article and journal titles, descriptions, and sometimes full articles.

While some databases are available to anyone, whether that person is a student or instructor at a college, most of the databases you'll use for research in college are offered through subscription and are available only

IN CLASS ❯ Use an analogy to illustrate that there are different databases for different resources: You wouldn't go to the grocery store to buy lumber. Not everything is available in the same location. This is why it's important that students ask their professor or a librarian where to look.

Research consists of considering multiple perspectives on a topic, analyzing the sources, and creating something new from your analysis. Signs of bias, such as overly positive or overly harsh language, hints of a personal agenda, or a stubborn refusal to consider other points of view, indicate that you should question the credibility and accuracy of a source. Although nothing is wrong with someone having a particular point of view, as a researcher you need to be aware that the bias exists. You may need to exclude strongly biased sources from your research. For example, if you are writing about climate change, you will want to examine sources for evidence of political or personal agendas. The following questions can help you evaluate your sources:

- Who is the author?
- Why is the author interested in this topic? What is the author's goal in writing about this topic?
- Does the author present facts or personal opinions about the topic?
- Does the author provide evidence that is based on research or information from other sources? Does the author cite these sources?
- Are the conclusions the author makes based on sound evidence, or are they just based on the author's personal interests and opinions?
- What do you think is missing from the article?

high-impact practice 3

HIGH-IMPACT PRACTICE ❯ By working together, students can begin to understand that not all individuals see bias in the same way. Check in to make sure that the group discussion is respectful of all perspectives.

RETENTION STRATEGY ❯ We know that students who feel empowered—meaning they have a strong locus of control—perform better in college, and that this correlates with retention. This chapter addresses how students can become self-reliant seekers and users of information, and hence become more empowered.

your turn Work Together

What Can You Believe?

Working with a group of your classmates, develop a list of Web sites, blogs, newspapers, magazines, or TV networks that you believe are biased. Why do you consider them biased? Do some members of your group have different opinions about what is biased and what is not?

USING YOUR RESEARCH IN WRITING

You have probably heard the saying "Knowledge is power." But knowledge gives you power only if you put it to use in the form of what might be called a product. You have to decide what form that product will take—a piece of writing or a presentation—and what kind of power you want it to hold. Who is your audience and how will you present the information? What do you hope to accomplish by sharing your conclusions? Remember that a major goal of information literacy is to use information effectively to accomplish a specific purpose. Make it a point to do something with the results of your research. Otherwise, why bother? You researched information to find the answer to a question. Now is the time to formulate that answer and share it with others.

Many students satisfy themselves with a straightforward report that summarizes what they found, and sometimes that's enough. More often, though, you'll want to analyze the information and use that analysis to form your own ideas. To do that, first consider how the facts, opinions, and details you found from your different sources relate to one another. What do they have in common, and how do they differ? What conclusions can you draw from those similarities and differences? What new ideas did they spark? How can you use the information you have on hand to support your conclusions? Essentially, what you're doing at this stage of any research project is **synthesis**, a process in which you put together parts of ideas to come up with a whole result. By accepting some ideas, rejecting others, combining related concepts, and pulling it all together, you'll create new information and ideas that other people can use. Working through the steps of the writing process will get you where you need to go with your paper.

Along with your original ideas, your final paper will include analysis and synthesis of the sources you found through your research. You must make sure that you clearly state which thoughts and ideas came from the sources you found, and which are yours.

THE WRITING PROCESS

In college, your writing provides tangible evidence of how well you think and how well you understand the ideas you are learning in your courses. Your writing is your chance to show what you discovered through your research and to demonstrate your ability to analyze and synthesize sources into a new product that is uniquely your own. Like research, writing takes practice, and asking for help is always a good idea. This section will get you started by providing guidelines for effective and efficient writing.

Steps to Good Writing

The writing process typically includes three steps: (1) prewriting, (2) drafting, and (3) revising. Let's look at each of these steps in depth.

FIGURE 10.2 ❯ The Writing Process

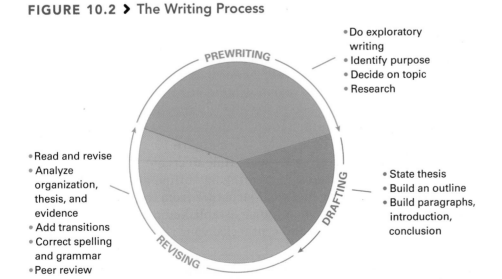

- Do exploratory writing
- Identify purpose
- Decide on topic
- Research

PREWRITING

DRAFTING

- State thesis
- Build an outline
- Build paragraphs, introduction, conclusion

REVISING

- Read and revise
- Analyze organization, thesis, and evidence
- Add transitions
- Correct spelling and grammar
- Peer review

Step 1: Using Prewriting to Discover What You Want to Say.

Engaging in prewriting activities is the first step in the writing process. Prewriting simply means writing things down as they come to mind—based on both the information you found through your research and your own ideas—without consciously trying to organize your thoughts, find exactly the right words, or think about structure. It can involve filling a page, whiteboard, or screen with words, phrases, or sentences.

The most commonly used prewriting activity is called **freewriting**. Freewriting simply means writing without worrying about punctuation, grammar, spelling, and background. Freewriting also helps you avoid the temptation to try to write and edit at the same time. It's impossible to write well while trying to organize, check grammar and spelling, and offer intelligent thoughts to your readers.[1] If you free-write on your computer or tablet, turn off the grammar and spelling checkers.

When you freewrite, you might notice that you have more ideas than can fit into one paper. This is very common. Fortunately, freewriting helps you choose, narrow, and investigate a topic. It helps you figure out what you really want to say as you make connections between different ideas. When you freewrite, you'll see important issues more clearly, and you can use these issues as keywords to help develop your theme. Remember, keywords are synonyms, related terms, or subtopics that we use to find materials for research papers.

high-impact practice 2

HIGH-IMPACT PRACTICE ❯ Free-writing is a strategy to get students to write without worrying about format and punctuation. It is the first step toward the more polished writing that students will do throughout their undergraduate years.

---

your turn   Write and Reflect

Give Freewriting a Try

Have you tried freewriting before? To see what freewriting feels like, write on this general prompt: important issues on our campus. Write for at least 10 minutes, nonstop, about that statement. Don't think about organization, grammar, punctuation, or spelling, and don't stop writing until the time is up.

Step 2: Drafting.

When you have completed your research with the help of your librarian, gathered a lot of information sources and ideas, and done some freewriting, it's time to move to the drafting stage. Before you start writing your draft, you need to organize all the ideas you generated in the freewriting step and form a **thesis statement**, a short statement that clearly defines the purpose of the paper (see Figure 10.3).

After you write your thesis, take some time to create an outline for your paper. Most students find that creating an outline helps them organize their thoughts, resulting in a clear structure from the thesis to the conclusion (see Figure 10.4). Once you've established the structure for your paper, you'll add analysis and synthesize your research findings, and

---

[1]Peter Elbow, *Writing without Teachers*, 2nd ed. (New York: Oxford University Press, 1998).

FIGURE 10.3 > Example of a Thesis Statement

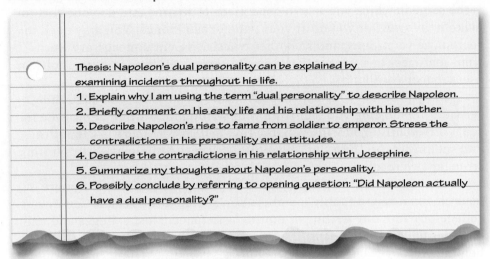

Thesis: Napoleon's dual personality can be explained by examining incidents throughout his life.
1. Explain why I am using the term "dual personality" to describe Napoleon.
2. Briefly comment on his early life and his relationship with his mother.
3. Describe Napoleon's rise to fame from soldier to emperor. Stress the contradictions in his personality and attitudes.
4. Describe the contradictions in his relationship with Josephine.
5. Summarize my thoughts about Napoleon's personality.
6. Possibly conclude by referring to opening question: "Did Napoleon actually have a dual personality?"

then you're well on your way to a final draft. Now, with your workable outline and thesis, you can begin to pay attention to the flow of ideas from one sentence to the next and from one paragraph to the next, including adding headings and subheadings where needed. If you have chosen your thesis carefully, it will help you evaluate whether each sentence relates to your main idea. When you have completed this stage, you will have the first draft of your paper in hand.

FIGURE 10.4 > Example of an Outline

An outline is a working document; you do not need a complete outline to begin writing. Note how this author has a placeholder for another example; she has not yet decided which example from her research to use.

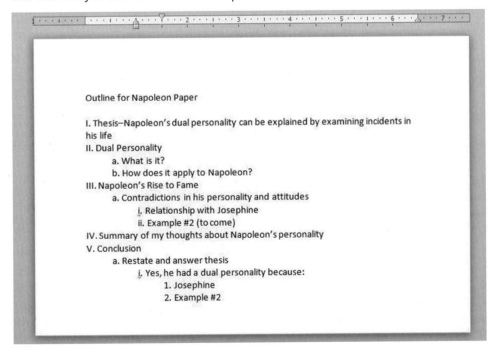

Outline for Napoleon Paper

I. Thesis—Napoleon's dual personality can be explained by examining incidents in his life
II. Dual Personality
    a. What is it?
    b. How does it apply to Napoleon?
III. Napoleon's Rise to Fame
    a. Contradictions in his personality and attitudes
        i. Relationship with Josephine
        ii. Example #2 (to come)
IV. Summary of my thoughts about Napoleon's personality
V. Conclusion
    a. Restate and answer thesis
        i. Yes, he had a dual personality because:
            1. Josephine
            2. Example #2

Step 3: Revising. The key to good writing is rewriting or revising, which is the stage in which you take a good piece of writing and do your best to make it great. After you draft your paper, read it once. You may need to reorganize your ideas, add smoother transitions, cut unnecessary words from sentences and paragraphs, rewrite some sentences or paragraphs, or use stronger vocabulary.

After you revise your paper, put it aside for at least a day and then reread it. Distancing yourself from your writing for a while allows you to see it differently. You will probably find and correct more grammatical and spelling errors, reorganize your written ideas, and make your writing stronger as a result.

It also might help to get feedback on your paper from one or more of your classmates or a family member. You should also check to see if your college provides any writing or editing assistance. Most colleges and universities have a writing center or learning center where students can get help during any stage of the writing process: finding a topic, narrowing a topic, creating a thesis, outlining, drafting, rewriting, or revising. Once you have talked with your reviewers about their suggested changes, it will be your decision to either accept or reject them.

At this point, you are ready to finalize your writing and turn in your paper. Reread the paper one more time, and double-check spelling and grammar.

Know Your Audience

Before you came to college, you probably spent much more time writing informally than writing formally. Think about all the time you've spent writing e-mails, Facebook posts, texts, and tweets. Now think about the time you've spent writing papers for school or work. The informal style that you use to write an e-mail, text, or post can become a problem if you try to apply it to a formal research paper. Be sure that you know when you can use abbreviations and when you have to write out an entire word or phrase. When you write research papers in college, you should assume that your audience is composed of instructors and other serious students who will make judgments about your knowledge and abilities based on your writing. You should not be sloppy or casual when writing a formal paper.

IN CLASS > Ask students why writing is an important skill in all their job choices. Stress that the ability to write well is a major criterion for almost any professional-level job.

RETENTION STRATEGY > Students who are focused on a career after college are more likely than those who are not to be retained, and virtually all careers require good writing skills. Help your students see the importance of writing to their future careers.

IN CLASS > Ask students to share examples of text messages that they have either sent or received. Ask if they have ever sent or received an e-mail or text message that could be interpreted in more than one way and, if so, to share problems that have resulted from these misunderstandings. Discuss how to prevent these kinds of problems and the ways texting has changed the way we write and communicate.

> **your turn** Make Good Choices
>
> **Facebook through an Employer's Eyes**
>
> Look at your own or a friend's Facebook page. Do you see anything that puts you or your friend in a negative light? Think about how you would alter the content and writing style if this Facebook page were part of a job application. Consider the changes that are needed to give you or your friend a good chance of getting the job. Remember that employers now routinely check Facebook to see what kinds of information potential employees might post. Choose to post only information that you are willing to share with anyone—*especially* a potential employer.

The Importance of Time in the Writing Process

Many students turn in poorly written papers because they skip the first step (prewriting) and the last step (rewriting/revising), and make do with the middle one (drafting). The best writing is usually done over an extended period of time, not as a last-minute task.

When planning the amount of time you'll need to write your paper, make sure to add enough time for the unexpected. You'll be glad you left enough time for the following:

- asking your instructor for clarification on the assignment
- seeking help from a librarian or from the writing center
- narrowing or expanding your topic, which might require finding some new sources
- balancing other assignments and commitments
- dealing with technology problems

Citing Your Sources

At some point you'll present your findings, whether you are writing an essay, a formal research paper, a script for a presentation, or a page for a Web site. Remember that you must include complete **citations**, which are references that enable a reader to locate a source based on information such as the author's name, the title of the work, and its publication date.

Citing your sources serves many purposes. For one thing, acknowledging the information and ideas you've borrowed from other writers distinguishes between other writers' ideas and your own and shows respect for their work. Source citations show your audience that you have based your conclusions on good, reliable evidence. They also provide a starting place for anyone who would like more information about the topic or is curious about how you reached your conclusions. Most important, citing your sources is the simplest way to avoid **plagiarism**—taking another person's ideas or work and presenting them as your own—which we will explore in more detail later in this chapter.

Source citation includes many details and can get complicated, but it all comes down to two basic rules. As you write, just remember these two points:

- If you use somebody else's exact words, you must give that person credit.
- If you use somebody else's ideas, *even if you use your own words to express those ideas,* you must give that person credit.

Your instructors will tell you about their preferred method for citation: footnotes, references in parentheses included in the text of your paper, or endnotes. If you're not given specific guidelines or if you simply want to be sure that you do it right, use a handbook or style manual. One standard manual is the MLA Handbook for Writers of Research Papers, published by the Modern Language Association (**mlahandbook.org**). Another is the Publication Manual of the American Psychological Association (**apastyle.org**). You can now download MLA and APA apps on your mobile devices from Google Play or iTunes.

About Plagiarism

Plagiarism is taking another person's ideas or work and presenting them as your own. Plagiarism is unacceptable in a college setting. Just as taking someone else's property is considered physical theft, taking credit for someone else's ideas is considered intellectual theft. In written reports and papers, you must give credit whenever you use another person's actual words, another person's ideas or theories, even if you don't quote them directly, or any other information that is not considered common knowledge.

Occasionally, writers and journalists who have plagiarized have jeopardized their careers. In 2012, columnist Fareed Zakaria was suspended for a week from *Time* and CNN for plagiarizing material from *The New Yorker,* an oversight for which he took full responsibility. In spring 2013, Fox News analyst Juan Williams was criticized for plagiarizing material from a Center for American Progress report in a column he wrote for a political insider publication, but he blamed his research assistant. Also in 2013, Republican senator Rand Paul of Kentucky found himself in trouble over accusations that he plagiarized portions of his book and several of his speeches. Even a few college presidents have been found guilty of borrowing the words of others and using them as their own in speeches and written documents. Such discoveries may result not only in embarrassment and shame but also in lawsuits and criminal actions.

Plagiarism can be a problem on all college campuses, so instructors are now using electronic systems such as Turnitin (**turnitin.com**) to identify plagiarized passages in student papers. Many instructors routinely check their students' papers to make sure that the writing is original. Some

A Speed Trap for Plagiarizers

If knowing that plagiarism is wrong isn't enough of a reason to prevent you from doing it, how about knowing that you will probably get caught? Turnitin's Originality Check checks submitted papers against billions of Web papers, millions of student papers, and leading library databases and publications. Just as known speed traps usually get you to slow down when you are driving, knowing about systems like Turnitin can help you resist the urge to plagiarize.

Courtesy Turnitin

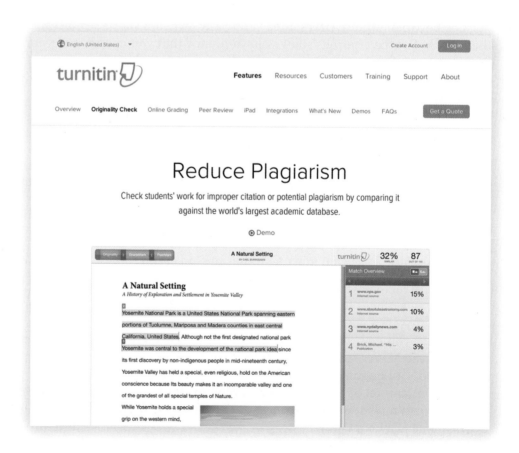

students consider cheating or plagiarizing because they think that doing so will help them get a better grade, but you can avoid the temptation if you keep in mind the high likelihood of getting caught, as well as the serious consequences that will follow if you do get caught.

Because there is no universal rule about plagiarism, ask your instructors about the guidelines they set in their classes. Once you know the rules, plagiarism is easy to avoid. Keep careful notes as you do your research, so that later on you don't mistake someone else's words or ideas for your own. Finally, be sure to check out your college's official definition of what constitutes plagiarism, which you will find in the student handbook, college catalog, college Web site, course syllabi, or first-year course materials. If you have any questions about what is and isn't acceptable, be sure to ask someone in charge.

It should go without saying (but we'll say it anyway) that intentional plagiarism is a bad idea on many levels. Aside from the possibility of being caught and the potential for punishment—a failing grade, suspension, or even expulsion—submitting a paper purchased from an Internet source, copying and pasting passages from someone else's paper, or lifting material from a published source will cause you to miss out on the discovery and skill development that research assignments are meant to teach.

USING YOUR RESEARCH IN PRESENTATIONS

What you have learned in this chapter about writing also applies to public speaking: Both are processes that you can learn and master, and each results in a product. Because the fear of public speaking is a common one—it is more common, in fact, than the fear of death—you might think: What if I plan, organize, prepare, and rehearse my speech, but my mind goes completely blank, I drop my note cards, or I say something totally embarrassing? Remember that people in your audience have been in your position and will understand your anxiety. Your audience wants you to succeed. Be positive, rely on your wit, and keep speaking. Your recovery is what they are most likely to recognize; your success is what they are most likely to remember. The following guidelines can help you improve your speaking skills significantly, including losing your fear of speaking publicly.

Guidelines for Successful Speaking

Just as there is a process for writing a paper, there is a process for developing a good speech. The following guidelines can help you both improve your speaking skills and lose your fear of public speaking.

Step 1: Clarify Your Objective.
Begin by identifying the goals of your presentation. Do you want to persuade your listeners that your campus needs additional student parking, or inform your listeners about the student government? What do you want your listeners to know, believe, or do when you are finished?

IN CLASS > Ask students to discuss how writing and speaking are both processes and products. Brainstorm a list of ways that writing and speaking are processes, and then create a second list of how they are products. Discuss the topic further with your students.

IN CLASS > Review your college's core requirements (found in the institution's print or online catalog) to determine whether a communications or speech course is mandated. If it is, show students the course description and discuss why speech and communication skills are important to students who want to become successful professionals.

They Make It Look So Easy

When television icon Ellen DeGeneres hosted the Academy Awards for the second time, she surprised everybody by having pizza delivered to the hungry celebrity audience. While this comedian's use of humor and creativity to engage with the audience seems effortless, she wasn't always so comfortable onstage. "I got so nervous I would choke," she has said when talking about her early days doing stand-up comedy. When you feel nervous about speaking in front of others, consider taking a cue from Ellen: How can you work some audience interaction into your presentation?

Kevin Winter/Getty Images

Step 2: Understand Your Audience. To understand the people you'll be talking to, ask yourself the following questions:

- What do they already know about my topic?
- What do they want or need to know?
- Who are my listeners?
- What are their attitudes toward me, my ideas, and my topic?

Step 3: Organize Your Presentation. Now comes the most critical part of the process: building your presentation by selecting and arranging blocks of information to guide your listeners through the ideas they already have to the new knowledge, attitudes, and beliefs that you would like them to have. You can use the suggestions from earlier in the chapter for creating a writing outline to create an outline for your speech.

Step 4: Choose Appropriate Visual Aids. You might use presentation software, such as Prezi or PowerPoint, to prepare your presentations. When creating PowerPoint slides or Prezi templates, you can insert images and videos to support your ideas while making your presentations animated, engaging, and interactive. You might also prepare a chart, write on the board, or distribute handouts. As you select and use your visual aids, consider these guidelines:

- Make visuals easy to follow.
- Make sure that words are large enough to be read, and don't overload your audience by including a lot of information on one slide.
- Use font colors to make your slides visually attractive. Use light colors for text on a dark background or dark colors on a light background.
- Explain each visual clearly.

- Allow your listeners enough time to process visuals.
- Proofread carefully. Misspelled words hurt your credibility as a speaker.
- Maintain eye contact with your listeners while you discuss the visuals. Don't turn around and address the screen.

A fancy slideshow can't make up for a lack of careful research or sound ideas, but using clear, attractive visual aids can help you organize your material and help your listeners understand what they're hearing. The quality of your visual aids and your skill in using them can help make your presentation effective.

Step 5: Prepare Your Notes. If you are like most speakers, having an entire written copy of your speech in front of you may tempt you to read much of your presentation, but a speech that is read word for word will often sound artificial. A better strategy is to memorize the introduction and conclusion, and then use a carefully prepared outline to guide you in between. You should practice in advance. Because you are speaking mainly from an outline, your choice of words will be slightly different each time you give your presentation, with the result that you will sound prepared but natural. Since you're not reading, you will be able to maintain eye contact with your listeners. Try using note cards; number them in case you accidentally drop the stack on your way to the front of the room. After you become more experienced, your visuals can serve as notes. A handout or a slide listing key points can provide you with a basic outline.

Step 6: Practice Your Delivery. Practice delivering your speech before an audience: a friend, your dog, even the mirror. As you rehearse, form a mental image of success rather than failure. Practice your presentation aloud several times to control your anxiety. Begin a few days before your speech date, and make sure you rehearse out loud, as thinking through your speech and talking through your speech have very different results. Consider making an audio or video recording of yourself to hear or see your mistakes and reinforce your strengths. If you ask a practice audience to give you feedback, you'll have some idea of what changes you might make.

Step 7: Pay Attention to Word Choice and Pronunciation.

As you reread your presentation, make sure that you have used the right words to express your ideas. Get help ahead of time with words that you aren't certain how to pronounce. Try your best to avoid *like, um, uh, you know,* and other fillers.

Step 8: Dress Appropriately and Give Your Presentation.

Now you're almost ready to give your presentation, but don't forget one last step: Dress appropriately. Leave the baseball cap, the T-shirt, and the tennis shoes at home. Don't overdress, but do look professional. Experts suggest that your clothes should be a "little nicer" than what your audience is wearing. Some speakers find that when they dress professionally, they deliver a better presentation!

Step 9: Request Feedback from Someone in Your Audience.

After you have completed your speech, ask a friend or your instructor to give you some honest feedback. If you receive written evaluations from your audience, read them and pay attention to suggestions for ways you can improve.

Your first public presentation in college might be a scary experience for you, and you might even try to select courses that allow you to avoid public speaking. You're really not doing yourself any favors, though. Nearly all employers will expect you to make an occasional speech or presentation, and the only way to improve as a speaker is through practice. If you receive negative feedback on a presentation, don't let it get you down. Show your instructors and your fellow students that you are resilient—you can bounce back from a less-than-perfect presentation and can use feedback to improve.

your**turn**   Stay Motivated

Learning from Motivational Speakers

Think about public speakers you have heard either in person or on TV. Which ones were the most effective? Which ones motivated you to accept their ideas? Why? What are some of the specific ways that the best public speakers communicate with and motivate an audience? What can you learn from them about what motivates you?

checklist **for** success

Information Literacy and Communication

☐ **Work to learn "information-literacy" skills.** These skills include the abilities to find, evaluate, and use information. They are important not only for college but also for your career because you will be working in the information economy, which uses and produces information.

☐ **Become comfortable in your campus library.** Use it as a place to read, relax, study, or just be by yourself.

☐ **Accept that research projects and papers are part of college life.** Learn how to do them well. Doing so will teach you how to "research" the information you need in life after college. After all, modern professional life is one big term paper after another!

☐ **Get to know your college librarians.** They are eager to help you find the information you need. Ask them for help, even if they look busy. If possible, get to know one as your personal "library consultant."

☐ **Early in your college career, take courses that require you to do research and use your library skills.** Yes, these will demand more of you, especially in writing, but you will be thankful for them later. Go ahead, bite the bullet.

☐ **Learn about as many new electronic sources as possible.** You must be able to do research and seek the information you need now and after college by doing more than using Google or Wikipedia.

☐ **When you use the ideas of others, be sure to give them credit; then create your own unique synthesis and conclusions.** Someday you will create your own "intellectual property," and you will want others to give you credit for your ideas.

☐ **Take the time and effort to develop your writing and speaking skills.** Effective writing and speaking are skills for success in college and in life after college. They are skills that employers seek in all their employees.

☐ **Learn and practice the three distinct steps of the writing process.** Prewriting, drafting, and revising are separate steps. Going through each step will improve the finished product. Ask for feedback on your writing. Accepting criticism and praise will make you a better writer.

☐ **Learn and practice the guidelines for effective speaking.** Clarify your objective, analyze your audience, organize your presentation, choose appropriate visual aids, prepare your notes, and practice delivery. Pay attention to word choice and pronunciation, give your presentation, and request feedback from someone in your audience.

REFLECT ON CHOICES

Your campus library is a valuable resource for finding information and a great place to study. While your instructors will sometimes require you to use the library, at other times, it will be your choice. Reflect on your use of the library so far in your college experience. Make a list of the pros and cons of going to the library to study or do research, and share that list with other students in your class.

APPLY WHAT YOU'VE LEARNED

Now that you have read and discussed this chapter, consider how you can apply what you have learned to your academic life and your personal life. The following prompts will help you reflect on chapter material and its relevance to you both now and in the future.

1. It is important to get familiar with all the resources in your campus library. Think about a book that you love that was turned into a movie (e.g., *The Lord of the Rings* or the Harry Potter series). Search your library catalog to find the print copy. See if the library has it as an audiobook or in a language other than English. Find the DVD and soundtrack in your library's media collection.

2. The importance of using information-literacy skills in college is a no-brainer, but think beyond your college experience. How will improving your information-literacy skills help you once you are out of college?

USE YOUR RESOURCES

> **Your Instructor**
Talk to your instructor after class, drop by during office hours, or make a one-on-one appointment. Check with your instructors to make sure that you understand their expectations for any writing, speaking, or research assignments.

> **Library**
Go to the library! Check out your campus library's Web site or ask for a calendar of upcoming events. Many libraries have drop-in classes or workshops to help you learn specific skills. Head over to the reference desk and talk with a librarian about an assignment that you are working on. If you are an online student, be sure to learn how you can gain access to library sources from your home.

> **Technology Support Centers**
Everyone faces some sort of computer crisis in their life. It seems that so many of these emergencies happen just before a deadline for a major paper. Prepare yourself! Check out your school's technology support services *before* you need them. Adult students sometimes feel uncomfortable with technology. If you are an adult student, get the help you need from the campus's technology experts.

> **Writing Center**
Most campuses have one. Frequently it is found within the English department.

> **Online Resources**
Take advantage of writing resources like Re:Writing 3 at **bcs.bedfordstmartins.com /rewriting2e.** Visit this free resource if you need help finding inspiration, building a bibliography, learning about citation styles, and more. It offers videos of real writers to inspire you, along with writing tutorials, checklists for better writing, grammar exercises, and research tips. Purdue University has an excellent resource on documenting both print and electronic sources. Visit **owl .english.purdue.edu/owl/resource/584/02.** Have you ever been confused by government jargon? Here's a guide to writing user-friendly documents for federal employees: **plainlanguage.gov/howto/guidelines /FederalPLGuidelines/index.cfm.**

 LaunchPad

LaunchPad for *Your College Experience* is a great resource. Go online to master concepts using the LearningCurve study tool and much more. **macmillanhighered.com/gardner12e**

PART THREE

PREPARING FOR LIFE

William Perugini/Shutterstock

11 RELATIONSHIPS

Student Goals

- Build positive relationships with your college instructors
- Understand the role that college friendships and romantic relationships play in your life
- Learn strategies to manage family relationships while in college
- Become skilled at using digital communication properly
- Get ideas for getting involved on campus

Blend Images-Andersen Ross/Getty Images

12 DIVERSITY

Student Goals

- Learn how to thrive in diverse environments
- Develop an awareness of the many kinds of diversity within the college environment and the value of gaining knowledge about various groups of people
- Understand how to identify and overcome discrimination, prejudice, and insensitivity on campus

PhotoAlto/Sandro Di Carlo Darsa/Getty Images

13 WELLNESS

Student Goals

- Manage the various aspects of wellness, including stress management, nutrition, exercise, weight management, sleep, and emotional health
- Maintain sexual health and protect yourself against sexual assault and violence
- Gain strategies for making good decisions about alcohol and other substances

Image Source/Getty Images

14 MONEY

Student Goals

- Create a budget and learn how to live within it
- Distinguish between different types of financial aid and understand how to qualify for and keep it
- Learn how to achieve a balance between working and borrowing
- Get strategies for using and managing credit wisely
- Know why you should plan for your financial future

William Perugini/Shutterstock

11

RELATIONSHIPS

YOU WILL EXPLORE

How to build positive relationships with your college instructors

The role that college friendships and romantic relationships play in your life

How to manage family relationships while in college

Strategies for using digital communication properly

Ways to get involved on campus

⚤ High-impact practices 2 (writing), 3 (collaboration), and 5 (service-learning)

Benjamin Smock, 37

Music Teacher
Graduate of Bunker Hill Community College and University of Massachusetts Boston

> **My wife encouraged me to enroll in college when I was just throwing around the idea.**

Even before he enlisted in the U.S. Navy and served for nine years as an electronics technician, Benjamin Smock had a passion for music. He played guitar in high school and on his ship, and he discovered a new interest in professional recording. If it hadn't been for his wife's encouragement, however, he may never have enrolled in Bunker Hill Community College (BHCC) in Boston and begun pursuing music as a career. "My wife encouraged me to enroll in college when I was just throwing the idea around," he said.

At BHCC, Benjamin developed an important relationship with one of his music instructors, Mari Black, who taught a course on arranging and composing. Professor Black also agreed to mentor Benjamin when he decided to participate in the honors program. "It was a wonderful experience to work so closely with a professor," he says. Benjamin also found plenty of support from friends and family while he was in college. "My father and sisters back in Illinois would listen to me talk about the classes I was taking. My friends were so supportive, to the point of asking about the research papers I was writing

and even attending events with me in support of my research."

During his time at BHCC, Benjamin became inspired to become a teacher, and he continued his studies in the music education program at the University of Massachusetts Boston (UMB). "I chose UMass Boston because I could use my military benefits, and I would be set up for job success right out of the gate," Benjamin explained. "I could tack a five-year initial [teaching] license onto my degree plan and teach K–12 music anywhere in the state."

While at UMB, Benjamin tutored second graders in math and reading. "That experience alone made me realize that teaching little kids is what I am meant to do," he said. He also created a ten-week middle school music program that he taught to sixth graders. After three years at UMB, Benjamin landed a job as a K–5 music teacher for the Framingham Public Schools. "I am so incredibly grateful that my college education path brought me here. This is what I was meant to do, and my wife is incredibly proud of my accomplishments. I'm the happiest I've ever been," he said. Benjamin plans to earn a master's degree within the next five years.

 **LaunchPad**

To access the LearningCurve study tool, video activities, and more, go to LaunchPad for *Your College Experience.* macmillanhighered.com /gardner12e

What does success in college have to do with relationships? As Benjamin's story shows, the quality of both the relationships students have when they begin college and those that they develop in college can have positive effects on their success. As college educators, we have learned from our own experiences and the experiences of others that relationships can also negatively affect success.

Relationships take many forms. Your relationships with your instructors will be very important while you're in college. You might choose to get to know your instructors or to ignore them outside of class, but the quality and frequency of the interactions you have with them can affect your academic performance.

Whether you live on campus or off, you will continue your existing relationships with your parents, spouse, children, or other family members. Sometimes, the assumptions and expectations that define family interactions will change, and negotiating that change is not always easy. Parents sometimes have trouble letting go of a son or daughter, and if you are fresh out of high school, you might think that your parents still want to control your life. If you are an adult with a spouse or partner, going to college will give you a new identity that might seem strange or threatening to your partner. If you have children, they might not understand what's going on as you try to balance your need for study time with their need for your undivided attention.

If your friends also go to college, you will have a great deal to share and compare. But if your friends are not college students, they, too, might feel threatened as you take on a new identity. In addition, romantic relationships can support you or can create major conflict and heartbreak, depending on whether your partner shares your feelings and whether the relationship is healthy or dysfunctional.

This chapter will help you think about all these different kinds of relationships, including those that you create and continue online.

your turn	Write and Reflect

Your Important Relationships

At this point in your life, what are the three relationships that are most important to you? In a journal entry, reflect on what makes these people special to you.

BUILDING RELATIONSHIPS WITH COLLEGE INSTRUCTORS

Some of the most important relationships you can develop in college are those with your instructors. The basis of such relationships is mutual respect. Instructors who respect students treat them fairly and are willing to help them both in and out of class. Students who respect instructors come to class regularly and take their work seriously.

What Your Instructors Expect from You

Although instructors' expectations might vary depending on a particular course, most instructors expect their students to exhibit attitudes and behaviors that are central to student success. First, and quite simply, be in class on time. In college, punctuality is a virtue. If you repeatedly arrive late for class or leave before class periods have officially ended, you are breaking the basic rules of etiquette and politeness, and you are intentionally or unintentionally showing a lack of respect for your instructors and your classmates. Being on time might be a difficult adjustment for some students, but you need to be aware of faculty members' expectations at your college or university.

Arrive early enough to class to shed your coat, shuffle through your backpack, and have your assignments, notebooks, and the writing utensils or devices that you need for class ready to go. Likewise, be on time for scheduled appointments. Avoid behaviors that show a lack of respect for both the instructor and other students, such as leaving class to feed a parking meter or answer your cell phone and then returning 5 or 10 minutes later, thus disrupting class twice. Similarly, texting, doing homework for another class, falling asleep, or talking (even whispering) disrupts the class. Make adequate transportation plans in advance, get enough sleep at night, wake up early enough to be on time for class, and complete assignments prior to the class session.

Your instructors expect you to come to class promptly, do the assigned work to the best of your ability, listen and participate, think critically about course material, and persist even when a concept is difficult to master. Instructors also expect honesty and candor. Many instructors will invite you to express your feelings about the course anonymously in writing through 1-minute papers or other forms of class assessment.

Generally speaking, college instructors expect you to be self-motivated to do your best. Your grade school and high school teachers might have spent a great deal of time thinking about how to motivate you, but college instructors usually consider motivation to be your personal responsibility.

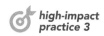
high-impact practice 3

HIGH-IMPACT PRACTICE ❯ This collaborative exercise will give students a chance to validate or refute any rumors they might have heard about college instructors. They will then be able to speak accurately with future incoming students about what to expect in the college classroom.

your turn Work Together

Evaluating the Rumor Mill: Were Those Stories True?

Make a list of any stories you heard or ideas you developed about college instructors before coming to college. Share these ideas in a small group. See how many stories or rumors were common among all students in the group. Talk about whether these stories are proving to be accurate or inaccurate in your college experience.

Exchanging Ideas

Most college instructors have a passion for their field and love to exchange ideas. Many successful college graduates can name a particular instructor who made a positive difference in their lives and influenced their academic and career paths. Embrace opportunities to develop meaningful relationships with your instructors. Doing so could change your life for the better.

What You Can Expect from Your Instructors

The expectations you have for college instructors may be based on the positive and negative things you have heard from friends, fellow students, and family members, but you will find that instructors vary in personality and experience. You might have instructors who are graduate students or new professors in their first year of teaching. Other instructors might be seasoned professors who have taught generations of new students. Some will be introverted and difficult to approach; others will be open, friendly, and willing to talk to you and your classmates.

However, no matter what their level of experience, personality, or skill as a lecturer, you should expect your instructors to grade you fairly and provide meaningful feedback on your papers and exams. They should be organized, prepared, and enthusiastic about their academic fields, and they should be accessible. You should always be able to approach your instructors if you need assistance or if you have a personal problem that affects your academic work.

Make the Most of the Learning Relationship

Most college instructors appreciate your willingness to ask for appointments. This may seem a little scary to some students, but most instructors welcome the opportunity to establish appropriate relationships with their students and to get to know them. As discussed in the first chapter of this book, it's up to you to take the initiative to visit your instructors during their office hours. Instructors are almost always required to keep office hours, so don't worry that you are asking for a special favor. Even part-time instructors, who are not required to have office hours, can be available to help you with your coursework or answer your questions.

You can visit your instructors, either in real time or online, anytime during the term to ask questions, seek help with a difficult topic or assignment, or discuss a problem. If you have a problem with the instructor, the course, or your grade, set up a meeting with him or her to work things out. If the problem is a grade, however, keep in mind that your instructors have the right to assign you a grade based on your performance, and no one can force them to change that grade.

People who become college instructors do so because they have a real passion for a particular subject. If you and your professor share an interest in a particular field of study, you will have the opportunity to develop a true friendship based on mutual interests. Instructors who know you well can also write that all-important letter of reference when you are applying to graduate or professional school or seeking your first job after college.

Understanding Academic Freedom

Colleges and universities have promoted the advancement of knowledge by granting instructors **academic freedom**, which is virtually unlimited freedom of speech and inquiry as long as human lives, rights, and privacy are not violated. Such freedom is not usually possible in other professions.

Most college instructors believe in the freedom to speak out, whether in a classroom discussion about economic policy or at a political rally. You will benefit by listening to what they have to say and respecting their ideas and opinions. Think of where education would be if instructors were required to keep their ideas to themselves. You won't always agree with your instructors, and you might find that different instructors within the same academic field have different viewpoints on a single topic. Don't let this confuse you. This "intellectual diversity" is one of the special features of almost all higher education environments, and it can help you understand that there is seldom one right answer to any complex question.

Academic freedom also extends to students. Within the limits of civility and respect for others, you will be free to express your opinions in a way that might be different from your experiences in high school or work settings.

Handling a Conflict between You and an Instructor

Although there is a potential in any environment for things to go wrong, only rarely are problems between students and instructors irresolvable. If you have a conflict with an instructor, you should first ask the instructor for a meeting to discuss your problem. See whether the two of you can work things out. If the instructor refuses, go up the administrative ladder, starting at the bottom: first the department head, then the dean, and so on. Above all, don't let a bad experience sour you on college. Even the most trying instructor will be out of your life by the end of the term. When all else fails, resolve to stick with the class until the final exam is behind you. Then shop carefully for instructors for next term by asking fellow students, your academic adviser, and others whose advice you can trust.

PERSONAL RELATIONSHIPS

One of the best things about going to college is meeting new people. In fact, scholars who study college students have found that you'll learn as much—or more—from other students as you'll learn from instructors. Although not everyone you meet will become a close friend, you will likely find a few relationships that are really special, that expose you to new backgrounds and worldviews, and that might even last a lifetime.

Roommates

Adjusting to a roommate is a significant transition experience. You might make a lifetime friend or end up with an exasperating acquaintance you wish you'd never known. A roommate doesn't have to be a best friend, just someone with whom you can share your living space comfortably.

Perhaps your current roommate is someone you wouldn't have selected if given a choice. The person may be of a different race or ethnic group or may have different attitudes or experiences than you. Although it's tempting to room with your best friend from high school, that friend might not make the best roommate. In fact, many students lose friends by rooming with them. Many students end up developing a lasting relationship with someone who at first was a total stranger. It's important for roommates to establish, in writing, their mutual rights and responsibilities. Many colleges provide contract forms that you and your roommate might find useful if things go wrong. If you have problems with your roommate, talk them out promptly. Talk directly—politely, but plainly. If the problems persist or if you don't know how to talk them out, ask your residence hall adviser for help; he or she is trained to help resolve roommate conflicts. Usually you can tolerate, and perhaps even learn from, a less-than-ideal situation, but if things get really bad and do not improve, insist on a change. If you live on campus, talk to your residence hall adviser or to a professional counselor in your campus's counseling center.

HIGH-IMPACT PRACTICE ❯ Problem roommates are one of the biggest threats to success, especially for new students. Use a regular form of written feedback (a weekly journal entry, an end-of-class note, etc.) for students to reflect on the topic "How I'm doing." If roommate problems surface, ask whether the student needs help solving the problem. Contact the residence hall adviser or the counseling center for assistance if the student grants you permission to do so.

RETENTION STRATEGY ❯ The influence of roommates connects to a major finding on the most important environmental influences during the college years: Very simply, the greatest influence is that of other students. Roommates can therefore have a profound effect on each other, for better or worse.

---

your turn Make Good Choices

What about Online Relationships?

Have you met someone interesting online? Do you plan to meet him or her in person? While some online relationships can blossom when the parties meet face-to-face, others can be disappointing or even dangerous. If you want to get together in person with someone you've met online, it's a good idea to meet in a public place and to bring a friend along for that first meeting. At that point, based on your interaction, you can choose whether you want to see this person again or whether one "date" was enough. Read "Communicating in a Digital Age" in this chapter for more information on this topic.

IN CLASS > Ask students how much time they have for relationships, how often relationships and other outside activities help or interfere with their studies, and whether they have a plan to balance their relationships and their academic responsibilities. Remind students that throughout life they will need to strike this balance by setting priorities according to their values.

IN CLASS > Engage students in a discussion about breaking up. Why do relationships end? How does being in college affect the way in which relationships start and end?

PEER LEADERS > Let your students know that you are available to talk if they are having problems with relationships. While you cannot solve their problems, you can be an important source of support. It is, however, important that you know when to refer students for professional help. Be aware of your limits, and always maintain appropriate boundaries between you and your students. If you are not sure how and when to draw the line, ask the course instructor for advice.

high-impact practice 2

HIGH-IMPACT PRACTICE > Giving advice or emotional support in writing to a friend who is facing a romantic breakup will probably come naturally to most of your students. Suggest that students save what they have written and read it back to themselves if a similar breakup happens to them at some point in the future.

IN CLASS > Many colleges and universities have policies forbidding relationships between instructors and students. Ask your students whether they think such policies make sense and why they think that the authors of this book take this stand. Talk about the dangers of having a relationship with an instructor. What do they think a student should do if he or she feels pressured by an instructor or boss?

Romantic Relationships

You may already be in a long-term, committed relationship as you begin college, or you might have your first serious romance with someone you meet on campus. Since college allows you to meet people from different backgrounds with whom you share common interests, you might find it easier to meet romantic partners in college than it ever was before. Whether you choose to commit to one serious relationship or keep yourself open to meeting others, you'll grow and learn a great deal about yourself and those with whom you become involved.

If you are seriously thinking about getting married or entering a long-term commitment, consider this: Studies show that the younger you are when you marry, the lower your odds are of enjoying a successful marriage. It is important not to marry before both you and your partner are certain of who you are and what you want. Many eighteen- to twenty-year-olds change their outlook and life goals drastically as they get older, which can negatively affect a romantic relationship.

Breaking Up. Breaking up is hard, but if it's time to end a romantic relationship, do it cleanly and calmly. Explain your feelings and talk them out. If you don't get a mature reaction, take the high road; don't join someone else in the mud.

If your partner breaks up with you, you might find yourself sad, angry, or even depressed. If that breakup happens through a text, an e-mail, or Facebook, ask to have a face-to-face meeting or at least a telephone conversation with that person. (See the "Communicating in a Digital Age" section later in this chapter.) Almost everyone has been rejected or "dumped" at one time or another. Let some time pass, be open to emotional support from your friends and your family, and, if necessary, pay a visit to your college counselor or a chaplain. These skilled professionals have assisted many students through similar experiences, and they can be there for you as well. You can also find many books in bookstores and your library that will have good information on the topic of surviving a breakup.

your turn   Write and Reflect

When Romantic Relationships End

On the basis of your experience or the experience of someone close to you, write a journal entry with advice or emotional support that you would give a student who is dealing with a breakup.

Relationship No-Nos. If you find yourself becoming attracted to an instructor or someone else who has the power to affect your grades or your job, remember this: It is never wise to get involved with someone who is in a "power relationship" with you, and if you date a subordinate and the relationship ends, you might find yourself accused of sexual harassment or being fired or sued. Even dating coworkers is risky; it will be much harder to heal from a breakup if you must continue to work with your ex. You won't be sorry if you choose to maintain strictly professional relationships in the classroom and in the workplace.

FAMILY CONNECTIONS

Almost all first-year students, no matter their age, are connected to other family members. Your family might be your parents and siblings, a partner, or a spouse and children. The relationships that you have with family members can be a source of support throughout your college years, and it's important that you do your part to maintain those relationships.

If you come from a cultural background that values family relationships and responsibilities above everything else, you will also have to work to balance your home life and your college life. In some cultures, if your grandmother or aunt needs help, that might be considered just as important—or more important—than going to class or taking an exam.

Negotiating the demands of college and family can be difficult. However, most college instructors will be flexible with requirements if you have genuine problems with meeting a deadline because of family obligations. But it's important that you explain your situation to your instructors; don't expect them to guess what you need. As the demands on your time increase, it's also important that you talk with family members to help them understand your role and responsibilities as a student.

Marriage and Parenting during College

Can marriage, parenting, or other family responsibilities coexist with being a college student? The answer, of course, is *yes*, although meeting everyone's needs—your own, a significant other's, your family's—is not easy. If you are married, with or without children, you need to become an expert at time management. If you do have children, make sure you find out what resources your college offers to help you with child care.

Sweet Success

Whether you are single or have a spouse or partner, being a parent while being a college student is one of the most challenging situations you can face. Find other students who have children so that you have a support system—it can make all the difference. You may not believe it now, but you are functioning as an important role model for your children. They will learn from you that education is worth striving for, even in the face of many obstacles.

© Paul Barton/Corbis

is**this**you?

In a Long-Distance Relationship

Are you a first-year college student who has a romantic partner at another college or university miles away from you? Negotiating long-distance relationships while trying to do well in college can be a significant challenge. You might find yourself feeling guilty if you enjoy activities on campus when your boyfriend or girlfriend isn't around. Try not to let this relationship get in the way of your enjoyment of the whole college experience and your commitment to doing well academically. Depending on you and your partner, the relationship may become stronger, or you may decide that absence doesn't really "make the heart grow fonder," but instead creates problems that seem insurmountable. If you find that it's difficult or impossible to negotiate a long-distance romance, seek some help from your counseling center before making any major decisions. Many students have been in the same situation as you.

Sometimes, going to college can create conflict within a family. Partners and children can be threatened and intimidated if you take on a new identity and a new set of responsibilities. Financial pressures are likely to put an extra strain on your relationship, so both you and your partner will have to work hard at paying attention to each other's needs. Be sure to involve your family members in your decisions. Bring them to campus at every opportunity and let them read your papers and other assignments. Set aside time for your partner and your family just as carefully as you schedule your work and your classes. Most family difficulties can be resolved with good communication. Trust your own ability to be resilient and to maintain your motivation in the face of occasional conflict.

Relationships with Your Parents

Whether you live on campus or at home, your relationship with your parents will never be quite the same as it was before you began college. Your father and mother may have made all or most of your decisions in the past, but now your instructors, academic advisers, and other administrators will expect you to make important choices for yourself, such as what your major will be, where and how much you work, and what you do on weekends. You might find that it's hard to make choices on your own without talking to your parents first. While you should continue to communicate with your parents, don't let them make all your decisions. Your college can help you draw the line between the decisions you should make alone and when you should seek advice from your parents. Many college students live in blended families, with more than one set of parents involved in their college experience. If your father or mother has remarried, you might even have to negotiate with both family units.

So how can you have a good relationship with your parents during this period of transition? A first step in establishing a good relationship with them is to be aware of their concerns. Your parents may be worried that you'll harm yourself in some way. They might still see you as young and innocent, and they don't want you to make the same mistakes that they might have made or experience negative aspects of the college experience that they have seen publicized in the media. They might be concerned that your family or cultural values will change or that you'll never really come home again, and, for some students, that is exactly what happens.

IN CLASS ▸ Have class members share thoughts about how their relationships with their parents have changed.

College on Screen

For decades, the college experience has been the basis of numerous television shows like *Felicity, Undeclared, Greek,* and *Community,* and movies like *Animal House, Revenge of the Nerds, Old School, Legally Blonde,* and *The Social Network.* What is it about college students that makes for such good storytelling? Have you seen any movies or TV shows that really struck a chord of familiarity with what you are experiencing as a college student?

NBC/Photofest

Remember, though, that parents generally mean well. Most of them love their children, even if their love isn't always expressed in the best way. Your parents have genuine concerns that you will understand even better if and when you become a parent yourself. To help your parents feel more comfortable with your life in college, try setting aside regular times to update them on how things are going for you. Ask for and consider their advice. You don't have to take it, but it can be useful to think about what your parents suggest, along with the other factors that will help you make decisions.

Even if you're successful in establishing appropriate boundaries between your life and your parents' lives, it's hard not to worry about what's happening at home, especially when your family is in a crisis. If you find yourself in the midst of a difficult family situation, seek help from your campus's counseling center or from a chaplain—people who are available for support even in "normal" times. Just reach out. When you receive help with your emotional needs, you can manage the tough times in more productive ways.

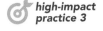

yourturn Stay Motivated

high-impact practice 3

Dealing with Family Meddling

In a small group, talk about how your family is adjusting to your college experience. Are they supportive, fearful, meddling, remote? How do their attitudes and reactions affect your motivation with regard to college? Share strategies with other students for handling issues that arise and staying motivated, even when family issues seem to get in the way.

COMMUNICATING IN A DIGITAL AGE

IN CLASS ❯ Be alert for students who might be engaging in online relationships instead of—rather than in addition to—real-world involvements. Although some evidence suggests that online connections might help students who use the Internet for necessary communications in their adjustment to college, there is also evidence that some students—those who use the Internet for purposes beyond necessary communications—can suffer negative emotional consequences from too much Internet use. Discuss sensible precautions that students should take with strangers online, but emphasize the positives of Internet socializing, too.

So much of our communication with others occurs through e-mail, text and photo messaging, mobile apps, and posting on social networking sites such as Facebook. Online communication enables us to connect with others, whether we're forming new friendships or romantic relationships or maintaining established ones. Online communication also gives us a broad sense of community.

Whereas people used to gather around the proverbial water cooler to chat, new media continually offer new virtual gathering places. Given how often we use technology to communicate with others, it becomes critically important to use it properly. Here are some helpful suggestions, which are also summarized in Table 1.1.[1]

- **Match the seriousness of your message to your communication medium.** Know when to communicate online versus offline. Texting a friend to remind her of a coffee date that you've already set up is likely quicker and less disruptive than calling her. E-mail may be best when dealing with problematic people or trying to resolve certain types of conflicts because it allows you to take the time to think and carefully draft and revise your responses before sending them, which isn't possible in person.

  Use face-to-face interactions for in-depth, lengthy, and detailed explanations of professional or personal problems or important relationship decisions. Although online communication is common, many people still expect important news to be shared in person. Most of us would be surprised if a close friend revealed a long-awaited pregnancy through e-mail, or if a family member disclosed a serious illness through a text message.

- **Don't assume that online communication is always more efficient.** Issues that may cause an emotional reaction are more effectively and ethically handled in person or over the phone. So are many simple things—like deciding when to meet or where to go to lunch. Often a 1-minute phone call or a quick face-to-face exchange can save several minutes of texting.

- **Presume that your posts are public.** You may be thinking of the laugh you'll get from friends when you post the funny picture of you drunkenly hugging a houseplant on Facebook. But would you want family members, future in-laws, or potential employers to see the picture? Even if you have privacy settings on your personal page, what's to stop friends from downloading your photos and posts and distributing them to others? Keep this rule in mind: Anything you've sent or posted online can potentially be seen by anyone.

- **Remember that your posts are permanent.** What goes online or is shared through a mobile app lives on forever, despite some sites' claims to the contrary. Old e-mails, photos, videos, tweets, blogs, you name it—all of these may still be accessible years later. As just one example, everything you have ever posted on Facebook is stored on

---

[1]Adapted from Steven McCornack, *Reflect & Relate: An Introduction to Interpersonal Communication*, 3rd ed. (Boston: Bedford/St. Martin's, 2013), pp. 24–27.

the Facebook server, whether or not you delete it from your profile, and Facebook legally reserves the right to sell your content, as long as they first delete personally identifying information such as your name. Think before you post.

- **Practice the art of creating drafts.** Get into the habit of saving text and e-mail messages as drafts, then revisiting them later and editing them for appropriateness, effectiveness, and ethics. Because online communication makes it easy to insult someone without thinking, many of us impetuously fire off messages that we later regret.
- **Protect yourself and your online identity, and protect yourself when online correspondence turns into face-to-face communication.** Choose secure passwords for your social networking sites and for course sites where your grades might be listed. Limit the amount of personal information available on any online profile, ratchet up your security settings, and accept friend requests only from people you know. Exercise caution and common sense when meeting someone you've met online in person. Keep in mind that some people lie in their profiles and posts.

TABLE 11.1 ❯ Best Practices for Online Communication

Key Points to Remember	Best Practices
1. Match the gravity of your message to your communication medium.	*Online* is best for transmitting quick reminders, linear messages, or messages that require time and thought to craft. *Offline* is better for sharing personal information such as engagement announcements or news of health issues.
2. Online communication is not necessarily more efficient.	If your message needs a quick decision or answer, a phone call or a face-to-face conversation may be better. Use online communication if you want the person to have time to respond.
3. Presume that your posts are public.	If you wouldn't want a message to be seen by the general public, don't post it or send it online.
4. Remember that your posts are permanent.	Even after you delete something, it still exists on servers and may be accessible.
5. Practice the art of creating drafts.	Don't succumb to the pressure to answer an e-mail immediately. Taking time to respond will result in a more competently crafted message.
6. Protect your online identity.	Choose passwords carefully and limit the personal information you put online.
7. Protect yourself when online correspondence turns into face-to-face communication.	Exercise caution and common sense when meeting any online acquaintances in person.

Source: Adapted from Steven McCornack, *Reflect & Relate: An Introduction to Interpersonal Communication*, 3rd ed. (Boston: Bedford/St. Martin's, 2013), pp. 24–27.

RETENTION STRATEGY ›
Long-standing research has
determined that students who
"get involved" are more likely
to persist than those who do
not; urge your students to get
involved on campus.

GET INVOLVED

A college or university can seem to be a huge and unfriendly place, especially if you went to a small high school or grew up in a small town. To feel comfortable in this new environment, it is important for you to get involved in campus life.

Getting involved is not difficult, but it will take some initiative on your part. Consider your interests and the high school activities you enjoyed most, and choose some related activities to explore. You might be interested in joining an intramural team, performing community service, running for a student government office, or getting involved in your residence hall, or you might prefer to join a more structured campuswide club or organization.

While involvement is the key, it's important to strike a balance between finding a niche where you are immediately comfortable and challenging yourself to have new and different interactions with others. Having an open mind and experiencing diversity will prepare you for the workforce you will enter after you graduate. Also, challenge yourself to learn about various cultural groups in and around your college and home community, and participate in campus ethnic and cultural celebrations to learn about unique traditions, ideas, and viewpoints.

Almost every college has numerous organizations you can join; usually, you can check them out through activity fairs, printed guides, open houses, Web pages, and so on. If a particular organization interests you, consider attending one of the organization's meetings before you decide to join. Find out what the organization is like, what the expected commitment is in terms of time and money, and whether you feel comfortable with its members. Students who become involved with at least one organization are more likely to complete their first year and remain in college.

Be careful not to overextend yourself when it comes to campus activities. Although it is important to get involved, joining too many clubs or organizations will make it difficult to focus on any one activity and will interfere with your studies. Future employers will see a balance in academics and campus involvement as a desirable quality in prospective employees. Don't fall into the trap of thinking that more is better. In campus involvement as in many things, quality is much more important than quantity.

PEER LEADERS › Your lead
instructor will appreciate
your introducing the students
in your class to campus
organizations. There are a
number of ways to do that:
taking your students to a
campus activities "fair," setting
up a discussion in your class
with student members of
organizations as the panelists,
or asking each of your
students to attend a meeting
of a campus organization
and report back to the class
on what they learned and
experienced.

*high-impact
practice 3*

HIGH-IMPACT PRACTICE › By
working together, students
can learn about involvement
opportunities and also share
their personal experiences
with the pros and cons of
involvement in some campus
organizations.

yourturn Work Together

Explore Involvement Opportunities

After you have been at your institution for a month or so, you will have been presented with opportunities to get involved. Get together with four or five other students in your class and share what you have learned about how to get involved and about participating in clubs or organizations. Share both the positives and the negatives of your involvement experiences, as well as your beliefs about how many extracurricular clubs or organizations a first-year student should join.

To Greek or Not to Greek?

Greek social organizations are not all alike, nor are their members. Fraternities and sororities can be a rich source of friendship and support. Some students love them. Other students find them philosophically distasteful, too demanding of time and finances, or too constricting. Members of Greek organizations sometimes associate exclusively with other members, and this exclusivity can cause them to miss opportunities to have a more varied group of friends. Greek rush (member recruitment) on your campus might happen before you have decided whether you want to go Greek or before you have determined which fraternity or sorority is right for you. There is nothing wrong with delaying a decision about Greek membership. In fact, we would argue that it's better to learn your way around campus and meet lots of different friends before committing to a particular organization. As you may have become aware through the news media, fraternities and sororities can be positive or negative social influences, so you'll definitely want to take a good look at the upperclass students who are members. If what you see is what you want to be, consider joining. If not, steer clear.

If Greek life is not for you, consider the many other ways that you can make close friends. Many campuses have residence halls or special floors for students with common interests or situations, such as first-year students; honors students; students in particular majors; students with strong ethnic or religious affiliations; students who do not use tobacco, alcohol, and drugs; environmentally conscious students; and so on. Check them out. Often, they provide very satisfying experiences.

Working

One of the best ways to develop meaningful relationships on your campus is to get an on-campus job, either through the federal work-study program or directly through the college.

Generally, your on-campus supervisors will be much more flexible than off-campus employers in helping you balance your study demands and your work schedule. You might not make as much money working on campus as you would in an off-campus job, but the relationships that you'll develop with influential people who care about your success in college and who will write those all-important reference letters make on-campus employment well worth it. Consider finding a job related to your intended major. For instance, if you are a pre-med major, you might be able to find on-campus work in a biology or chemistry lab. That work could help you gain knowledge and experience, as well as make connections with faculty experts in your field.

If an on-campus job is not available or if you don't find one that appeals to you, an off-campus job can allow you to meet new people in the community. If you plan to continue a job you had before starting college, talk to your employer about the new demands on your time. Also keep in mind that some employers offer tuition assistance, so be sure to ask whether that benefit is available to you.

Wherever you decide to find a job, it's important that you limit work to a reasonable number of hours per week. Although some students have to work to pay their tuition or living expenses, many college students work

IN CLASS ❯ Many new students flock to Greek rush on campuses where it is available. Make it clear that although the Greek system might be right for some students, the majority find ways to participate on campus through other organizations. Tell students that if they feel pressured to join a Greek organization, it might not be the right choice for them. Ask whether any of the students have already been approached or involved with a Greek organization. Ask them to share their experiences.

IN CLASS ❯ Students can be conflicted about whether to rush or not. What can they do to make the correct decision? Help students generate a list of questions that they can use to make an educated decision.

FYI ❯ Greek organizations, especially those for men, have had a controversial history since the early twentieth century. In fact, U.S. President Woodrow Wilson attempted unsuccessfully to abolish the student "eating clubs" at Princeton when he was president of that institution. The pros and cons of Greek life or any recent issues involving these organizations can make for lively class discussions.

BUILD A DIGITAL PERSONA

You are active on social media—Facebook, Instagram, Twitter, and others—but you have been told that employers or others might be looking at your profiles, posts, and pictures. You are concerned that people might see parts of your private life that will embarrass you.

If you wonder what people might see, find out. Type your full name into a search engine like Google or Bing and see what comes up. You will see what is connected to you, and you might also see information connected to people who share your name. How can you take charge in order to enjoy a safe digital life?

The Problem

You don't know how to create a professional digital profile that will ensure that employers or other professionals see you at your best.

The Fix

Join social networking sites and connect with people in ways that reflect the person you want the world to know.

© Jens Kalaene/dpa/Corbis

How to Do It

1. *Build your online professional self.* Find a professional social networking site and begin to build a professional persona on that site. Currently, many professionals connect with each other at sites like LinkedIn (linkedin.com). Build your professional profile to show where you have gone to college, where you have worked, and awards you have received. The information in this profile should match other professional documents that prospective employers will see, such as your résumé and your job applications.

   A professional profile that you control will allow you to connect to other people in your profession, give and receive recommendations and endorsements, join groups of people who share your professional interests, and post comments in those groups. When someone conducts an online search for you, your professional profile will come up first.

2. *Exercise caution.* The best way to manage your image online is to be proactive and aware. Make sure that your privacy settings on all social media sites are up to par. For instance, make your profile and all photos posted to your wall and time line available to friends only, and if you list your birthday, don't include the year. If you provide access to your personal information, you are providing access to you. If you're choosy about who can have your phone number and address in the real

3. You want your online persona to be a version of yourself that you will be proud to be connected to for the rest of your life. If you find yourself tagged in a compromising picture, address it right away. Remember that once something goes online, it is public forever, regardless of your privacy settings or if it is taken down.

4. *Delete old accounts.* Delete any accounts that are open to the public but are not updated. Not only do these accounts include out-of-date and possibly embarrassing information, it's likely that you rarely, if ever, check these sites and won't notice if your account has been hacked. The last thing you want is for an employer to find a site full of spam and questionable promotional links.

5. *Stay one step ahead.* Google yourself regularly, especially when applying for jobs or to graduate schools. Make sure that you know what potential employers can see. For more on protecting your virtual reputation, visit blog.kgbpeople.com.

EXTRA STYLE POINTS: Have the right mind-set when it comes to posting and sharing photos—or even taking them at all—and help adjust the mind-set of others. Remind your friends and family to check with you before posting anything about you—espetoo many hours just to support a certain lifestyle. Be careful to maintain a reasonable balance between work and study. Don't fall into the trap of thinking, "I can do it all." Too many college students have found that trying to do it all means not doing anything well.

Community Service

high-impact practice 5

As a first-year student, one way to get involved with your college or university or with the community is to consider volunteering for a community-service project such as serving the homeless at a soup kitchen or helping to build or renovate homes for needy families. Your campus's division of student affairs might have a volunteer or community-service office that offers other opportunities such as tutoring elementary school students in literacy skills, working at an after-school program, participating in a campus cleanup, or working at a local animal shelter. You can also check the Volunteer Match Web site (**volunteermatch.org**) for opportunities in your area. Simply enter your ZIP code and, if you wish, keywords to help you find volunteer work in your field of interest.

checklist for success

Relationships

- **Do your part to build a learning relationship with your instructors.** Ask good questions in and out of class, and visit instructors during their posted office hours.

- **Be open to new relationships.** College may be a great time for you to test out serious relationships, including romantic ones.

- **Don't hesitate to get help from your campus counseling center.** When counselors are asked, "What is the most common type of problem you help students address?" the answer is "relationship issues."

- **Work to have a good relationship with your family during the college years.** Family members have your best interests at heart, and college is a time to become closer to them while also setting boundaries.

- **Get involved.** Join other students in groups sponsored by your educational institution. Students who are involved on campus are more likely to graduate from college than those who are not. Getting involved is fun, easy, free, and rewarding, and employers will be interested in your extracurricular activities.

- **Know that social organizations, such as fraternities and sororities, can be very supportive of college success.** They can also be very disruptive, so make careful choices regarding your involvement with these groups.

- **Look for the right on- or off-campus job.** Working during college is a good thing, depending on where you work, how much you work, and what you do. Get help on this important decision from your adviser and career center.

- **Consider performing some kind of community service during college.** By doing so, you will develop meaningful relationships that will help you clarify your career choices.

REFLECT ON CHOICES

🎯 *high-impact practices 2, 5* | College is a great time to build and nurture relationships with instructors, students your age, and students who are younger or older. The choice of whether to find new relationships is up to you. College offers lots of ways to meet new and interesting people. Consider finding an on-campus job, participating in community service, and becoming involved in a campus activity. Write a brief summary of the new relationships you've developed so far and the activities in which you're involved. Then write about whom you'd like to meet and how you would like to be involved during the rest of your college experience.

APPLY WHAT YOU HAVE LEARNED

Now that you have read and discussed this chapter, consider how you can apply what you have learned to your academic life and your personal life. The following prompts will help you reflect on chapter material and its relevance to you both now and in the future.

1. If you are not already involved in on-campus activities and clubs, visit your campus's Web site or activities office to learn more about the kinds of clubs, organizations, sports teams, and volunteer work that are offered. Find at least one activity that seems interesting to you and learn more about it. When does the group meet, how often, and how many students are involved?

2. Check out some of your fellow students' profiles on a social networking site such as Facebook or Twitter. What kinds of personal information do they share? What kinds of issues are they writing about? Do they use the privacy settings that are available? Do you think that it is important for college students to be careful about the kinds of information they post on social networking sites? Why or why not?

USE YOUR RESOURCES

> **Counseling Center**
A helpful campus resource where you can obtain expert, confidential counseling from professionals at no charge.

> **Chaplains**
An often under-recognized resource for getting help with relationship issues is a session (or more) with a campus chaplain. Your academic adviser might be able to refer you to an appropriate chaplain, or you can seek out the one who represents your faith.

> **Student Organizations**
The variety of student groups designed to bring together students is virtually unlimited. Explore student organizations on your campus.

> **Your College Success Instructor**
Whether you are a student or a peer leader in the classroom, your course instructor can help you locate resources that will help you negotiate relationship issues.

> **Online Resources**
The University of Chicago's "Student Counseling Virtual Pamphlet Collection" (**dr-bob .org/vpc**) takes you to dozens of Web sites devoted to problems in relationships. Browse among the many links to see whether any information applies to you. The University of Texas Counseling Center offers an online brochure that explores the ups and downs of romantic relationships. Visit **cmhc.utexas .edu/healthyrelationships.html**.

🅜 LaunchPad

LaunchPad for *Your College Experience* is a great resource! Go online to master concepts using the LearningCurve study tool and much more. **macmillanhighered.com/gardner12e**

Blend Images-Andersen Ross/Getty Images

12
DIVERSITY

YOU WILL EXPLORE

Opportunities to thrive in diverse environments and various kinds of diversity

The value of gaining knowledge about and experience with various groups

How to identify and help overcome discrimination, prejudice, and insensitivity on campus

⚹ High-impact practices 2 (writing), 3 (collaboration), and 4 (global learning/diversity)

Olivia Castilla, 19 / **Undecided major**
Simone Hisakawa, 20 / **Graphic Design major**
Darrell Stiehl, 25 / **Sociology major**
Wei Zhan, 21 / **Marine Biology major**
Leticia Turner, 19 / **Computer Science major**

Florida Atlantic University Students

" Diversity is like a salad of people . . . mixed well. "

Diversity can mean many things to many people. For the purposes of introducing this chapter, we spoke to a number of students about their personal experiences with diversity. At Florida Atlantic University in Boca Raton, Florida, we asked students to tell us about themselves, where they were from, why they decided to attend college, and how diversity has played a part in their lives, both in college and elsewhere.

The students ranged in age from nineteen to twenty-five and grew up in places as varied as New Zealand, the state of Florida, China, New York City, and Mexico City. Most of the students chose Florida Atlantic University because of its numerous academic opportunities and its diverse community. Leticia is the first person in her family to attend college, and she explained, "The reason I decided to go to college was to ensure a better future for myself and set a good example for my younger sister." Some of the students are adjusting to life in America for the first time, while others were born and raised here.

Being an international student and living far away from his family was a tough transition for Wei, but he said that "despite the challenges, the opportunity to meet and interact with students from diverse backgrounds has been enriching for me personally and academically." Some of these students came to Florida Atlantic straight from high school, while others returned to college after a break. These students bring their own unique experiences to Florida Atlantic, and they strive to learn about the differences and similarities among them.

We asked the students to talk a bit about diversity and how it has played a part in their education. Darrell believes that it is important to seek out other people and other opinions. He said, "Your view in life is one of billions. Get to know what your peers' thoughts are!" Leticia, Olivia, and Simone emphasized getting involved on campus so that you can learn to work with many people toward a common goal. As Simone put it, "Diversity brings language skills, new ways of thinking, and creative solutions to different problems." Darrell reminded us that diversity is international, adding, "The Internet and improved transportation mean that contact between countries is increasing. Learning about diversity equals learning people skills." Olivia summed it all up: "Diversity is like a salad of people . . . mixed well."

To access the LearningCurve study tool, video activities, and more, go to LaunchPad for *Your College Experience.* macmillanhighered.com /gardner12e

As demonstrated by the diverse group profiled here, a college or university serves as a microcosm of the real world—a world that requires us all to work, live, and socialize with people from various ethnic and cultural groups. In few settings do members of ethnic and cultural groups interact in such close proximity to one another as they do on a college campus. Whether you are attending a four-year university or an open-enrollment college, you will be exposed to new experiences and opportunities, all of which can enhance learning and understanding.

Through self-assessment, discovery, and open-mindedness, you can begin to understand your perspectives on diversity. This work, although difficult at times, will intensify your educational experiences, personal growth, and development. Thinking critically about your personal values and belief systems will allow you to have a greater sense of belonging and to make a positive contribution to our multicultural society.

THRIVING IN DIVERSE ENVIRONMENTS

Colleges and universities attract students from different backgrounds, and therefore the ethnicity, cultural background, economic status, and religion of students may vary widely on college campuses. These differences provide opportunities for students to experience diversity.

Diversity is the difference in social and cultural identities among people living together. A diverse community has many advantages that include exposure to various cultures, historical perspectives, and ways of thinking. Diversity, however, can also be a source of misunderstanding and suspicion of the beliefs and behaviors of others. Because almost all colleges and universities value rationality and fairness, they offer an ideal environment for exploring, understanding, and appreciating human differences.

In 2013, thirty-seven U.S. higher education associations representing hundreds of colleges and universities came together to issue this statement, which was printed in a full-page ad in the *New York Times*:

> A diverse student body enables all students to have the transformational experience of interacting with their peers who have varied perspectives and come from different backgrounds. These experiences, which are highly valued by employers because of their importance in the workplace, also prepare students with the skills they need to live in

high-impact practice 4

IN CLASS › As you introduce this chapter to your students, remind them that diversity and global learning are high-impact practices that educational research suggests increase rates of student retention and student engagement. Encourage your students to take advantage of courses and programs that help them explore cultures, life experiences, and worldviews different from their own, especially "difficult differences" such as racial, ethnic, and gender inequality, or continuing struggles around the globe for human rights, freedom, and power.

IN CLASS › Ask students what the word *diversity* means to them. Ask them to reflect on experiences that they have had with people who are racially or ethnically different from themselves. Were the experiences positive or negative?

an interconnected world and to be more engaged citizens. Our economic future, democracy, and global standing will suffer if the next generation is not ready to engage and work with people whose backgrounds, experiences, and perspectives are different from their own. Our nation's higher education institutions, whether they are community colleges or four-year institutions, public or private, nonprofit or for-profit, religiously affiliated or secular, professional, vocational, or liberal-arts focused, stand committed to furthering the goals of equal opportunity and diversity in education. (*New York Times*, June 30, 2013, Advertisement)

Because of this stated commitment, you will likely find that your college or university provides many opportunities for you to familiarize yourself with diverse ideas and people. By taking advantage of ways that you can experience diversity, you will find that your college experience opens the door to new and engaging ideas—ideas that challenge your worldview and enhance your learning.

high-impact practice 3

---

your turn Work Together

Exploring Diversity in Your College Success Classroom

Look around your classroom. What kinds of diversity do you see? What other kinds of diversity might exist but can't be seen? With a small group of students, discuss the reasons some college students have an interest in diversity, both seen and unseen, and why other students avoid the topic. Share your ideas with the whole class.

Ethnicity, Culture, Race, and Religion

Often the terms *ethnicity* and *culture* are used interchangeably, but their definitions are different. **Ethnicity** refers to the identity that is assigned to a specific group of people who are historically connected by a common national origin or language. For example, Latinos are one of the largest ethnic groups in the U.S., consisting of people from more than thirty countries within North, Central, and South America. **Culture** is defined as the aspects of a group of people that are passed on or learned. Traditions, food, language, clothing styles, artistic expression, and beliefs are all part of culture.

Race commonly refers to biological characteristics that are shared by groups of people, including skin tone, hair texture and color, and facial features. Making generalizations about someone's racial group affiliation is risky. Even people who share some biological features—such as similar eye shape or skin color—might be ethnically distinct.

All of us come into the world with our own unique characteristics. Aspects of our physical appearance, our personalities, and our experiences make us who we are. As unique as each one of us is, people around the world have one thing in common: We want to be respected, even if we are

Let Diversity Energize You

While you may initially feel overwhelmed in a diverse campus environment, don't hide from it. Be resilient and make the most of all the opportunities you have to meet, interact, enjoy, and learn from new and different people.

AP Photo/Elaine Thompson

different from others in some ways. Whatever the color of your skin or hair, whatever your life experiences or cultural background, you want others to treat you fairly and acknowledge and value your contributions to your community and the world. And, of course, others want the same from you.

Religion is a specific, fundamental set of beliefs and practices generally agreed on by a number of persons or sects. Freedom to practice one's religion has been central to the American experience from its inception. In fact, many settlers of the original thirteen colonies came to North America to escape religious discrimination.

IN CLASS > Ask students to share their cultural backgrounds and make a list of interesting examples of their cultural traditions.

RETENTION STRATEGY > A campus characterized by respect for all is the kind of environment in which students will want to persist. Make sure that your class also exemplifies that respect.

Other Differences You Will Encounter in College

When you think about diversity, you might first think of differences in race or ethnicity. Although it is true that those are two forms of diversity, you will most likely experience many other types of diversity in college and in the workplace, including age, religion, economic status, physical challenges, learning challenges, and sexuality.

Age. Although many students enter college around age eighteen, others choose to enter or return in their thirties and beyond. Age diversity in the classroom gives everyone the opportunity to learn from others who have different life experiences. Many factors determine when students enter higher education for the first time or when they leave college and then reenter. If you are attending a college that has a large population of students who are older or younger than you, this can be an advantage. A campus where students of different ages are in classes together can be an invigorating learning environment.

Gender. The words *gender* and *sex* are often used interchangeably, but as you become part of an academic community, you will start to think differently about terms and ideas you've always known. Generally speaking, *sex* is used when discussing someone's biological makeup, whereas *gender* refs to the things a person says, does, or wears that help display to the world what the person's gender affiliation is. While *sex* is often thought of as either male or female, *gender* is generally understood as a continuum consisting of many different ways of identifying oneself. Many colleges and universities are now paying more attention to their *transgendered* students and are offering special support to this important, and sometimes neglected, population.

While in college, make friends with all kinds of people, avoid stereotyping what is "appropriate" for one group or another, and don't limit your interests. For example, consider taking a gender studies course if your school has a gender studies department. Gender studies courses are generally interdisciplinary and look at subject matter from the perspective of gender. These classes aren't necessarily about women or men; rather, they consider how the concept of gender influences the way we see and shape the world around us. Such a course could open up new ways of thinking about many aspects of your world.

high-impact practice 2

HIGH-IMPACT PRACTICE ▶ This writing assignment will encourage students to consider the role of gender in the choices available to them. Students' papers can then be used as a framework for an interesting class discussion on how gender plays a role in societal opportunities, even in the 21st century.

OUTSIDE CLASS ▶ Ask students to gather news from the Internet about religious discrimination.

IN CLASS ▶ Have students discuss the findings from their Internet research on religious discrimination.

your turn   Write and Reflect

Gender and Opportunities

Has anyone ever tried to convince you to forgo an educational or job opportunity based on your gender? Are there special jobs or other life experiences that should be restricted to one gender or the other? Write a short paper in which you argue that gender should or should not narrow life choices or options.

Religion. Many students come to college with deeply held religious views. Some will create or join faith communities on campus. These faith communities will encompass those with a common Judeo-Christian heritage, Islam, Hinduism, Buddhism, and more. Learning about different faith perspectives is another way you can explore human differences. Some students and instructors may consider themselves atheists or agnostics, either denying or doubting the existence of a divine creator.

Whatever *your* religious views may be, it is important that you respect the views of others. Learning more about world religions can help you better understand your own faith perspective.

Economic Status. The United States is a country of vast differences in wealth. This considerable economic diversity can be either a positive or a negative aspect of college life. On the positive side, you will be exposed to, and can learn from, students who have had vastly different life experiences as a result of their economic backgrounds. Meeting others who have grown up with either more or fewer opportunities than you is part of learning how to live in a democracy.

Try to avoid developing exaggerated feelings of superiority or inferiority. What matters now is not what you had or didn't have before you came to college; what matters is what you do in college. You have more in

From Another Country

Are you a student who has recently come to the United States from another country? Perhaps you have immigrated to the United States with family members, or perhaps you immigrated on your own. Whatever your particular situation, learning the unique language, culture, and expectations of an American college or university can be a challenge, especially if English is not your primary language. You might find that instructors' expectations seem different from what you experienced in your home country. In the United States, instructors want students to speak up in class and work in groups. You will also find that American students sometimes challenge their instructors in ways that might seem disrespectful to you. Even if you don't feel comfortable with your language skills, don't give up. Your college or university probably offers English as a Second Language courses or programs to help you with your English skills. Also, visit the international student office or center to investigate ways to increase your understanding of life in the United States, both on and off campus.

common with other students than you think. Now your individual efforts, dreams, courage, determination, and ability to stay focused can be the determinants of your success.

Learning and Physical Challenges. Although the majority of college students have reasonably average learning and physical abilities, the numbers of students with physical or learning challenges are rising on most college campuses, as are the services that are available to these students. Physical challenges can include hearing impairment, visual impairment, paralysis, or specific disorders such as cerebral palsy or multiple sclerosis. As discussed earlier in this book, many students have a learning disability that makes college work a challenge.

A person with a physical or learning challenge wants to be treated just as you would treat anyone else—with respect. If a student with such a challenge is in your class, treat him or her as you would any student; too much eagerness to help might be seen as an expression of pity.

If you have, or think you might have, a learning disability, visit your campus learning center for testing, diagnosis, and advice on getting extra help for learning problems. Unlike in high school, college students with disabilities need to inform the appropriate office if they require accommodations.

IN CLASS > Ask students whether they have been around people with learning or physical disabilities. If so, how did they act and feel in their company? Did the disability make them feel uncomfortable? If so, why? Would they do things differently now? Why or why not?

Sexuality. The word *sexuality* refers to the people to whom you are romantically attracted. You are probably familiar with the terms *gay, straight, homosexual, heterosexual,* and *bisexual.* In college you will likely meet students, staff members, and instructors whose sexual orientation differs from yours. While some people are lucky enough to come from welcoming environments, for many students, college is the first time they have been able to express their sexual identity openly. Sexual orientation can be difficult to talk about, and it is important that you respect all individuals that you meet. Check to see if your campus has a center for the lesbian, gay, bisexual, transgendered, and questioning (LGBTQ) community. If there are educational events about sexual identity on your campus, consider going to hear some speakers and expanding your worldview.

IN CLASS › Ask students to define and discuss the words *bias*, *stereotyping*, and *prejudice*. What are the sources of these attitudes and beliefs? You might want to introduce students to the lyrics of "You've Got to Be Carefully Taught," a song about prejudice from the Rodgers and Hammerstein musical *South Pacific*.

Stereotyping: Why We Believe What We Believe

Many of our beliefs are the result of our personal experiences. Others are a result of a **stereotype**, which is a generalization—usually exaggerated or oversimplified, and often offensive—that is used to describe or distinguish a group. A negative experience with members of a particular group may result in the stereotyping of people in that group. We may acquire stereotypes about people we have never met before, or we may have bought into a stereotype without even thinking about it. Children who grow up in an environment in which dislike and distrust of certain types of people are openly expressed might adopt those judgments, even if they have had no direct interaction with those being judged.

In college, you might encounter personal values and belief systems that run counter to yours. When your friendships with others are affected by differing values, tolerance is generally a good goal. Talking about diversity with someone else whose beliefs seem to conflict with your own can be very rewarding. Your goal in this kind of discussion is not to reach agreement, but to enhance your understanding of why people have different

Expand Your Worldview

How has coming to college changed your experience with diversity? Are you getting to know people of different races or ethnic groups? Do your classes have both traditional-aged and older students? Are you seeking out people who are different from you and sharing personal stories and worldviews?

© Ocean/Corbis

values and beliefs, and how this understanding can enrich your college experience and your life beyond college.

Before coming to college, you might never have coexisted with most of the groups you now see on campus. In college, you have the opportunity to learn from many kinds of people, possibly many more than in your home community. Your lab partner in biology may be a veteran, and your sociology study group may include international students. Even your roommate or suitemate in a residence hall may be someone of a different racial or ethnic group. If you are taking one or more online courses, explore the diversity among other online students. You may get to know students from other states, adult students, students with disabilities, and others who could be taking classes on campus but prefer to learn in an online format. Your college experience will be enriched if you are open to the possibility of learning from all members of the college or university community.

While in college, your openness to diversity will add to your understanding of the many ways in which people are different from one another. Learn not to make assumptions, rely on stereotypes, or rush to judgment. Give yourself time to get to know someone before forming an opinion about him or her.

IN CLASS > Discuss with students why understanding perspectives on diversity is an important element of a college education. Why is it important for personal growth and development? Why will learning about others help us better understand ourselves?

SEEKING DIVERSITY IN COLLEGE

high-impact practice 4

Because research in higher education[1] confirms the importance of diversity to learning, colleges and universities have committed to assuring diversity in college admissions and in learning opportunities. Your campus will provide you with opportunities to interact with and learn alongside a kaleidoscope of individuals who represent diversity in religious affiliation, sexual orientation, gender, ethnicity, age, culture, economic status, and ability.

The Curriculum

Many institutions offer an **inclusive curriculum**, one that offers courses that introduce students to diverse people, worldviews, and approaches. Today you can find many courses with a diversity focus, and many of them meet graduation requirements. The college setting is ideal for promoting education about diversity because it allows students and faculty of varying backgrounds to come together for the common purpose of learning and critical thinking.

College students have led the movement that resulted in a curriculum that reflects disenfranchised groups such as women, people of color, the

IN CLASS > *Eyes on the Prize* is an excellent video series on the civil rights movement. After watching parts of the series, have students share their reactions. How could racism like this exist in the United States? What was the role of youth in the civil rights movement?

IN CLASS > At your college, how is multiculturalism reflected in the curriculum? Are there multicultural organizations? Ask students to discuss their feelings about multiculturalism. Are there any negative points of view? If so, what are they, and why do you think that they exist?

---

[1]*Does Diversity Make a Difference: Three Research Studies on Diversity in College Classrooms* (Washington, DC: American Council on Education and American Association of University Professors, 2000) and Gloria M. Ameny-Dixon, "Why Multicultural Education Is More Important in Higher Education Now Than Ever: A Global Perspective." *National Forum*. Accessed January 9, 2015.

Commit to Coexist

In a college or university environment, students often learn that they have a lot in common with others who have been on the opposite side of the fence for centuries. By learning to coexist respectfully and peacefully, students can take the first step toward building a better world.

Jamie Smith-Skinny Genes Photography

elderly, the disabled, gays, lesbians, bisexuals, and the transgendered. In public protests, students have demanded the hiring of more instructors from different ethnic groups, the creation of ethnic studies departments, and a variety of initiatives designed to support diverse students academically and socially, including multicultural centers, women's resource centers, enabling services, and numerous academic-support programs.

In almost all colleges and universities, you will be required to take some general education courses that will expose you to a wide range of topics and issues. We hope that you will take a course or two with a multicultural focus. Such courses can provide you with new perspectives and an understanding of issues that affect your fellow students and community members. They can also affect you, possibly in ways you had not considered. Just as your college or university campus is diverse, so too is the workforce you will enter. Therefore, a multicultural education can improve the quality of your entire life.

your turn   Make Good Choices

Go for Diversity

Whether or not your college or university requires you to include a diversity or multicultural course in your curriculum, you should choose to take at least one. These courses will introduce you to different views on common issues and will help prepare you for the contemporary and multicultural world in which you live and work.

Study Abroad

If your college or university offers study-abroad opportunities, take advantage of them. Visiting or living in another country for a period of time (a few weeks to an entire year) is a great way to expand your horizons, learn about another culture, and become competent speaking another language. Many colleges and universities offer scholarships or grants for study abroad, and some even have student residential accommodations in the host country.

Student-Run Organizations

Student-run organizations can provide multiple avenues to express ideas, pursue interests, and cultivate relationships. According to our definition of culture, all student-run organizations provide an outlet for the promotion and celebration of a culture. Let's take, for instance, a gospel choir and an animation club and apply the components of culture to both of them. Both groups promote a belief system that is common among their members: The first is based on a love of music in the gospel tradition, and the second is based on the appreciation of animation as an art form. Both have aspects that can be taught: the musical tradition of gospel singing and the rules and techniques used in drawing. Both groups use a specific language related to the group's belief system. Most campus organizations bring like-minded students together and are open to anyone who wants to be involved.

To promote learning and discovery both inside and outside the classroom, colleges and universities provide programming that highlights ethnic and cultural celebrations, such as Chinese New Year and Kwanzaa; gender-related activities, such as initiatives sponsored by the group Sexual Assault and Relationship Violence Activists; and a broad range of entertainment, including concerts and art exhibits. These events expose you to new and exciting ideas and viewpoints, enhancing your education and challenging your current views.

Career/Major Groups. You can also explore diversity through your major and your career interests. Groups that focus on a specific field of study can be great assets as you explore your interests. Are you interested in helping minority and majority groups interact more effectively? Consider majoring in sociology or social work. Do you want to learn more about human behavior? Study psychology. If you join a club that is affiliated with the major that interests you, not only will you find out more about the major, but you can also make contacts in the field that could lead to career opportunities.

Political/Activist Organizations. Organizations devoted to specific political affiliations and causes—such as Campus Republicans, Young Democrats, Students for Human Rights, and Native Students in Social Action—add to the diversity mix on campus. These organizations provide debating events and forums and contribute diverse ideas on current issues and events.

Special-Interest Groups. Perhaps the largest subgroup of student organizations is the special-interest category, which encompasses everything from

PEER LEADERS > Introduce your class to study-abroad or student-exchange options at your college or university. Find someone who can visit your class to talk about these opportunities.

OUTSIDE CLASS > Students will have fun seeking campus events that have multicultural themes. Assign students to attend such an event on their own or with classmates.

IN CLASS > Have students report on what they experienced at one or more multicultural events.

OUTSIDE CLASS > Have students attend an orientation event sponsored by a campus organization.

RETENTION STRATEGY > There is evidence that minority or under-represented students who join co-curricular organizations devoted specifically to supporting those students realize higher retention and graduation rates than those who do not join. Recommend such participation to your students.

OUTSIDE CLASS > If some students have a hard time finding their niche in an existing club or organization, encourage them to start their own club. By using social media, they can find others who have the same interests.

recreational interests to hobbies. On your campus, you might find special-interest clubs such as the Brazilian jujitsu club, a belly dance club, the flamenco club, Ultimate Frisbee, and the video gamers' society. Students can cultivate an interest in bird watching or indulge their curiosity about ballroom dance without ever leaving campus. If a club for your special interest is not available, create one yourself.

Intramural Sports. Believe it or not, you can often experience multiculturalism through intramural sports, especially soccer, tennis, and basketball. These sports and others may be a way for you to develop close friendships with teammates whom you might never have met in any other way.

high-impact practice 4

IN CLASS > Confusion can arise when students use the words *prejudice* and *racism* interchangeably. Racism is prejudice directed at a racial group that often stems from one group's fear of losing power and privilege to another. Ask students whether they understand the difference between prejudice and racism, and how and why power can often be misdirected. The bottom line is that neither racism nor prejudice is tolerable; the latter is merely a prelude to the former.

OVERCOMING DISCRIMINATION, PREJUDICE, AND INSENSITIVITY ON COLLEGE CAMPUSES

You might feel uncomfortable when asked about your views on diversity. We all have **biases,** tendencies against or in favor of certain groups or value systems, but it is what we do with our individual beliefs that separates an unbiased and open-minded person from the racist, the bigot, and the extremist. Colleges strive to provide a welcoming and inclusive campus environment for all students. Because of acts of violence, intimidation, and stupidity occurring on campuses, college administrations have established policies against any and all forms of discriminatory actions, racism, and insensitivity. Many campuses have adopted zero-tolerance policies that prohibit verbal and nonverbal harassment and hate crimes such as physical assault, vandalism, and intimidation.

Some students instigate hate crimes because of deeply held negative views or fears about people who represent a different race, ethnic group, or sexual orientation. Other students might "follow the crowd" or feel pressured by peers to participate in organized harassment of a certain group. Commit to becoming involved in making your campus a safe place for all students. If you have been a victim of a racist, insensitive, or discriminatory act, report it to the proper authorities.

Raising Awareness

HIGH-IMPACT PRACTICE > Most college campuses have policies against discrimination and intolerance. Ask students to research your campus policy and write a short paper on the subject. Have there been any recent incidents involving discrimination, racism, or insensitivity? If so, how did students react? What would students do if they observed this kind of activity?

While hate crimes on college and university campuses are, thankfully, infrequent, they do happen. In 2013, three first-year students at San Jose State University in California were suspended as a result of taunting their black roommate with racial slurs and references to slavery and trying to clamp a bicycle lock on his neck. In 2015, Sigma Alpha Epsilon fraternity at the University of Oklahoma was shut down because members engaged in racial chants; two members were expelled from the university. In 2014, students at both the University of Massachusetts and Colgate University protested acts of racism.

Although such actions are deliberate and hateful, others occur out of a lack of common sense. Consider a campus party to celebrate Cinco de Mayo. Party organizers asked everyone to wear sombreros. On arrival, guests encountered a mock-up of a border patrol station on the front lawn and were required to crawl under or climb over a section of chain-link fencing. Student groups voiced their disapproval over such insensitivity, which resulted in campus probationary measures for the organization that had thrown the party. At a Halloween party at a large university, members of a campus organization decided to dress in Ku Klux Klan outfits while other members dressed as slaves and wore black shoe polish on their faces. The group then simulated slave hangings during the party. When photos of the events surfaced, the university suspended the group from campus, and the community demanded that the group be banned indefinitely.

For a number of years, stereotypes that are used to identify school sports teams and their supporters have disturbed ethnic and cultural groups such as Native Americans. Mascots that incorporate a bow and arrow, a tomahawk, feathers, and war paint have raised awareness about the promotion and acceptance of stereotypes associated with the concept of the "savage Indian." Some schools have responded by altering the images while retaining the mascot. Other schools, such as Southeastern Oklahoma State University and the University of Illinois Urbana-Champaign, have changed their mascots to move away from references to Native Americans.

---

your turn   Stay Motivated

Don't Let Harassment Ruin Your College Experience

Think back on your life. Can you recall an occasion in school or college when you were harassed for any reason, or when you witnessed harassment? Did that experience reduce your motivation to work toward a college degree? Discuss the event with a classmate, how it made you feel, and how you reacted. Don't let someone rob you of an important milestone like your college degree through harassment based on your race, ethnic group, gender, sexual orientation, or other characteristics.

What You Can Do to Fight Hate on Campus

Hate crimes, regardless of where they occur, should be taken very seriously. A hate crime is any prejudicial activity and can include physical assault, vandalism, and intimidation. One of the most common forms of hate crime on campus is graffiti that expresses racial, ethnic, and cultural slurs.

IN CLASS ❯ Does your campus have a program that promotes diversity and understanding within the student body? If so, invite a speaker from this program to your class to describe the program's goals and activities.

Whatever form these crimes might take on your campus, it is important to examine your thoughts and feelings about their occurrence. The most important question to ask yourself is: Will you do something about it, or do you think that it is someone else's problem? If you or a group to which you belong is the target of the hate crime, you might be compelled to take a stand and speak out against the incident, but will you feel strongly enough to express your discontent if you are not a member of the target group?

Just because you or your particular group has not been targeted in a hate crime doesn't mean that you should do nothing. Commit to becoming involved in making your campus a safe place where students with diverse views, lifestyles, languages, politics, religions, and interests can come together and learn. If nothing happens to make it clear that hate crimes on campus will not be tolerated, it's anyone's guess as to who will be the next target.

Many students, whether or not they were directly targeted in a hate crime, find strength in unity, forming action committees and making it clear that hate crimes will not be ignored or tolerated. In most cases, instead of dividing students, hate crimes bring students together to work toward denouncing hate. It is important not to respond to prejudice and hate crimes with violence. It is more effective to unite with fellow students, faculty, staff, campus police, and administrators to address the issue, educate the greater campus community, and work to promote an environment of respect and tolerance. Recent news reports have also described the use of Twitter to identify and arrest perpetrators of hate crimes, whether the crime is hate speech or more serious instances of physical assault. The use of social media can make identifying harassers and responding to hate crimes quick and effective.

IN CLASS > Talk with your students about the career world of the future, when diversity will be the norm as demographics change. Preparing for future professional success will require a multicultural perspective.

Encouraging College Students to Vote

One of the simplest and most important ways to participate in your community is to vote. College students can have a significant impact on the outcome of an election, and the more regularly you vote, the more the politicians who represent you will pay attention to you. Be sure to exercise your right and privilege to "rock the vote."

Ann Hermes/*The Christian Science Monitor* via Getty Images

How can you get involved? Work with existing campus services such as the campus police, the multicultural center, faculty members, and the administration to plan and host educational opportunities, including training sessions, workshops, and symposiums centered on diversity, sensitivity, and multiculturalism. Organize an on-campus antidiscrimination event at which campus and community leaders address the issues and provide solutions. Join prevention programs to come up with ideas to battle hate crimes on campus or in the community. Finally, look into the antidiscrimination measures your college has in place. Do you think that they need to be updated or revised?

Challenge Yourself to Experience Diversity

Diversity enriches us all, and understanding the value of working with others and the importance of having an open mind will enhance your educational and career goals. Your college campus is diverse, and so is the workforce you will enter.

Challenge yourself to learn about various groups in and around your community, both at school and at home. These two settings might differ ethnically and culturally, giving you an opportunity to develop the skills you need to function in and adjust to a variety of settings. Attend events and celebrations outside of your regular groups. Whether they are in the general community or on campus, it is a good way to see and hear traditions that are specific to the groups being represented. Exposing yourself to new experiences through events and celebrations can be gratifying. Understanding viewpoints different from yours and learning from such differences will help you see similarities where you didn't think they existed.

You can also become active in your own learning by making time for travel. Seeing the world and its people can be an uplifting experience. Finally, if you want to learn more about a culture or group, ask a member of that group for information. If you do so in a tactful, genuine way, most people will be happy to share information about their viewpoints, traditions, and history. It is only through allowing ourselves to grow that we really learn.

techtip

GO BEYOND THE FILTER

When people learn new things, they increase their capacity to learn even more.

Technology can help us explore new ideas, products, and opportunities. However, when we are on the Internet, our preferences are tracked. The more we use Internet technology, the more information we make available about our opinions. Our online experience is continually shaped by our past searches, likes, and preferences. Author Eli Pariser defines this effect as our "filter bubble," which he describes as an unintended consequence of Web companies tailoring their services, including news and search results, to our personal tastes.[1] This effect causes us to miss all kinds of information that we might like or learn from—we never see it because it is being filtered away from us.

[1]Eli Pariser, *The Filter Bubble: What the Internet Is Hiding from You* (New York: Penguin Press, 2011).

The Problem

You want to be exposed to new things, but past preferences are shaping your current online experience.

The Fix

Push back on the "filter bubble." Be aware that it exists, and make a concerted effort to get exposure to information that could challenge or broaden your worldview. Shape your online research and reading so that you automatically receive a variety of sources of online information. And don't restrict yourself to the online world. Get out and experience the diverse world in which you live, in person!

How to Do It

1. *Join clubs or student groups to expand your interests.* Check with your campus center for student services. Most colleges have student activities, clubs, and events. College can be a time for you to meet new people and learn about new things, and not all of this will happen in the classroom. You can develop new interests by talking to new people about new things.

2. *Find ways to be of use.* Volunteering or interning can help you meet new people, explore new interests, understand others, and learn new skills. It can be tempting to avoid these kinds of activities because of the existing demands of your schoolwork or job. But the people you meet, the interests you explore, and the skills you learn can be important to your future career and long-term goals.

3. *When you are online, search in places other than Google or YouTube for new things to see, hear, or experience.* As you saw in the chapter on "Information Literacy and Communication," your college maintains access to a number of databases containing all kinds of cool information. These are not searchable by external search engines like Google or Bing, and your preferences and interests are not automatically tracked and mirrored back to you. If you take time to explore videos and music as well as text, you will become a better researcher and find new things to guide your professional interests.

4. *Expand your world.* Travel can be a great way for you to experience new people, music, food, history, and culture. No one will electronically track your interests if you explore the Camden Market in London or the Divisoria, a major market district in Manila. Travel will expose you to diverse ways of thinking that will challenge your ideas about who you are and what you have been taught—things you cannot learn in books or by watching television.

checklist for success

Diversity

- **Know that successful college students have strong skills in understanding, appreciating, and embracing diversity.** Given the growing diversity of the American workforce, most employers now hold these skills as an expectation, too. It is just good business.

- **Gain an understanding of the various differences you will encounter in college.** Beyond race, ethnicity, culture, and religion are differences in age, economic status, gender, sexuality, and physical and learning abilities. In college, you have the opportunity to learn from many kinds of people, and these experiences will likely affect any stereotypes you have brought to college with you.

- **Use college as the ideal environment to learn about and get to know people who are different from you.** Practice acknowledging and respecting other people, even if you don't agree with them.

- **Take advantage of opportunities to enroll in courses designed to expose you to a wide range of topics and issues.** You can and should study diverse people and diverse ideas in both the curriculum and the co-curriculum.

- **Be alert for examples of racism and discrimination.** College is a microcosm of our society. You may, therefore, see examples of discrimination, prejudice, and insensitivity on your campus. Become aware of what you can do to combat hate on campus.

- **Don't fear diversity.** The best students allow themselves to break out of their comfort zones and be challenged by new people and new experiences.

REFLECT ON CHOICES

high-impact practices 2, 4 | Your college experience will probably expose you to more diversity than you have experienced before—diversity of race and ethnicity and diversity of opinions and attitudes. By choosing to get to know others who are different you will enrich and energize your learning. Write a one-page essay about someone you have already met who helped expose you to a different way of thinking.

APPLY WHAT YOU HAVE LEARNED

Now that you have read and discussed this chapter, consider how you can apply what you have learned to your academic life and your personal life. The following prompts will help you reflect on the chapter material and its relevance to you both now and in the future.

1. Use your print or online campus course catalog to identify courses that focus on topics of multiculturalism and diversity. Why do you think that academic departments have included these issues in the curriculum? How would studying diversity and multiculturalism help you succeed in different academic fields?

2. Reflecting on our personal identities and values is a step toward increased self-awareness. Read and answer the following questions to the best of your ability: How do you identify and express yourself ethnically and culturally? Are there practices or beliefs in your culture to which you have difficulty subscribing? If so, what are they? Why do you have difficulty accepting these beliefs? What aspects of your identity do you truly enjoy?

USE YOUR RESOURCES

Most colleges and university campuses take an active role in promoting diversity. In an effort to ensure a welcoming and supportive environment for all students, institutions have established offices, centers, and resources to provide students with educational opportunities, academic guidance, and support networks. Look into the availability of the following resources on your campus, and visit one or more.

> **Office of Student Affairs** Small institutions may group all services into a comprehensive office of student affairs.

> **Office of Diversity or Multicultural Center** An office that provides resources for educating students about diversity or multiculturalism is a good place to find the information you need.

> **Women's and Men's Centers** Some institutions provide specialized services to both women and men.

> **Lesbian, Gay, Bisexual, and Transgendered Student Alliances** These student-run organizations provide valuable programming and sources of support for LGBTQ students, their friends, and their families.

> **Centers for Students with Disabilities** Students with either learning or physical disabilities can access special services through these campus offices.

> **Academic support programs for underrepresented groups** While academic support programs are generally available for all students, your institution may offer special types of academic support for certain student populations.

> **Diversity Resources** The Diversity Web (**diversityweb.org**) lists resources related to diversity on campus.

> **Tolerance.org** This Web site, a project of the Southern Poverty Law Center, provides numerous resources for dealing with discrimination and prejudice, both on and off campus.

 LaunchPad

LaunchPad for *Your College Experience* is a great resource. Go online to master concepts using the LearningCurve study tool and much more. **macmillanhighered.com/gardner12e**

13
WELLNESS

YOU WILL EXPLORE

The many aspects of wellness, including stress management, nutrition, exercise, weight management, sleep, and emotional health

Ways to maintain your sexual health and protect yourself and others against sexual assault and violence

Strategies for making good decisions about alcohol and other substances

⚲ High-impact practices 2 (writing) and 3 (collaboration)

Rahm Patel, 19

Accounting major
University of West Florida

> **I realized that eating, exercising, and sleeping well made me less irritable and better able to control my emotions.**

When Rahm Patel started attending the University of West Florida, he expected to have a lot of fun. However, when he received the syllabus for each of his courses during the first week of classes, he could tell he was going to have to work hard. "To make more study time, I cut back on going to the gym each week," he explained. "And I started skipping lunch to save time and ate snacks from vending machines between classes instead." He also found himself sleeping less and eating more junk food.

Rahm was particularly stressed out and anxious about a class presentation he had been working on for his psychology class. He e-mailed his instructor and asked for an extension, which she granted. The day for the presentation came, and Rahm was really nervous. He felt flushed and his voice was shaking. After delivering the speech, Rahm was upset about his performance. He knew he hadn't done well, but he was especially upset about the critique from the instructor. After class, he skipped dinner and went back to his residence hall room. He reviewed his syllabus and saw that this presentation was the first of three that he was required to give during the term. He hardly slept at all and finally decided that he would just drop the class. He could take a psychology class later, hopefully from an instructor who didn't require oral presentations.

The next day he went to the instructor's office to let her know his decision. His face was beet red, and it was all he could do to keep from crying. His instructor, Dr. Wilson, told him, "Lots of people are afraid of public speaking, and their stress causes them to perform poorly. But please keep in mind that the goal of my class is to help you get better." She encouraged Rahm to stay in the class, and she promised that she would help him.

"I was really embarrassed," Rahm admitted, "but Dr. Wilson convinced me that I couldn't escape public speaking for the rest of my life, and I needed to learn how to control my anxiety." Dr. Wilson helped Rahm make an appointment at the counseling center. He was surprised to learn that dealing with anxiety starts with eating, exercising, and sleeping well. His sessions with the counselor helped Rahm understand that his fear was common and that through preparation and practice, he could, over time, become more comfortable speaking before a class or even a larger group. He also learned about resilience—his ability to bounce back when things don't go well.

 **LaunchPod**

To access the LearningCurve study tool, video activities, and more, go to LaunchPad for *Your College Experience.*
macmillanhighered.com
/gardner12e

The first year of college can be one of life's most interesting and challenging transitions. Much of what you experience will be new—new friends, new freedoms, and new responsibilities. You will notice that many students use sensible and healthy coping strategies to handle the transition to college successfully. They watch what they eat and drink, exercise regularly, and get enough sleep. However, some students go in the opposite direction, staying up late, drinking too much, smoking, overeating, or engaging in risky sexual behaviors.

assess your strengths

Maintaining your health in college will enable you to feel good about yourself and succeed academically. By making smart choices, developing an exercise regimen, and eating a healthy diet, you will be ready to make the most of your college experience. As you read this chapter, consider the healthy behaviors that you already practice.

set goals

What are your most important objectives in learning the material in this chapter? Think about the challenges that you have had in the past in the areas of health and wellness. Think of reasonable goals that you would like to achieve, such as maintaining a healthy weight or increasing the number of days per week that you exercise.

The college experience shouldn't only be about studying. To make the most of the college years, it's also important to spend time with friends and enjoy all the activities your college has to offer. The freedoms you experience in this new environment bring challenges and risks, and your success in college depends on your ability to make sensible decisions about your personal habits and behaviors. If you stay healthy, you are more likely to achieve your academic and personal goals, and that is what this chapter is all about.

UNDERSTANDING WELLNESS

Wellness is a concept that encompasses the care of your mind, body, and spirit. Wellness involves making healthy choices and achieving balance throughout your life. It includes reducing stress in positive ways, keeping fit, fostering your spirituality, deepening your self-knowledge, maintaining good sexual health, and taking a safe approach to alcohol and other drugs—assuming that you are of legal age to consume them.

Take this short quiz. As you consider each question, rate yourself on a scale of 1–5, with 1 being "never" and 5 being "always."

1. Are you able to manage your stress successfully? _____
2. Do you eat a wide range of healthy foods? _____
3. Do you exercise at least once a day? _____
4. Do you get seven or more hours of sleep each night? _____
5. Do you say "no" to others in order to manage your obligations? _____
6. Do you seek help from friends, family, or professionals when you need it? _____
7. Are you in control of your sexual health? _____
8. Do you avoid abusing alcohol, tobacco, or other substances? _____
9. Do you live a balanced life? _____

In what areas did you mark a 4 or 5? _____
In what areas did you mark a 1 or 2? _____

As you read the preview of the nine components of wellness described on the next page, pay special attention to the areas that you scored as ones or twos, so that you can get yourself on track.

IN CLASS ❯ Begin this chapter by discussing how the mind, the spirit, and the body are all integral parts of a healthy person. Ask students what that means. Make a list of those ideas under each category, and share those ideas on how the mind, the spirit, and the body complement each other.

1. **Stress management:** Occasional stress is a normal reaction to the new demands of college life. It is important, though, to recognize when your stress level is getting out of control and to seek help before stress gets in the way of your academic performance.

2. **Diet and nutrition:** Eating fast food will often increase your cholesterol and your weight. Limit the number of diet sodas you drink, and opt for fresh, unprocessed foods.

3. **Exercise:** Exercising stimulates the release of the endorphins needed for stress relief and helps with weight management. If you don't have time to work out every day, start with a smaller goal of three or four times a week.

4. **Sleep:** Going without sleep will negatively affect your overall health and ability to perform academically. Seven or eight hours of sleep per night can significantly improve your ability to handle stress.

5. **Saying "no" when you need to:** In order to manage your obligations, sometimes you have to say "no" to friends or even family. Know what your priorities are and stick to them. You might want to review the chapter on "Time Management" for more help in this area.

6. **Seeking help for emotional problems:** If your emotions are out of control, if you are feeling depressed, or if you are becoming anxious about what's happening in your life, consider professional counseling or talking to a friend or family member. Even writing in a journal can be an effective way for you to combat this kind of stress.

7. **Sexual health:** Be sure that you practice safe sex. Understand the resources available to you when you have questions or problems, and remember that communication with your partner is key to navigating your sexual experiences in college.

8. **Substance abuse:** During the college years, you will encounter substances like alcohol, tobacco, and drugs. First and foremost, you must know the laws that govern the use of these substances in your state. If you are of legal age, remember that moderation is key. Are you a smoker? If so, quit now. There is no such thing as a safe level of smoking.

9. **Balance:** Wellness is about mind, body, and spirit. When you take care of all aspects of your personal wellness, it will be easier for you to identify and handle problems when they develop.

Nothing but Blue Skies

When you feel stressed, take a moment to breathe. Focusing on inhaling and exhaling slowly and picturing a serene scene, like a blue sky or a sunny beach, can help slow your heart rate and calm you down. Visualization techniques can be powerful tools.

Filipe Frazao/Shutterstock

Managing Stress to Maintain Wellness

Everyone experiences stress at one time or another—it's a normal part of being a human being—but the level of stress affecting college students can undermine their ability to succeed academically.

Consider the level of stress you feel today. Rate your current level of stress on a scale of 1–5: 1 is "little or no stress" and 5 is "extremely stressed."

My current stress level: _____

If your stress level is a 3 or above, describe the symptoms of stress that you are experiencing.

_____

_____

Can you identify *why* you are feeling this level of stress?

_____

_____

If your stress level is a 1 or 2, can you identify why?

_____

_____

When you are stressed, your body undergoes physiological changes. Your breathing becomes rapid and shallow; your heart rate increases; the muscles in your shoulders, forehead, neck, and chest tighten; your hands become cold or sweaty; your hands and knees may shake; your stomach becomes upset; your mouth goes dry; and your voice may sound strained. Over time, stress can develop into chronic health issues such as irritable bowel syndrome, common colds, migraines, and fatigue.

A number of psychological changes also occur when you are under stress. You might experience a sense of confusion, trouble concentrating, memory lapses, and poor problem solving. As a result of stress, you may also make decisions that you regret later. High stress levels can lead to emotions such as anger, anxiety, depression, fear, frustration, and irritability, which might cause you to be unable to go to sleep at night or to wake up frequently. These stress-related changes can turn into more serious psychological ailments such as anxiety disorder, depression, or panic attacks.

Stress has many sources, but two seem to be prominent: life events and daily hassles. Life events are those that represent major adversity, such as the death of a parent, spouse, partner, or friend. Researchers believe that an accumulation of stress from life events, especially if many events occur over a short period of time, can cause physical and mental health problems. Daily hassles are the minor irritants that we experience every day, such as losing your keys, having three tests on the same day, quarreling with your roommate, or worrying about money.

The best starting point for handling stress is to be in good physical and mental shape. If you pay attention to your body and mind, you will be able to recognize the signs of stress before they escalate and become uncontrollable.

HIGH-IMPACT PRACTICE › In class, ask students to write down their top ten stressors. Then break students into small groups and have them reach a consensus on the top stressors for first-year college students. Finally, have each group share its consensus list with the other groups. How different are the lists? How similar are they? What does that suggest?

your turn — Stay Motivated

Being Mindful of Stress

Do you get stressed before an exam or graded performance? Some level of stress might motivate you to do well, but a high stress level can have the opposite effect. The next time that you are stressed before a test or performance, note how you feel, both physically and mentally. Are you more energized, more alert? Or does your stress negatively affect your concentration or self-confidence? Manage your stress so that it helps, not hurts, your preparation and performance. If your stress is out of control, seek help from the campus counseling center.

IN CLASS ❯ Ask students how many of them think that they are constantly juggling one deadline to meet another, or skipping one class to finish an assignment for another one. Assure them that although they will need to work on both time and stress management, most other students are facing the same challenges, and most will learn to handle these challenges successfully.

IN CLASS ❯ Have students identify stressors that they might be able to reduce through lifestyle modifications. What would those modifications be?

Take Control. Modifying your lifestyle is the best overall approach to stress management. You have the power to change your life so that it is less stressful. Lifestyle modification involves identifying the parts of your life that do not serve you well, making plans for change, and then carrying out the plans. For example, if you are stressed because you are always late for classes, get up 10 minutes earlier. If you get nervous when you talk to a certain negative classmate before a test, avoid that person when you have an exam coming up. Learn test-taking skills so that you can manage test anxiety better. If doing poorly on a test causes you to give up or become depressed, work to develop your resilience and belief in yourself. Learn from your mistakes, but trust yourself to do better in the future.

Another way students can take control of their lifestyle is by knowing their boundaries and making priority lists. This might mean saying *no* to friends or family members who distract you from your tasks and obligations—for instance, telling a roommate that you have to stay in to study instead of going to open mic night. It is OK to say *no*, and you don't have to feel guilty about doing so. Students have obligations from clubs, classes, and peers, and you will have to work hard to manage all of these obligations and still maintain good grades.

Check your college Web site, counseling center, health center, student newspaper, or fitness center for classes that teach relaxation techniques. Learning new techniques for managing stress takes knowledge and practice. You'll find apps, Web sites, books, and other resources that guide you through many options.

The Importance of Good Nutrition

There is a clear connection between what you eat and drink, your overall health and well-being, and stress. Eating a lot of junk food will add pounds to your body and reduce your energy level. When you can't keep up with your work because you're slow or tired, you will experience more stress.

Caffeine is probably the best example of a commonly ingested substance that is linked to high stress levels. College students, like many adults, use caffeine to help with productivity. Caffeine increases alertness and reduces feelings of fatigue if used moderately. Up to 400 milligrams (mg) of caffeine a day appears to be safe for most healthy adults. That's roughly the amount of caffeine in four cups of brewed coffee, ten cans of cola, or two "energy shot" drinks.[1] However, too much caffeine can cause nervousness, headaches, irritability, upset stomach, and sleeplessness—all symptoms of stress. It is important to monitor your daily use of caffeine. Many students consume energy drinks, which can contain more than the recommended amount of caffeine. Be careful to limit your caffeine intake. Using coffee or energy drinks when you're cramming for exams, or even to get through the day, can become a crutch. Find other sources of energy, like jogging or power napping.

isthisyou?

My Favorite Pants Don't Fit

Have your eating habits changed since you started college, and have those changes caused you to put on some weight? Are you struggling to make the right decisions about what to eat? Have you found that fitting exercise into your daily schedule is nearly impossible? This chapter offers nutrition and exercise strategies. Which of these strategies are you willing to try? Pick one nutrition strategy and one exercise strategy, and chart your progress for a week. Are you willing to continue for a second week? What about incorporating a second strategy?

IN CLASS ❯ Check on campus or with one of your local hospitals to see if you can find a dietitian who is willing to talk to your class. A dietitian might help students think about the benefits of eating a healthy diet at this stage in their lives, as well as suggest how to escape a constant diet of pizza.

IN CLASS ❯ The 2004 film *Super Size Me* deals in a humorous, yet serious, way with the effects of eating fast food for a month. This film will spark a lively discussion.

IN CLASS ❯ Poll students to find out how many cups of coffee and how many caffeinated soft drinks they drink each day. Have them calculate the total number of milligrams of caffeine they ingest each day.

yourturn   Make Good Choices

Resist Junk Food Temptations

Food—especially savory or sweet items—may be one of life's greatest temptations. Remember that your choices of what and how much you eat now will affect what you feel like and look like twenty, thirty, or forty years from now. Look around you and take note of people in their forties, fifties, and sixties. Which ones do you think made healthy food choices when they were your age, and as they grew older?

Many of us find that gaining weight is really easy; a few days of donuts, pizza, and soft drinks can pack on unexpected pounds. Losing weight, even a small amount, is far more difficult. Let's face it—food is one of life's greatest pleasures, and having the self-discipline to say no to a giant piece of birthday cake is difficult. Weight gain also will reduce your energy and interest in exercise.

---

[1]Mayo Clinic reference: www.mayoclinic.org/caffeine/ART-20045678?p=1.

If you are gaining weight and losing energy, what can you do about your eating habits? It might not be easy at first, but if you start making small, positive changes, you can build toward a new way of eating. You will not only feel better, but also be healthier and probably happier. Here are some commonsense suggestions:

- Limit snacks to healthy options such as fruit, vegetables, yogurt, hummus, and small portions of nuts, like pistachios, almonds, cashews, or walnuts.
- Be careful about "fad" diets. Before using diet pills or beginning a diet regimen such as the Paleo, Atkins, or South Beach diet, check with your physician. These diets may show results quicker than maintaining a balanced diet and exercising, but they might cause you to miss essential nutrients, especially if you are an athlete. Simply changing your portion sizes can be a first step toward weight loss.
- Drink plenty of water. Drinking 64 ounces of water a day helps flush your system, keep your skin healthy, and manage weight. A rule of thumb: To keep hydrated, drink water before and after a workout and between meals.
- Add variety to your meals. Dining halls can offer several options, and the most important strategy is to eat a balanced and well-portioned meal that includes protein, vegetables, grains, salad, and fruit. Stay away from fried and sugary foods. Choose grilled or broiled lean meat and fish instead. A good reference is **ChooseMyPlate.gov**, shown in Figure 13.1. Watch your portion sizes. Avoid large, jumbo, or king-size fast-food items and all-you-can-eat buffets.
- Eat a healthy breakfast! Your brain will function better if you eat a power-packed meal first thing in the morning. Try oatmeal, smoothies, eggs, and foods high in protein to help you focus and boost your metabolism for the rest of the day.

FIGURE 13.1 › MyPlate Eating Guidelines

This is the new MyPlate icon, which was introduced by the federal government in 2011 to replace the food guide pyramid. **ChooseMyPlate.gov** provides tips and recommendations for healthy eating and understanding the plate's design.
Courtesy USDA

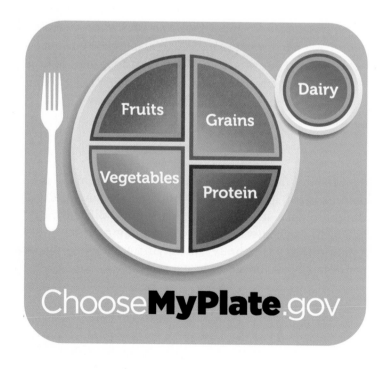

A Serving Is a Slice, Not the Whole Pizza

Have you ever found yourself staring at the remains of a pizza like this one and realizing that your eating is a bit out of control? Start to rein yourself back in that moment. Stop at the grocery store on the way home to pick up some healthy snacks. Throw out half-eaten bags of chips. Take a long walk, or give yourself an extra half hour in the morning to take a walk or a jog. It's never the wrong time or too late to take better care of yourself, and no step in the right direction is too small.

© Image Source/Corbis

- Always read the nutrition label on packaged foods. Be skeptical of marketing on labels. Instead, look for the number of grams of fat, sugars, protein, and carbohydrates. Check the sodium content: Sodium (table salt) will make you retain water, which increases your weight, and can possibly increase your blood pressure. Do not let "nonfat/low-fat" options entice you. Often, these products contain chemicals and unhealthy by-products that are worse for you than their full-fat counterparts.
- If possible, take time to cook your own food, bring your lunch, and pack your own snacks. Preparing your own meals and snacks is almost always healthier and more cost-effective than eating out or buying snack food at convenience stores.

your turn Work Together

Portion Size and Your Meal Plan

How does portion size factor into what you put on your plate, whether you're home, in a dining hall, or in a restaurant? Do you fill up your plate? Do you eat everything on it? Do you monitor whether you feel satisfied or full during the meal? Do chicken fingers and toasted ravioli appeal to you more than grilled chicken and sautéed vegetables? Do you think that college students are less likely to eat in a healthy manner than the general population? Why or why not? Discuss your thoughts on these questions in a small group.

high-impact practice 3

HIGH-IMPACT PRACTICE ❯ Students can collaborate on strategies for healthy eating and can also challenge their own eating habits. These questions can prompt class discussions, writing assignments, or even in-class debates.

Risky Eating Habits. Although we advise you to think about what you eat from day to day, we also advise you not to overthink your diet. Remember that the key to good health is achieving balance, and an obsession with food intake may be a sign that things are out of balance. Over the last few decades, an increasing number of both male and female college students have been developing eating disorders such as anorexia nervosa (an extreme fear of gaining weight), bulimia (overeating followed by self-induced vomiting or laxative use), or binge eating disorder (compulsive overeating long past the feeling of being full).

Anyone who is struggling with an eating disorder should seek immediate medical attention. Eating disorders can be life-threatening if they are not treated by a health care professional. Contact your student health center for more information, or contact the National Eating Disorder Association (**nationaleatingdisorders.org** or 1-800-931-2237) to find a professional in your area who specializes in the treatment of eating disorders.

Exercising to Maintain Wellness

Exercise is an excellent stress-management technique, the best way to stay fit, and an important element in effective weight management. Whether it's walking to class, going to the campus recreation center, or going for a bike ride, it is important to get outside and be active every day. Any kind of exercise benefits your body and spirit and is a great choice for stress and weight management. Choose activities that you enjoy so that you look forward to your exercise time and make it a regular part of your routine. People who exercise report higher energy levels, less stress, better sleep, healthier weight, and an improved self-image compared with people who do not exercise.

IN CLASS > Have students write down the kinds of exercise they do regularly, including the type of activity, how long each day, and how many days a week they exercise—and yes, walking counts. Ask some of the students to read what they wrote about their exercise regimen. It is generally accepted that it takes 30 to 40 minutes of aerobic exercise at least three times a week to gain the health benefits that exercise affords, such as lower cholesterol, weight loss, stress relief, increased strength, etc. Ask how many of the students are meeting that requirement. Discuss the factors preventing them from getting the proper amount of exercise.

IN CLASS > Discuss the "freshman fifteen." Have your students experienced this weight problem? If so, what can they do about it? If not, how do they think that they avoided it?

Get Moving!

Whether it's running, walking, or playing a sport, every student needs to get moving. What are your exercise habits? Remember that daily exercise can be a great, no-cost way to reduce stress while keeping you in good physical and mental shape.

Jonathan Stark

Besides doing wonders for your body, aerobic exercise keeps your mind healthy. When you do aerobic exercise, your body produces hormones called beta-endorphins. These natural narcotics cause feelings of contentment and happiness and help manage anxiety and depression. Your mood and general sense of competence improve with regular aerobic exercise. In fact, people who undertake aerobic exercise report more energy, less stress, better sleep, weight loss, and an improved self-image.

Think about ways to combine activities and use your time efficiently. Maybe you can leave your car at home and walk or ride a bike to class. If you must drive, then park at the far end of the parking lot to get in extra steps. Try going to the gym with a friend and asking each other study questions while you're on the treadmills. Take the stairs whenever possible. Wear a pedometer, and aim for a certain number of steps each day. If you're a parent, run around with your kids. Play organized sports or use your campus fitness center. Most important, remember that exercise is most effective if you make it part of your day-to-day life.

Another way to monitor your weight management and progress during exercise is not just to focus on your weight, but also to be aware of your body mass index (BMI). Knowing your BMI is a good way to understand your optimum size. According to the U.S. Centers for Disease Control and Prevention (CDC), BMI is calculated by weight and height, and provides an effective way to screen for health issues. For an adult, BMI is calculated with this formula:[2] weight (lb) / [height (in)]^2 x 703

Calculate BMI by dividing weight in pounds (lbs.) by height in inches (in.) squared and multiplying by a conversion factor of 703.

Example: Weight = 150 lbs., Height = 5'5" (65")

Calculation: [150 ÷ (65)^2] x 703 = 24.96

Per **cdc.gov**, a BMI of under 18.5 indicates "underweight," 18.5 to 24.9 is "normal," 25 to 29.9 is "overweight," and 30 or higher is "obese."

Getting Enough Sleep to Maintain Wellness

Getting adequate sleep is another way to protect yourself from stress. When you wake up in the morning, you should feel fresh and sharp. According to the National Sleep Foundation, 63 percent of American adults do not get the recommended eight hours of sleep per night. Lack of sleep can lead to anxiety, depression, and academic problems. Researchers found that students who studied all week but then stayed up late partying on the weekends forgot as much as 30 percent of the material they had learned during the preceding week. Try the following suggestions to establish better sleep habits:

- Avoid long daytime naps that last more than 30 minutes.
- Try reading or listening to a relaxation tape before going to bed.
- Exercise during the day.
- Get your clothes, school materials, and food together for the next day before you go to bed.
- Sleep in the same room and bed every night.
- Stick to a regular schedule for going to bed and getting up.

[2]Indianapolis: American College of Sports Medicine, 2003.

OUTSIDE CLASS › Ask students to do an Internet search on the effects of sleep deprivation. They might be surprised at what they find.

IN CLASS › Follow up the investigation on the effects of sleep deprivation with a discussion. What happens to the body if we do not get sufficient sleep? Do students think that they are getting enough sleep? Why or why not?

Catch Some Z's

When you aren't getting enough sleep, you cannot do your best. A brief, 20-minute nap can revive you when you're feeling tired during the day. Establish good sleeping habits and grab opportunities for power naps when you can.

© Randy Faris/Corbis

Emotional Health

Your emotional or mental health is an important component of your overall health. Particularly in the first year of college, some students have difficulty establishing positive relationships with others, dealing with pressure, or making wise decisions. Other students are optimistic and happy, and seem to believe in their own abilities to address problems successfully. Your ability to deal with life's challenges is based on your emotional intelligence (EI); this book devotes a chapter to this topic, with tools for assessing your EI and strategies for improving it. Emotional intelligence is part of your personality; if you take a psychology course in college, you will learn more about it.

Taking care of your emotional health is a big part of maintaining wellness. When one's emotional health declines, the consequences can be very serious.

Depression. According to the American Psychological Association, depression is one of the most common psychiatric disorders in the United States, affecting more than fifteen million adults. College students are at especially high risk for both depression and suicide because of the major life changes and high stress levels some of them experience during the college years.

Depression is not a weakness; it is an illness that needs medical attention. Many college students suffer from some form of depression. The feelings are often temporary and may be situational. A romantic breakup, a disappointing grade, or an ongoing problem with another person can create feelings of despair. Although most depression goes away on its own, if you or a friend has any of the following symptoms for more than two weeks, it is important to talk to a health care provider:

- feelings of helplessness and hopelessness
- feeling useless, inadequate, bad, or guilty

- self-hatred, constant questioning of one's thoughts and actions
- loss of energy and motivation
- loss of appetite
- weight loss or gain
- difficulty sleeping or excessive need for sleep
- loss of interest in sex
- difficulty concentrating for a significant length of time

Suicide. The CDC reports that students aged fifteen to twenty-four are more likely than any other group to attempt suicide. Most people who commit suicide give a warning of their intentions. The following are common indicators of someone's intent to commit suicide:

- recent loss and inability to let go of grief
- change in personality—sadness, withdrawal, indifference
- expressions of self-hatred
- change in sleep patterns
- change in eating habits
- a direct statement about committing suicide (e.g., "I might as well end it all")
- a preoccupation with death

If you or someone you know threatens suicide or displays any of these signs, it's time to consult a mental health professional. Most campuses have counseling centers that offer both one-on-one sessions and support groups for their students, usually for free.

Finally, remember that there is no shame attached to having high levels of stress, depression, anxiety, or suicidal tendencies. Unavoidable life events or physiological imbalances can cause such feelings and behaviors. Proper counseling, medical attention, and in some cases prescription medication can help students cope with depression and suicidal thoughts.

Difficulty Coping

Many events in life can trigger feelings of despair. Know the signs of depression. If you or someone you care about seems to be having trouble, reach out. College campuses have resources to help.

© Wavebreak Media Ltd/Veer/Corbis

Cyberbullying. In recent years, cyberbullying has been on the rise, not just in grade school and high school, but on college campuses as well. Experts define cyberbullying as "any behavior performed through electronic or digital media by individuals or groups who repeatedly communicate hostile or aggressive messages intended to inflict harm or discomfort on others."[3] According to a recent study, the prevalence of cyberbullying among college populations ranges from 10 to 28.7 percent.[4] These may seem like low numbers, but cyberbullying can go unreported because of embarrassment or privacy concerns. Tragic cyberbullying stories that have resulted in the victim's clinical depression or suicide have been reported in recent years.

Cyberbullying is a serious issue that harms individuals in many ways. It is a crime that should be dealt with immediately. If someone you know has experienced cyberbullying or if you have been a cyberbullying victim, you should report it as soon as possible. Several foundations and resources are available to help students report cyberbullying:

- **stopbullying.org**
- The Megan Meier Foundation, **meganmeierfoundation.org**
- National Crime Prevention Council, **ncpc.org**

---

[3]P. K. Smith et al., "Cyberbullying: Its Nature and Impact in Secondary School Pupils," *Journal of Child Psychology and Psychiatry*, no. 49 (2008): 375–76.

[4]Carlos P. Zalaquett and SeriaShia J. Chatters, "Cyberbullying in College: Frequency, Characteristics, and Practical Implications," *SAGE Open* (Jan.–Mar. 2014): 1–8. Web.

Victimized by Cyberbullying?

Have you or a friend ever felt victimized by something someone posted about you on social media? It's tempting to lash out with an equally negative post, but the best strategy is to disengage. Don't let what others say or write about you define who you are, and don't join them in the mud.

© Owen Franken/Corbis

your turn	Work Together

The Link between Cyberbullying and Suicide

Google *college students and cyberbullying*. As you read through the articles that you find, write down common triggers that seem to cause student suicide. Bring your notes to class and share them with other students in a small group. Discuss why college students are at risk for cyberbullying, depression, and suicide, and share ideas for what colleges and universities can do to decrease this risk.

MAINTAINING SEXUAL HEALTH

Numerous studies report that about 75 percent of traditional-age college students have engaged in sexual intercourse at least once. Whether or not you are part of this percentage, it can be helpful to explore your sexual values and consider whether sex is right for you at this time in your life. Many students have had different levels of exposure to sex education and have a different view and knowledge base about their sexual experiences. If it is the right time for you to become sexually active, you should know what resources are available and adopt strategies for avoiding the unwanted consequences of unprotected sex. This section provides resources to help you make informed and educated decisions regarding your sexual health.

Communicating about Safe Sex

Communication is the most important aspect of both casual and long-term sexual relationships. You and your partner must share your experiences and communicate needs, backgrounds, and how to be safe. Without communication, partners do not know each other's expectations, intentions can get confused, and emotions can become muddled. Here are some strategies to help with communication:

- Discuss testing for sexually transmitted infections (STIs). Make sure both partners have been tested recently. The rule of thumb for a sexually active person is to get tested at least once a year, and after any unprotected encounter.
- Share expectations. Partners should talk about what they expect from the sexual encounter. Partners should be clear about what they are comfortable with and what they want to get out of the experience.
- Use protection. Protecting yourself and your partner from unwanted consequences—pregnancy or the transmission of STIs—is important, and so is communicating about protection ahead of time. Do you and your partner have what you need, or does one of you need to buy it? One night can change your entire life, so make sure you are prepared.

- Communicate in "I" statements. "I" statements help facilitate open communication. When you use "I" statements, you accept responsibility for your feelings, you do not accuse or threaten another. A statement like "I feel like we need to explore our options," is more useful than "You don't know what you're talking about." Remember, each person brings his or her previous experiences into an encounter or a relationship; being aware of this helps with communication, whether you are talking or listening.

Avoiding Sexually Transmitted Infections (STIs)

RETENTION STRATEGY > STIs need to be a topic instructors in this course address because they are sources of great stress for affected students, and hence interfere with concentration and academic success. Of course, they also can have long-term negative health consequences. Make sure to tell students where they can go on campus to obtain confidential diagnosis and treatment.

IN CLASS > Topics such as masturbation, celibacy, monogamy, and condom negotiation are often uncomfortable to discuss and have stigmas and myths attached. Students should know that it is perfectly natural and normal for individuals to have sexual desires, feelings, and urges. The key point of this section is to let students know that there are alternatives to intercourse, including a range of behaviors that carry varying degrees of risk.

You can avoid STIs and unwanted pregnancies by abstaining from sex entirely. Apparently, 25 percent of college students choose this option, according to national research. For many people, masturbation is a reasonable alternative to sex with a partner.

If you're in the remaining 75 percent, you'll be safer, in terms of STI transmission, if you have only one partner. As a responsible adult, you have the option to choose your sexual experiences. Whether you're monogamous or not, you should always protect yourself by using a condom or being sure your partner uses one.

In addition to offering contraceptive protection, a condom can help prevent the spread of STIs, including human immunodeficiency virus (HIV) and human papillomavirus (HPV). A condom offers effective protection against the spread of disease during anal, vaginal, and oral intercourse. The most up-to-date research indicates that condoms are 90 to 99 percent effective at both preventing the transmission of STIs and preventing pregnancy when used correctly and consistently for every act of anal, vaginal, and oral intercourse. Note that only latex rubber condoms and polyurethane condoms—not lambskin or other types of natural membrane condoms—provide this protection. The polyurethane condom is a great alternative for individuals who have allergies to latex. Use a water-based lubricant such as K-Y Jelly rather than an oil-based lubricant, which can cause a latex condom to break.

The problem of STIs on college campuses has received growing attention in recent years as epidemic numbers of students have become infected. In general, STIs continue to increase faster than other illnesses on campuses today, and approximately 5 to 10 percent of visits by U.S. college students to college health services are for the diagnosis and treatment of STIs. STIs are usually spread through genital contact. Sometimes, however, these infections can be transmitted mouth-to-mouth. Leaving the light on before intercourse can give you an opportunity to notice symptoms of an STI on your partner, and it can also help with proper condom use.

There are more than twenty known types of STIs; seven are most common on college campuses. One particularly common STI is HPV, a sexually transmitted infection that is closely linked to cervical cancer. In fact, the CDC estimates that 20 million people in the United States are currently infected with HPV. Gardasil, a vaccine that became available in 2006, provides protection for both men and women against the strains of HPV that cause genital warts, anal cancer, and cervical cancer. For more information about this vaccine or to receive the three-injection series, contact your college or university health services or your local health care provider.

Using Birth Control

Sexually active, heterosexual students have to take steps to prevent unwanted pregnancies. Planning is the key. The best method of contraception is any method that you use correctly and consistently each time you have intercourse. Always discuss birth control with your partner so that you both feel comfortable with the option you have selected. For more information about a particular method, consult a pharmacist, your student health center, a local family-planning clinic, or your private physician. Remember, birth control is not the answer to safe sex—it only protects against pregnancy. Use condoms for protection against STIs, in addition to your chosen method of pregnancy prevention.

What if the condom breaks or you forget to take your birth control pill? Emergency contraceptive pills can reduce the risk of pregnancy. According to the Planned Parenthood Federation of America, if emergency contraceptive pills are taken within 72 hours of unprotected intercourse, they can significantly reduce the risk of pregnancy. Most campus health centers and local health clinics dispense emergency contraception.

IN CLASS > Research shows that alcohol is often involved in unplanned, unintended sexual activity, whether consensual or not. Ask students to brainstorm ideas for preventing or managing such a situation. Refer them to the content later in this chapter on making good decisions regarding alcohol consumption.

Protecting Yourself and Others against Sexual Assault and Violence

Sexual assault that happens on college campuses is a problem that has existed for many years. Everyone is at risk for becoming a victim of sexual assault, but the majority of victims are women. Between the time women start college and when they graduate, an estimated one out of four of them will be the victim of attempted rape, and one out of six will be raped. According to statistics, 85 to 90 percent of these victims will be raped by someone they know—a date or an acquaintance—and most will not report the crime. Alcohol is a factor in nearly 75 percent of the incidents.

Many sexual assaults on college campuses happen during the first two weeks of classes. Moving to college can bring students into contact with new people and new places that are unfamiliar and may be unsafe. Students should have a heightened sense of awareness when going to social events in their first few months on campus. Always be sure to take a friend with you, bring your cell phone, carefully monitor what you are drinking, trust your intuition, and be sure to become familiar with your surroundings so you know how to leave or get help if needed.

If you observe a sexual assault or a potential sexual assault, make your presence known. Don't be a bystander; intervene in any way you can. Create a distraction, and if you need help, ask a friend, a resident assistant, or even a bartender or bouncer to help you.

In 2013, the federal government instituted an initiative called the Campus Save Act. The act mandates that all universities must provide sexual assault, violence, and harassment education to students. The Campus

IN CLASS > Although today's college students are more sophisticated and experienced than earlier generations, they are also exposed to a great deal of misinformation. They might have heard about abstinence and perhaps the importance of condoms, but have they learned how to negotiate for safer sex, to communicate with potential partners, or to be assertive about their own bodies and sexuality? If they had, would we be experiencing the high levels of unwanted pregnancies and STIs that are still prevalent on college campuses?

PEER LEADERS > Students will have questions about how to intervene if they observe a sexual assault without putting themselves at risk or causing greater risk to the victim. Talk with your campus counseling center about this issue and learn about the center's recommendations. The **itsonus. org** Web site also provides excellent tips on intervening to prevent a sexual assault.

Save Act provides an amendment to the Clery Act of 1990, which the federal government implemented after a woman was raped and killed. The Clery Act required postsecondary institutions to report sexual crimes and related statistics. Colleges can report cases of sexual misconduct, but as always, the student's information must remain confidential. It is always up to the victim to decide how he or she would like to proceed after a sexual assault has occurred. You can find out more about the Campus Save Act by visiting **campussaveact.org**, contacting your campus security office, or contacting your student judicial office.

Whether sexually assaulted by a date or by a stranger, a victim can suffer long-term traumatic effects and mental health consequences such as depression, anxiety, and even suicide. Many victims essentially blame themselves, but the only person at fault for a sexual assault is the perpetrator. If you are a victim of sexual assault, regardless of whether you choose to report it to the police, it is very helpful to seek counseling from a campus sexual assault coordinator, a local rape crisis center, the campus police department, student health services, women's student services, a local hospital emergency room, or a campus chaplain. Here are some steps you can take to help a sexual assault victim:

- Remain empathetic and nonjudgmental.
- Keep information private and ensure his or her confidentiality.
- Listen.
- Ask the victim how he or she would like to proceed—discuss options like contacting campus police or the campus counseling center.
- Seek out advice from a professional on how to help the student.
- Stay in touch and follow up to see if the victim is getting the help he or she needs.

IN CLASS > Students might claim that they have heard this speech before. Have them defend their right to party; that is, ask them to explain why campus authorities should have no business interfering with a student's social life.

RETENTION STRATEGY > There is a clear-cut relationship between whether students use or abuse alcohol, their level of academic functioning, and their retention rates.

ALCOHOL AND OTHER SUBSTANCES

In this section, our purpose is not to make judgments, but to warn you about the ways in which irresponsible use of substances can have a negative impact on your college experience and your life. In today's world, it is easy to obtain substances, both legal and illegal, that can cause serious harm to your health and well-being. For college students, tobacco, alcohol, and marijuana are the substances most commonly used and abused.

The Use and Abuse of Alcohol

In college, many students will encounter alcohol or other legal and illegal substances. Of course, there are legal age restrictions to consuming alcohol; to avoid potential legal consequences, you should not drink alcohol if you are under age twenty-one. If you decide to consume risky substances, you can still make responsible decisions about your consumption by using the harm-reduction approach. The next pages list some simple harm-reduction approaches to consuming alcohol.

Consider the Consequences
This party looks like fun, but if you drink too much, you may find yourself hooking up with someone you hardly know. What started off as a good time could end up being your worst nightmare.
© 2/Ocean/Corbis

- Slow down drinking. One way to maintain a "buzz"—the euphoric sensation you experience from drinking—is by drinking one beer per hour or less. Pacing yourself and limiting your drinks help prevent you from attaining a high blood alcohol content (BAC) level. (You will learn more about BAC levels later in this section).
- Eat while you drink. Sometimes eating while you consume alcohol helps slow down your drinking and slows down the processing of alcohol. Body weight and gender play a large role in this as well.
- Drink water. Alcohol dehydrates your body, so it is important to drink plenty of water while consuming alcohol.
- Designate a driver before you go out. Walking is always a better option than driving a vehicle, but if you are going to take a vehicle to a destination with alcohol, you should always designate the sober driver before you leave.

Because 50 percent of college students reported helping a drunken friend, classmate, or study partner in the previous year, it's important that all students learn about the effects of alcohol consumption. Alcohol can turn even people who don't drink into victims, such as people who are killed by drunk drivers or family members who suffer as a result of the destructive behavior of an alcoholic relative. Over the course of one year, about 20 to 30 percent of students report serious problems related to excessive alcohol use. You might have heard news reports about college students who died or were seriously or permanently injured as a result of excessive drinking. Just one occasion of heavy or high-risk drinking can lead to problems.

HIGH-IMPACT PRACTICE > In class, ask students to write anonymously about whether they believe they drink more or less than their peers. Now ask them to estimate the number of drinks they consume in a week. Tell them to be as accurate as possible. Collect the unsigned papers, and determine the average number of drinks per week per student. What can the class derive from these data?

IN CLASS > Ask students whether drinking alcohol, especially during the week, affects one's schoolwork. Ask for examples. How can these issues be better managed?

IN CLASS > Ask students to identify as many effects of alcohol on the body as they can. What are some of the early effects? What are the later effects? Some research might be of interest here.

IN CLASS > Ask students to make a list of times or situations when it would be unwise to drink alcohol. Ask some of the students to share what they wrote, and then discuss their lists with the class.

IN CLASS ❯ Ask the class to share their experiences with intoxicated friends. What was the situation? What was their role?

HIGH-IMPACT PRACTICE ❯ In class, ask students to write for several minutes on what the statement "You do not have to be an alcoholic to experience problems with alcohol" means to them. Ask students to volunteer their answers and discuss them as a class.

People experience the pleasurable effects of alcoholic beverages as the alcohol begins to affect several areas in the brain. How fast you drink makes a difference, too. Your body gets rid of alcohol at a rate of about one drink—defined as one 12 ounce beer, one 5 ounce glass of wine, or 1.5 ounces of hard liquor—per hour. Drinking more than one drink an hour may cause a rise in BAC because the body is absorbing alcohol faster than it can eliminate it. We should also note here that popular home remedies for sobering up, like drinking coffee or water or taking a cold shower, don't work.

At BAC levels of .025 to .05, a drinker may feel animated and energized. At a BAC level of around .05, a drinker may feel rowdy or boisterous. This is where most people report feeling a buzz from alcohol. At a BAC level between .05 and .08, alcohol starts to act as a depressant, so as soon as you feel that buzz, remember that you are on the brink of losing coordination, clear thinking, and judgment.

Driving is measurably impaired even at BAC levels lower than the legal limit of .08. In fact, an accurate safe level for most people may be half the legal limit, or .04. As BAC levels climb past .08, people become progressively less coordinated and less able to make good decisions. Most people become severely uncoordinated at BAC levels higher than .08 and may begin falling asleep, falling down, or slurring their speech.

Most people pass out or fall asleep when their BAC level is above .25. Unfortunately, even after you pass out and stop drinking, your BAC level can continue to rise as alcohol in your stomach is released to the intestine and absorbed into the bloodstream. Your body may try to get rid of alcohol by vomiting, but you can choke on your vomit if you are unconscious, semiconscious, or severely uncoordinated. Worse yet, at BAC levels higher than .30, most people will show signs of severe alcohol poisoning, such as an inability to wake up, slowed breathing, a fast but weak pulse, cool or damp skin, and pale or bluish skin. Anyone exhibiting these symptoms needs medical assistance immediately.

IN CLASS ❯ Be aware that one or more students in the class might know someone who has died or come close to dying from acute alcohol poisoning, or some might have suffered acute intoxication themselves. Be prepared for emotional reactions to this topic.

Tobacco and Marijuana

IN CLASS ❯ Discuss why people choose to smoke tobacco or marijuana or to try the new e-cigarette products. What is the role of peer pressure? Why do some athletes use smokeless tobacco?

Tobacco is a legal drug that contains nicotine, a highly addictive substance, and is the cause of many serious medical conditions, including heart disease, lung disease, and some forms of cancer. One concern that particularly relates to college students is *social smoking*. This term describes smoking by students who do so only when hanging out with friends, drinking, or partying. Most college students feel they will be able to give up their social smoking habit once they graduate, but some find that they have become addicted to cigarettes.

You may have noticed advertisements for electronic cigarettes (e-cigarettes or e-cigs) or seen them in stores. According to the U.S. Food and Drug Administration, e-cigarettes are battery-operated products designed to deliver nicotine, flavors, and other chemicals in the form of vapor. Vaping, the term for using e-cigarettes, has not been fully studied, so consumers currently don't know the potential risks.

TABLE 13.1 › Average Cost of Smoking across the United States
(packs of cigarettes continue to increase in cost, but prices differ by geographical location)

Half-Pack-a-Day Smoker
$5.51/pack × 3.5 packs/week = $19.29/week
$19.29/week × 52 weeks/year = $1,002.82/year
$1,002.82/year × 4 years of college = $4,011.28
In 25 years, you will have spent $25,070.50

Pack-a-Day Smoker
$5.51/pack × 7 packs/week = $38.57/week
$38.57/week × 52 weeks/year = $2,005.64
$2,005.64/year × 4 years of college = $8,022.56
In 25 years, you will have spent $50,141.00

A final reason for smokers to quit, and for others never to start, is the cost, as reported by the American Lung Association (see Table 13.1). Contact your campus health center for more information about quitting.

Recently, Colorado, Washington, Oregon, Alaska, and Washington, D.C. became the first places in the U.S. to legalize recreational marijuana use for individuals twenty-one years or older. It is still not legal in other states or federally, however. College students sometimes get caught with marijuana, and as with tobacco, there are health risks associated with smoking it. Some impacts of marijuana use include an increase in anxiety, paranoia, short-term memory loss, and depression. In addition, marijuana smoke increases your risk for lung cancer, much like tobacco. It is important to know the risks and acknowledge your state and federal laws.

your turn Write and Reflect

The Legalization of Marijuana

Four states and the District of Columbia have recently legalized the recreational use of marijuana. Reflect on and write about the consequences associated with consuming marijuana legally. What are potential problems? What are the benefits?

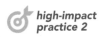

high-impact practice 2

HIGH-IMPACT PRACTICE › Ask students to write a persuasive one- or two-page paper arguing either for or against the legalization of marijuana. By doing do, they will explore this social issue, gain experience in persuasive writing, and have the opportunity to share their ideas with other students in the classroom.

techtip

SURF FOR HEALTH

We all want to be healthy and look fit, but we live in a world that makes us inactive and presents us with convenient but unhealthy food options. Many of us spend lots of time in front of television and computer screens. Even when we aren't watching a particular show or presentation, we view videos on our phones at the gas pump, in restaurants, or while we wait for the elevator. When we are bored, we have game systems and games on our phones that often keep us sitting right where we are. It seems like we are in front of digital screens almost 24 hours a day. So instead of letting technology make you a couch potato, how can you use it to help you become and stay fit?

The Problem

You want to stay healthy, but hours sitting in front of a computer or eating too much fast food are getting in your way.

The Fix

Enlist technology to get you moving and making healthier choices.

How to Do It

Learn how to filter out the fiction. When it comes to fitness and nutrition, there's a lot of conflicting advice and bad information out there, and more than a few scams. Zero in on a few reputable, well-vetted sources of information. You can find everything from healthy menu plans to yoga training to fitness tips on the following Web sites and smart phone apps:

FITNESS WEB SITES	
Site Name	Web Address
FitDay	fitday.com
fitness.com	fitness.com
fitness partner	primusweb.com/ fitnesspartner
Livestrong	livestrong.com
Men's Fitness	mensfitness.com
Nutrition Data	nutritiondata.self.com
WeightWatchers	weightwatchers.com

HEALTH-RELATED PHONE APPS	
App Name	Function
FitStar	Makes workout dynamic
Argus	Tracks physical activity
Human	Tracks casual activity
Fooducate	Features shopping guide to help you buy good food
Diet Point Weight Loss	Helps track food/ calorie intake
Healthy Out	Guide when eating out or getting takeout
Spark People	Connects you to a range of health sites

Clear some floor space. Make some of the time you spend in front of a screen active time. The Internet can be a valuable ally if you're struggling to find time to work out. Free Web sites like YouTube and online services like Netflix, which charges a low monthly fee, let you stream a huge variety of workout videos with no need to hit the gym.

Exergame: Video gaming systems like Xbox let you enjoy real-life workouts in the virtual world. Try Dance Dance Revolution or virtual baseball, bowling, boxing, golf, or tennis. While you're at it, get your roommates or family members to join in.

EXTRA STYLE POINTS: Use your electronic calendar to send periodic alerts to your cell phone throughout your school day and workday to take breaks or work out. When you are studying, working, or attending classes, it is very easy to forget to give your body time to be active. You don't necessarily have to change clothes or go to the gym. Sometimes a brisk walk or 15 minutes of stretching and relaxed breathing can reset your body and your mind.

checklist **for** success

Wellness

◼ **Understand that wellness is about your body, mind, and spirit.** These components can influence each other and can, in turn, affect your success in college.

◼ **Remember that managing stress is a key college success strategy.** College, with its very demanding nature, increases stress. Use the strategies from your college success course to learn how to reduce stress in college and beyond.

◼ **Learn strategies for managing your diet and your exercise regimen.** There are many sources of advice on ways to maintain your physical and mental health through proper diet and exercise. Check in your library or online for a reputable source that works for you.

◼ **Appreciate the role that your emotional health plays in your overall wellness, and recognize the warning signs of depression in yourself and others.** Remember that depression can negatively affect your college experience. It's important for any student who is depressed to seek help from the campus counseling center.

◼ **Consider the powerful connections between things you control through your decisions.** Make good decisions concerning diet, exercise, sleep, your schedule, and your stress levels.

◼ **Practice making good decisions about sexual health.** Make wise choices to protect yourself against unwanted pregnancy and sexually transmitted infections. Learn to communicate about sex, and work to develop and maintain respectful relationships.

◼ **Learn about sexual assault.** Know how to define sexual assault, what laws are in place to protect victims, and what you should do if you witness a sexual assault.

◼ **Practice moderation in using alcohol and other legal drugs.** Successful college students can still have a good time in college and not let alcohol or marijuana use interfere with their academic success or personal health. Contrary to prevalent stereotypes, it is not the norm for students to abuse these substances.

◼ **Learn about the costs of smoking.** Not only will you spend a lot of money purchasing tobacco products, you will also have a higher likelihood of developing significant and costly health problems than if you don't smoke.

13 buildyourexperience

REFLECT ON CHOICES

Successful college students reflect deeply on their wellness and experiences. From the strategies you learned in this chapter, what do you remember as being most important? How will you change behaviors and check in with yourself in the future? Reflect on the information found in this chapter.

APPLY WHAT YOU HAVE LEARNED

Now that you have read and discussed this chapter, consider how you can apply what you have learned to your academic life and your personal life. The following prompts will help you reflect on the chapter material and its relevance to you both now and in the future.

1. Identify one area in your life where you need to make changes to become healthier. How do you think that becoming healthier will improve your performance in college? What challenges do you face in becoming healthier?

2. If you could make only three recommendations to an incoming first-year college student about managing stress in college, what would they be? Use your personal experience and what you have learned in this chapter to make your recommendations.

USE YOUR RESOURCES

> **Counseling Center** Locate your college or university's counseling center. Professionals there offer individual and group assistance and lots of information. Remember that their support is confidential and that you will not be judged.

> **Health Center or Infirmary** Pay a visit to your campus health center or infirmary. On most campuses, the professionals who staff the health center are especially interested in educational outreach and practicing prevention. You should be able to receive treatment as well.

> **Campus Support Groups** Many campuses provide professionally-led support groups for students dealing with problems related to excessive alcohol and drug use, abusive sexual relationships, and other issues. Your campus counseling center can help you identify support groups at your college or in your community. If you are a member of a minority group on campus in terms of your age, sexual orientation, race or ethnic group, or veteran or active-duty status, seek out services that are designed specifically for you.

> **Online Resources**

The Go Ask Alice Web site, sponsored by Columbia University, has answers to many health questions: **goaskalice.columbia.edu**

The Web site of the American Dietetic Association provides advice and information on healthy eating and nutrition: **eatright.org**

Learn more about the health effects of tobacco at the American Cancer Society's Web site: **cancer.org**

The Web site of the Center for Young Women's Health has helpful advice on sexual health and other issues: **youngwomenshealth.org/collegehealth10.html**

The National Clearinghouse for Alcohol and Drug Information provides up-to-date information about the effects of alcohol and drug use: **ncadi.samhsa.gov**

The Web site of the Centers for Disease Control and Prevention is an excellent resource for information on all the topics covered in this chapter: **cdc.gov**

If you or someone you know is having suicidal thoughts, contact the National Suicide Prevention Lifeline at 1-800-273-TALK or visit their Web site: **suicidepreventionlifeline.org.**

National Eating Disorders Association: **nationaleatingdisorders.org**

U.S. Government's Nutrition Information: **nutrition.gov**

 LaunchPad

LaunchPad for *Your College Experience* is a great resource. Go online to master concepts using the LearningCurve study tool and much more. macmillanhighered.com/gardner12e

14
MONEY

YOU WILL EXPLORE

The importance of living on a budget

Different types of financial aid and how to qualify for and keep them

How to achieve a balance between working and borrowing

Strategies for using and managing credit wisely

Why you should plan for your financial future

⌖ High-impact practices 2 (writing) and 3 (collaboration)

Juliana Henry, 19

Business major
University of Arizona

> ❝ **I have had to keep my spending to the bare minimum in college. That was a tough transition.** ❞

Juliana Henry was born in Bogota, Colombia, and was adopted as an infant by a family in Massachusetts, where she attended high school. During the college application process, she decided that she wanted to attend a big university, one with Greek life and lots to do, and she wanted to find an institution with a highly-ranked business program. The University of Arizona fit the bill, and the warm weather far from the harsh New England winters didn't hurt either.

Juliana had worked hard during high school, and she managed to save a lot of money the summer before she left for college, so she opted to try attending the university without holding an outside job. The trade-off was that she had to keep her spending low. "It was a tough transition from having lots of money while working full time," she says, but she quickly learned how important it was to have a balanced budget. "When I first got to school I wasn't able to immediately adjust to the thought of not buying things when I wanted them. I have had to keep my spending to the bare minimum in college. That was a tough transition." Like many students, Juliana also has a credit card now, which she got to begin building a good credit score. She has to be careful with that, too, and she tries to use it only for necessities. "My parents cosigned for it," she says, "but I am still the one who has to make the monthly payments!"

After a year at the University of Arizona, Juliana has realized that she actually misses New England more than she thought she would and has decided to transfer to a college back East. "The process of applying to colleges as a transfer was exhausting, but worth it in the end," she says. "I am at a point in my life where I need to make decisions that will truly benefit my future and help me set up my career." She sees herself working in hotel management in the future and hopes to get a job at one of Boston's many fine hotels. Her advice for other first-year students? "Save much more than you think you will need. That money can come in handy!"

To access the LearningCurve study tool, video activities, and more, go to LaunchPad for *Your College Experience.* macmillanhighered.com /gardner12e

Juliana made a hard choice; she had just enough money to manage expenses without working, but her strict budget didn't allow her to spend her hard-earned dollars on anything but the necessities. Living within a budget during the first year of college can be tough, and that's why some students begin to depend on credit cards. Counting on credit cards to extend your available financial resources can be a slippery slope, however. Problems with managing money can make it more difficult to establish a strong academic record and complete your degree. Money issues can also affect your specific academic goals, causing you to select or reject certain academic majors or degree plans because of their future earning potential.

assess your strengths

Whether they work, receive financial aid, or receive money from their families, successful college students must learn to live on a budget. As you begin to read this chapter, remember areas where you think that you have had some success managing your money in the past.

set goals

What are your most important objectives in learning the material in this chapter? Think about challenges you have had in the past with money management, or areas that confuse you or make you nervous. Write down three money-management goals, such as tracking your spending and expenses for one month and using that information to create a monthly budget.

Money is often symbolically and realistically the key ingredient to independence and even, some people have concluded, to a sense of freedom. Money can also stir up problems. You probably know of instances when money divided a family or a relationship, or seemed to drive someone's life in a direction that person would not have taken otherwise.

The purpose of this chapter is to provide some basics of financial literacy—a specialized form of information literacy—and suggestions so that money issues will not be barriers to your success in college. Sources of financial assistance are available through loans, grants, and work-study programs, and this chapter will help you develop a strategy for investigating your options. Think of this chapter as a summary of needed financial skills; if you want more information, consider taking a personal finance class at your college or in your community.

LIVING ON A BUDGET

Face it: College is expensive, and most students have limited financial resources. Not only is tuition a major cost, but day-to-day expenses can also add up quickly. No matter what your financial situation, a budget for college is a must. A **budget** is a spending plan that tracks all sources of income (student loan disbursements, money from parents, etc.) and expenses (rent, tuition, etc.) during a set period of time (weekly, monthly, etc.). Creating and following a budget will allow you to pay your bills on time, cut costs, put some money away for emergencies, and finish college with as little debt as possible. A budget can help you become realistic about your finances so that you have a basis for future life planning.

Creating a Budget

A budget will condition you to live within your means, put money into savings, and possibly invest down the road. Here are a few tips to help you get started.

Gather Income Information. To create an effective budget, you need to learn more about your income and your spending behaviors. First, determine how much money is coming in and when. Sources of income

HIGH-IMPACT PRACTICE ❯ In class, ask students to write about their financial situations, either anonymously or with attribution. Without using names, summarize their responses during the next class and ask students what they might do to solve any financial problems. Provide students with information on where they can go on campus or in the community for help with financial problems.

IN CLASS ❯ Share the methods you use to keep your finances in order (e.g., balancing your checkbook, saving credit card and debit slips, reviewing your credit report). Ask the class whether these methods seem appropriate and manageable. Why or why not?

Too Much Month, Too Little Money

Are you having serious problems managing your money? Were you counting on a source of income that isn't going to be available after all? Do you need a budget, even though you aren't sure how to create one that will work for you? Are you using credit cards to buy things that you don't really need? To stay in college and do your best academically, you have to learn to manage your money. That might mean seeking out loans or scholarships, destroying or hiding your credit cards until they are paid off, or seeking financial counseling at your institution or through a community resource. This chapter will help you figure out what you need to do to be resilient—to stay on top of your financial situation so that money problems don't derail your college plans.

might include a job, your savings, gifts from relatives, student loans, scholarship dollars, or grants. List all your income sources, making note of how often you receive each type of income (weekly or monthly paychecks, quarterly loan disbursements, one-time gifts, etc.) and how much money you can expect. Knowing when your money is coming in will help you decide how to structure your budget. For example, if most of your income comes in on a monthly basis, you'll want to create a monthly budget. If you are paid every other week, a biweekly budget might work better.

Gather Expense Information for Your College or University. Your expenses will include tuition, residence hall fees if you live on campus, books and course materials, lab fees, and membership fees for any organizations you join. Some institutions offer a separate January or May term. Although your tuition for these one-month terms is generally covered in your overall tuition payment, you would have extra expenses if you wanted to travel to another location in the United States or abroad.

Gather Information about Living Expenses. First, do a "reality check." How do you *think* that you are spending your money? To find out for sure where your money is going and when, track your spending for a few weeks—ideally for at least a full month—in a notebook, a table, or a spreadsheet. The kinds of expense categories you should consider will vary depending on your situation. If you are a full-time student who lives with your parents or family members, your living expenses won't be the same as students living in a campus residence hall or in an off-campus apartment. If you are a returning student who holds down a job and has a family of your own to support, you will calculate your expenses differently. Whatever your situation, keeping track of your expenses and learning about your spending behaviors are important habits to develop. Consider which of the following expense categories are relevant to you:

- rent/utilities (electricity, gas, water)
- cell phone/cable/Internet/wi-fi
- transportation (car payment, car insurance, car repairs, gas, public transportation)
- child care
- groceries
- medical expenses (prescriptions, doctor visits, hospital bills)
- clothing/laundry

- entertainment (dining out, hobbies, movies)
- personal grooming (haircuts, toiletries)
- miscellaneous (travel, organization dues)

Be sure to recognize which expenses are fixed and which are variable. A *fixed expense* is one that will cost you the same amount every time you pay it. For example, your rent is a fixed expense because you owe your landlord the same amount each month. A *variable expense* is one that may change. Your textbooks are a variable expense because the number and cost of them will be different each term.

Find Out How You Are Doing. Once you have a sense of how your total income compares to your total weekly or monthly expenses, you can get a clearer picture of your current financial situation.

Make Adjustments. Although your budget might never be perfect, you can strive to improve it. In what areas did you spend much more or much less than expected? Do you need to reallocate funds to better meet the needs of your current situation? Be realistic and thoughtful in how you spend your money, and use your budget to help meet your goals, such as planning for a trip or getting a new pair of jeans.

Whatever you do, don't give up if your bottom line doesn't end up the way that you expected it would. Budgeting is a lot like dieting; you might slip up and eat a pizza (or spend too much buying one), but all is not lost. If you stay focused and flexible, your budget can lead you to financial stability and independence.

---

your turn Make Good Choices

Miscellaneous Expenses

Trying to get a handle on your "miscellaneous" expenses can be a challenge. Choose to write down everything you purchase over a two-week period, and see how many of those expenses don't fit into any of the categories listed above. Which of your miscellaneous expenses are necessary, and which aren't? The unnecessary expenses are places to reduce your spending. Make some tough choices to cut back, and start immediately. Track your spending for another two weeks. Can you tell the difference?

Cutting Costs

Once you have put together a working budget, have tried it out, and have adjusted it, you're likely to discover that your expenses still exceed your income. Don't panic. Simply begin to look for ways to reduce those expenses. Here are some tips for saving money in college:

- **Recognize the difference between your *needs* and your *wants*.** A *need* is something that you must have. For example, tuition and textbooks are considered *needs*. On the other hand, your *wants* are goods, services, or experiences that you wish to purchase but could reasonably live without. For example, concert tickets and mochas are *wants*. Your budget should always provide for your *needs* first.

- **Share expenses.** Having a roommate (or several) can be one of the easiest ways to cut costs on a regular basis. In exchange for giving up a little bit of privacy, you'll save hundreds of dollars on rent, utilities, and food. Make sure, however, that you work out a plan for sharing expenses equally and that everyone accepts his or her responsibilities. For instance, remember that if only your name is on the cable account, you (and only you) are legally responsible for that bill. You'll need to collect money from your roommates so that you can pay the bill in full and on time.

- **Consider the pros and cons of living on campus.** Depending on your school's location, off-campus housing might be less expensive than paying for a room and a meal plan on campus. Be aware, however, that although you might save some cash, you will give up a great deal of convenience by moving out of your campus residence. You almost certainly won't be able to roll out of bed 10 minutes before class, and you will have to prepare your own meals. Living on campus also makes it easier to make friends and develop a sense of connection to your college or university. Before you make the decision about where to live, weigh the advantages and disadvantages of each option.

- **Use low-cost transportation.** If you live close to campus, consider whether you need a car. Take advantage of lower-cost options such as public transportation or biking to class to save money on gasoline and parking. If you live farther away, check to see whether your institution hosts a ride-sharing program for commuter students, or carpool with someone in your area.

Go Vintage

Saving money doesn't mean you have to deprive yourself. Shopping at thrift stores for your clothes or apartment furnishings is a fun, affordable way to get one-of-a-kind pieces that won't break the bank.

© ANDREW WINNING/Corbis

- **Seek out discount entertainment options.** Take advantage of discounted or free programming through your college. Most institutions use a portion of their student fees to provide affordable entertainment options such as discounted or free tickets to concerts, movie theaters, sporting events, or other special events.
- **Embrace secondhand goods.** Use online resources such as Craigslist and thrift stores such as Goodwill to expand your wardrobe, purchase extras such as games and sports equipment, or furnish and decorate your room or apartment. You'll save money, and you won't mind as much when someone spills a drink on your "new" couch.
- **Avoid unnecessary fees.** Making late payments on credit cards and other bills can lead to expensive fees and can lower your credit score, which in turn will raise your interest rates. You might want to set up online, automatic payments to avoid making this costly mistake.

PEER LEADERS > Some students might be embarrassed to share money-saving strategies in class because they don't want to be identified as someone who needs to keep a careful eye on expenses. You can play a major role in helping students understand that most of them have to live on a budget. Facilitate a class discussion in which you describe ways you save money, and invite students to share their ideas as well.

IN CLASS > Consider sharing a time when you didn't handle your finances very well, perhaps when you were in college. Explain what went wrong and how long it took you to resolve your financial problem. Students can certainly learn from another person's mistakes.

> **your turn** Stay Motivated
>
> **Using Money-Saving Strategies**
>
> Are you a bargain shopper or a coupon-clipper? Do you get a good feeling when you know you've saved money on a purchase or a service? Be on the lookout for ways to trim your budget, and let your successes motivate you to cut your expenses even more. Share your strategies with other students in your college success class.

UNDERSTANDING FINANCIAL AID

Few students can pay the costs of college tuition, fees, books, room and board, bills, and random expenses without some kind of help. Luckily, financial aid—student loans, grants, scholarships, work-study programs, and other sources of money to support your education—is available to help cover your expenses.

Types of Aid

While grants and scholarships are unquestionably the best forms of aid because they do not have to be repaid, the federal government, states, and colleges offer many other forms of assistance, such as loans, work-study opportunities, and cooperative education. A student loan is a form of financial aid that must be paid back with interest. We will discuss student loans in more detail later in this chapter.

Grants are funds provided by the government to help students pay for college. They are given to students based on their financial needs, and they do not need to be repaid. Some grants are specific to a particular academic major. Grants are awarded by the federal government, state

IN CLASS > Ask students to share their thoughts about financial aid and any experiences they have had in applying for financial aid. What advice would they give to other students about financial aid?

RETENTION STRATEGY > Even though the term has already begun, many of your students may have registered without fully understanding or taking advantage of all the options available to them for financial aid. Financial aid could make the difference between leaving and persisting in college.

IN CLASS ❯ Invite a financial aid adviser to visit class, or have the class meet in the financial aid office. Your students might not be aware of scholarship opportunities offered by your college or university. A financial aid adviser can give them up-to-date information and encourage them to apply for available scholarships.

governments, and educational institutions. Students meet academic qualifications for grants by being admitted to a college and maintaining grades that are acceptable to the grant provider.

A **scholarship** is money from your college or another institution that supports your education; it does not have to be repaid. Some scholarships are need-based—that is, they are awarded on the basis of both talent and financial need. "Talent" can refer to your past accomplishments in the arts or athletics, your potential for future accomplishments, or even where you are from. Some colleges and universities place importance on admitting students from other states or countries. "Need" in this context means the cost of college minus a federal determination of what you and your family can afford to contribute toward that cost. Your institution might provide scholarships from its own resources or from individual donors. Donors themselves sometimes stipulate the characteristics of scholarship recipients, such as age or academic major.

Other scholarships are known as **merit scholarships**. These are based on talent as defined above, but they do not require you to demonstrate financial need. It can be challenging to match your talent with merit scholarships. Most of them come through colleges and are part of the admissions and financial aid processes, which are usually described on the college's Web site.

Web-based scholarship search services are another good source for information on merit scholarships. Be certain that the Web site you use is free, will keep your information confidential unless you release your name, and will send you a notice—usually through e-mail—when a new merit scholarship that matches your qualifications is posted. Also be sure to ask your employer, your family's employers, and social, community, or religious organizations about any available merit scholarships.

Work-study programs provide part-time employment opportunities for students who receive financial aid if their aid amount is not enough to cover all their education costs. Students receive work-study notices as part of the overall financial aid notice and then can sign up to be interviewed for work-study jobs. Although some work-study jobs are relatively menial, the best options provide experience related to your academic studies while allowing you to earn money for college. Your salary is based on the skills required for a particular position and the hours involved. Keep in mind that you will be expected to accomplish specific tasks while on duty, although some supervisors might permit you to study during any down-time.

Cooperative (co-op) education allows you to alternate a term of study (a semester or quarter) with a term of paid work. Co-op opportunities are very common in the field of engineering, and the number of co-op programs in health care fields is growing. Colleges make information about co-ops available through the admissions office and individual academic departments.

Navigating Financial Aid

Financial aid seems complex because it can come from so many different sources. Each source may have a different set of rules about how to receive the money and how not to lose it. Your college's financial aid office and its Web site can help you find the way to get the largest amount of money that doesn't need to be repaid, the lowest interest rate on loans, and work opportunities that fit your academic program. Do not overlook this valuable campus resource, even if you dread having to fill out lots of forms that ask for personal financial information. In order to get the assistance you need and deserve, you'll have to be resilient and overcome any negative feelings you might have about asking for money.

Other organizations that can help students find the right college and the money to help them attend are located throughout the United States. Many of these organizations are members of the National College Access Network (which helps manage the National College Access Program Directory at **collegeaccess.org/accessprogramdirectory**) or participate in a national effort called KnowHow2Go (**knowhow2go.acenet.edu**). You might also be able to obtain funds from your employer, a local organization, or a private group.

The majority of students pay for college through a combination of various types of financial assistance: scholarships, grants, loans, and paid employment. Financial aid professionals refer to this combination as a *package.*

Qualifying for Aid

Most financial assistance requires you to fill out some kind of application form. The application used most often is the Free Application for Federal Student Aid (FAFSA). Every student should complete the FAFSA by the earliest deadline of the colleges you are applying to. Be sure to log on to the FAFSA Web site at **fafsa.ed.gov;** you will find it very informative. If additional forms are also required, such as the College Board's PROFILE form (**student.collegeboard.org/css-financial-aid-profile**) or individual scholarship applications, they will be listed in colleges' financial aid or

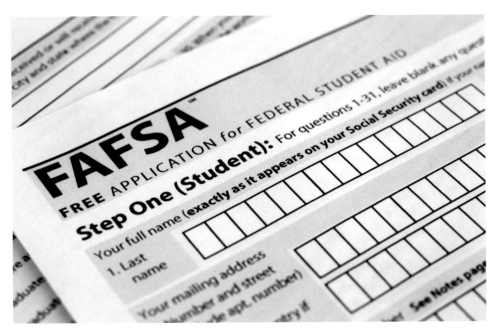

Show Me the Money

Don't let the paperwork scare you away. If you're not already receiving financial aid, be sure to investigate all the available options. Remember that your institution may also offer scholarships or grants that you don't have to repay.

AP Photo/Jon Elswick

admissions materials or by the organizations that offer scholarships. The box on this page outlines the steps you must take to qualify for most scholarships and grants, especially those sponsored by the federal government or state governments.

The amount of financial aid that you receive will depend on the cost of your academic program and what you or your family can pay as determined by the FAFSA. The cost includes average expenses for tuition and fees, books and supplies, room and board, transportation, and personal expenses. The financial aid office will subtract from the cost the amount that you and your family are expected to pay. In some cases, that amount can be as little as zero. Financial aid is designed to make up as much of the balance or "need" as possible.

Steps to Qualifying for Financial Aid

1. Enroll half-time or more in a certificate or degree program at one of the more than 4,500 colleges and universities certified to distribute federal financial aid. A few aid programs are available for less than half-time study; check with your department or college.

2. Complete the FAFSA. The first FAFSA you file is intimidating, especially if you rush to complete it right before the deadline. Completing the FAFSA in subsequent years is easier because you only need to update items that have changed. To make the process easier, get your personal identification number (PIN) a few weeks before the deadline. This PIN will be the same one you'll use throughout your college career. Try to do the form in sections rather than tackling all of it at once. Most of the information is basic: name, address, driver's license number, and things you will know or have in your personal files and records. For many undergraduates, the financial section will require your own and your parents' information from tax materials. However, if you are at least twenty-four, are a veteran, or have dependents, you do not need to submit your parents' tax information. If you are

married, your spouse's tax information will be needed.

3. Complete the College Board PROFILE form if your school or award-granting organization requires it. Review your college's admission information, or ask a financial aid adviser to determine whether this form is required.

4. Identify any additional applications that are required. These are usually scholarship applications with personal statements or short essays. The organizations, including the colleges that are giving the money, will provide instructions about what is required. Most have Web sites with complete information.

5. Follow instructions carefully, and submit each application on time. Financial aid is awarded from a fixed pool of funds. Once money is awarded, there is usually none left for those who file late.

6. Complete the classes for which you were given financial aid with at least a minimum grade point average as defined by your academic department or college, or by the organization that provided you the scholarship.

How to Keep Your Funding

If you earn average or better grades, complete your courses each term, and finish your program or degree on time, you should have no trouble maintaining your financial aid. It's a good idea to check with the financial aid office before you drop classes to make sure that you will not lose any aid.

Some types of aid, especially scholarships, require that you maintain full-time enrollment and make satisfactory academic progress. Dropping or failing a class might jeopardize all or part of your financial aid unless you are enrolled in more credits than the minimum required for financial aid. Full-time financial aid is often defined as twelve credit hours per term. If you initially enrolled in fifteen credit hours and dropped one three-hour course, your aid should not change. Even so, talk with a financial aid counselor before making the decision to drop a course, just to be sure.

Remember that although the financial aid office is there to serve you, you must be your own advocate. These tips should help:

- **File for financial aid every year.** Even if you don't think that you will receive aid for a certain year, you must file annually in case you become eligible in the future.
- **Meet all filing deadlines.** Students who do not meet filing deadlines risk losing aid from one year to the next.
- **Talk with a financial aid officer immediately if you or your family experiences a significant loss** (e.g., loss of a job, death of a parent or spouse). Don't wait for the next filing period; you might be eligible for funds for the current year.
- **Inquire every year about criteria-based aid.** Many colleges and universities have grants and scholarships for students who meet specific criteria. These might include grants for minority students, grants for students in specific academic majors, and grants for students of single-parent families.
- **Inquire about campus jobs throughout the year,** as these jobs might be available at any time, not just at the beginning of the term. If you do not have a job and want or need to work, keep asking.
- **Consider asking for a reassessment of your eligibility for aid.** If you have reviewed your financial aid package and think that your circumstances deserve additional consideration, you can ask the financial aid office to reassess your eligibility. The office is not always required to do so, but the request might be worth your effort.

ACHIEVING A BALANCE BETWEEN WORKING AND BORROWING

RETENTION STRATEGY > Even though it may sound counterintuitive to you and your students, explain the positive correlation between degree attainment and borrowing money for tuition to enable full-time enrollment versus not borrowing money, working more hours, and attending part-time.

After you have determined your budget, decided what (if anything) you can pay from savings, and taken your scholarships and grants into consideration, you might find that you still need additional income. Each term or year, you should decide how much you can work while maintaining good grades, and how much you should borrow from student loans.

Advantages and Disadvantages of Working

The majority of students today find that a combination of working and borrowing is the best way to gain experience, finance college, and complete their educational goals on time. Paid employment while you are in college has benefits beyond the money you can earn. Having a job in a field related to your major can help you develop a credential for graduate school and make you more employable later because it shows that you have the capability to manage several priorities at the same time. Working while you are in college can help you determine whether a particular career is what you will really want after you complete your education. And students who work a moderate amount (fifteen to twenty hours per week) typically get better grades than students who do not work at all.

On the other hand, it's almost impossible to get great grades if you work full time while also trying to be a full-time student. Some students prefer not to take a job during their first year in college while they're making adjustments to a new academic environment. You might find that you're able to work some terms but not others, as family obligations or challenging classes can sometimes make the added burden of work impractical or impossible.

PEER LEADERS ❯ Attempting to work too many hours while maintaining a full-time course load often results in poor grades or even academic failure. Students will be more willing to listen to this message if it comes from you. Identify some options for students who are trying to work too many hours—such as borrowing money or reducing their overall course load—but be sensitive to students' reluctance to take on debt for any reason.

Part-time off-campus jobs that relate to your major or career plan are hard to come by. You'll likely find that most part-time employment has little or no connection to your career objectives. A better option may be to seek a job on campus. Students who work on campus develop relationships with instructors and staff members who can help them make plans for the future and negotiate the academic and social sides of campus life. While off-campus employers are often unwilling to allow their student employees time off for study and exam preparation, college employers will want you to put your studies and exam preparation first. The downside to on-campus employment is that you'll likely earn less than you would in an off-campus job, but if success in college is your top priority, the upside of working on campus outweighs the downside.

Student Loans

Although you should be careful not to borrow yourself into a lifetime of debt, avoiding loans altogether could delay your graduation and your progress up the career ladder. For most students, some level of borrowing is both necessary and prudent.

The following list provides information about the most common types of student loans. The list reflects the order in which you should apply for and accept loans to get the lowest interest rates and the best repayment terms.

- **Subsidized federal student loans** are backed by the government, which pays the loan interest on your behalf while you are enrolled in undergraduate, graduate, or professional school. These loans require at least half-time enrollment and a submitted FAFSA application.
- **Unsubsidized federal student loans** may require that you make interest payments while you are enrolled. If not, the interest is added to the amount you owe; this is called *capitalization*.

- **Parent Loan for Undergraduate Students (called PLUS loans)** are applied for and owed by parents but disbursed directly to students. The interest on PLUS loans is usually higher than the interest on federal student loans but lower than that on private loans. Parents who apply must provide information on the FAFSA.
- **Private student loans** are offered through banks and credit unions. Private loans often have stricter credit requirements and higher interest rates than federal loans do, and interest payments on private loans begin immediately.

Student loans are a very important source of money for college, but like paid employment, loans should be considered carefully. Loans for costs such as books and tuition are good investments. Loans for a more lavish lifestyle are likely to weigh you down in the future. As one wise person put it, if by borrowing you live like a wealthy graduate while you're a student, you'll live like a student after you graduate. Student loans can be a good way to begin using credit wisely, a skill you are likely to need throughout your life.

MANAGING CREDIT WISELY

RETENTION STRATEGY › Evidence suggests that some students drop out of college because they abuse credit cards and accumulate unsustainable debt, especially for purposes unrelated to education. One of the financial-literacy skills students must therefore acquire is credit card management.

When you graduate, you will leave your institution with two significant numbers. The first is your grade point average (GPA), which represents the level of academic success you attained while in college. The second, your credit score, is a numerical representation of your fiscal responsibility. Although this second number might be less familiar to you than the first, it could be a factor that determines whether you get your dream job, regardless of your GPA. In addition, years from now you're likely to have forgotten your GPA, while your credit score will be more important than ever.

Your credit score is derived from a credit report that contains information about accounts in your name. These accounts include credit cards, student loans, utility bills, cell phones, and car loans, to name a few. This credit score can determine whether or not you will qualify for a loan (car, home, student, etc.), what interest rates you will pay, how much your car insurance will cost, and your chances of being hired by certain organizations. Even if none of these things are in your immediate future, now is the time to start thinking about your credit score.

Although using credit cards responsibly is a good way to build credit, acquiring a credit card has become much more difficult for college students. In May 2009, President Barack Obama signed legislation that prohibits college students under the age of twenty-one from obtaining a credit card unless they can prove that they are able to make the payments, or unless the credit card application is cosigned by a parent or guardian.

IN CLASS › Ask students to share their opinions about the 2009 credit card legislation and its effect on college students. Do they think that the government was justified in changing the way that credit cards are made available? Consider organizing an in-class debate on the pros and cons of this legislation.

Understanding Credit

Even if you can prove that you have the means to repay credit card debt, it is important for you to thoroughly understand how credit cards work and how they can both help and hurt you. Several frequently asked

MASTER BUDGETING, VERSION 2.0!

Technology can really help you when it comes to keeping track of your money—knowing how much you have, how much you need, and whether there are any problems with transactions moving through your accounts.

The Problem

You want to keep track of your finances, but you are afraid of making mistakes and you don't know where to begin.

The Fix

Start with the financial institutions you already work with and see what technology tools they offer.

How to Do It

1. *Create a budget.* As you learned earlier in this chapter, a budget is a spending plan that tracks all of your sources of income and expenses during a set period of time. Working within a budget helps you meet your goals and obligations.

2. *Check with your banking institution.* See what apps and online services they offer. Many banks offer free online access to your accounts so that you can deposit funds, make purchases, transfer funds, and receive deposit or withdrawal notifications via your cell phone or e-mail. Many banks will also send you electronic notifications of these transactions so you are always aware of how much money is currently in your account and when activity occurs that will affect your account. These services allow you to review your account information and help you make better decisions about when you use your money.

3. *Use your bank's apps and online tools to help you with your budget.* Check out some of these cool apps:

    *Mint* mint.com
   This Web site and phone app allows you to combine information from all of your financial accounts in one place, so you can see how much money you have in investments, income, loans, and payments. While it is not a bank, it does allow you to see your whole financial picture at once.

    *PayPal Mobile* paypal.com
   This app allows you to spend money and allows other people to give you money, including money you earn from part-time jobs, gigs, or monetary gifts from friends or family members.

    *Pocket Budget* mapeapps.com
   This is a simple way to keep track of your budget that installs on your phone.

4. *Beware of scams.* As you improve how you track your finances, remember to exercise caution in dealing with banks, credit card companies, and all financial institutions:

   - Do not transmit personal information (social security number, bank details, credit or debit card numbers, passwords, etc.) through e-mail. Doing so could put you at risk of identity theft. (Read more about identity theft in the box later in this chapter.) If you need to contact a financial institution by phone, place the call yourself, and deal only with banks or other financial institutions you trust.
   - Do not answer questions about vital personal information over the phone if you didn't originate the call.
   - Do not reply to e-mail, pop-ups, or text messages that ask you to reveal personal information.
   - Never click on links in unsolicited e-mails or paste URLs or lines of code into your browser bar.
   - Use good judgment. If an offer sounds too good to be true—like a huge line of credit with 0% annual percentage rate—it probably is.

EXTRA STYLE POINTS: Keep tabs on your credit report. Regularly reviewing your credit history pays off in major ways. It alerts you to any new accounts that might have been opened in your name. It also lets you catch unauthorized activity on accounts that you've closed or haven't used lately.

questions about credit cards are answered in the box later in this chapter. Simply put, a credit card allows you to buy something now and pay for it later. Each month, you will receive a statement listing all the purchases you made using your credit card during the previous thirty days. The statement will request a payment toward your balance and will set a payment due date. Your payment options will vary: You can pay your entire balance, pay a specified amount of the balance, or pay only a minimum payment, which may be as low as $10.

But beware: If you make only a minimum payment, the remaining balance on your card will be charged a finance fee, or interest charge, causing your balance to increase before your next bill arrives, even if you don't make any more purchases. Paying the minimum payment is almost never a good strategy and can add years to your repayment time. In fact, assuming an 18 percent interest rate, if you continually pay only $10 per month toward a $500 credit card balance, it will take you more than seven years to pay it off, and you'll pay an extra $431 in interest, almost doubling the amount you originally charged.

Avoid making late payments. Paying your bill even one day late can result in a finance charge of $30 or more; it can also raise the interest rate not only on that card, but also on any other credit accounts you have. If you decide to use a credit card to build credit, you might want to set up online, automatic payments to avoid incurring expensive late fees. Remember that the payment due date is the date that the credit card lender should receive your payment, not the date that you should send it.

If you decide to apply for a credit card while you're in college, remember that it should be used to build credit and for emergencies. Credit cards should not be used to fund a lifestyle that you cannot otherwise

In Case of Emergency
Having a credit card for emergencies is a good practice. Circumstances that might warrant the use of credit include paying critical expenses to care for yourself or your family, dealing with an auto accident or an unforeseen medical expense, or traveling on short notice to handle a crisis. Spring break is *not* an emergency.

© Britt Erlanson/cultura/Corbis

Frequently Asked Questions about Credit Cards and Identity Theft

- **I have a credit card with my name on it, but it is actually my parents' account number. Is this card building credit for me?** No. You are considered an authorized user on the account, but your parents are the primary account holders. To build credit, you must be the primary account holder, or at least a joint account holder.

- **I have a credit card and am the primary account holder. How can I resist abusing it?** Use your credit card to help you build credit by making small charges and paying them off in full each month. Stick to two expense categories only, such as gas and groceries, and don't make any exceptions unless you have a serious emergency.

- **I choose the "credit" option every time I use my debit card. Is this building credit for me?** No. Using the credit function of your debit card is more like writing an electronic check because you are still taking money directly out of your checking account. Even if your debit card has a major credit card (Visa, MasterCard, etc.) logo on it, it is not building credit for you.

- **I have a few store credit cards (Target, Best Buy, etc.). Are these accounts included on my credit report?** Yes. However, though they will affect your credit score, store credit cards do not carry as much weight as major credit cards such as Visa or MasterCard. It is OK to have a few store credit cards, but a major credit card will do more to help you build credit.

- **Where can I apply for a major credit card?** A good place to begin is your bank or credit union. Remember that you might have to prove your ability to make payments in order to obtain a card.

- **If one credit card will help me build credit, will several build my credit even more?** Research shows that there is no benefit to having more than two major credit cards. And even if you're able to pay the required monthly amounts, having too many accounts open can make you appear risky to the credit bureaus determining your credit score.

- **What if I forget and make a late payment? Is my credit score ruined?** Your credit report reflects at least the past seven years of activity, but it puts the most emphasis on the most recent two years. In other words, the farther you get from your mistakes, the less impact they will have on your credit score. There is no quick fix for improving a credit score, so beware of advertisements that say otherwise.

afford, or to buy things that you want but don't need (see the "Living on a Budget" section in this chapter). On the other hand, if you use your credit card just once a month and pay the balance as soon as the bill arrives, you will be on your way to a strong credit score in just a few years.

Debit Cards

Although you might want to use a credit card for emergencies and to establish a good credit rating, you might also look into the possibility of applying for a debit card (also called a checkcard). The big advantage of a debit card is that you don't always have to carry cash, and thus you don't run the risk of losing your money. Because the amount of your purchases will be limited to the funds in your bank account, a debit card is also a good way to constrain your spending.

- **If building credit is a wise decision, what's so bad about using credit cards to buy some things that I really want but can't afford right now?** It is not wise to use credit cards to purchase things that you cannot afford. Living within your means is always the way to go.

- **What is identity theft?** In this insidious and increasingly common crime, someone assumes your identity, secretly opens up accounts in your name, and has the bills sent to another address.

- **How can I protect myself from identity theft?** *Be password savvy.* The more sensitive the information, the stronger your password should be. Aim for passwords with eight to fourteen characters, including numbers, both uppercase and lowercase letters, and, if allowed, a few special characters like @ and #. Never use an obvious number like your birthday or wedding anniversary. Don't use the same username and password for every site. Change the password to your online credit card or bank account at least once a year. If you must keep a written record of your usernames and passwords, keep the list in a secure place at home, not in your wallet. *Beware of scams.* Don't make yourself vulnerable. A few tips: Research a company or organization before submitting your résumé. Don't e-mail any personal information (social security number, bank details, credit or debit card numbers, passwords, etc.) that could put you at risk of identity theft. Don't answer questions about vital personal information over the phone if you didn't originate the call. Don't reply to e-mails, pop-ups, or text messages that ask you to reveal sensitive information. Don't send sensitive data by e-mail. Call instead, and deal only with businesses you trust. Never click on links in unsolicited e-mails or paste URLs or lines of code into your browser bar. If an offer sounds too good to be true, it probably is.

- **Where can I get my credit report?** You can keep an eye on your credit report by visiting the free (and safe) Web site **annualcreditreport.com** at least once a year. Regularly reviewing your credit history pays off in major ways. It alerts you to any new accounts that might have been opened in your name. It also lets you catch unauthorized activity on accounts that you've closed or haven't used lately. Everyone is entitled to one free credit report a year from each of the three major credit bureaus.

The only real disadvantage is that a debit card provides direct access to your checking account, so it's very important to keep your card in a safe place and away from your personal identification number (PIN). The safest way to protect your account is to commit your PIN to memory. If you lose your debit card—or your credit card—notify your bank immediately.

high-impact practice 3

HIGH-IMPACT PRACTICE > This Your Turn exercise will enable your students to collaborate and share valuable information about how they choose to manage their money. By working together, they can also recognize the pros and cons of each method.

yourturn Work Together

Credit or Debit: Which Works Better for You?

With a small group, discuss your use of credit or debit cards. Which of these do you have, and which do you prefer? Make a list of the advantages and disadvantages of each, and share your list with the whole class.

Don't Let This Happen to You

The 2013 comedy *Identity Thief* tells the story of an identity theft victim, played by Jason Bateman, who confronts the thief, played by Melissa McCarthy. In the movie, the victim answers questions about vital personal information in a phone call that he did not initiate—a big no-no—and his life is turned upside down. If identity theft happens to you, it's not so funny.

Bob Mahoney/© Universal/courtesy Everett Collection

your turn Write and Reflect

Beware: It's Easy to Waste Money in College

Write a "warning letter" to a younger sibling (real or imaginary) about ways that students are tempted to waste money in college and what can happen as a result. In your letter, include strategies from this chapter for carefully managing money.

PLANNING FOR THE FUTURE

It's never too early to begin thinking about how you will finance your life after graduation and whether you will begin working immediately or pursue a graduate or professional degree. Your work, whether on or off campus, will help you make that decision. Here are some tips that will help you plan now for your future:

- **Figure out your next step—more education or work?** If you are working on campus, get to know faculty or staff members and seek their advice about your future plans. If you are working off campus, think carefully about whether your current job is one that you would want to continue after you graduate. If not, keep your options open and look for part-time work in a field that more closely aligns with your career plans or long-term educational objectives.
- **Keep your address current with the registrar.** Even when you have finished your degree or program, and especially if you stop classes for a term, alert the registrar of any changes in address. This is doubly important if you have a student loan; you don't want to get a negative report on your credit rating because you missed information about your loan.
- **Establish a savings account.** Add to it regularly, even if you can manage to deposit only a few dollars a month. The sooner you start, the greater your returns will be.

Your education is the most productive investment that you can make for your future and the future of your family. Research shows that completion of programs or degrees after high school increases earnings, opens up career options, leads to greater satisfaction in work, results in more engaged citizenship such as voting and community service, and greatly increases the probability that your children will go to college. Although college is a big investment of time and money, it's an investment you'll be glad you made.

checklist for success

Money

■ **Make learning financial-literacy skills a key college success skill.** Understanding how to manage money has life-long benefits.

■ **Create a budget and then live on it.** Remember that it's your budget, tailor-made by and for you.

■ **Act on some of the suggestions offered in this chapter for cutting your costs.** For most college students, cutting costs is even more important than increasing their income.

■ **Learn as much as you can about the different types of financial aid.** Find out what is offered to U.S. college students by the government and by your particular college, even though the term has already started. It's never too late to take advantage of these opportunities.

■ **Consider the pros and cons of working while in college.** If you do work, consider how much and where you will work. Realize that students who borrow money and attend college full time are more likely to attain their degrees than those who use a different strategy.

■ **Remember that you will finish college with two key numbers: your GPA and your credit score.** Potential employers will check both your transcript and your credit report.

■ **Learn the strategies in this chapter for wise credit card management.** College is a time to learn how to use credit wisely.

■ **Take advantage of help offered on your campus to learn financial-management skills.** You can't help it if you didn't learn these skills before; you may not have had any money to manage!

REFLECT ON CHOICES

high-impact practice 2 Successful college students learn to manage their money. They are careful to manage their income and their expenditures. Write about the choices you have already made about how to spend your money? This chapter offers lots of good strategies for handling your finances. Which of them will you practice this term?

APPLY WHAT YOU'VE LEARNED

Now that you have read and discussed this chapter, consider how you can apply what you have learned to your academic life and your personal life. The following prompts will help you reflect on chapter material and its relevance to you both now and in the future.

1. Sometimes it's hard to plan for the future. Describe two ways that you can save money each week, such as using public transportation to reduce the expense of owning a car.

2. Money is a difficult subject to talk about, and sometimes it seems easier not to worry about it. Ask yourself hard questions. Do you spend money without much thought? Do you have a lot of debt? Describe your ideal financial picture.

USE YOUR RESOURCES

> **Your Institution's Financial Aid Office** Be sure to visit your institution's financial aid office to take advantage of financial aid opportunities and to learn how to apply for scholarships.

> **Special Scholarships** If you are a veteran, an under-represented student, or an adult student, your institution may have special scholarship opportunities designed for you. Check with the financial aid office for leads on special scholarship opportunities.

> **Local United Way Office** If your college or university doesn't offer credit counseling, look online or in the telephone book for credit counseling agencies within the local United Way office.

> **Campus Programs** Be on the lookout for special campus programs on money management. These programs are often offered in residence halls or through the division of student affairs.

> **Business School or College** Faculty or staff members within a school or college of business or a division of continuing education sometimes offer a course in personal finance. Check your college catalog or Web site, or call the school, college, or division office to see if there are options that you can take advantage of either this term or next.

> **Counseling Center** If money problems are related to compulsive shopping or gambling, be sure to seek counseling at your institution's counseling center.

> **Budget Wizard: cashcourse.org.** The National Endowment for Financial Education (NEFE) offers this free, secure, budgeting tool.

> **Free Application for Federal Student Aid: fafsa.ed.gov.** The online form allows you to set up an account, complete the application electronically, save your work, and monitor the progress of your application.

> **FastWeb: FastWeb.com.** Register for this free scholarship-search service and discover sources of educational funding you never knew existed.

> **Bankrate: bankrate.com.** This free site provides unbiased information about the interest rates, fees, and penalties associated with major credit cards and private loans. It also provides calculators that let you determine the long-term costs of different kinds of borrowing.

> **Susan Knox, _Financial Basics: A Money-Management Guide for Students._** (Columbus: Ohio State University Press, 2004.) The author blends money-management experience with her desire to inform and help students master their finances, sharing experiences about money lessons learned in college, and offering sound solutions and advice for students and their families.

 LaunchPad

LaunchPad for _Your College Experience_ is a great resource. Go online to master concepts using the LearningCurve study tool and much more. macmillanhighered.com/gardner12e

PART FOUR
NEXT STEPS

Hero Images/Getty Images

15

MAJORS AND CAREERS

Student Goals

- Appreciate the characteristics of today's economy and learn ways to build the right mind-set for the future
- Understand the role of self-exploration in career planning
- Become career-minded during your college experience
- Get familiar with the various ways you can gain valuable experience
- Acquire effective job search strategies
- Become aware of the skills that employers seek in job candidates

15
MAJORS AND CAREERS

YOU WILL EXPLORE

The characteristics of today's economy and how to build the right mind-set for the future

The role of self-exploration in career planning

The value of being career-minded in college

How to gain experience through experiential learning and work opportunities

Effective job search strategies

The skills employers seek in college graduates

⚲ High-impact practices 2 (writing), 3 (collaboration), 4 (study abroad), 8 (research), and 9 (internships)

Tia Roy, 19

Psychology major, Interpersonal Communications minor
Merrimack College

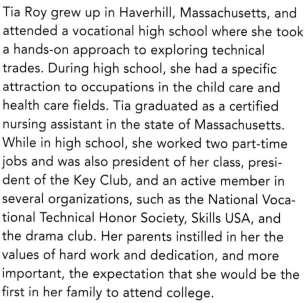

❝ **The more I learn about myself, and the more exploration I do, the more refined my decision making becomes.** ❞

Tia Roy grew up in Haverhill, Massachusetts, and attended a vocational high school where she took a hands-on approach to exploring technical trades. During high school, she had a specific attraction to occupations in the child care and health care fields. Tia graduated as a certified nursing assistant in the state of Massachusetts. While in high school, she worked two part-time jobs and was also president of her class, president of the Key Club, and an active member in several organizations, such as the National Vocational Technical Honor Society, Skills USA, and the drama club. Her parents instilled in her the values of hard work and dedication, and more important, the expectation that she would be the first in her family to attend college.

Knowing that she would have to commute, Tia applied to four colleges, all within a 30-mile radius of her home. Her parents, although emotionally supportive, were unable to provide financial or informational support during the college applications process. If Tia was going to be successful, she would have to find her own way. "Being told I needed to pay for my college education all by myself was a real shock," she says. "I basically was forced to grow up overnight. I realized that working harder than ever was no longer a choice, but a necessity. I knew if I was truly going to be the first in my family to go to college, I was on my own." When Tia is not in class or studying, she splits her time between working as a peer adviser, waiting tables, and being an in-home health care aide. "Being a commuter student, juggling academics, family, and three part-time jobs is definitely difficult,"

says Tia. "It is hard to explain to my parents that sometimes finishing a ten-page paper takes precedence over contributing to Sunday morning house cleaning. They didn't go to college. They don't understand. Making it all work—holding all of this responsibility on my shoulders—is difficult but important. I understand myself as a first-generation college student better now, in that I have unique challenges associated with the college experience."

Tia entered Merrimack College as an undeclared first-year student, unsure of what she wanted to study but knowing that eventually she wanted to work with those suffering from intellectual and developmental disabilities. "I am so grateful to have had such a nontraditional high school experience because I was able to immerse myself as a professional in the workforce earlier than my peers. At sixteen, I was working in a facility through the cooperative education program, supporting twelve adults with various developmental disabilities. I believe this has allowed me to have a clearer understanding of my post-college career goals, as well as giving me a greater appreciation for what college has to offer," she explains. Now in her sophomore year, Tia has decided to major in psychology and minor in interpersonal communications. "I've changed my major twice since coming to Merrimack," she says. "The more I learn about myself, and the more exploration I do, the more refined my decision making becomes. I've settled on psychology because I believe it will provide me with a foundation on which to build my education and experiences."

One of the reasons most students go to a college or university is to acquire knowledge that they will apply to a career. As a first-year student, it is not necessary to know exactly what you want to do when you graduate from college. After all, you just got here! What is important, however, is to take advantage of the resources and support available. Consider some of the things you are doing or have already done to make use of the help provided.

As you read this chapter, think of what is important as you begin mapping out your career path. Do you need to make a decision about your major? Have you thought about joining a campus club or organization? In what industry could you see yourself building a career? Commit to exploring and using the resources available to you, starting with a visit to the career center and a goal of getting familiar with the excellent online occupational resources described in this chapter.

Your choice to attend college enhances your possibilities for employment and will likely contribute to a satisfying career path. College is a time not only for gaining academic knowledge, but also for understanding who you are as a person, exploring available opportunities, being exposed to diverse ideas and cultures, and growing from a student into a contributing member of our global economy.

Some students come to college with a clear direction, firm knowledge of what major they want to study, and awareness of their likely career path. Others, like Tia, enter college undecided, understanding that their exposure to diverse subject matter will help solidify their academic choices. Still others enter with a declared major but are not certain how this course of study translates to the world of work. Each of these scenarios is normal. According to research conducted by Pennsylvania State University, 80 percent of entering college students at Penn State and other institutions are uncertain about their major, regardless of their decision to declare a major, and 50 percent of students change their major at least once.[1] Participating in co-curricular activities, such as joining a club or working part-time, helps solidify some decision making and allows you to learn a bit more about yourself in the process. Students who make connections between what they learn both inside and outside the classroom have a more profound and satisfying college experience than those who do not. In this chapter, you will learn how self-exploration influences the career decision-making process, as well as helpful tips and guidance about the resources available to prepare you for your career exploration in college and beyond.

 **LaunchPad**

To access the LearningCurve study tool, video activities, and more, go to LaunchPad for *Your College Experience.* macmillanhighered.com /gardner12e

---

[1] Jennifer A. Coffey, "Addressing the Distinctive Needs of Guaranteed Entrance to Medical School," *The Mentor*, Pennsylvania State University Division of Undergraduate Studies. Web. 28 Jan. 2004.

CAREERS AND THE NEW ECONOMY

For some, the reason to attend college is to get a good job. For others, it is to fulfill a dream of getting an education. For many first-generation college students like Tia, it's both. College not only helps you land a better job but also helps you become an effective leader, prepares you for graduate school, enhances your critical-thinking and problem-solving skills, and elevates your societal status based on merit.

Over the past few years, the economy has experienced extreme ups and downs, but the employment situation for college graduates is beginning to improve. In 2013, the unemployment rate for recent bachelor's degree recipients with some work experience was about 4.7 percent, but the overall unemployment rate in the U.S. was 7.9 percent.[2] The good news is that employers will likely hire many college students in the next few years.

Economic uncertainty is a reality, and although earning a college degree is one of the best ways for you to increase your chances of being employed, it is important to make decisions about your major and career path based on information about yourself and the long-term demands of the job market.

 **high-impact practice 2**

your turn   Write and Reflect

The Economy and Your Future Plans

In a journal entry, describe how the current state of the economy makes you feel. Do some online research into the economic forecast associated with the major you are considering, and make notes in your journal about what you find and its effect on your plans.

Characteristics of Today's Economy

Today's economy has characteristics that are new and quite different from those of previous years—it is global, unstable, innovative, without boundaries, customized, ever-changing, and social. The most motivated and successful college students will work hard to understand these characteristics, and will consider them carefully as they make decisions that relate to their futures. As we take a look at each characteristic, think about the potential impact on the program of study and possible career path you are envisioning for yourself.

It's Global.
Many corporations are multinational; they look for cheap labor, capital, and resources both within and outside the United States. Competition on a global level presents challenges for American workers. College graduates in the United States now compete for jobs with others around the world, particularly in industries that involve science, technology, engineering, and mathematics (STEM).

---

[2] A. P. Carnevale, B. Cheah, and J. Strohl, Hard Times: Not All College Degrees Are Created Equal, Georgetown Public Policy Institute p. 3. Web. May 2013.

It's Unstable. In late 2008, the world economy began suffering from a series of events that led to bankruptcies, foreclosures, failing businesses, downturns in stock markets, and lost jobs. The nation's economic situation gradually improved in subsequent years, but that improvement may have halted or even begun to reverse by the time you graduate. Economic instability is troubling, but having a college education gives you a great advantage over those without a degree.

It's Innovative. The economy has always depended on creativity to generate consumer interest in new products and services around the world. As a leader in industry innovation, the United States needs college graduates who possess imagination and a desire to move forward.

It's without Boundaries. You might be an accountant and find yourself working with the public relations division of your company, or you might be a nurse who does staff training. The ability to work outside of traditional boundaries while expanding your skills, abilities, and knowledge will be essential to your professional success.

It's Customized. More and more, consumers demand products and services tailored to their specific needs. This is especially true of those born after 1970, who were raised on the individualistic concept of consumer choice. For instance, the popular frozen yogurt franchise, Orange Leaf, allows patrons to "become the master of your dessert" by building their very own yogurt treats, boasting that "the possibilities are endless!" We customize our cell phone ringtones, our coffee, and our iPod playlists. Some universities even allow students to customize their own majors. Such market segmentation requires constant adaptation of ideas to identify new products and services as new customer demands emerge.

It's Ever-Changing. As we rebuild our economy, new jobs in nearly every industry will demand more education and training. As we have stated in this book, the most important skill that you need to learn in college is how to keep learning throughout your life. To give yourself the best chance at avoiding a negative employment situation, it's important to adapt your skills to the job market that exists. Doing so requires both flexibility and the desire to continually develop yourself.

It's Social. Technology has allowed us to stay more connected in our personal lives and in business; however, it has also decreased our need for, and exposure to, face-to-face social interactions (or so we think—the long-term effects of having less face-to-face contact have not been

isthisyou?

No Plan for Life after College
Whenever someone asks you about your plans for employment after college, do you fumble for a response? Do you feel clueless? Are you hoping a flash of insight will put you on the right career path? If so, you're not alone. Many students come to college without firm career plans. This chapter will give you some new ways to think about your major and career choices. It will introduce you to resources that you may not have thought about before. So don't panic. Just make your first year a time to explore your options.

definitively measured yet). Employers rank the following abilities as the most important skills or qualities they look for in job candidates: the ability to work in a team structure; the ability to make decisions and solve problems; the ability to plan, organize, and prioritize work; and the ability to communicate verbally with people inside and outside the organization.[3] In this world of ever-increasing technological advancements, the ability to be a team player is the top asset organizations look for when hiring new employees.

These characteristics of the economy—that it is global, unstable, innovative, without boundaries, customized, ever-changing, and social—should provide a roadmap for you as you make decisions throughout your college experience.

Building the Right Mind-Set for the Future

Even after you have landed a job, you will be expected to continue learning and developing yourself. Whether you are preparing to enter a career for the first time or to change careers after many years on the job, keep in mind the following:

A College Degree Does Not Guarantee Employment. If competition within a struggling economy isn't enough, consider what it will be like competing with hundreds of other college graduates earning the same degree as you and graduating at the same time! With a college degree, however, more opportunities, financial and otherwise, will be available to you than if you do not have a degree. For those who pursue a degree and

---

[3] NACE Research, *Job Outlook 2012*, National Association of Colleges and Employers, p. 3. Web. 2011.

Stiff Competition

The information and strategies in this chapter will help you prepare for job interviews so that when it's your turn to be interviewed, you can walk in with confidence.

AP Photo/Lynne Sladky, File

complete it, the payoff is substantial. On average, for example, Americans with bachelor's degrees or higher make twice as much in annual income as those with a high school education or less.[4]

You Are, More or Less, Solely Responsible for Your Career. Career development is a lifelong process, controlled only by you. Many employers offer some degree of training, and some might also offer assessments and information on available positions in the industry.

However, the ultimate task of creating a career path is yours. Students who realize that they are responsible for managing their careers actively throughout their lifetime will be more successful and more satisfied than those who think someone else will come along to manage things for them.

To Advance Your Career, You Must Accept the Risks That Accompany Employment and Plan for the Future. Organizations grow or downsize in response to economic conditions, so you must do your best to prepare for the unexpected. As we have stated at several points in this book, perhaps the most vital skill you can gain in college is learning how to learn. Lifelong learning will help keep you employable and can provide you with many opportunities, regardless of the economy.

A First Career Choice Might Not Be Permanent. College students often view the choice of a career as a monumental and irreversible decision. However, a career is based on your professional development decisions over a lifetime. No single right occupation is just waiting for you to discover it. Rather, many career choices could fulfill and satisfy you. The question to consider is this: What is the best choice for me right now?

Now for the good news: Hundreds of thousands of graduates find jobs every year, even in recessionary times. Some graduates might have to work longer to get where they want to be, but persistence pays off. If you start preparing now and continue to do so over the next few years in college, you'll have time to build a portfolio of academic and **co-curricular** experiences—learning that occurs outside the classroom—that will begin to add substance to your career profile.

OUTSIDE CLASS ❯ Suggest that students research an industry aligned with their declared major or with majors that they are considering. This chapter includes guidelines for doing this research. Have students report on their findings.

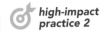 *high-impact practice 2*

your turn Make Good Choices

Ponder Your Academic Major Choice
This week, find another student who has the same major as you. Ask that person his or her reasons for selecting this major. Does that person seem passionate about this major? Why or why not? Why did *you* choose this major? Are you excited or do you have a "ho-hum" attitude about it? Reflect on your choice of major in a journal entry.

---

[4] A. P. Carnevale, S. J. Rose, B. Cheah, *The College Payoff: Education, Occupations, Lifetime Earnings,* Georgetown Public Policy Institute, p. 4. Web. 2011.

WORKING WITH AN ACADEMIC ADVISER

Academic planning is a vital step in your college career, and it should be an ongoing process that starts on your first day of school. Students who engage in academic planning are more likely to stay in college. Before you register for classes next term, sit down for a strategy session with your academic adviser. On most campuses, you are assigned an adviser who is usually either an instructor or staff person in your field or a professional adviser. A good adviser can help you choose courses, decide on a major, weigh career possibilities, and map out your degree and certificate requirements. He or she can also recommend instructors and help you simplify the different aspects of your academic life. Here are a few ways to make sure that your first meeting with your adviser is a valuable experience:

- Prepare by looking at the course catalog, thinking about the available majors, and familiarizing yourself with campus resources. If you haven't already decided on a major, ask your adviser about opportunities for taking an aptitude test or a self-assessment to help you narrow down your options. (Read more about self-assessments and self-exploration below.)
- Prepare materials to bring to the meeting. Even if you submitted your academic transcript with your application, bring a copy of the transcript to the meeting. The transcript—your complete high school record—is an important tool; it shows your academic adviser where you've been, what your academic strengths are, and where your interests lie.
- Make a list of majors that appeal to you. Academic advisers love it when students come prepared—it shows that they're passionate and are taking their futures seriously.
- Map out your time frame and goals. Do you plan to enroll full-time or part-time? If you're at a four-year college or university, when do you plan to graduate, and with what degree? Are you planning to go on to graduate school to finish your studies? If you are at a two-year college, do you want an associate's degree? A certificate? Do you plan to transfer to a four-year institution?
- Know the right questions to ask. Once you've chosen a major, you'll need to understand how to move forward in your academic program to meet the necessary requirements. You will have *prerequisites*—the basic core courses you need to take before you can enroll in upper-level classes in your major. Your major may also have *corequisites:* courses you have to take in conjunction with other courses during the same term, such as a chemistry lab alongside your chemistry class. With this knowledge under your belt, here is what you need to find out:
  - How many credits must I take each term to graduate on time? Note that if you are on financial aid, are doing work-study, or are a college athlete, you may have to take a minimum number of credits per term.
  - What are the prerequisites for my major? What are the corequisites?

- If I have any AP credits or have taken any placement exams, can I use them to fulfill some of my major's requirements?
- What career opportunities will I have once I graduate? What will the salary potential look like?

- Know what to take away from your meeting. When you leave the meeting, have in hand a printout of your current course schedule and plans for classes you might take in the next term and beyond. At many institutions, you and your adviser will set up a five- to seven-term plan online.
- Know these rules of thumb about selecting your classes:

  - Most full-time students take four to six courses a term. Decide which classes you want to take, find out which days and times they meet, and make sure they don't overlap.
  - To get the classes you want, make sure to register as early as possible—in person or online.
  - Resist the temptation to cram all of your classes into one or two days. It's better to aim for a manageable workload by spreading your classes throughout the week.
  - Go for a mix of hard and easy classes. Especially at the beginning, you might not realize how challenging college classes can be or how much outside work they entail. If you load up on organic chemistry, Russian 101, and advanced thermodynamics, your grades and general well-being could suffer.

- Know what to do if your academic adviser isn't very helpful. If you think you and your adviser are not a good match, go to the admissions office and ask to be assigned to a different adviser. Whatever you do, don't throw in the towel. Academic planning is so critical to your success in college that it's worth persevering until you find an adviser with whom you feel comfortable.
- Set up subsequent meetings with your academic adviser. Check in with your adviser at least once a term, if not more often. It's important to stay connected and make sure you're on a positive track, especially if you plan to transfer or apply to graduate school. Programs change requirements occasionally, so it's smart to touch base with your adviser periodically in case you need to make any necessary adjustments.

SELF-EXPLORATION IN CAREER PLANNING

Are you confident in your skills and abilities? Do you know what you want or can accomplish? How well you know yourself and how effectively you can do the things you need to do are integral to your success, not only as a college student, but also as a person. Self-assessment is the process of gathering information about yourself in order to make informed decisions. Self-assessment is a good first step in setting your academic and career goals. While you might know what you like to do and what you are good at doing, you may lack a clear idea of how your self-knowledge can help you explore different career possibilities. Factors that can affect your career choices include your values, skills, aptitudes, personality, life goals and work satisfaction, and interests. Learning about these factors is an important step in career planning.

Values

OUTSIDE CLASS > Have students visit myplan.com/assess /values.php to take a free values assessment.

IN CLASS > Have a discussion about the values assessment and how students' results might affect their career choices.

Your values, formed through your life experiences, are the things you feel most strongly about. For career planning, values generally refer to the things we most desire in a career in relation to how we want to live. For example, some people value job security, money, structure, and a regular schedule. Others value flexibility, excitement, independence, variety, or a particular work environment such as the outdoors. Some career choices pay higher salaries than others but may require hard work and long hours.

Thus, knowing your personal wishes and needs in relation to your values is important. You might find that what you value most is not money, but rather the chance to work for a specific cause or the opportunity to have a particular lifestyle. In general, being aware of what you value is important because a career choice that is closely related to your core values is likely to be the best choice.

Skills

The ability to do something well can usually be improved with practice. You may bring different skills to different situations, and it is important to know both your assets and your weaknesses. Skills typically fall into three categories:

1. **Personal.** Some skills come naturally or are learned through experience. Examples of these skills are honesty, punctuality, teamwork, self-motivation, and conflict management.
2. **Workplace.** Some skills can be learned on the job; others are gained through training designed to increase your knowledge or expertise in a certain area. Examples include designing Web sites, bookkeeping, and providing customer service.
3. **Transferable.** Some skills gained through your previous jobs or hobbies or through everyday life can be transferred to another job. Examples include planning events, motivating others, paying attention to detail, and organizing workspaces.

By identifying your skill set, you can turn your current skills into career possibilities. During the college years, build on your strengths and develop your weaker skills. Whether in or out of class, find ways to practice what you are good at and get help with what you need to improve.

Aptitudes

IN CLASS > Ask students what they believe are their natural abilities or what others have told them they are "a natural" at doing. Can they explain where such aptitudes came from?

Aptitude is your acquired or natural ability for learning and proficiency in a particular area, which makes it easier for you to learn or do certain things. The chapter, "How You Learn," introduced the differences in learning styles and the importance of understanding your unique learning style

A Passion for the Outdoors?

Are you interested in American history? Do you enjoy talking with the public? Do you value education? Do you value the preservation of our natural resources and historical landmarks? People who answer "yes" to these questions might find that a career as a park ranger suits them. How does the career that you plan to pursue align with your values, interests, and personality? If you're coming up empty, you might want to reconsider your plans.

Matt McClain for *The Washington Post*/Getty Images

and its effect on your success as a student. Manual dexterity, musical ability, spatial visualization, and memory for numbers are examples of aptitudes that have a lot to do with the way you learn. Similar to skills, each of us has aptitudes that we can build on. The trick is to shine a light on your aptitudes and discover a path in which your strengths become your best intellectual assets.

Personality

Your personality makes you who you are, and it can't be ignored when you make career decisions. The quiet, orderly, calm, detail-oriented person will probably make a different work choice than the aggressive, outgoing, argumentative person will. The chapter, "How You Learn," introduced you to the Myers-Briggs Type Indicator, one of the best-known, most widely used personality inventories. This assessment can help you understand how you make decisions, perceive the world, and interact with others.

Life Goals and Work Values

Each of us defines success and satisfaction in his or her own way, and the process of defining them is complex and personal. Two factors can change how we feel about our success and happiness: knowing that we are achieving the life goals we've set for ourselves and finding that we gain satisfaction from our work. If your values are not in line with the values of the organization where you work, you might be in for trouble.

Interests

From birth, we develop particular interests. These interests help shape our career paths and might even define them. Good career exploration begins

Thinking Things
Through

Your experiences in
college will help you
make thoughtful
decisions about your
future.

Blend Images/Peathegee Inc./Getty
Images

with considering what you like to do and relating that to your career
choices. For example, if you enjoyed writing for your high school newspaper, you might be interested in writing for the college newspaper with an
eye on a career in journalism. On the flip side, you might enroll in Psych
101 if you have an interest in human behavior, but then realize halfway
through the course that psychology is not what you imagined and that you
have no desire to become a psychologist. Because your interests are unique
to you, you are the only person who should determine what you want to do
in the future.

your turn   Make Good Choices

Let Previous Work Experience Guide Future Career Choices

What kinds of jobs have you had, either for pay or as a volunteer? Why
did you choose those jobs? Which of them was your favorite, and which
did you dislike? How could your prior job experience help you make good
choices in the future? Be prepared to discuss your ideas in class and offer
thoughts about what your work experience has taught you about yourself
and which careers you should choose—or avoid—in the future.

EXPLORING YOUR INTERESTS

Most students want their major to lead directly to a career, although this
doesn't always happen. You might be encouraged to select a major in a subject about which you are really passionate. Most academic advisers would

agree with this decision-making advice: Try a major you think you'll like and that makes sense given the attributes described above—your values, strengths, aptitudes, skills, personality, goals, and interests—and see what develops. Take advantage of available self-assessments to help you learn more about yourself.

John Holland, a psychologist at Johns Hopkins University, developed a number of tools and concepts that can help you organize the various dimensions of yourself so that you can identify potential career choices (see Table 15.1). Holland suggests that people are separated into six general categories based on differences in their interests, skills, values, and personality characteristics—in short, their preferred approaches to life. Holland's system organizes career fields into the same six categories. Career fields are grouped according to what a particular career field requires of a person (the skills and personality characteristics most commonly associated with success in those fields) and what rewards those fields provide (interests and values most commonly associated with satisfaction). As you view Table 15.1, highlight or note characteristics that you believe that you have, as well as those that are less closely matched.

Your career choices will ultimately involve a complex assessment of the factors that are most important to you. To display the relationship between career fields and the potential conflicts people face as they consider them, Holland's model is commonly presented in a hexagonal shape (Figure 15.1). The closer the types, the closer the relationships among the career fields; the farther apart the types, the more conflict between the career fields.

Holland's model can help you address the questions surrounding career choice in two ways. First, you can begin to identify career fields that are consistent with what you know about yourself. Once you have identified potential fields, you can use the career center at your college to get more information about those fields, such as the daily activities for specific jobs, the interests and abilities required, the preparation required for entry, the working conditions, salary and benefits, and employment outlook. Second, you can begin to identify the harmony or conflicts in your career choices. Doing so will help you analyze the reasons for your career decisions and be more confident as you make choices.

OUTSIDE CLASS > For more information or to research career fields of interest, have students read and discuss this chapter's Tech Tip.

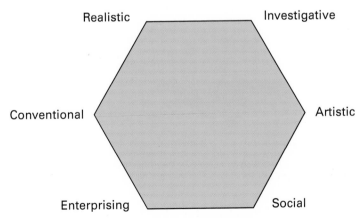

FIGURE 15.1 > Holland's Hexagonal Model of Career Fields

TABLE 15.1 › Holland Personality and Career Types

Category	Personality Characteristics	Career Fields
Realistic (R)	These people describe themselves as concrete, down-to-earth, and practical doers. They exhibit competitive/assertive behavior and show interest in activities that require motor coordination, skill, and physical strength. They prefer situations involving action solutions rather than tasks involving verbal or interpersonal skills, and they like taking a concrete approach to problem solving, rather than relying on abstract theory. They tend to be interested in scientific or mechanical areas rather than the arts.	Environmental engineer, electrical contractor, industrial arts teacher, navy officer, fitness director, package engineer, electronics technician, Web designer
Investigative (I)	These people describe themselves as analytical, rational, and logical problem solvers. They value intellectual stimulation and intellectual achievement, and they prefer to think rather than to act and to organize and understand rather than to persuade. They usually have a strong interest in physical, biological, or social sciences. They are less apt to be people oriented.	Urban planner, chemical engineer, bacteriologist, flight engineer, genealogist, laboratory technician, marine scientist, nuclear medical technologist, obstetrician, quality-control technician, computer programmer, environmentalist, physician, college professor
Artistic (A)	These people describe themselves as creative, innovative, and independent. They value self-expression and relating with others through artistic expression and are also emotionally expressive. They dislike structure, preferring tasks involving personal or physical skills. They resemble investigative people but are more interested in the cultural or the aesthetic than the scientific.	Architect, film editor/director, actor, cartoonist, interior decorator, fashion model, graphic communications specialist, journalist, editor, orchestra leader, public relations specialist, sculptor, media specialist, librarian
Social (S)	These people describe themselves as kind, caring, helpful, and understanding of others. They value helping and making a contribution. They satisfy their needs in one-on-one or small-group interaction using strong speaking skills to teach, counsel, or advise. They are drawn to close interpersonal relationships and are less apt to engage in intellectual or extensive physical activity.	Nurse, teacher, social worker, genetic counselor, marriage counselor, rehabilitation counselor, school superintendent, geriatric specialist, insurance claims specialist, minister, travel agent, guidance counselor, convention planner
Enterprising (E)	These people describe themselves as assertive, risk-taking, and persuasive. They value prestige, power, and status and are more inclined than other types to pursue it. They use verbal skills to supervise, lead, direct, and persuade rather than to support or guide. They are interested in people and in achieving organizational goals.	Banker, city manager, FBI agent, health administrator, judge, labor arbitrator, salary and wage administrator, insurance salesperson, sales engineer, lawyer, sales representative, marketing manager
Conventional (C)	These people describe themselves as neat, orderly, detail oriented, and persistent. They value order, structure, prestige, and status and possess a high degree of self-control. They are not opposed to rules and regulations. They are skilled in organizing, planning, and scheduling and are interested in data and people.	Accountant, statistician, census enumerator, data processor, hospital administrator, insurance administrator, office manager, underwriter, auditor, personnel specialist, database manager, abstractor/indexer

Source: Table 15.1 and Figure 15.1 reproduced by special permission of the Publisher, Psychological Assessment Resources, Inc., 16204 N. Florida Ave., Lutz, FL 33549. From *The Self-Directed Search Professional User's Guide*, by John L. Holland, Ph.D. Copyright © 1985, 1987, 1994, 1997. Further reproduction is prohibited without permission from PAR, Inc.

Throughout this book, you have been introduced to a variety of self-assessments designed to provide a clearer picture of who you are as an individual. These assessments are designed as tools to assist the career exploration process. Never think that you have to make a decision based on the results of only one assessment. Career choices are complex and involve many factors; furthermore, these decisions are reversible. It is important not only to take time to talk your interests over with a career counselor but also to shadow individuals in the occupations that interest you. Obtaining a better understanding of what an occupation entails in terms of skills, commitment, and opportunity will help you make informed decisions about your own career choices.

BEING CAREER-MINDED IN COLLEGE

So far, the chapters in this book have covered strategies that will help you succeed in college and in life, so that upon graduation you are prepared to begin a career or continue your education in graduate school. The process of making choices about life after college should begin in the first year. Here are some important steps to take and ways to be career-minded as you move through your college experience:

- **Visit the career center yearly.** There is a misconception that graduating students have the most immediate need for career services, when in fact research suggests that students benefit from active involvement with career services *throughout the entire course of their educational experience.* From helping you choose a major and career direction to getting an internship to helping you understand which careers will require a graduate degree, the career center is a valuable source of guidance. Take advantage of what your institution's career professionals have to offer. After all, your tuition is paying for it! You are the driver of your career trajectory.
- **Explore the career center Web site.** You'll find listings for part- and full-time positions, internships, cooperative (co-op) programs, and seasonal employment. You'll also find on-campus interviewing opportunities for internships and for full-time employment after graduation.

---

your turn Stay Motivated

Planning an Exciting Future

Have you explored your institution's career center? If so, did your visit allow you to think about the relationship between your academic work and planning for your ideal job? Thinking about your dream career can motivate you to succeed in the present. While you're making those big plans, it's always a good idea to have a back up plan that builds on your strengths and your interests, just in case the dream career doesn't happen.

Attend workshops on advanced résumé writing, internship placement, interviewing, and other job-search skills. Participate in mock interview activities to improve your interviewing skills.

- **Attend your college's career fairs.** Employers in the area visit your campus to hire students. Get to know more about the employers who hire graduates in your major, and check your career center Web site for the dates of upcoming career fairs. Some career fairs may be specific to disciplines such as health care, information technology, or business.

- **Take a variety of classes, and pay attention to your grades.** College gives you the opportunity to get exposure to various knowledge areas. Remember, though, that employers and graduate schools want candidates with good grades. Good grades show that you have a solid knowledge base and a strong work ethic—two characteristics that all employers value. Don't risk your chances for a great career or admission to graduate school by letting your grades slide.

- **Network.** Connect with instructors, family members, and friends to find contacts in your fields of interest so that you can learn more about those areas. If possible, participate in mentoring programs hosted by **alumni,** past graduates of your college or university. Spend the summer completing internship, service-learning, and co-op experiences.

- **Discover leadership opportunities.** Companies want to hire leaders, and they look for leadership experience in college students when hiring for internships or postgraduate employment. It is actually the top characteristic employers look for on a résumé, after GPA.[5] Being active in a campus club or organization helps develop your skills in leadership and teamwork. Volunteer to be team leader when working with a group on classroom projects. Seek out campus leadership employment opportunities, such as orientation leader or resident adviser. Active involvement in these opportunities will help you exercise your inner leader.

- **Build communication skills.** The ability to communicate verbally with persons inside and outside an organization is an important attribute that employers seek in new graduates. Again and again, company and graduate school recruiters complain about the lack of communication skills among college graduates. You should take every available opportunity to practice communicating, whether through classroom presentations, group work, leadership, or employment opportunities.

- **Develop computer skills.** Today's college students have never been more technologically savvy, but not all technology experience is equal. Just because you hold the record for sending the fastest text message or have conquered the highest level on your favorite video game does not mean that you are proficient in the *right* kinds of technology. As you begin to make decisions about your career path, explore and become familiar with technologies used in your field. Take advantage of the computer courses and workshops your college offers, or learn by experimenting with different software packages on your own. It is also helpful to develop your own Web page or

---

[5] NACE, *Job Outlook 2012.*

Web-based portfolio. Many Web-design software tools make this easy. Contact your college's information technology department for information on how to get started.

- **Create and monitor your digital footprint.** Have you Googled yourself lately? Do you like what you see online? Would an employer? Your online representation matters, and it can influence how others see you and what they think of you. Make sure nothing inappropriate is posted about you on Facebook, Instagram, Twitter, or other social media sites. Over 50 percent of employers use social networks in recruiting. However, fewer college students use social networks as part of their job search.[6] This discrepancy indicates that college students still do not realize the effect of social networks as a resource for researching career possibilities, connecting to employers, searching for opportunities, and applying for positions. For more on your digital footprint, turn to the "Relationships" chapter to review both the Tech Tip on Building a Digital Persona and the section on Communicating in a Digital Age.

As you plan for your career, you want to develop your qualifications, make good choices, and take advantage of opportunities on and off campus to learn more about your career preferences. Keep your goals in mind as you select courses and look for employment, but also keep an eye out for special opportunities. The route you think you want to take might change as you grow.

**high-impact
practice 3**

HIGH-IMPACT PRACTICE > By working together to come up with ways to put their best foot forward in obtaining a job, your class members will practice being assertive about their own strengths and will gain important self-knowledge through others' opinions.

your turn   Work Together

Marketing Yourself to Employers

Working with a small group of your classmates, help one another develop a "marketing strategy" that each of you could develop to sell yourself to a potential employer. Which characteristics and aptitudes would each group member emphasize? Do other group members agree or disagree? Be honest and respectful in your comments to each other.

GETTING EXPERIENCE

Developing a career plan, getting a handle on your interests, and doing industry research are all part of becoming career-minded. Another step to take in this journey is to test the waters—to get some experience in areas that interest you and for which you are well suited. Employers prefer to hire people with experience, so how can you get some? Fortunately, there are several ways you can gain experience while you are in college. Engaging in experiential learning opportunities such as service learning, volunteer activities, internships, co-op programs, and student competitions and projects are all great ways to get career-based experience.

---

[6] NACE, *Job Outlook 2012.*

JOIN THE PROFESSIONAL COMMUNITY

If you have ever been to a party where you don't know many people, you know how awkward it can be to stand near a group and not feel comfortable joining it.

Getting started in a new career or profession is similar. Members of different professions have their own ways of doing things, their own terminology, particular leaders, and important events. As a college student, you have to learn about how to join your intended professional community, and you can and should start now.

The Problem

You want to research a professional community that you're interested in joining, but you don't know how.

The Fix

Learn about the industries, companies and professional groups you would like to work with.

How to Do It

1. *Conduct industry and career research.* A great place to start is O*NET OnLine (onetonline.org), a site with an interactive application for exploring occupations. Also, get in the habit of visiting the U.S. Bureau of Labor Statistics' Occupational Outlook Handbook (bls.gov/ooh). These sites will give you a very clear picture of thousands of professions. Identify specific companies or organizations that interest you, as well as roles in which you could see yourself. Research individual employers of interest, too. How do your expectations match up with reality? Be sure to ask for help from a librarian if you need it.

2. *Do some research on yourself.* Even if you already have an idea about what you want to pursue, online resources, like the O*NET OnLine Interest profiler (mynextmove.org/explore/ip) or iSeek (iseek.org/careers/clusterSurvey) will give you important feedback about what professions would match your interests, personality, values, and skills.

3. *Get familiar with professional organizations.* Every profession has groups whose members exchange ideas, hold events, or conduct training. Explore their Web sites to find local chapters of the organization or local events you can attend to learn more. For a list of associations, check out Weddle's Association Directory (weddles.com /associations). Also, many professional groups have a presence on LinkedIn, where you can see who is in a group and join an online conversation about an area of interest.

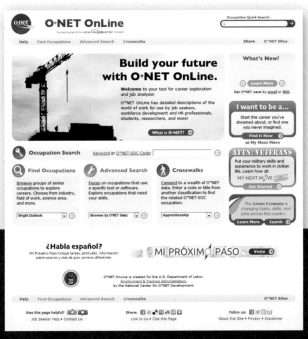

Courtesy U.S. Department of Labor

4. *Find ways to gain real experience:* Check with your college's career center to find out what kinds of internship opportunities are available. You can look online, too:

   - internships.com
   - indeed.com
   - mediabistro.com
   - idealist.com
   - experience.com

EXTRA STYLE POINTS: Visit work environments you want to explore. Find a person, either through LinkedIn or your college's alumni or career center, who will grant you an informational interview. You can also seek an opportunity for job shadowing. Here are a few questions to get your interview off to a strong start:

   - Describe the moment when you knew this was the job for you.
   - What is the most interesting thing that has happened to you in this profession?
   - What changes would you make in your career preparation if you were entering this field today?
   - Describe the most satisfying professional accomplishment you have had.

Experiential Learning

Gaining experience in your field while in college can help you meet people who may later serve as important employment references. The experience can also teach you things you won't learn in the classroom. Here are a number of ways to pursue such experience:

Volunteer. Giving back to your community has many benefits to the community you serve, but it can also have tremendous personal and professional advantages. Whether you give your time to a nonprofit organization, a school, or a business, volunteering can help you develop your skill set, explore career possibilities, network, and contribute to lifelong learning, and it offers the personal satisfaction that comes when you know you are making a difference. The longer and more detailed your volunteer experience, the more benefits it will bring.

HIGH-IMPACT PRACTICE ❯ Have someone from your campus's service-learning or community service office visit your class to acquaint students with all the possibilities for service-learning in the local area.

Service-Learning. Service-learning is a special category of volunteering that allows you to apply what you learn in class to actual practice. Some instructors build service-learning into their courses, but if this option isn't available, consider making that link yourself. Ask your college success instructor for help in finding a service opportunity that would enrich your classroom learning.

high-impact practice 5

OUTSIDE CLASS ❯ Consider building a service-learning requirement into your course.

Study Abroad. Awareness of other cultures expands your diversity of thought and your exposure to people different than you. If possible, take courses in another country so that you can learn about a different culture, experience new traditions, and practice a different pace of life. Many colleges provide short- and long-term options, so find an opportunity that works best for your class and work schedule. Some study-abroad programs also include options for both work and service-learning experiences. If that interests you, find out how financial aid applies to study abroad.

high-impact practice 4

Internships and Co-Ops. What you learn in the classroom can be applied to the real world through internships and co-ops. An **internship** is a short-term, structured method of on-the-job training. As an intern, you are not likely to be paid, but you might be able to receive academic credit. Check with your academic department and career center to find out what internships are available in your major. Remember that with one or more internships on your résumé, you'll be a step ahead of students who ignore this valuable experience. A **co-op program** allows you to alternate work experience and classes. As a co-op student, you can also have paid work assignments that provide you with an opportunity to apply what you learn to the workplace.

high-impact practice 9

Student Projects and Competitions. In many fields, students engage in competitions based on what they have learned in the classroom. They might compete against teams from other colleges. In the process, they learn teamwork, communication, and problem-solving skills.

Trash or Treasure?

This student intern in the campus recycling department empties a bin of food into a container that will be sent to an off-campus composting center. Imagine what he is learning about the business of recycling, composting, and food waste reduction with regard to an academic area like environmental or sustainability studies.

Mark Crosse/*Fresno Bee*/MCT via Getty Images

 **high-impact practice 8**

Research. An excellent way to extend your academic learning is to work with a faculty member on a directed research project. Research extends your critical-thinking skills and provides insight into a subject above and beyond your books and class notes. This experience also allows you greater exposure to faculty members, who can become mentors and professional advocates.

Working in College

Paid opportunities for getting experience are also beneficial because they can support the attainment of your college goals, provide you with the financial means to complete college, and help you structure your time so that you are a much better time manager. Overextending yourself, however, can potentially interfere with your college success, your ability to attend class, your homework, and your participation in many other valuable parts of college life, such as group study or academic preparation. Take some time to determine how involved you are able to be, and stay within reasonable limits. If you want or need to work, explore on-campus opportunities as soon as possible after you arrive at college.

Working while taking classes means enjoying benefits such as:

- gaining professional experience
- earning money for tuition, books, and living expenses
- networking/making connections

- learning more about yourself and others
- developing key skills, such as communication, teamwork, problem solving, work ethics, and time management

Your first decision will be whether to work on campus or off. If you choose to work on campus, look for opportunities early in the term. You might be pleasantly surprised at how varied on-campus opportunities are, such as tutoring in the writing or math center, being an attendant in the fitness center, or serving as a student ambassador for the admissions office or career center. One benefit of on-campus employment is that the work schedules are often flexible. Another benefit is that you might be able to connect with instructors and administrators you can later consult as mentors or professional references. Plus, your boss will understand that you occasionally need time off to study or take exams. Finally, students who work on campus are more likely to graduate from college than students who work off campus; keep this fact in mind as you think about mixing college and work.

RETENTION STRATEGY ❯ There is a very positive correlation between working on campus and persistence, when compared to working off campus. Use this finding to encourage students to work on campus if possible.

Some on-campus jobs are reserved for work-study students. The federal work-study program is a form of government-sponsored financial aid that provides part-time employment to help with college expenses. Once you accept the work-study award on your financial aid notification, you will be sent information regarding the steps you should take for getting a job within the program. Keep in mind that your work-study award will be limited to a certain amount each term; once you reach your limit in earnings, you can no longer work until the next term begins. Generally, you will have to interview for a work-study position, whether on or off campus. Check with your college's financial aid office or career center to get a list of available jobs and to get help preparing your application materials and getting ready for the interview.

As a college student, you may decide that you would rather work off campus. An off-campus job might pay better than an on-campus one, or be closer to your home, or be in an organization where you want to continue working after you finish college. The best place to start looking for off-campus jobs is your campus career center, which might have listings or Web sites featuring off-campus employment opportunities. Feel free to ask a career counselor for suggestions.

Whether you choose to work on or off campus, keep in mind that over-extending yourself can interfere with your college success and your ability to attend class, do your homework, and participate in many other valuable parts of college life, such as group study. Students who work in paid jobs more than fifteen hours a week have a lower chance of success in college.

JOB SEARCH STRATEGIES

It may be hard to imagine yourself searching for a job—after all, you've just begun college—but the strategies discussed below can also be applied to an internship or part-time job. In addition, some preparation requires you to plan and get organized ahead of time. Here are a few things to consider:

- Learn the names of the major employers in your college's geographic area: manufacturers, service industries, resorts, and so on. Once you know who the major employers are, check them out and visit their Web sites. If you like what you see, visit your career center to arrange an informational interview or job shadow opportunity.
- Check the Web site for the agency in your state that collects and disseminates information about available employment opportunities. Find out whether this agency has an office in the community where you are attending college.
- Visit employment agencies, particularly those that seek part-time, temporary workers. It is a convenient, low-risk (for both you and the employer) way to "shop" for a job and obtain flexible, short-term, low-commitment employment.
- Visit online job boards and look at the classified ads in the local newspaper, either in print or online. Don't forget the classifieds in the national press. Some national firms will have jobs that can be done part-time in your area, or even from your own living space.
- Check your college's student newspaper. Employers who favor hiring college students (such as UPS) often advertise there. Be cautious about work opportunities that seem unrealistic, such as those offering big salaries for working at home or those that ask you to pay an up-front fee for a job. When in doubt, consult your career center for advice.
- Be aware that many jobs are never posted. Employers often find it easier to hire people who are recommended to them by current employees, friends, or the person vacating the position. Faculty members often hire students for their research labs based on performance in the classroom.
- Realize that who you know is important. Your friends who already work on campus or who have had an internship can be the best people to help you when you are ready to search for your job. In fact, nearly 50 percent of all student jobs are found through family and friends.

Market Yourself

Some think that marketing yourself is what you do when you need a job, but that's not the case at all. It's actually about developing a presence on campus and within your industry. Marketing yourself is about creating a name and a reputation that will shape your future. It is important to start building your brand now and looking at it as a personal challenge with no end date. Here are a few points to consider:

- **If you don't do it, no one else will.** Taking control of your own image is your responsibility. No one is better equipped to portray *you* as accurately as *you*. Remember to share your career goals with instructors, advisers, friends, and family; they can't help market you if they don't know you! The more others know about your professional goals, the more they can help you make professional connections.
- **Actions speak louder than words.** It is important to develop and continuously update professional documents such as a résumé and a

well-written cover letter. It is *more* important, however, to have a professional *voice*.

- **Got ideas? Share them.** People are often hesitant about sharing their ideas or providing direction to others, but guess what? If you don't, others establish themselves as the go-to person, and you may be left with a good idea that no one else knows about.
- **Get an edge over your competition.** You need to stand out from your peers if you want to go far in your career. Think carefully about what you are doing to advance yourself professionally outside the classroom, such as becoming a co-op student, an intern, or a volunteer.
- **It isn't all about you.** Really, it isn't. Sharing the accomplishments of your peers is one way to promote yourself indirectly. The smartest way to market yourself is actually to make it not about you. In turn, your peers will do the same for you and your accomplishments. In the end, everyone wins.

Build a Résumé

A good résumé is an excellent and necessary way to market yourself. Before you finish college, you'll need a résumé, whether it's for a part-time job, an internship or co-op position, or to show to an instructor who agrees to write you a letter of recommendation. Typically, there are two types of résumés. One is written in chronological format, and the other is organized by skills. If you have related job experience, choose the chronological résumé; if you can group skills from a number of jobs or projects under several meaningful categories, choose the skills-based résumé. Your career center can help you choose the format that is right for you given your experience and future goals.

On average, an employer spends 7 to 10 seconds screening each résumé to glean their first-round picks when it's time to fill a job. Many employers also use résumé-scanning software to identify key terms and experiences that are most important to the employer. If you are a new professional, a one-page résumé is usually appropriate. Add a second page only if you have truly outstanding skills or work experiences that won't fit on the first page, but consult with your career center for guidance on this point. If you are in college to get retrained and change your career, make sure to update the information on your résumé.

Write a Cover Letter

A cover letter is *more important* than a résumé, and much harder to write well. When sending a cover letter, think about who will receive it. Different fields will have different requirements. Your academic adviser or career counselor can help you address your letter to the right person; so can the Internet. Never write, "To whom it may concern." Use the proper formats for date, address, and salutation. These are details that employers pay attention to, and a mistake in your letter may cost you an interview. Make sure to ask someone whose writing ability you trust to proofread your cover letter.

IN CLASS > Students might wonder why they should create a résumé when they have just started college. The answer is this: Practice! Suggest that students contact a faculty member in their department to ask about the accepted résumé format and structure for their academic major, as standards can vary.

IN CLASS > Writing about yourself can be hard. Tell students to expect this as they draft a cover letter that sings their praises without sounding as if they are bragging. One suggestion is to have them pretend they are writing a close friend to describe some of their recent accomplishments, what they are thinking of doing after college, and why.

IN CLASS > If a student asks, "Why send a cover letter AND a résumé?" the answer is simple: The résumé tells what you have done; the cover letter tells who you are and how well you express yourself in writing.

A cover letter, written to explain how hiring you will benefit the organization, is an excellent way of marketing yourself to a potential employer. It is important to review the organization's Web site and find out what skills and experience its employees have. Use the cover letter to highlight your skills for every requirement of the position. Your career center can help you write a cover letter that talks about your education and your experience related to the position. Spending time on writing an excellent cover letter also prepares you for the interview by allowing you to think about how your background matches the needs of the position and the organization.

Interview

The first year of college might not seem like a time to be concerned about interviews. However, students often find themselves in interview situations soon after arriving on campus. You might be vying for positions in student government, finding an on-campus job, competing for a second-year scholarship, applying for a residence hall assistant position, choosing a summer job opportunity, or up for selection for an internship or as a research assistant. As you explore different industries and careers, you might set up information interviews, which are a great form of networking that can lead to job opportunities.

Interview Preparation. Preparing for an interview begins the moment that you arrive on campus because, as a first-year student, the interview is about you and how college is changing you. Students who haven't clarified their sense of purpose or who have taken only a little time to reflect on who they are and how they have changed can feel lost in an interview. Luckily, the chapters in this book have begun preparing you for the interview process.

The purpose of the interview is to exchange information. The interviewer's goal is to evaluate you on your abilities and competencies in terms of what the organization seeks. For you, the interview is an opportunity to learn more about the employer and whether the opportunity would be a good fit with your aptitudes and preferences. Ideally, you want to find a match between your interests and abilities and the position or experience you seek. It is important to research the organization and the people you may work with prior to any interview. Doing so will help prepare you for the interview and help you know what questions to ask. Review the Tech Tip in this chapter and consider the following advice:

1. **Start with the organization's or company's Web site.** It is usually the single best resource. Note details you can use to develop good questions to ask in your interview, as well as prepare relevant answers to anticipated interview questions. If the company does not have its own Web site, try **hoovers.com,** a site that provides extensive information about companies and industries.
2. **Review competitors' Web sites.** Gather information on developments in the company's industry or sector.
3. **Ask for advice.** Ask faculty or your career center whether they have information or feedback about the company.
4. **Use your library.** Find articles in business publications and industry trade magazines. Remember to ask a librarian for help if you need it.
5. **Note the employer's goals and values.** This information tells you about the company culture and can help you decide whether you would be a good fit.
6. **Research details about the company's products and services.** When you can speak a company's language, you're showing that you have prepared yourself.
7. **Find out the company's strategic goals, special projects, and new developments.** Use this information in your interview to prepare insightful questions to ask about the direction of the company.
8. **Take your research with you to the interview.** Show that you have taken the time to find out about the company prior to the interview.

After you've done your company research, the next step is to prepare for and practice interviewing *before* the actual interview. First, check with your career center to find out whether you can participate in a mock interview. Mock interviews help students strategize and feel comfortable in interview situations. Your counselor might ask you for a position description, your résumé, and a company profile prior to the interview to simulate an actual interview as closely as possible. Many career centers also have virtual practice interview software for you to gain experience. InterviewStream is a popular program that allows you to record answers to interview questions asked by the computer for replay and review. You can record your answers multiple times, which allows you to practice and perfect your response, and you can send your recorded interview to faculty members or others for feedback. Because the interview is recorded using a Web cam, you can review not only your words but also your body language! Nonverbal communication is often more important than what you actually say in the interview. Even if a mock interview session is not

IN CLASS > Have students' role-play mock interviews. Identify some jobs for which your students could currently apply. Make a list of questions for each job. You could also involve more students by allowing some of them to be the mock interviewer and giving them specific questions for students to practice answering. Because this is impromptu practice, you might need to help and encourage students who struggle with it.

available, the career center can offer tips on handling an interview situation. Check your career center's Web site for sample interview questions so that you can practice before an interview.

If you are changing your career and have been interviewed before, make sure to think about the best and worst interviews you have had and try to avoid repeating the mistakes you made in the past; more important, build on the positive interview strategies you used in previous successful interviews.

Appropriate Interview Conduct.

In any interview situation, certain things you do might make the difference whether you are considered for a position. Here are a few suggestions:

- **Dress appropriately.** First impressions matter, so always dress neatly and appropriately. You can be somewhat casual for some types of employers, but it is better to dress too professionally than too informally. Check with your career center to get advice about proper dress. Also, many two-year colleges have suits to loan to students who cannot yet afford to buy expensive clothes for an interview.
- **Arrive to the interview on time.** If your interview is off campus, consider taking a trial run to the location prior to the day of your interview to determine how long it takes to travel to the interview site. Be mindful of traffic volume at certain times of the day, and plan accordingly. The interviewer expects you to be on time, regardless of the weather or commuting time.
- **Follow up.** It is important to follow up any interview with a thank-you e-mail. Many times, the person to whom you addressed your cover letter is not the person with whom you actually interview. Prior to leaving the interview, ask for business cards of the professionals you met so that you have their contact information. Send a handwritten thank-you note or well-written thank-you e-mail to every person who interviewed you. In your follow-up, you can once more highlight how your skills and experience match the organization's goals.

PEER LEADERS > Although your campus career center can be the "official" source for practicing interview skills, you can also offer to conduct mock interviews with your students to give them additional practice.

SKILLS EMPLOYERS SEEK

One of the many important purposes and outcomes of your college experience is gaining a combination of knowledge and skills. Two types of skills are essential to employment and to life: content skills and transferable skills. **Content skills** are intellectual, or "hard," skills that you gain in your academic field. They include writing proficiency, computer literacy, and foreign language skills. Computer literacy is now a core skill like reading, writing, and mathematics. You can apply content skills to jobs in any field or occupation.

Certain types of employers will expect extensive knowledge in your academic major before they will consider hiring you; for example, to get a job in accounting, you must demonstrate knowledge of Quickbooks or Microsoft Excel's advanced features. Employers will not train you in basic applications or knowledge related to your field, so remember to be prepared to speak about your qualifications during the interview process. Remember, for most college students it's sufficient to have some fundamental knowledge. You will learn more on the job as you move from entry-level work to more advanced positions.

Transferable skills are skills that are general and apply to, or transfer to, a variety of settings. Transferable skills give you flexibility in your career planning, as they are valued by many employers and in various professions. You develop transferable skills through a variety of activities, such as volunteer work, studying abroad, involvement in a student professional organization or club, and the pursuit of hobbies or interests. All of these pursuits can build teamwork, leadership, interpersonal awareness, and effective communication abilities. Internships and career-related work are also valuable opportunities to practice these skills in the real world.

Some transferable skills are listed and described below in Table 15.2.

TABLE 15.2 > Transferable Skills

Skills	Abilities
Communication	Being a clear and persuasive speaker Listening attentively Writing well
Presentation	Justifying Persuading Responding to questions and serious critiques of presentation material
Leadership	Taking charge Providing direction
Teamwork	Working with different people while maintaining control over some assignments
Interpersonal	Relating to others Motivating others to participate Easing conflict between coworkers
Personal traits	Showing motivation Recognizing the need to take action Being adaptable to change Having a strong work ethic Being reliable and honest Acting in an ethical manner Knowing how to plan and organize multiple tasks Being able to respond positively to customer concerns
Critical thinking and problem solving	Identifying problems and their solutions by combining information from different sources and considering options

PEER LEADERS > Ask your students to list the seven skills from the table on a piece of paper and to rate themselves on each using a scale of 1 (I need help in this area) to 5 (I am strong in this area). The rating should be anonymous. Collect the rating sheets and let students know the areas in which the most students are strong or weak. Facilitate a discussion about how to improve the weaker skills.

Job Candidate Skills and Qualities Ranked as *Very Important* by Employers

Employers seek job candidates who can:

- work in a team structure

- make decisions and solve problems

- plan, organize, and prioritize work

- verbally communicate with persons inside and outside the organization

- obtain and process information

- analyze quantitative data

- demonstrate that they have technical knowledge related to the job

Therefore, the ideal candidate is a team player and a good communicator who can make decisions, solve problems, and prioritize. Does this describe you? If not, don't panic. This chapter is intended as a guide for you to *develop into* the ideal candidate!

Source: National Association of Colleges and Employers, *Job Outlook 2014* (Bethlehem, PA: National Association of Colleges and Employers, 2013).

Time to Celebrate!

When you are a first-year student, it may be hard for you to imagine graduation day, but we can confidently tell you that successful completion of this course is a good predictor that you will succeed and graduate with a college degree and perhaps a graduate degree some day. Before you know it, you, along with your family and friends, will celebrate your achievements. By making the most of what you have learned in your college success course and your other college experiences, both in and out of class, you will be ready to take the next steps toward a successful career and a bright future.

© Corbis

checklist for success

Majors and Careers

☐ **Understand the nature of the new economy that you will be entering.** It is global, unstable, innovative, without boundaries, customized, ever-changing, and social.

☐ **Learn which of your characteristics could and should affect your career choices.** Strive to define your interests, skills, aptitudes, personality, life goals, and work values. Talk them through with a career counselor. It's a normal thing for college students to do.

☐ **Keep in touch with your instructors.** Consider keeping in touch with the instructor of this course and with other instructors. Later in college, you may need to ask them to write letters of reference for you as you seek employment or admission to graduate school. When an instructor becomes part of your larger support group, it is a form of networking.

☐ **Be responsible for planning your own career.** No one else is going to do it for you, but plenty of people on your campus are willing to help you. Think seriously about your major. You eventually have to get a degree in something, and you want to feel confident and comfortable about the major that you select. Use the insights into yourself that you have gotten from this course as motivation, now and in the future.

☐ **Get familiar with online resources for industry research and career exploration.** The more knowledge you have about the industries that interest you, the better your chances of making a sound career decision. Great places to start are **O*NET OnLine (onetonline.org)** and the U.S. Bureau of Labor Statistics' Occupational Outlook Handbook (**bls.gov/ooh**).

☐ **Enhance your employability by getting different kinds of work and travel experience during college.** You can get different experiences while taking classes, but better yet, consider maintaining your momentum during the summer. Continuous enrollment is a good thing. See your adviser and career center to learn about experiences that your college offers: volunteer or service learning, study abroad, internships and co-ops, employment on campus, and student projects and research.

☐ **Get professional help from your career center.** When writing your résumé and cover letters, learning and practicing interview skills, and much more, advisers can help you. For example, you can learn how your personality characteristics have been shown to align with particular career fields.

☐ **Be aware of what today's employers seek from new employees.** Make sure you can demonstrate both the content and transferable skills necessary for the jobs that interest you most.

15 build your experience

REFLECT ON CHOICES

high-impact practice 2 | Most students are in college to prepare for a career. This chapter provides essential information on how you can structure your college experience, both in and out of class, to gain knowledge and skills that will help you, no matter what your employment future holds. Think about careers you are considering, and jot down some steps you can take while you're a college student to help you prepare for your first job after graduation.

APPLY WHAT YOU HAVE LEARNED

Now that you have read and discussed this chapter, consider how you can apply what you have learned to your academic life and your personal life. The following prompts will help you reflect on chapter material and its relevance to you both now and in the future.

1. Sometimes it's hard to know if you're headed in the right career direction. Describe two steps you can take to make sure your career plans are realistic.

2. Finding a career is about more than just the job itself. It's also about how and where you want to live. Does the career you envision fit with the way you want to live your life?

USE YOUR RESOURCES

> **Your College Web Site and Campus Resources** Continue using the institutional services and resources that you learned about in this course, such as the learning center or career center.

> **Academic Advising and First-Year Counselors** More and more advisers have been trained to help you throughout your college experience. If you are an adult student seeking a new career direction, your academic adviser can help make sure you're taking the right courses and can assist you in finding the help you need.

> **Faculty** On many campuses, faculty members take an active role in helping students connect academic interests to careers. A faculty member can recommend specific courses that relate to a particular career. If you are a racial or ethnic minority student on your campus, seek out faculty or staff members who share your racial or ethnic profile and experiences.

> **Library** All campuses have a main library that contains a wealth of information on careers. Some campuses have a separate library in the career center, staffed by librarians whose job is to help you locate career-related information resources.

> **Upperclass Students and Your Peer Leader** More experienced students can help you navigate courses and find important resources. Many colleges have established peer mentoring programs that connect you to upperclass students for one-on-one guidance. Because they have tested the waters, they can alert you to potential pitfalls or inform you of opportunities.

> **Student Organizations** Professional student organizations that focus on specific career interests meet regularly throughout the year and provide excellent leadership development opportunities. Join them now. If you are a veteran or active duty military student, your campus may have a special organization designed to help you take advantage of special veterans or military benefits.

> **Career Center** Go to your campus career center's home page and check its resources.

> **U.S. Bureau of Labor Statistics' Occupational Outlook Handbook: bls.gov/ooh.** This guide to career information about hundreds of occupations is maintained by the U.S. Department of Labor.

> **Mapping Your Future: mappingyourfuture .org.** This comprehensive site provides support for those who are just starting to explore potential careers.

 LaunchPad

LaunchPad for *Your College Experience* is a great resource. Go online to master concepts using the LearningCurve study tool and much more. macmillanhighered.com/gardner12e

glossary

abstract   A paragraph-length summary of the methods and major findings of an article in a scholarly journal.

abstract conceptualization   A learner's ability to integrate observations into logically sound theories. One of the four stages of the Kolb Inventory of Learning Styles.

academic adviser   A faculty or staff member who provides official advice to students on course selection and academic planning.

academic calendar   A calendar that shows all the important dates specific to your campus: financial aid, registration, and add/drop deadlines; midterm and final exam dates; holidays; graduation deadlines; and so forth.

academic freedom   The virtually unlimited freedom of speech and inquiry granted to professors to further the advancement of knowledge as long as human lives, rights, and privacy are not violated.

academic integrity   Intellectual honesty; the avoidance of cheating and plagiarism.

academic plan/map   A list of the courses you need to take and complete in a program of study to graduate with a degree.

academic planning   Creating a plan of coursework that leads to a college degree.

accommodators   Individuals who prefer hands-on learning. They are skilled at making things happen, rely on their intuition, and might use trial and error rather than logic to solve problems. Accommodators often major in business. One of the learner groups of the Kolb Inventory of Learning Styles.

acronym   A memory device created by forming new words from the first letters of several words.

acrostic   A verse in which certain letters of each word or line form a message.

active experimentation   A learner's ability to make decisions, solve problems, and test what he or she has learned in new situations. One of the four stages of the Kolb Inventory of Learning Styles.

active learning   Learning by participation, such as listening critically, discussing what you are learning, and writing about it.

active reading   A four-step process to reading that involves using strategies, such as highlighting and taking notes, to help you stay focused. The steps in the active reading process are previewing, marking, reading with concentration, and reviewing.

adaptability   The ability to adjust your thinking and behavior when faced with new or unexpected situations.

analysis   The process of breaking down material into its parts so that you can understand its structure. Includes categorizing, comparing, contrasting, and questioning. One of the six levels of Bloom's Taxonomy.

annotate   To add critical or explanatory margin notes on a page as you read.

annotation   Note or remark written in the margin about a piece of writing.

application   The process of using what you have learned, such as rules and methods, in new situations. Application includes choosing, illustrating, practicing, and interpreting. One of the six levels of Bloom's Taxonomy.

aptitude   Natural talent or an ability an individual has acquired through life experience, study, or training.

argument   Reason and evidence brought together in logical support of a claim.

assertiveness   Standing up for yourself when you need to, without being too aggressive.

assimilators   Individuals who like to develop theories and think about abstract concepts. Assimilators often major in math, physics, or chemistry. One of the learner groups of the Kolb Inventory of Learning Styles.

attention deficit hyperactivity disorder (ADHD)   A disorder characterized by difficulty organizing tasks, completing work, and listening to and following directions.

aural learner   A person who prefers to learn by listening to information. One of the preferences described by the VARK Learning Styles Inventory.

autonomy   Self-direction or independence. College students usually have more autonomy than high school students.

behavioral interview   An interview in which the interviewer questions the candidate about past experiences and how they helped the candidate learn and grow. This type of interview helps assess skills and behaviors.

bias   A tendency against or in favor of certain groups or value systems.

biorhythms   The internal mechanisms that drive our daily patterns of physical, emotional, and mental activity.

bodily/kinesthetic learner   An individual who prefers learning by moving around and is good at sports, dance, and acting. One of the eight intelligences described by the theory of multiple intelligences.

Campus SAVE Act   A federal law passed in 2013 mandating that all colleges and universities provide sexual assault, violence, and harassment education to students.

campus wide common intellectual experience A program in which students take required "common-core" courses, participate in a required learning community, or engage in other shared experiences such as a "common reading" (a high-impact practice).

capstone course or project A course or experience taken during the senior year that requires students to reflect on what they learned in all their courses and create a project of some sort that integrates and applies that knowledge (a high-impact practice).

cheating Dishonesty in academic work. Each campus has its own definition, which could include looking over a classmate's shoulder for an answer, using a calculator when it is not permitted, obtaining or discussing an exam or individual questions from an exam without permission, copying someone else's lab notes, purchasing term papers over the Internet, watching the video instead of reading the book, and copying computer files.

chunking A previewing method that involves making a list of terms and definitions from the reading and then dividing the terms into smaller clusters of five, seven, or nine to learn the material more effectively.

citation A source or author of certain material. When browsing the Internet for sources, use only material that has citations crediting the author, where it came from, and who posted it.

cloud computing A term that describes using the Internet as a storage device and sharing files and folders with others.

co-curricular experience Learning that occurs outside the classroom through on-campus clubs and groups, co-op programs, internships, or other means.

cognitive restructuring A technique of applying positive thinking and giving oneself encouraging messages rather than self-defeating, negative ones.

collaborative assignment A learning activity in which you work and solve problems with your classmates (a high-impact practice).

comprehension Understanding the meaning of material. Comprehension includes classifying, describing, explaining, and translating. One of the six levels of Bloom's Taxonomy.

computerized test A test that is often taken in a computer lab or testing center and is usually not administered online.

computer literacy Facility with electronic tools, both for conducting searches and for presenting to others what you have found and analyzed.

concrete experience Abilities that allow learners to be receptive to others and open to their feelings and specific experiences. One of the four stages of the Kolb Inventory of Learning Styles.

content skills Cognitive, intellectual, or "hard" skills acquired as one gains mastery in an academic field. They include writing proficiency, computer literacy, and foreign language skills.

convergers People who enjoy the world of ideas and theories and are good at thinking about how to apply those theories to real-world, practical situations. Convergers tend to choose health-related and engineering majors. One of the learner groups of the Kolb Inventory of Learning Styles.

cooperative (co-op) education Paid work assignments that provide students with an opportunity to use their education and apply it to the workplace. In cooperative education, a period of work alternates with a period of school.

co-op programs Programs offered at many institutions that allow students to work in their field of study while enrolled in college. They offer valuable experiences and an excellent preview of what work in the chosen field is actually like. Also called cooperative education.

Cornell format A method for organizing notes in which one side of the notebook page is designated for note taking during class, and the other serves as a "recall" column where main ideas and important details for tests are jotted down as soon as possible after class.

credit hours A representation of the number of clock hours you spend in each class every week during a term, and the number of credits you will earn if you satisfactorily complete a course. A one-credit course generally meets for 50 to 60 minutes once a week.

credit score A numerical representation of your level of fiscal responsibility, derived from a credit report that contains information about all the accounts in your name. This score can determine your ability to qualify for loans, the interest rates and insurance rates you pay, and can sometimes affect your employability.

critical thinking Thoughtful consideration of the information, ideas, observations, and arguments that you encounter; in essence, a search for truth.

cultural literacy Knowing what is going on around you and what has happened in the past.

culture The aspects of a group of people that are passed on or learned. Traditions, food, language, clothing styles, artistic expression, and beliefs are all part of culture.

cyberbullying Any behavior performed through electronic or digital media by individuals or groups who repeatedly communicate hostile or aggressive messages intended to inflict harm or discomfort on others.

database An organized and searchable set of information. Like a special search engine, a database is often classified by a certain subject area, such as chemistry or U.S. history.

deep learning Understanding the "why" and "how" behind the details.

degree The type of diploma students receive after graduation.

delayed gratification The ability to resist the temptation for an immediate reward and wait for a later reward.

digital footprint How you represent yourself—and how others represent you—online on Facebook, Instagram, Twitter, and other social media sites.

digital persona/profile The version of yourself that you present online on Facebook, Instagram, Twitter, and other social media sites.

discipline An area of academic study, such as sociology, anthropology, or engineering.

discrimination The act of treating people differently because of their race, ethnicity, gender, socioeconomic class, or other identifying characteristics, rather than on their merits.

divergers Individuals who are adept at reflecting on situations from many viewpoints. They excel at brainstorming and are imaginative and people-oriented but sometimes have difficulty making decisions. Divergers tend to major in the humanities or social sciences. One of the learner groups of the Kolb Inventory of Learning Styles.

diversity Variations in social and cultural identities among people living together.

drafting Step two of the writing process, during which a writer organizes information and ideas into sentences and paragraphs.

dyslexia A widespread developmental learning disorder that can affect the ability to read, spell, or write.

e-book A book in electronic format that can be read on a computer or other digital device.

emotional intelligence (EI) The ability to recognize, understand, use, and manage moods, feelings, and attitudes.

emotional self-awareness Knowing how and why you feel the way you do.

empathy Recognition and understanding of another person's feelings, situation, or point of view.

episodic memory An aspect of long-term memory that deals with particular events, their time, and their place.

essay exam An exam made up of questions that require students to write a few paragraphs or a short essay in response to each question.

ethnicity The identity that is assigned to a specific group of people historically connected by a common national heritage or language.

evaluation The ability to judge the value of ideas and information you are learning according to internal or external criteria. Evaluation includes appraising, arguing, defending, and supporting. The highest level of Bloom's Taxonomy.

explanatory writing Writing that is "published," meaning that others can read it.

exploratory writing Writing that helps you first discover what you want to say. It is private and is used only as a series of steps toward a published work.

extraverts Individuals who are outgoing, gregarious, and talkative. Extraverts are good communicators who are quick to act and lead. One of the personality preferences described by the Myers-Briggs Type Indicator.

feeling types Individuals who are warm, empathetic, compassionate, and interested in the happiness of others as well as themselves. They need and value harmony and kindness. One of the personality preferences described by the Myers-Briggs Type Indicator.

fill-in-the-blank question A test question that consists of a phrase, sentence, or paragraph with a blank space indicating where the student should provide the missing word or words.

financial aid Monetary sources to help pay for college. Financial aid can come in the form of scholarships, grants, loans, work study, and cooperative education.

first-year seminars The course in which you find yourself now, designed to prepare you for your college experience (a high-impact practice).

fixed expense An expense that will cost you the same amount every time you pay it.

flash cards A card with words or numbers that is displayed or reviewed as part of a study routine.

flexibility Adapting and adjusting your emotions, viewpoints, and actions as situations change.

forgetting curve The decline of memory over time.

freewriting Writing that is temporarily unencumbered by mechanical processes, such as punctuation, grammar, spelling, context, and so forth.

gender A continuum that accounts for many different ways of identifying oneself based on the things a person says, does, or wears.

general education Introductory courses—such as English, math, history, or psychology—that almost every student must take in order to earn a degree.

global learning or diversity experience Courses and programs in which you explore cultures, life experiences, and worldviews different from your own (a high-impact practice).

grants A form of financial aid awarded by the federal government, state governments, and institutions themselves. Students meet academic qualifications for grants by being admitted to the college and maintaining grades that are acceptable to the grant provider.

happiness Being satisfied with yourself, with others, and with your situation in general.

humanities Branches of knowledge that investigate human beings, their culture, and their self-expression. They include the study of philosophy, religion, literature, music, and art.

impulse control Thinking carefully about potential consequences before you act and delaying gratification for the sake of achieving long-term goals.

inclusive curriculum A curriculum offering courses that introduce students to diverse people, worldviews, and approaches.

independence Making important decisions on your own without having to get everyone's opinion.

information age Our current times, characterized by the primary role of information in our economy and our lives, the need for information retrieval and information-management skills, and the explosion of available information.

informational interview A meeting used to gather information on a field or company and expand one's professional network.

information literacy The ability to find, interpret, and use information to meet your needs.

intellectual property Ownership over nonphysical creative works such as slogans, artwork, and inventions. Copyright, trademarks, and patents are kinds of intellectual property.

interdisciplinary Linking two or more academic fields of study, such as history and religion. Encouraging an interdisciplinary approach to teaching can offer a better understanding of modern society.

interlibrary loan A service that allows you to request an item at no charge from another library at a different college or university.

internship Direct experience in a work setting often related to your career interests.

interpersonal Relating to the interaction between yourself and other individuals. Friendships, professional networks, and family connections are interpersonal relationships that can be mutually beneficial.

interpersonal learner An individual who likes to have many friends and is good at understanding people, leading others, and mediating conflicts. One of the eight intelligences described by the theory of multiple intelligences.

intrapersonal Relating to how well you know and like yourself, as well as how effectively you can do the things you need to do to stay happy. Knowing yourself is necessary in order to understand others.

intrapersonal learner Someone who likes to work alone, understands him- or herself well, and is an original thinker. One of the eight intelligences described by the theory of multiple intelligences.

introverts Individuals who like quiet and privacy and who tend to think a lot and reflect carefully about a problem before taking action. One of the personality preferences described by the Myers-Briggs Type Indicator.

intuitive types Individuals who are fascinated by possibilities, the meaning behind the facts, and the connections between concepts. They are often original, creative, and nontraditional. One of the personality preferences described by the Myers-Briggs Type Indicator.

judging types Individuals who approach the world in a planned, orderly, and organized way. They strive for order and control, making decisions relatively quickly and easily so they can create and implement plans. One of the personality preferences described by the Myers-Briggs Type Indicator.

keyword A term used to tell a search engine what you're looking for. Keywords are synonyms, related terms, or subtopics of your search topic.

kinesthetic learner A person who prefers to learn something through experience and practice, rather than by hearing or reading about it. One of the preferences described by the VARK Learning Styles Inventory.

knowledge Awareness or understanding gained through study or experience. Knowledge includes arranging, defining, and recognizing.

laboratory test Given in many science courses, a test that requires you to move from one lab station to the next to solve problems, identify parts of models or specimens, or explain chemical reactions.

learning community A program in which students take two or more "linked" courses with a group of other students, allowing them to work closely with each other and with instructors (a high-impact practice).

learning disability A disorder such as dyslexia that affects people's ability to either interpret what they see and hear or connect information across different areas of the brain.

learning management system (LMS) A Web site that helps you connect with the material you're studying—as well as with your instructors and classmates.

learning objectives The main ideas or skills that students are expected to learn from a particular course, from an entire program of study, or from reading a particular article, chapter, or book.

learning styles Particular ways of learning, unique to each individual. For example, one person may prefer reading to understand how something works, while another may prefer using a "hands-on" approach.

list format A method for organizing notes that is most effective for taking notes on lists of terms and definitions, facts, or sequences. This format is effective when combined with the Cornell format, with key terms in the left column and their definitions and explanations in the right column.

logical fallacy A false belief or misconception resulting from incorrect reasoning.

logical/mathematical learner An individual who likes to work with numbers and is good at problem solving and logical processes. One of the eight intelligences described by the theory of multiple intelligences.

long-term memory The type of memory that is used to retain information and can be described in three ways: procedural, semantic, and episodic.

major An area of study such as psychology, engineering, education, or nursing, in which you can earn a degree.

mapping A previewing strategy of drawing a wheel or branching structure to show relationships between main ideas and secondary ideas. This strategy also helps you see how different concepts and terms fit together and helps you make connections between the material at hand and what you already know about the subject.

marking An active reading strategy of underlining, highlighting, or writing margin notes or annotations in your text.

matching question A test question that is set up with terms in one column and descriptions or definitions in the other. The student must match the proper term with its definition.

media literacy The ability to think critically about material distributed to a wide audience through television, film, advertising, radio, magazines, books, and the Internet.

merit scholarships Scholarships based on talent, which do not require you to demonstrate financial need. Most merit scholarships are granted by colleges and are part of the admissions and financial aid processes.

mind map A review sheet with words and visual elements that jog the memory to help you recall information more easily.

mnemonics Various methods or tricks to aid memory, including acronyms, acrostics, rhymes or songs, and visualization.

motivation The process that initiates, guides, and maintains goal-oriented behaviors; the desire to do things.

multiculturalism The active process of acknowledging and respecting the diverse social groups, cultures, religions, races, ethnicities, attitudes, and opinions within a community.

multimodal An individual who learns through two or more modes described by the VARK Learning Styles Inventory.

multiple intelligences A theory developed by Dr. Howard Gardner based on the premise that the traditional notion of human intelligence is very limited. According to Gardner, all human beings have at least eight different types of intelligence, including verbal/linguistic, logical/mathematical, visual/spatial, bodily/kinesthetic, musical/rhythmic, interpersonal, intrapersonal, and naturalistic.

multiple-choice question A test question that provides a number of possible answers, often between three and five. The answer choices are usually numbered (1, 2, 3, 4, . . .) or lettered (a, b, c, d, . . .), and the test taker selects the correct or best one.

multitasking Doing more than one thing at a time, requiring that you divide your time and attention among tasks.

musical/rhythmic learner An individual who likes to sing or play an instrument and is good at remembering melodies and noticing pitches and rhythms. One of the eight intelligences described by the theory of multiple intelligences.

naturalistic learner An individual who likes to be outside and is good at preservation, conservation, and organizing a living area. One of the eight intelligences described by the theory of multiple intelligences.

need-based scholarship A scholarship based on both talent and financial need.

online test A test that is administered online.

open-book or open-note test A test during which you are permitted to refer to your book or notes.

optimism Looking for the "bright side" of any problem or difficulty and being confident that things will work out for the best.

outline format A method for organizing notes that uses Roman numerals to represent key ideas and then transitions to using uppercase letters, then numbers, and then lowercase letters to represent other ideas relating to each key idea.

paragraph format A method for organizing notes that consists of writing summary paragraphs on what you are reading.

peer review A process by which experts in a field read and evaluate the articles in a journal before it is published.

perceiving types Individuals who are flexible and can comfortably adapt to change. They tend to delay decisions to keep their options open to gather more information. One of the personality preferences described by the Myers-Briggs Type Indicator.

periodical A resource that is published multiple times a year, such as a magazine.

plagiarism The act of taking another person's idea or work and presenting it as your own. This gross academic misconduct can result in suspension or expulsion, and even the revocation of the violator's college degree.

prejudice A preconceived judgment or opinion of someone that is not based on facts or knowledge, such as prejudging someone based entirely on his or her skin color.

previewing Taking a first look at your assigned reading before you really tackle the content.

prewriting The first stage of the writing process, during which you write things down as they come to mind—based on both the information you found through your research and your own ideas—without consciously trying to organize your thoughts, find exactly the right words, or think about structure.

primary sources   The original research or documentation on a topic, usually referenced either at the end of a chapter or at the back of a book.

problem solving   Approaching challenges step by step and not giving up in the face of obstacles.

procedural memory   An aspect of long-term memory that refers to knowing how to do something, such as solving a mathematical problem or playing a musical instrument.

procrastination   The habit of delaying something that needs your immediate attention.

punctuality   Being on time.

race   A term that refers to biological characteristics shared by groups of people, including skin tone, hair texture and color, and facial features.

read/write learner   A person who prefers to learn information displayed as words. One of the preferences described by the VARK Learning Styles Inventory.

reality testing   Ensuring that your feelings are appropriate by checking against external, objective criteria.

reflective observation   A learner's ability to reflect on his or her experiences from many perspectives. One of the four stages of the Kolb Inventory of Learning Styles.

religion   A specific set of beliefs and practices generally agreed on by a number of persons or groups.

research   A process of steps used to collect and analyze information to increase understanding of a topic or issue. Those steps include asking questions, collecting and analyzing data related to those questions, and presenting one or more answers.

resilience   The ability to adapt to and bounce back from life's hardships and difficulties.

reviewing   The final step in active textbook reading. Reviewing involves looking through your assigned reading again.

review sheet   A list of key terms and ideas developed from your notes. It is valuable as a study aid.

revision   The third and final stage of the writing process, which involves polishing your work until it clearly explains what you want to communicate and is ready for your audience.

scholarly article   Articles written by experts in their fields, such as researchers, librarians, or professors, and then assessed and edited by other experts in a process called peer review.

scholarly journals   Published collections of original, peer-reviewed research articles written by experts or researchers in a particular academic discipline.

self-actualization   Being satisfied and comfortable with what you have achieved in school, work, and your personal life.

semantic memory   An aspect of long-term memory that involves remembering facts and meanings without regard to where and when you learned those things.

sensing types   Individuals who are practical, factual, realistic, and down-to-earth. Relatively traditional and conventional, they can be very precise, steady, patient, and effective with routine and details. One of the personality preferences described by the Myers-Briggs Type Indicator.

service-learning   Unpaid volunteer service that is embedded in courses across the curriculum (a high-impact practice).

sex   One's biological makeup, typically categorized as male or female.

short-term memory   How many items you are able to perceive at one time. Memory that disappears in less than 30 seconds (sometimes faster) unless the items are moved to long-term memory.

social responsibility   The establishment of a personal link with a group or community and cooperation with other members toward shared goals.

stacks   The areas in libraries containing shelves that are full of books available for checkout.

stereotype   A generalization—usually exaggerated or over-simplified, and often offensive—that is used to describe or distinguish a group.

stress tolerance   Recognizing the causes of stress and responding in appropriate ways; staying strong under pressure.

summary   A section at the end of a textbook chapter that sums up a larger section of material and highlights the most important ideas.

Supplemental Instruction (SI)   Classes that provide further opportunity to discuss the information presented in lectures.

syllabus   A formal statement of course requirements and procedures or a course outline that an instructor provides to all students on the first day of class.

synthesis   The process of combining separate information and ideas to formulate a more complete understanding. Includes collecting, organizing, creating, and composing. Also, a level of learning on Bloom's Taxonomy.

take-home test   Tests taken outside class, for which you can refer to your textbook, notes, and other resources.

thesis statement   A short statement that clearly defines the purpose of a paper.

thinking types   Individuals who are logical, rational, and analytical. They reason well and tend to be critical and objective without being swayed by their own or other people's feelings. One of the personality preferences described by the Myers-Briggs Type Indicator.

transcript Your official academic record; it shows your major, when you took particular courses, your grades for each course, and your overall GPA.

transferable skills General skills that apply to or transfer to a variety of settings. Examples include solid oral and listening abilities, leadership skills, critical-thinking skills, and problem-solving skills.

true/false question A test question that asks students to determine whether a statement is correct or not.

undergraduate research A program that gives you the opportunity to participate in systematic investigation and research working one-on-one with a faculty member.

variable expense An expense that may change over time.

verbal/linguistic learner An individual who likes to read, write, and tell stories and is good at memorizing information. One of the eight intelligences described by the theory of multiple intelligences.

visualization A memory technique used to associate words, concepts, or stories with visual images.

visual learner A person who prefers to learn by reading words on a printed page or by looking at pictures, charts, graphs, symbols, video, and other visual means. One of the preferences described by the VARK Learning Styles Inventory.

visual/spatial learner An individual who likes to draw and play with machines and is good at puzzles and reading maps and charts. One of the eight intelligences described by the theory of multiple intelligences.

wellness A catchall term for taking care of your mind, body, and spirit that includes keeping fit, making healthy choices, achieving balance, and reducing stress in positive ways.

work-study award A form of federal financial aid that covers a portion of college costs in return for on-campus employment.

writing-intensive courses Courses across the curriculum that engage students in multiple forms of writing for different audiences. This textbook offers various writing activities that make your first-year seminar a writing-intensive course (a high-impact practice).

index

Counseling services, 194
Counselors, 13. *See also* Academic advisers;
    Career counselors
    academic planning and, 18, 21
    ADHD (attention deficit hyperactivity
        disorder) and, 81
    career choices and, 319, 327, 333
    course withdrawal and, 192, 293
    emotional intelligence and, 59, 60
    first-year students and, 334
    international students and, 10
    off-campus employment and, 325
    procrastination and, 34
    public speaking and, 260
    relationships and, 230, 239
    roommate situations and, 229
    text anxiety and, 186
    time management and, 44
    tutors and, 173
Course catalog, 16, 18, 104, 215, 302, 312
Course management system (CMS), 70, 133,
    142. *See also* Learning management
        system (LMS)
Courses. *See also* Classes; Lectures
    argument, 104
    capstone (high-impact practice 10), 9
    communications, 46, 106, 306
    critical thinking, 104
    on diversity, 249–250
    emotional intelligence, 60
    foreign language, 179, 185
    gender studies, 246
    humanities and social science, 71, 120, 121(*f*)
    linked, 9, 63
    logic, 104
    math, 18, 71, 80, 116, 117–118, 123, 143–145,
        150, 152, 170, 177, 179, 186, 224, 308
    online, 180, 196, 249
    personal finance, 302
    psychology, 18, 84, 88, 120, 123, 131, 260,
        306, 316
    science, 15, 62, 63, 109, 116–117, 118–120,
        119(*f*), 143–145, 152, 170, 174, 175(*f*),
        177–178, 179, 308
    teaching styles in, 65, 77, 79, 79(*t*), 83
    writing-intensive (high-impact practice 2),
        9, 14, 20, 22, 40, 44, 59, 60, 72, 74, 84, 100,
        101, 104, 114, 125, 143, 150, 155, 168, 189,
        194, 207, 209, 210, 225, 230, 240, 246, 258,
        279, 300, 302, 308, 311, 334
Course schedules, 19, 32, 38, 42, 43, 232, 313, 323
Cover letters, 327–328, 333
Creativity, 93–94, 309
Credibility of sources, 102, 200, 206, 208
Credit, and money management, 295–298, 301
Credit cards, 284, 286, 289, 296, 298–299, 302.
    See also Debit cards
Credit counseling agencies, 302
Credit reports, 299, 300, 301
Credit unions, 295
Crime, on campus, 272, 275, 276
Criteria-based aid, 293
Critical thinking, 8, 87–104
    arguments considered in, 96–97, 104
    asking questions in, 89, 91, 93, 94–95, 97, 103
    building experience in, 104
    challenging assumptions and, 89, 97, 103
    collaboration and, 92–93
    in college life, 89–90, 103
    conclusions in, 88, 89–90, 91, 95–96, 103
    courses on, 104
    creativity and, 93–94
    defined, 89
    essay exams and, 181

evaluating sources and, 104
examining evidence in, 90, 96, 97–98, 103
faulty reasoning and, 98–100
importance of, 88, 89–90
information literacy and, 197
multiple points of view in, 93, 95–96, 103
new ideas and, 95, 134
problem solving and, 90, 91, 96
research and, 102, 196, 200, 204, 206
self-assessment of skills in, 92
slow and fast thinking in, 88, 91
student profile for, 88
tech tips for, 102, 204
Cultural differences, 9, 132. *See also* Diversity;
    Multiculturalism
Cultural literacy, 197
Culture, 244, 247, 249, 251
Current information, 206–207
Curriculum, diversity in, 249–250
Customized products, 309
Cyberbullying, 272–273

D

Daily planners, 28, 29(*f*), 30, 36
Daily to-do lists, 37, 37(*f*), 43, 171
Dartmouth College, 128
Databases, 102, 196, 198, 201, 202, 203–205,
    214, 256
Deadlines, 26, 28, 32, 36, 39, 44, 192, 231, 293
Debating skills, 104, 251. *See also* Arguments
Debit cards, 296, 298–299. *See also* Credit cards
Decision making, 15, 25, 47, 49, 53, 70, 71, 73, 74
    critical thinking and, 8, 88, 90, 91, 94, 97
    parents and, 232–233
Deep learning, 156–157
Definitional information, 206
Depressants, 278
Depression, 230, 262, 263, 264, 269, 270–271,
    272, 276, 279, 281
Developmental arithmetic disorder, 81
Developmental disabilities, 306
Dictionaries, 114, 122, 124, 126
Diet. *See* Eating habits (diet)
Digital footprints, 321
Digital readers, 122. *See also* E-books
Disabilities, 79–82, 84, 150, 249, 258, 306.
    See also Learning disabilities
Disability services, 60, 82, 84, 150, 258
Discrimination, 245, 252, 255, 257, 258
Discussion forums, online, 78
Discussion groups, 63, 77
Discussions, classroom, 11, 56, 63, 77, 93, 103,
    130, 135, 136, 145, 149, 228
    note taking in, 143, 145
    recording, 131
Dishonesty. *See* Academic honesty
Disorders
    attention, 80–81
    eating, 268, 282
    reading, 80, 81
    writing, 81
Distractions, 80, 136, 264
    studying and, 114, 164, 167
    time management and, 30, 33, 35–36, 35(*t*)–
        36(*t*), 43
Divergers, 70, 70(*f*)
Diversity, 9, 11, 100, 101, 236, 241–258
    building experience in, 258
    challenges of, 255
    commitment to, 232–244
    curriculum and, 249–250
    discrimination, prejudice, and insensitivity,
        252–255
    forms of, 245–248

hate crimes and, 253–255
multiculturalism and, 243, 250, 252, 255, 258
stereotypes and, 246, 248–249, 253, 257
student profile for, 242
tech tip for, 256
Diversity experiences (high-impact practice 4),
    9, 101, 243, 249, 252, 258, 323
Diversity Web, 258
Dorsey, Jack, 93
Drafts, in writing, 22, 36, 162, 209, 209(*f*), 210–
    211, 212, 213, 219, 235
Dress code, for interviews, 218
Drinking, alcohol. *See* Alcohol use
Driving, and drinking, 277
Drug use, 56, 261, 262, 281, 282
Dyslexia, 80, 81

E

Earning power of college graduates, 6, 6(*f*)
Eating disorders, 268, 282
Eating habits (diet), 51, 165, 260, 265, 266–268,
    266(*f*), 271, 282
    before exams, 175
    fast (junk) food, 262, 264
E-books, 122, 206
Economic Institute, 6
Economics courses, 24, 120, 121(*f*)
Economic status, and diversity, 243, 245,
    246–247, 249, 257
Economy, and careers, 308–311, 333
Editing, 158, 212. *See also* Revising; Rewriting
EI. *See* Emotional intelligence
Elbow, Peter, 210
Electronic calendars, 26, 28–29, 30, 32, 43, 280
Electronic communication, 93. *See also*
    Cell phones; E-mail; Internet resources;
    Online communication
    blogs, 58, 102, 234
    instant messaging, 180
    social networking, 8, 58, 234, 235, 238, 240,
        321. *See also* Facebook
    text messaging (texting), 30, 41, 156, 226,
        234, 296, 299
E-mail, 12, 13, 32, 114, 122, 212, 234, 235, 296,
    299, 330
Emotional intelligence (EI), 45–60, 270
    academic success and, 56–57
    adaptability in, 53(*f*), 54
    anger management and, 51–52
    assessing, 48–49
    balance and priority management and, 51
    building experience in, 60
    competencies in, 47–49
    defined, 47–49
    developing, 52–55
    in everyday life, 49–52
    first-year seminars and, 57
    identifying, 53–55
    improving, 57–59
    impulse control and, 54, 56
    interpersonal skills in, 53(*f*), 54
    intrapersonal skills in, 53, 53(*f*), 56
    mood and, 55
    motivation and, 50–51
    questionnaire on, 48
    resilience and, 51
    stress management and, 53(*f*), 54, 56, 57
    student profile for, 46
Emotional problems, 60, 262
Emotions
    in preparing for exams, 176
    stress and, 263
    understanding and managing, 48–50, 59, 260
    well-being and, 56–57